M000235785

Promise and Fulfillment

Letter & Spirit 8 (2013): 3–5

CONTRIBUTORS

~: Scott W Hahn :~

Scott W. Hahn, founder of the St. Paul Center for Biblical Theology, holds the Father Michael Scanlan, TOR Chair of Biblical Theology and the New Evangelization at Franciscan University of Steubenville. He has held the Benedict XVI Chair of Biblical Theology and Liturgical Proclamation at St. Vincent Seminary in Latrobe, Pennsylvania and the Pio Cardinal Laghi Chair for Visiting Professors in Scripture and Theology at the Pontifical College Josephinum in Columbus, Ohio, and has served as adjunct faculty at the Pontifical University of the Holy Cross and the Pontifical University, Regina Apostolorum, both in Rome. Hahn is the general editor of the Ignatius Catholic Study Bible and Catholic Bible Dictionary, and is author or editor of more than thirty books, including *Politicizing the Bible: The Roots of Historical Criticism and the Secularization of Scripture 1300-1700* (2013), *Consuming the Word: The New Testament and The Eucharist in the Early Church* (2013), *Kinship By Covenant: A Canonical Approach to the Fulfillment of God's Saving Promises* (The Anchor Yale Bible Reference Library, 2009), *Covenant and Communion: The Biblical Theology of Pope Benedict XVI* (2009), *Letter and Spirit: From Written Text to Living Word in the Liturgy* (2005), and *The Lamb's Supper: The Mass as Heaven on Earth* (1999).

~: Brant Pitre :~

Brant Pitre is professor of Sacred Scripture at Notre Dame Seminary in New Orleans, Louisiana. He holds a Ph.D. in Theology from the University of Notre Dame, where he specialized in the study of the New Testament and ancient Judaism. He is the author of several articles and the books, *Jesus, the Tribulation, and the End of the Exile* (Baker Academic, 2005), *Jesus and the Jewish Roots of the Eucharist* (Image Books, 2011), *Jesus the Bridegroom* (Image Books, 2014), and *Jesus and the Last Supper* (Eerdmans, forthcoming).

~: Jeremy Holmes :~

Jeremy Holmes is academic dean and assistant professor of theology at Wyoming Catholic College. He received his doctoral degree in theology with an emphasis in New Testament from Marquette University, where he wrote his dissertation on the formula citations in the Gospel of Matthew. His scholarly work has focused on the relationship between ancient and modern exegesis. His articles and translations have appeared in *Nova et Vetera*, *Letter and Spirit*, *Faith and Reason*, and various volumes of essays.

❧ Leroy A. Huizenga ❧

Leroy Huizenga is chair of the department of theology and director of the Christian Leadership Center at the University of Mary in Bismarck, N.D. Dr. Huizenga received his Ph.D. in New Testament from Duke University. During his doctoral studies he received a Fulbright Grant to study and teach at Johann Wolfgang Goethe-Universität in Frankfurt, Germany. After teaching at Wheaton College (Ill.) for five years, Dr. Huizenga was reconciled with the Catholic Church at the Easter Vigil of 2011. Dr. Huizenga is the author of *The New Isaac: Tradition and Intertextuality in the Gospel of Matthew.*

❧ Michael Patrick Barber ❧

Michael Patrick Barber is the chair of the graduate program in biblical theology at John Paul the Great University in San Diego, California. He completed his Ph.D. in Theology at Fuller in Pasadena, CA, writing a dissertation entitled, "The Historical Jesus and Cultic Restoration Eschatology: The New Temple, the New Priesthood, and the New Cult" (2010). Barber also earned an M.A. in Theology from Franciscan University and a B.A. in Theology and Philosophy from Azusa Pacific University. He has published a number of popular books on Scripture. With two other Senior Fellows of the St. Paul Center, John Bergsma and Brant Pitre, Dr. Barber writes for the weblog, www.TheSacredPage.com, a site affiliated with the Society of Biblical Literature.

❧ Edward Sri ❧

Edward Sri is professor of theology and Scripture at the Augustine Institute's Master's in Catechetics and Evangelization program in Denver, Colorado. He also serves as a visiting professor at Benedictine College, where he taught full-time for nine years. Edward holds a doctorate from the Pontifical University of St. Thomas Aquinas in Rome. He is author or co-author of over ten books including *Walking with Mary: A Biblical Journey from Nazareth to the Cross* (Image, 2013), *The Gospel of Matthew* in the Catholic Commentary on Sacred Scripture series (Baker Academic, 2010), *Men, Women and the Mystery of Love: Practical Insights on John Paul II's Love and Responsibility* (Servant, 2007), and *Queen Mother: A Biblical Theology of Mary's Queenship* (Emmaus Road, 2005)

❧ John Bergsma ❧

John Bergsma is associate professor of theology at the Franciscan University of Steubenville (Ohio). He holds a B.A. in Classical Languages from Calvin College (Grand Rapids, MI), the M.Div. and Th.M. from Calvin Theological Seminary (Grand Rapids, MI), and a Ph.D. in Theology from the University of

Notre Dame. He is the author of *The Jubilee from Leviticus to Qumran* (VTSup 115; Brill, 2007), and several articles in *Biblica, Vetus Testamentum, Journal of Biblical Literature, Letter and Spirit,* and other scholarly journals, festschrifts, and essay collections.

~: Sean Innerst :~

Sean Innerst is the Theology Cycle Director at St. John Vianney Theological Seminary and a founding professor at the Augustine Institute in Denver, Colorado. He is the author of *From Blessing to Blessing: The Catechism as a Journey of Faith* and the recently released series *Pillars: A Journey through the Catechism,* both from Ascension Press.

~: Jeffrey L. Morrow :~

Jeffrey L. Morrow is assistant professor at Immaculate Conception Seminary School of Theology at Seton Hall University in South Orange, New Jersey, where he teaches courses in systematic theology and Sacred Scripture. He earned his Ph.D. in theology from the University of Dayton and has published articles in the *International Journal of Systematic Theology, New Blackfriars, Pro Ecclesia, Toronto Journal of Theology,* and *Logos.*

~: Nathan Eubank :~

Nathan Eubank is professor of Scripture at Notre Dame Seminary in New Orleans, LA. He holds a Ph.D. in New Testament from Duke University. He is the author of *Wages of Cross-Bearing and Debt of Sin: The Economy of Heaven in Matthew's Gospel* (2013), as well as recent and forthcoming articles in *Journal of Biblical Literature, New Testament Studies, Journal for the Study of the New Testament,* and *Catholic Biblical Quarterly,* among others. His current book project focuses on almsgiving, grace, and atonement in the Pauline corpus. He is also writing a commentary on 1-2 Thessalonians for *Catholic Commentary on Sacred Scripture* series.

Letter & Spirit 8 (2013): 7-11

INTRODUCTION

On the day of his resurrection, Jesus' exposition to two of his disciples on the road to Emmaus (Luke 24:25–27, 32) and shortly afterwards to his eleven apostles and other disciples (Luke 24:44–47) included "all the scriptures" "beginning with Moses and all the prophets." An idea implicit and underlying Jesus' expositions in these two episodes is that a unity of purpose exists throughout the many diverse sacred books of the Old Testament. Jesus discerned there a story line, an orderly plan—a *Divine economy*—unfolding throughout history and expressed in the inspired record that would culminate in his own saving work.

The idea of *Typology* is implicit and flows from this unified story—this *Divine economy*—that we find in the Bible. The scriptures encompass a single story, but it is composed of two parts: the Old Testament and the New. Typology is the literal sense in which the New Testament reads the Old. Indeed, typology refers precisely to those things that Christ revealed in his exegesis on the road to Emmaus—"the things concerning him" "in all the scriptures."

By unveiling the "things concerning him" "in all the scriptures," Christ established a normative approach to the work of New Testament exegesis and of biblical theology.

The other New Testament writers follow his example in applying "all the scriptures" to the doctrine on the church and Christian moral, ascetical, and sacramental life. It is not merely, or even primarily, a correspondence of prediction and fulfillment. It is, rather, a pattern of analogy. What began in the Old Testament is fulfilled partially even within the Old Testament, but definitively in the New, in a way that is both restorative and transformative.

Christ's life has fulfilled the types in a sacrifice that was "once for all" (Heb. 9:26). But the mysteries of his life—all that was hidden in his life—are now extended in time through the church's sacraments. After his resurrection, the ordinary way the disciples come to know the mysteries of his life is through the breaking of the bread. In the sacraments, he is made known to his disciples, but it is more than a knowledge of doctrine, more than wisdom about the world. In "the breaking of the bread," what happens is something far more profound than mere learning, surpassing the mere conversation of wayfarers, no matter how exalted that may be. What happens is *Mystagogy*: the leading of the Christian not just into a deeper understanding of the sacraments, but to personal *restoration* and *transformation*, and indeed—mysteriously and supernaturally, to *replication*—of Christ himself in the life of the Christian. The end or goal of mystagogy is for the Christian to become an *alter Christus*, another Christ, living a life of Christ-like love, sacrifice, death, resurrection, and ultimate glorification.

But the *end* is dependent on the *means*. Jesus' interpretation of the Hebrew scriptures on the Emmaus Road functioned to effectively give his imprimatur to

the notion of a *Divine Economy*, from Genesis to Revelation, and to the legitimacy—indeed, to the *necessity*—of *Typological Exegesis*, both of which will then
lead to the miracle of *Mystagogy*.

This issue of Letter & Spirit seeks to explain and demonstrate the propri-
ety and necessity of interpreting the Bible using the hermeneutics of the divine
economy and typology; hence the title for this issue: Promise and Fulfillment: The
Relationship Between the Old and New Testaments.

In his article, "From Old to New: 'Covenant' or 'Testament' in Hebrews 9?"
Scott Hahn investigates the meaning of "covenant" in Hebrews 9:15-18. "Covenant"
(διαθήκη) occurs more frequently in Hebrews (17x) than in the rest of the NT
(16x). For a majority of interpreters, the author's use of διαθήκη in Hebrews
9:15–17 is based on an analogy of the contemporary Greco-Roman legal institution
of "testament," and thus represents a brief but radical departure from the ancient
Israelite understanding of "covenant" which the author employs everywhere else in
Hebrews (chaps. 7–13). In this article, Dr. Hahn takes a social-scientific approach
to the *legal* and *liturgical* aspects of "covenant" (διαθήκη) in the Old Testament
to demonstrate that in Hebrews 9:15-18 the author did not abandon the ancient
Israelite understanding of "covenant"—with its close relationship between liturgy
and law—but actually bases his argument on the deeper inner logic of the liturgical and legal aspects involved in Israel's making—and breaking—of the covenant at
Sinai (Exod. 24-34). In Hebrews 9:15–19, the author draws out the *legal* implications of the *liturgical* ritual of the old (Sinai) covenant: a covenant that is solemnly
sworn—and then broken—requires the death of the covenant-maker (Heb. 9:16),
which thus implies that it is not "in force" (that is, *enforced*) while the offending
covenant-maker still lives (Heb. 9:17). Hebrews 9:16–17 is therefore not an abrupt,
unannounced shift in context from 9:15, nor does the author argue for a tortuous
analogy between "covenant" and "testament." In Hebrews 9:16–17 the author simply restates a theological principle summarized just prior in 9:15: the first covenant
entailed the curse-of-death for those who broke it, which Christ now takes upon
himself as Israel's redemptive representative, thus freeing those who, under the old
(broken) covenant, had become subject to the curse-of-death.

In his article, "Jesus, the Messianic Wedding Banquet, and the Restoration
of Israel," **Brant Pitre** interprets the parable of the Royal Wedding Feast (Matt.
22:1-14) against the backdrop of Jewish Scripture and tradition. Jesus seems to be
alluding to the Passover feast of King Hezekiah, to which all Israel was invited but
many refused to come (2 Chron. 30; Josephus, *Antiquities* 9:263-67). Seen in this
light, Jesus is using this parable to reveal the liturgical nature of the restoration of
Israel. As Jesus' parable reveals, the twelve tribes of Israel and the Gentile nations
will not be restored and gathered by means of a geographical return to the land, but
by accepting the invitation to the new Passover banquet of the heavenly Kingdom
of God, inaugurated at the Last Supper.

In his article, "Matthew as Exegete: The Unity and Function of the Formula Citations in Matthew 1:1-4:16," **Jeremy Holmes** takes up Matthew's so-called "formula citations," in which Matthew explicitly cites Old Testament texts with a formulaic "this happened to fulfill that" phrase. While New Testament scholars have often criticized the formula citations for supposedly twisting the Scriptures, Holmes argues that Matthew's citations must be understood in relation to one another and against the background of Matthew's more allusive use of Scripture. Seen in this light, the formula citations are not apologetic proof-texts in defense of Jesus but a network of contextually sensitive interpretations that build a positive, typological understanding of Jesus' identity and mission. Matthew presents Jesus as reliving the past history of Israel and inaugurating the New Exodus.

Many modern readers of the Bible eschew allegory, believing it to be the illegitimate importation of one's own wishes and desires into the text. But **Leroy Huizenga,** in his article, "The Tradition of Christian Allegory Yesterday and Today," argues that reading the Scriptures using the spiritual sense commonly called "allegory" is a natural and normal way to read religious texts, is seen in the biblical texts themselves—as well as the pre-modern tradition— and is for Catholics affirmed by contemporary authorities from the Second Vatican Council to the present. Dr. Huizenga's essay explores what "allegory" has meant in the Western ecclesial tradition from the New Testament to the present, how it finds its culmination in liturgical mystagogy, and how it calls biblical scholars and theologians to a disciplined and fruitful return to it.

In his article "The New Temple, the New Priesthood, and the New Cult in Luke-Acts," **Michael Barber** demonstrates how Luke's Gospel displays clear expectations for a new temple, a new priesthood, and a new cult. While contemporary scholars downplay the significance of cultic elements in Luke, his emphasis on such matters was not lost on the early Church fathers. Irenaeus, Ambrose, Jerome, and Augustine all identified his Gospel with the symbol of the "ox," precisely because of the evangelist's perceived focus on cultic imagery. Contemporary scholarship's lack of interest in these features can be traced to a centuries-old methodological blunder pioneered by certain Protestant scholars which held that the priestly and cultic elements of the Old Testament represented the degeneration of Israel's religion in the post-exilic era and thus embodied the very antithesis of the Gospel Jesus came to proclaim. Such biases have led scholars to overlook the role of the cult in Luke-Acts. Dr. Barber demonstrates how the threefold hope for a new temple, a new priesthood, and a new cult—proclaimed by the prophets and hoped for in Jesus' day—finds its fulfillment in the New Covenant established by Christ. Barber shows how Luke describes Jesus and the Church as the new temple, Jesus and the apostles as the new priests, and the celebration of the Lord's Supper as the new cult.

In his article, "New Approaches to Marian Typology in Luke 1: Mary as Daughter Zion and Queen Mother," **Ted Sri** considers two Marian types that appear in the first chapter of Luke's Gospel: Mary as "Daughter Zion" and Mary as "queen mother." Dr. Sri's methodological approach precinds from using extra-Scriptural agents such as the Church Fathers, the liturgy, or magisterial teaching and focuses instead on an examination of Mary in the context of Old Testament Scripture and Luke's presentation of Mary in Luke 1. While reference to "extra-Scriptural" agents could certainly and properly be made, Dr. Sri demonstrates that interpretations of Mary as Daughter Zion and Queen are not just the result of later theological reflection by the Church. These typological connections are firmly grounded in Luke's own scripturally-based presentation of Mary in the first chapter of his Gospel. Thus the angel's greeting to Mary in Luke 1:28 presents her in ways that recall the prophecies about lady Zion in the Old Testament. Likewise, Luke's accounts of the annunciation to Mary and her visit to Elizabeth invite us to view Mary in light of the Davidic kingdom traditions which those passages evoke. Considering Mary against the Davidic kingdom backdrop sheds important Biblical light on why we should see Mary, the mother of the Davidic king, as the queen mother. Dr. Sri demonstrates that by considering Mary by using the methodology of what he terms "inter-Biblical typology," the case for these and other typological connections involving Mary in the New Testament is strengthened.

Is his article, "Qumran and the Concept of Pan-Israelite Restoration," **John Bergsma** argues that although it is sometimes claimed otherwise, the members of the Qumran community practically never self-identify in their sectarian documents as "Jews," "Judeans," or "Judah." Instead, the Qumran sectarians conceive of themselves as "Israel," that is, as representatives of the twelve tribes of the LORD. This self-conception as the eschatological restoration of the pan-Israelite twelve-tribe union bears striking resemblance to certain motifs and images employed by the New Testament authors, showing that the Qumranites and the early Church had strong parallels in their self-identities.

The *General Directory for Catechesis* enjoins upon catechists the recital of *narratio* (the narration of salvation history) to accompany the explication of the mysteries of faith. After showing that the reason for the GDC's call for revival of *narratio* is rooted in its insistence upon the primacy of God's own pedagogy, **Sean Innerst**, in his article, "Divine Pedagogy and Covenant Memorial: The Catechetical *Narratio* and the New Evangelization," examines the character of that pedagogy. He first examines *narratio* in the classic patristic source text, Augustine of Hippo's *De catechizandis rudibus*. Then, by reflecting upon Old Testament covenant practices, he demonstrates that God's pedagogy required the people of Israel to engage in haggadic recitals of His saving works to form and maintain their covenant identity. Dr. Innerst's article concludes that a positive response to the GDC's call is warranted by the biblical and post-biblical Jewish and Christian practices of ritual/covenantal remembrance. A positive response to the GDC's call will constitute one important way of advancing the New Evangelization.

Historical criticism is often understood as a scientific exegesis that emphasizes the literal sense of Scripture and eschews recourse to the more imaginative allegorical interpretation of the church fathers. In his article, "Historical Criticism as Secular Allegorism: The Case of Spinoza," **Jeffrey Morrow** employs the example of Baruch Spinoza to demonstrate how some of what passes for historical criticism is little more than secular allegory, where the literal sense of the biblical text is ignored in favor of a hypothetical history behind it. Spinoza is key here as one of the earliest pioneers of modern historical criticism of the Bible. His method, inherited by later historical critical exegetes, fragments the biblical text in order to undermine traditional interpretations which he supplants with alternative histories. These historical-critical reconstructions often serve particular political ends, ends which are secular, anti-Jewish, and anti-Catholic.

Matthew's Gospel is packed with economic imagery, especially in passages dealing with sin, righteousness, and divine recompense. Sin incurs a debt with God, righteous deeds earn treasure in heaven, and the second coming of Jesus will be the great settling of accounts. New Testament scholars have tended to downplay or even ignore this material as a theological embarrassment. As a result, the theologic of salvation in Matthew has remained opaque in contemporary scholarship. **Nathan Eubank**, in his article, "Purchasing the Rewards of Eternal Life: The Logic of Resurrection and Ransom in Matthew's Gospel," examines Matthew's portrayal of Jesus as an earner of treasure in heaven by analyzing three key passages occurring after the pivotal moment when Jesus begins predicting his death and resurrection (16:13-28; 19:16-29; 20:17-28) with a particular focus on the ransom saying in 20:28. Dr. Eubank argues that careful attention to Matthew's economic language illuminates how Jesus saves his people from their sins (1:21) and is enthroned in fulfillment of Daniel 7.

Letter & Spirit 8 (2013): 13-34

FROM OLD TO NEW
"Covenant" or "Testament" in Hebrews 9?

❖: Scott W. Hahn :❖

Franciscan University of Steubenville

1. Legal and Liturgical Dimensions of "Covenant"

The Book of Hebrews has typically been regarded as anomalous in biblical stud-ies for a variety of reasons, one of which is its unusual emphasis on the concept of "covenant" (διαθήκη), which is treated differently and much more extensively in Hebrews than in any other New Testament book. Just over half of the occur-rences of the word διαθήκη in the New Testament (17 of 33) are in Hebrews alone. Moreover, Hebrews is unique in the emphasis it places on "covenant" as a *cultic* and *liturgical* institution.

A new phase in modern studies of the biblical concept of "covenant" (בְּרִית MT, διαθήκη LXX) began in the middle of the last century with George E. Mendenhall's work comparing the form of Hittite vassal treaties to the Sinai covenant of Exodus.[1] Scholars since Mendenhall have either challenged or defended his arguments for the antiquity of the covenant concept in Israelite religion, but have generally stayed within the framework Mendenhall established for the discussion, viewing "covenant" as a legal institution and using the extant treaties between ancient Near Eastern states as the primary texts for comparison and engagement with the biblical mate-rials.[2] Thus, covenants in biblical scholarship have generally been considered under the aspect of "law."

Scholarship has tended, however, to neglect the pronounced cultic-liturgical dimension of these ancient Near Eastern treaty-covenants.[3] The covenants were often concluded by lengthy invocations of nearly the entire Near Eastern pantheon,

---

1 George E. Mendenhall, *Law and Covenant in Israel and the Ancient Near East* (Pittsburgh: The Biblical Colloquium, 1955).

2 Notice how often "law" or "treaty" occurs in the titles of the following important studies on biblical covenants: Herbert B. Huffmon, "The Covenant Lawsuit," *Journal of Biblical Literature* 78 (1959): 285–295; Dennis J. McCarthy, *Treaty and Covenant*, Analecta biblica 21 (Rome: Pontifical Biblical Institute, 1963 [2d ed., 1978]); Meredith G. Kline, *Treaty of the Great King: The Covenant Structure of Deuteronomy: Studies and Commentary* (Grand Rapids: Eerdmans, 1963); Rintje Frankena, "The Vassal Treaties of Esarhaddon and the Dating of Deuteronomy," *Oudtestamentische studiën* 14 (1965):140–154; Hayim Tadmor, "Treaty and Oath in the Ancient Near East: A Historian's Approach," in *Humanizing America's Iconic Book*, eds. Gene M. Tucker and Douglas A. Knight (Chicago: Scholars Press, 1982), 125–152; George E. Mendenhall, "The Suzerainty Treaty Structure: Thirty Years Later," in *Religion and Law* (Winona Lake: Eisenbrauns, 1990), 85–100.

3 An exception is the essay by John M. Lundquist, "Temple, Covenant, and Law in the Ancient

calling upon the gods to witness elaborate sacred oaths confirmed by ritual sacrifices and to enforce those oaths with blessings for faithfulness and curses for transgression.[4] Thus, the establishment of covenants consisted essentially of a liturgy: ritual words and actions performed in the presence of divinity. The liturgical dimension of covenant-making appears quite clearly in the Old Testament, where the covenant is established through cultic ritual (see, for example, Exod. 24:4–11), and where liturgical functionaries or "celebrants" (that is, priests and Levites) mediate the covenant blessings and curses on behalf of God (Num. 6:22–27; Deut. 27:14–26).

Reflecting on the Old Testament traditions of "covenant," the author of Hebrews, while not forgetting the legal dimension, places the *liturgical* (or cultic) in the foreground. This is most obvious in chapters 8–9 of Hebrews,[5] in which the author contrasts two covenant orders: the old (Heb. 8:3–9:10) and the new (Heb. 9:11–28). Both covenant orders have a cultus which includes a high priest (Heb. 8:1, 3; 9:7, 11, 25, ἀρχιερεύς) or "celebrant" (Heb. 8:2, 6, λειτουργός) who performs ministry (Heb. 8:5; 9:1, 6, λατρεία) in a tent-sanctuary (Heb. 8:2, 5; 9:2–3, 6, 8, 11, 21, σκηνή), entering into a holy place (Heb. 8:2; 9:2–3, 12, 24, ἅγια) to offer (Heb. 8:3; 9:7, 14, 28, προσφέρω) the blood (Heb. 9:7, 12, 14, 18–23, 25, αἷμα) of sacrifices (Heb. 8:3–4, 9:9, 23, 26, θυσίαι) which effects purification (Heb. 9:13, ἁγιάζω; Heb. 9:14, 22–23, καθαρίζω) and redemption (Heb. 9:12, 15, λύτρωσις) of worshippers (Heb. 8:10, 9:7, 19, λαός; Heb. 9:9, 14, λατρεύοντες) who have transgressed cultic law (Heb. 8:4; 9:19, νόμος).[6] The mediation of both covenants is primarily cultic, the sacred realm of liturgy.

The legal nature of the covenant is not absent, however. The two aspects of the covenant, legal and liturgical, are inextricably bound in a reciprocal relationship. On the one hand, cultic acts (that is, sacrificial rites) establish the covenant (Heb. 9:18–21, 23), and also renew it (Heb. 9:7; 10:3). On the other hand, the covenantal law provides the legal framework for the cult, determining the suitable persons, ma-

---

Near East and in the Hebrew Bible," in *Israel's Apostasy and Restoration: Essays in Honor of Roland K. Harrison*, ed. Gileadi Avraham (Grand Rapids: Baker, 1988), 293–305.

4   See J. B. Pritchard, ed., *Ancient Near Eastern Texts*, 200–201; 205–206; 532–535; 538–541.

5   On the cultic background of chapter 9, see James Swetnam, "A Suggested Interpretation of Hebrews 9,15–18," *Catholic Biblical Quarterly* 27 (1965): 375; Johannes Behm, "διαθήκη," *Theological Dictionary of the New Testament*, G. Kittel and G. Friedrich, eds., 2:131–132; Ceslas Spicq, *L'Épître aux Hébreux*, 2 vols. (Paris: Gabalda, 1952), 2:246–247; Albert Vanhoye, *Old Testament Priests and the New Priest According to the New Testament*, trans. J. B. Orchard; Studies in Scripture (Petersham, MA: St. Bede's, 1986), 176–177.

6   See William L. Lane, *Hebrews 9–13*, Word Biblical Commentary 47b (Dallas: Word, 1991), 235: "The manner in which the argument is set forth presupposes the cultic orientation of 9:1–10 and its leading motif, that access to God is possible only through the medium of blood (9:7). The basis for the exposition in 9:11–28 is not primarily theological. It is the religious conviction that blood is the medium of purgation from defilement. . . . The essence of the two covenants is found in their cultic aspects; the total argument is developed in terms of cultus. . . . The interpreter must remain open to the internal logic of the argument from the cultus."

terials, acts, and occasions for worship (Heb. 7:11–28; 9:1–5). Thus, the liturgy mediates the covenant, while covenant law regulates the liturgy.

The unity of the legal and liturgical aspects of the covenant are united in Christ himself, who is simultaneously king (the highest legal authority) and high priest (the highest liturgical celebrant). This dual role of Christ as priest and king, running as a theme throughout the book, is announced already in Hebrews 1:3, where Christ "sits down at the right hand of the Majesty in heaven" (a royal act) after having "provided purification for sins" (a priestly function). It is brought to its quintessential expression by the use of Melchizedek—both "King of Salem" and "Priest of God Most High" (Heb. 7:1)—as a principal type of Christ.

Hebrews' vision of a cultic covenant, with close integration of law and liturgy, is difficult for modern scholarship to appreciate. Western modernity, as heir to the Enlightenment concept of "separation of church and state," has tended to privatize liturgy and secularize law, resulting in an irreconcilable divorce between the two. On the occasions when liturgy does appear in the public square, it is generally either dismissed as superstition or explained away as ritualized politics. In any case, Hebrews confronts us with a radically different vision: law and liturgy as distinguishable but inseparable aspects of a single covenant relationship between God and his people.

In order to understand the Book of Hebrews, we must be prepared to enter into its own cultural worldview, with its unity of liturgy and law. Doing so will elucidate a long-standing interpretive *crux*: the meaning of διαθήκη in Hebrews 9:15–18. The methodology that I employ is in some ways classical textual exegesis, that is, examining the grammar and syntax of the text in the light of its historical and religious context. But since I emphasize the legal and liturgical aspects of the covenant in their integration, a more deliberate application of the social-scientific approach is appropriate. This methodology is associated with the scholarship of Bruce J. Malina, John J. Pilch, Richard Rohrbaugh, and others.[7] David A. deSilva has applied social-scientific methods specifically to the interpretation of Hebrews.[8]

---

7   Bruce J. Malina, *The New Testament World: Insights from Cultural Anthropology*, 3d ed. (Louisville, KY: Westminster John Knox, 2001); Bruce J. Malina, *Christian Origins and Cultural Anthropology: Practical Models for Biblical Interpretation* (Atlanta: John Knox, 1986); Bruce J. Malina, *Windows on the World of Jesus: Time Travel to Ancient Judea* (Louisville: Westminster/ John Knox, 1993); John J. Pilch, *Introducing the Cultural Context of the New Testament* (New York: Paulist, 1991); John J. Pilch and Bruce J. Malina, *Handbook of Biblical Social Values* (Peabody, MA: Hendrickson, 1998); Richard Rohrbaugh, ed., *The Social Sciences and New Testament Interpretation* (Peabody, MA: Hendrickson, 1996); David G. Horrell, *Social-Scientific Approaches to New Testament Interpretation* (Edinburgh: T&T Clark, 1999); Philip F. Esler, ed., *Modelling Early Christianity: Social-Scientific Study of the New Testament in its Context* (London: Routledge, 1995).

8   David A. deSilva, *Despising Shame: Honor Discourse and Community Maintenance in the Epistle to the Hebrews*, Society of Biblical Literature Dissertation Series 152 (Atlanta: Scholars Press, 1995); David A. deSilva, *Perseverance in Gratitude: A Socio-Rhetorical Commentary on the Epistle "To the Hebrews"* (Grand Rapids: Eerdmans, 2000).

Regrettably, most of the social-scientific study of the New Testament in the past few decades has focused on the Greco-Roman world and not on the significance of the unique cultural institutions of First and Second Temple *Israel* (or Judea) themselves—the covenant, cult, priesthood, temple, etc.—and how these institutions shaped the cultural worldview of the New Testament authors. John Dunnill's monograph *Covenant and Sacrifice in the Letter to the Hebrews* represents a breakthrough in this regard.[9] Dunnill not only applies social-scientific methods to the analysis of the distinctly Israelite-Jewish values and cultural institutions characterizing the Book of Hebrews, but also incorporates methodological insights from the religious anthropology of Mary Douglas and Victor Turner.[10] In what follows, I will build on Dunnill's work while attempting to unravel the difficulties presented by Hebrews 9:15–18.

2. *Hebrews* 9:15–18: A Crux Interpretum

Hebrews' concept of covenant, with liturgy and law intertwined, may actually be at work in the one passage of Hebrews where the author seems to dispense with his usual cultic categories for understanding covenant. Ironically, the problematic passage occurs in the middle of Hebrews 9, the chapter with the densest concentration of cultic language and imagery in the book. In Hebrews 9:16–17, according to most commentators, the author abandons his Israelite, cultic understanding of διαθήκη, "covenant,"[11] and appeals to the Greco-Roman, secular definition of διαθήκη as "last will or testament."[12] In the usual translations, the author seems, in the course of Hebrews 9:15–18, to slip between the two quite distinct meanings in a facile manner:

> For this reason he is the mediator of a new covenant (διαθήκη),
> so that those who are called may receive the promised eternal in-
> heritance, because a death has occurred that redeems them from
> the transgressions under the first covenant (διαθήκη). For where
> a will (διαθήκη) is involved, the death of the one who made it
> must be established. For a will (διαθήκη) takes effect only at

---

9   John Dunnill, *Covenant and Sacrifice in the Letter to the Hebrews*, Society for New Testament Studies Monograph Series 75 (Cambridge: Cambridge University Press, 1992). For an expansion of Dunnill's groundbreaking insights into the inseparable link between the legal and liturgical aspects of "covenant" in ancient Israel, see Scott Hahn, *Kinship by Covenant* (New Haven: Yale University Press, 2009).

10   Mary L. Douglas, *Natural Symbols: Explorations in Cosmology*, 2d ed. (New York: Routledge, 1996); Mary L. Douglas, *Purity and Danger: An Analysis of Concepts of Pollution and Taboo* (New York: Routledge, 1966); Victor W. Turner, *The Ritual Process: Structure and Anti-Structure* (Ithaca, NY: Cornell University Press, 1966).

11   On the use of διαθήκη with the meaning "covenant" in most Jewish Hellenistic literature, see Behm, *Theological Dictionary of the New Testament*, G. Kittel and G. Friedrich, eds., 2:126–129.

12   For διαθήκη in secular Greek, see Behm and Quell, *Theological Dictionary of the New Testament*, G. Kittel and G. Friedrich, eds., 2:106–134, especially 124–126.

death, since it is not in force as long as the one who made it is alive. Hence not even the first covenant (διαθήκη) was inaugurated without blood. (Heb. 9:15–18 NRSV)

As can be seen, the NRSV follows the majority of commentators and translators by taking διαθήκη in the sense of "will" or "testament" in Hebrews 9:16–17, even though the word clearly has the meaning "covenant" in verses 15 and 18, and indeed in every other occurrence in Hebrews.[13] Nonetheless, it is not difficult to see why this approach enjoys majority support.[14] In Hebrews 9:15, the context seems to demand the sense of "covenant," since only a covenant has a mediator (μεσίτης) and reference is made to the first διαθήκη, which the author clearly regards as a covenant. However, in Hebrews 9:16, the requirement for the "death of the one who made it" would seem to suggest the translation "will" or "testament," since covenants did not require the death of their makers. Likewise, in Hebrews 9:17, the statement that a διαθήκη takes effect only at death and is not in force while the maker is alive seems to apply only to a testament. However, in Hebrews 9:18, the topic returns again to "the first διαθήκη," that is, the Sinai event, which can scarcely be anything but a covenant.

While there seems to be a semantic requirement that the meaning of διαθήκη alternates between "testament" and "covenant," the resulting argument is, logically speaking, *very* unsatisfying. A "testament" simply is not a "covenant," and it is hard to see how the analogy between the two has any validity. In a "testament," one party dies and leaves an inheritance for another. In a "covenant," a relationship is established between two living parties, often through a mediator. Testaments do not require mediators, and covenants do not take effect upon the death of one of the parties. Moreover, it is hard to understand either the "new" or the "old" covenants—as portrayed in Hebrews—as a "testament." If the old covenant is understood as a "testament," God would be the "testator"; yet it is absurd to think of God dying and leaving an inheritance to Israel. In the new covenant, Christ indeed dies, but he is a mediator (Heb. 9:15; 12:24), not a "testator." Moreover, he does not die in order to *leave* an inheritance to the Church, but rather to *enter* the inheritance himself (Heb. 1:3–4; 2:9; 9:11–12; 10:12–13), which he then shares with his "brothers" (Heb. 2:10–3:6).

---

13 See the NEB, JB, TEV, NIV, NAB (only the NASB translates "covenant" in vv. 16–17). Commentators endorsing "testament" in vv. 16–17 include: Gerhardus Vos, *The Teaching of the Epistle to the Hebrews* (Grand Rapids: Eerdmans, 1956), 27–48; George W. Buchanan, *To the Hebrews*, Anchor Bible 36 (Garden City: Doubleday, 1972), 151; Thomas G. Long, *Hebrews*, Interpretation: A Bible Commentary for Teaching and Preaching (Louisville: John Knox, 1997), 99; Harold W. Attridge, *Hebrews*, Hermeneia (Philadelphia: Fortress, 1989), 253–256; Paul Ellingworth, *Commentary on Hebrews*, New International Greek Testament Commentary (Grand Rapids: Eerdmans, 1993), 462–463; Victor C. Pfitzner, *Hebrews*, Abingdon New Testament Commentaries (Nashville: Abingdon, 1997), 131; Craig R. Koester, *Hebrews*, Anchor Bible 36 (New York: Doubleday, 2001), 418, 424–426.

14 See Swetnam, "Suggested Interpretation," 374–375, for a succinct summary of the case.

Clearly, then, the mode of the inheritance of salvation in Hebrews is based on a Jewish covenantal and not a Greco-Roman testamentary model.[15] Therefore, it is hard to see how the analogy the author draws in Hebrews 9:15–18 has any cogency. The awkwardness of the argument has led a few commentators to propose taking διαθήκη as "covenant" in Hebrews 9:16–17 (see below), but most retain the sense of "testament" while expressing their discomfort. Here are two examples:

> Among the many references to covenants, new and old, the word-play on διαθήκη which compares them to a secular will seems strangely banal, and the argument that Jesus' death was necessary because "where there is a will the death of the testator must be established" ([Heb.] 9:16) is simply irrelevant to the theology of the new covenant.[16]

> [The author] jumps from the religious to the current legal sense of διαθήκη . . . involving himself in contradictions which show that there is no real parallel.[17]

It is manifest that the idea of "testament" fits very awkwardly into the passage.[18] One must therefore ask the question: is it really the case that the author of Hebrews, usually so theologically and rhetorically brilliant, has committed here a logical and theological *faux pas*, tearing the otherwise seamless coherence of his homiletical

---

15 See Dunnill, *Covenant and Sacrifice*, 46–47: "Though Hebrews exhibits Alexandrian [that is, Hellenistic] terminology . . . in every case the substance of the thought is Jewish. . . . The Hellenistic element overlays a mind thinking in the categories of the Old Testament cultus." Although it came to be used in later periods, the institution of the testament is not native to Israelite-Jewish culture, which traditionally practiced *intestate* (non-testamentary) succession, in which the first-born son enjoyed a privileged share. The first-born had no privileged status in Greco-Roman succession (see Larry R. Helyer, "The *Prōtotokos* Title in Hebrews," *Studia Biblica et Theologica* 6 [1976]: 17). That the author of Hebrews thinks in terms of Israelite-Jewish inheritance custom can be seen in the strategic use of the concept πρωτότοκος (first-born) in Heb. 1:6 and 12:23.

16 Dunnill, *Covenant and Sacrifice*, 250–251.

17 Behm, *Theological Dictionary of the New Testament*, G. Kittel and G. Friedrich, eds., 2:131. Many other advocates of διαθήκη-as-testament also feel the tension caused by the abrupt switch in meaning. See, for example, Bruce, *Hebrews*, 461; Pfitzner, *Hebrews*, 131; Ellingworth, *Hebrews*, 462; Swetnam, "Suggested Interpretation," 373. Currently it seems popular to defuse this tension somewhat by describing the author as engaged in "playful" rhetorical argument which—while not logically valid—would amuse the audience or readership with its clever word-play (Attridge, *Hebrews*, 253–254; similarly Long, *Hebrews*, 98–99). Unfortunately, in order to be rhetorically effective an argument must at least appear to be valid. A blatantly false example cited as proof, or a syllogism whose errors are apparent to all, tends to discredit the speaker and his argument. It is doubtful whether the argument of Heb. 9:16–17 would have had even apparent validity under a testamentary interpretation.

18 See George D. Kilpatrick, "Διαθήκη in Hebrews," *Zeitschrift für die neutestamentliche Wissenschaft* 68 (1977): 263.

masterpiece?[19] I am inclined to think not. In what follows, I will propose that if διαθήκη is understood as "covenant" in Hebrews 9:16–17, there is a way of interpreting the passage which confirms the coherence of thought of the author, who seems to be explicating the *legal implications* of the *liturgical act* which established the first covenant.

First, I will point out certain frequently-overlooked difficulties with the usual interpretation of διαθήκη as "testament" in Hebrews 9:16–17. I will then critique some previous attempts to understand διαθήκη as "covenant" in these verses. Finally, I will outline an original interpretive proposal which has greater explanatory power than others have offered to date.

2.1 Difficulties with διαθήκη as "Testament"

The troubles with διαθήκη as "testament" in Hebrews 9:15–18 go deeper than the mere fact that the word so translated renders the argument of the passage obscure if not simply fallacious. John J. Hughes has pointed out these difficulties at length elsewhere.[20] I will summarize some of Hughes' observations here, focusing on the lexical, grammatical, and legal problems with rendering διαθήκη as "testament" in these verses.

2.1.1 Lexical Issues

Outside of Hebrews 9:16–17, the author of Hebrews uses διαθήκη only in its Septuagintal sense of "covenant" (בְּרִית).[21] Moreover, the term διαθήκη (and the concept of "covenant") occurs more often and receives greater attention and emphasis in Hebrews than in any other New Testament book.[22] Most of the occurrences of the

---

19 On the coherence and brilliance of Hebrews' thought and expression, see Attridge, *Hebrews*, 1: "[Hebrews is] the most elegant and sophisticated . . . text of first-century Christianity. . . . Its argumentation is subtle; its language refined; its imagery rich and evocative . . . a masterpiece of early Christian rhetorical homiletics"; Vanhoye, *Structure and Message*, 32–33: "Pause for a moment to admire the literary perfection of [this] priestly sermon. . . . One sees how the author is concerned about writing well. . . . [His] talent is seen especially in the harmony of his composition"; Dunnill, *Covenant and Sacrifice*, 8: "[The interpreter must] capitalize on the strong impression of the *unity* of its imaginative world which any reading of Hebrews communicates. . . . It is generally agreed that Hebrews exhibits a marked theological *coherence*"; and Brooke F. Westcott, *The Epistle to the Hebrews: The Greek Text with Notes and Essays*, 2d ed., 1892, reprint (Grand Rapids: Eerdmans, 1980), xlvi–xlvii: "The style is . . . characteristic of a practised scholar. It would be difficult to find anywhere passages more exact and pregnant in expression. . . . The writing shows everywhere the traces of effort and care. . . . Each element, which seems at first sight to offer itself spontaneously, will be found to have been carefully adjusted to its place, and to offer in subtle details results of deep thought." See also Swetnam, "Suggested Interpretation," 375.

20 John J. Hughes, "Hebrews IX 15ff. and Galatians III 15ff.: A Study in Covenant Practice and Procedure," *Novum Testamentum* 21 (1976–77): 27–96.

21 See Behm, *Theological Dictionary of the New Testament*, G. Kittel and G. Friedrich, eds., 2:132; Lane, *Hebrews*, 230.

22 See Vos, *Hebrews*, 27.

word (15 of 17) occur in the extended discussion of Christ-as-high-priest from Hebrews 7–10, with seven occurrences in Hebrews 9 alone. Since the word is central to the author's thought, and in every instance outside of Hebrews 9:16–17 has the meaning "covenant," Hughes remarks: "As a matter of a priori concern one should at least be exceedingly cautious in attributing a meaning to διαθήκη in [Heb.] 9:15–22 that is so foreign to the author's use of the word elsewhere."[23]

2.1.2 Grammatical Issues

Several scholars have noted grammatical irregularities in the use of φέρεσθαι (Heb. 9:16b) and ἐπὶ νεκροῖς (Heb. 9:17a).[24] If Hebrews 9:16b had testamentary practice in view, one would expect ὅπου γὰρ διαθήκη, διαθέμενον ἀνάγκη ἀποθανεῖν, "where there is a testament, it is necessary for the testator *to die*" (italics added). The circumlocution actually found in 9:16, θάνατον ἀνάγκη φέρεσθαι τοῦ διαθεμένου, seems unnecessary. The NRSV translates, "the death of the one who made it must *be established*" (italics added), but similar usage in the rest of the New Testament or the LXX cannot be found. Φέρω frequently occurs in legal contexts (biblical and non-biblical), but in the sense of "bring a report, claim, or charge," not a *death*. The expression should be φέρεσθαι ἀνάγκη τὸν λόγον τοῦ θανάτου, "it is necessary for the report of the death to be brought."[25]

Another grammatical strain occurs at Hebrews 9:17a, διαθήκη γὰρ ἐπὶ νεκροῖς βεβαία, which the NRSV renders, "a will takes effect only at death." A literal translation, however, would read "for a διαθήκη is confirmed *upon dead [bodies]*." The phrase ἐπὶ νεκροῖς cannot be taken as "at death" (ἐπὶ νεκρῷ or ἐπὶ νεκρώσει), although this is the sense demanded by a testamentary interpretation of διαθήκη.[26] The use of the plural (νεκροῖς, "dead [bodies]") is particularly awkward if indeed the author was intending to speak of the death of the testator.[27]

Both of these grammatical irregularities become intelligible when διαθήκη is taken as "covenant" in the manner I will outline below.

---

23   Hughes, "Hebrews IX 15ff.," 32–33.

24   See Kilpatrick, "Διαθήκη," 265; Westcott, *Hebrews*, 301.

25   Lexicographers treat it as a special case of φέρω, being unable to produce any analogous citations. See Liddell-Scott-Jones, *Greek-English Lexicon* 1923a (def. A.IV.4, "announce"), W. Bauer, W. F. Arndt, and F. W. Gingrich, 3d ed., rev. by F. W. Danker, *Greek-English Lexicon of the NT* 855b (def. 4.a.b, "establish"), L&N 667b–668a (§70.5, "show"). Note Ellingworth's honesty: "Exact parallels to this statement have not been found" (*Hebrews*, 464); and Attridge's polite understatement: "The sense of φέρεσθαι is somewhat uncertain" (*Hebrews*, 256).

26   Lane, *Hebrews*, 232; George Milligan, *The Theology of the Epistle to the Hebrews* (Edinburgh: T& T Clark, 1899), 169.

27   Attridge admits, "The phrase referring to the testator's death, 'for the dead' (ἐπὶ νεκροῖς), is somewhat odd" (*Hebrews*, 256). Likewise, Swetnam recognizes the oddity and offers a singular explanation for it ("Suggested Interpretation," 378).

2.1.3 *Legal Issues*

Hughes demonstrates that the characteristics of a διαθήκη in Hebrews 9:16–17 do not, in fact, correspond to those of secular Hellenistic or Roman διαθῆ καɩ (covenants). For example, the ratification or validation (βεβαίωσɩς) of wills in Hellenistic, Egyptian, and Roman law was not "over the dead [bodies]" (Heb. 9:17, ἐπὶ νεκροῖς):

> It is simply untrue and completely lacking in classical and papy-rological support to maintain that, given the legal technical terms (βέβαɩος, ἰσχύω, and perhaps ἐγκαɩνίζω) and their consistent meanings, a will or testament was only legally valid when the tes-tator died . . . It is impossible, not just unlikely, that [Heb. 9:16–17] refer to any known form of Hellenistic (or indeed any other) legal practice.[28]

A Hellenistic will was legally valid (βέβαɩος) not when the testator died, but when it was written down, witnessed, and deposited with a notary.[29] Moreover, the in-heritance was not always subsequent to the death of the testator, as Hebrews 9:17 would imply. Distribution of the estate while the testator(s) was/were still living (*in-ter vivos*) was widespread in the Hellenistic world.[30] Only a few instances of *donatio inter vivos* ("distribution while still living") known to the readers of Hebrews would have subverted the emphatic statement of Hebrews 9:17b (ἐπεὶ μήποτε ἰσχύεɩ ὅτε ζῇ ὁ διαθέμενος ["since it is not in force while the testator is alive"])[31] and destroyed its rhetorical effectiveness.[32]

---

28 Hughes, "Hebrews IX 15ff.," 61.

29 Hughes, "Hebrews IX 15ff.," 60.

30 Hughes, "Hebrews IX 15ff.," 62, citing Hans J. Wolff, "Hellenistic Private Law," in *The Jewish People in the First Century: Historical Geography, Political History, Social, Cultural and Religious Life and Institutions*, 2 vols., eds. Shemuel Safrai and Manahem Stern, Compendia rerum Iudaicarum ad Novum Testamentum, sec. 1 (Assen: Van Gorcum, 1974), 1:534–560, at 543; and Rafal Taubenschlag, *The Law of Greco-Roman Egypt in Light of the Papyri 322 BC–640 AD*, 2d ed., (Warsaw: Panstwowe Wydawnictwo Naukowe, 1955), 207–208.

31 On μήποτε as a strong negative, see Ellingworth, *Hebrews*, 464. The sense would not be "wills do not usually have force while the testator lives," but "they *certainly* do not," or perhaps "they *never* do" (see NIV, ASV).

32 Subsequent responses to Hughes' demonstration ("Hebrews IX 15ff.," published 1979) of the lack of correspondence between Heb. 9:16–17 and Greco-Roman testamentary law have been surprisingly weak. Curiously, Attridge, publishing almost thirteen years after Hughes' seventy-page *Novum Testamentum* article, makes no reference to Hughes or his arguments (see Attridge, *Hebrews*, 255–256 n. 25, 419). Ellingworth, while aware of Hughes, does not rebut him, although his comment "ἀνάγκη is here used [in v. 16] not strictly of a legal requirement" (*Hebrews*, 464) seems a concession to Hughes' evidence that testaments were validated by a notary and not by death. Likewise, Koester, who feels Hughes' arguments more strongly, has to nuance and mitigate the sense of Heb. 9:17 to accommodate Hughes' point that the language is not legally accurate (*Hebrews*, 418, 425). Koester also cites a papyrus death-notice as proof of his

2.2 Previous Proposals for διαθήκη as "Covenant" in Hebrews 9:16–17

The various difficulties with reading διαθήκη as "testament" noted above have led several scholars to maintain the author's usual meaning "covenant" for διαθήκη in Hebrews 9:16–17.[33] These scholars have, in my opinion, moved the discussion in the proper direction by seeking to explain Hebrews 9:16–17 in terms of the cultic rituals involved in biblical and ancient Near Eastern covenant-making. In these rites, the covenant-maker (ὁ διαθέμενος) swore a self-maledictory oath (that is, a curse upon himself), which was then ritually enacted by the death of animals representing the covenant-maker.[34] The bloody sacrifice of the animal(s) symbolized the fate of the covenant-maker should he prove false to his covenantal obligations.[35] The meaning of Hebrews 9:16–17 may be paraphrased as follows: Where there is a covenant, it is necessary that the death of the covenant-maker be represented (by animal sacrifices); for a covenant is confirmed over dead bodies (sacrificial animals), since it is never valid while the covenant-maker is still ritually "alive."

2.2.1 The Covenantal Background of Hebrews 9:16–17

As background for the covenantal interpretation of Hebrews 9:16–17, it may be useful to cite some relevant examples to demonstrate the following: (1) biblical and ancient Near Eastern covenant-making entailed the swearing of an oath, (2) this oath was a conditional self-malediction, that is, a curse, (3) the content of the curse usually consisted of the covenant-maker's death, and (4) the curse-of-death was often pre-enacted through sacrificial rituals.

(1) COVENANT-MAKING AND OATH-SWEARING

The swearing of an oath was closely associated with the making of a covenant. In fact, the two terms, oath (אָלָה) and covenant (בְּרִית), are sometimes used interchangeably, for example, in Ezekiel 17:13–19:

> And he took one of the seed royal and made a *covenant* (בְּרִית) with him, putting him under *oath* (אָלָה). (The chief men of the land he had taken away, that the kingdom might be humble and not lift itself up, and that by keeping his *covenant* it might stand.) But he

---

assertion that "legally people had to present evidence that the testator had died for a will to take effect" (*Hebrews*, 418, 425), but the papyrus cited does not actually mention a will or inheritance as being at issue in the notice of death.

33   See, for example, Westcott, *Hebrews*, 298–302; Milligan, *Hebrews*, 166–170; Brown, *Hebrews*, 407–419; Hughes, "Hebrews IX 15ff.," 27–96; Lane, *Hebrews*, 226–252; Darrell J. Pursiful, *The Cultic Motif in the Spirituality of the Book of Hebrews* (Lewiston, NY: Edwin Mellen, 1993), 77–79.

34   For example, Westcott, *Hebrews*, 301; Hughes, "Hebrews IX 15 ff.," 40–42; Lane, *Hebrews*, 241–243.

35   Hughes, "Hebrews IX 15ff.," 41; Lane, *Hebrews*, 242.

rebelled against him by sending ambassadors to Egypt, that they might give him horses and a large army. Will he succeed? Can a man escape who does such things? Can he break the *covenant* and yet escape? As I live, says the Lord God, surely in the place where the king dwells who made him king, whose *oath* he despised, and whose *covenant* with him he broke, in Babylon he shall die. . . . Because he despised the *oath* and broke the *covenant*, because he gave his hand and yet did all these things, he shall not escape. Therefore thus says the Lord God: As I live, surely my *oath* which he despised, and my *covenant* which he broke, I will requite upon his head (italics added, RSV).

In light of Ezekiel 17:13–19 and similar texts, the close inter-relationship between "covenant" and "oath" is a commonplace among scholars who work with ancient Near Eastern covenant materials:[36]

> It is now recognized that the *sine qua non* of "covenant" in its normal sense appears to be its ratifying oath, whether this was verbal or symbolic (a so-called "oath sign").[37]

> [B]erith as a commitment has to be confirmed by an oath: Gen. 21:22ff.; 26:26ff.; Deut. 29:9ff.; Josh. 9:15–20; 2 Kings 11:4; Ezek. 16:8; 17:13ff.[38]

(2) Covenant Oath as Conditional Self-Malediction

The oath by which a covenant was ratified was a conditional self-malediction (self-curse), an invocation of the divinity to inflict judgment upon the oath-swearer should he fail to fulfill the sworn stipulations of the covenant. A fourteenth-century

---

36 See Gordon P. Hugenberger, *Marriage as a Covenant: A Study of Biblical Law & Ethics Governing Marriage, Developed from the Perspective of Malachi*, Vetus Testamentum Supplements 52 (Leiden: Brill, 1994), 183–184. Oath (אָלָה) and covenant (בְּרִית) appear in semantic proximity in the following texts: Hos. 10:4, Deut. 29:11, 13 MT (ET 29:12, 14); Ezek. 16 as shown above; and Gen. 26:28. In Gen. 24:1–67, אָלָה and שְׁבֻעָה are used interchangeably; and elsewhere (Deut. 4:31; 7:12; 8:18; 31:20; Josh. 9:15; 2 Kings 11:4; Ezek. 16:8; Ps. 89:3) it is apparent that נִשְׁבַּע שְׁבֻעָה (to "swear an oath") and כָּרַת בְּרִית (to "cut" or "make a covenant") are functionally equivalent. For a Phoenician example of the relationship between curse and covenant, see Ziony Zevit, "A Phoenician Inscription and Biblical Covenant Theology," *Israel Exploration Journal* 27 (1977): 110–118.

37 Hugenberger, *Marriage as Covenant*, 4; citing James Barr, "Some Semantic Notes on the Covenant," in *Beiträge zur Alttestamentlichen Theologie: Festschrift für Walther Zimmerli zum 70. Geburtstag*, eds. Herbert Donner, Robert Hanhart, and Rudolf Smend (Göttingen: Vandenhoeck & Ruprecht, 1977), 23–28.

38 Moshe Weinfeld, "בְּרִית b'rith," *Theological Dictionary of the Old Testament*, G. J. Botterweck et al. (eds.), 2:256. See also Hugenberger, *Marriage as Covenant*, 182–184.

B.C.E. Hittite covenant expressed this principle as follows: "May the oaths sworn in the presence of these gods break you like reeds, you ... together with your country. May they exterminate from the earth your name and your seed."[39] Likewise, in Ezekiel 17:13–19, it is evident from the divine threats to enforce the oath that the making of the covenant involved a conditional curse-of-death (see, for example, Ezek. 17:16, 19). The word "curse" came to be functionally equivalent to "covenant" and "oath." Hugenberger remarks, "The fact that אָלָה (originally meaning "curse," cf. Gen. 24:41; Deut. 29:19 MT [ET 29:20]; 30:7; Isa. 24:6; Jer. 23:10; Pss. 10:7; 59:13) is used [to mean "covenant"] serves to emphasize the hypothetical self-curse which underlies biblical oaths—that is, if the oath should be broken, a curse will come into effect."[40]

(3) DEATH AS THE CONTENT OF THE CURSE

That the curse for covenant violation was typically death can be seen quite clearly in the passage from Ezekiel cited above (17:16), in the covenant curses of Leviticus 26 and Deuteronomy 28,[41] and in other biblical passages which explicitly mention the violation of the covenant being sanctioned by death[42] or mortal punishment.[43] Likewise, among extant ancient Near Eastern covenant documents, death by excruciating or humiliating means, accompanied by various other calamities, is frequently the content of the oath-curse.[44] At Qumran it is a commonplace that "the sword avenges the covenant"[45] resulting in death.[46] Dunnill's observation is apposite:

> In both Greek and Hebrew [oaths] often take the form of a *conditional self-curse*, the swearer invoking upon his or her own head penalties to follow any breach of the undertaking.... Even where the context is non-legal and the vagueness of the penalty shows

---

39   J. B. Pritchard (ed.), *Ancient Near Eastern Texts* 206b.

40   Hugenberger, *Marriage as Covenant*, 194. Sometimes the curse is only implicit. See Hugenberger, *Marriage as Covenant*, 200–201. Some biblical examples are 1 Sam. 3:17; 14:44; 20:13; 25:22; 2 Sam. 3:9, 3:35; 19:14 MT; 1 Kings 2:23; 2 Kings 6:31; Ruth 1:17; Jer. 42:5, in all of which the content of the curse is left unexpressed, but may be presumed to be death.

41   See Lev. 26:14–39, especially v. 30, but also vv. 16, 22, 25, 38; Deut. 28:15–68, especially vv. 20, 22, 24, 26, 48, 51, 61.

42   Deut. 4:23, 26; 17:2–7; Josh. 7:11, 15; 23:16; Jer. 22:8–12 (both death and death-in-exile); Jer. 34:18–21; Hos. 8:11.

43   For example, to be "devoured" (Deut. 31:16); "consumed" and "burned" (Isa. 33:8–12; Jer. 11:10, 16); "destroyed" (Hos. 7:13 [see 6:7]).

44   See J. B. Pritchard (ed.), *Ancient Near Eastern Texts* 179–180, 201, 205, 532, 534, 538–541. Note, too, that while not all the curses are death *per se*, usually they are means of death: plague, famine, siege, military defeat, etc.

45   See *Damascus Document* from the Genizah in Cairo I, 3; I, 17–18; III, 10–11; 4Q266 2 I, 21; 4Q269 2 I, 6; 4Q390 1 I, 6. The reference to the "sword" is probably inspired by Lev. 26:25.

46   See *Damascus Document* from the Genizah in Cairo XV, 4–5; 1Q22 1 I, 10.

the formula on the way to becoming a figure of speech, in every case the invocation of death is the guarantee of sincerity, placing the whole person behind the promise made.[47]

(4) The Curse of Death Ritually Enacted

Several ancient Near Eastern documents record the symbolic enactment of the curse-of-death during the covenant-making ritual. One of the most celebrated examples is the eighth-century treaty of Ashurnirari V and Mati'ilu, the King of Arpad, which includes the following enacted curse-ritual or *Drohritus*:

> This spring lamb has been brought from its fold . . . to sanction the treaty between Ashurnirari and Mati'ilu. If Mati'ilu sins against (this) treaty made under oath by the gods, then, just as this spring lamb . . . will not return to its fold, alas, Mati'ilu . . . [will be ousted] from his country, will not return to his country, and not behold his country again. This head is not the head of a lamb, it is the head of Mati'ilu. . . . If Mati'ilu sins against this treaty, so may, just as the head of this spring lamb is torn off . . . the head of Mati'ilu be torn off.[48]

Hugenberger draws the following conclusion:

> In light of this and many similar examples [for example, *Ancient Near Eastern Texts* 539f], it is possible . . . that the prominence of such cutting oath-signs in the ratification ceremony for covenants gave rise to the widespread terminology of "cutting" [כָּרַת] a covenant as well as "cutting" a curse.[49]

The Bible records similar curse-rituals. Abraham's bisection of animals in the covenant of Genesis 15 represented a self-curse of death for the covenant-maker—in this case, God himself. The significance of the *Drohritus* is elucidated by Jeremiah 34:18–20,[50] where the Lord addresses the leaders of Jerusalem and Judah, who had

---

47 Dunnill, *Covenant and Sacrifice*, 249. See O. Palmer Robertson: "The death of the covenant-maker appears in two distinct stages. First it appears in the form of a symbolic representation of the curse, anticipating possible covenantal violations. Later the party who violates the covenant actually experiences death as a consequence of his earlier commitment" (*The Christ of the Covenants* [Grand Rapids: Baker, 1980], 11–12).

48 J. B. Pritchard (ed.), *Ancient Near Eastern Texts* 532b.

49 Hugenberger, *Marriage as Covenant*, 195; Quell, *Theological Dictionary of the New Testament*, G. Kittel and G. Friedrich, eds., 2:108. In light of the evidence that Hugenberger and others have adduced, Koester's statement that "there is little evidence that sacrifices represented the death of the one making the covenant" is in error (*Hebrews*, 418).

50 The scholarly support for viewing Gen. 15 as a self-maledictory ritual enactment in light of Jer.

made a solemn covenant to release their slaves during the siege of Jerusalem but promptly reneged on their commitment when the siege was lifted:

> I will make the men who violated My covenant, who did not ful-
> fill the terms of the covenant which they made before Me, [like]
> the calf which they cut in two so as to pass between the halves:
> The officers of Judah and Jerusalem, the officials, the priests, and
> all the people of the land who passed between the halves of the
> calf shall be handed over to their enemies, to those who seek to
> kill them. Their carcasses shall become food for the birds of the
> sky and the beasts of the earth. (NJPS)

Significantly, each of the biblical covenants that concern the author of Hebrews involves a *Drohritus* symbolizing the curse-of-death. The covenant (or covenants) with Abraham (Heb. 6:13–18; 11:17–19) is confirmed by the bisection of animals (Gen. 15:9–10), the rite of circumcision (Gen. 17:10–14, 23–27), and the "sacrifice" of Isaac (Gen. 22:13; Heb. 6:14; 11:17–19).[51] The Sinai covenant is solemnized by the sprinkling of the people with the blood of the animal sacrifices after their solemn promise to obey the covenant stipulations (Exod. 24:3–8), conveying the concept, "As was done to the animals, so may it be done to us if we fail to keep the covenant."

2.2.2. The Exegesis of Hebrews 9:16–17 with διαθήκη as "Covenant"

The advocates of διαθήκη-as-covenant propose this biblical and ancient Near East-ern background of covenant-by-self-maledictory-oath as the context for Hebrews 9:16–17. In Hebrews 9:16, according to this view, φέρεσθαι should be translated "bring into the picture" or "introduce."[52] The "death" (θάνατος) that must be "brought into the picture" (φέρεσθαι) is the death of the covenant-maker (ὁ διαθέμενος), symbolically represented by the sacrificial animals. Thus, Hebrews 9:16 (ὅπου γὰρ

---

34 is strong, although some dispute it. See Quell, *Theological Dictionary of the New Testament*, G. Kittel and G. Friedrich, eds., 2:116; Hugenberger, *Marriage as Covenant*, 195 n. 109.

51   On the possibility that the covenant-making ceremonies in Gen. 15 and 17 are not parallel accounts of the same event but intentionally different covenants, see T. Desmond Alexander, "A Literary Analysis of the Abraham Narrative in Genesis" (Ph.D. diss.; The Queen's University of Belfast, 1982), 49, 160–182. Heb. 6:13–18 and 11:17–19 focus on the formulation of the Abrahamic covenant-oath found in Gen. 22:15–18. On the self-maledictory symbolism of circumcision, see Meredith G. Kline, *By Oath Consigned: A Reinterpretation of the Covenant Signs of Baptism and Circumcision* (Grand Rapids: Eerdmans, 1968), 39–49, 86–89, especially 43; Hugenberger, *Marriage as Covenant*, 196; and Dunnill, *Covenant and Sacrifice*, 177 n. 72. On the interrelationship of the three Abrahamic covenant-making rituals, see Dunnill, *Covenant and Sacrifice*, 177; Hahn, *Kinship by Covenant*, 101–135.

52   Hughes cites 2 Pet. 2:11, John 18:29, and *1 Clem.* 55:1 as examples of similar usage ("Hebrews IX 15ff.," 42–43). See W. Bauer, W. F. Arndt, and F. W. Gingrich (3d ed.; rev. by F. W. Danker), *Greek-English Lexicon of the NT* 855b (def. 4.a.β).

διαθήκη, θάνατον ἀνάγκη φέρεσθαι τοῦ διαθεμένου) should be translated, "For where there is a covenant, it is necessary to introduce the [symbolic] death of the covenant-maker." The following statement of Hebrews 9:17, "for a covenant is ratified over dead [bodies]," is a fairly accurate description of biblical and ancient Near Eastern covenant-making practice. Hebrews 9:17b, "since it [a covenant] is never in force while the covenant maker lives," makes sense if ὅτε ζῇ ὁ διαθέμενος ("while the covenant-maker lives") is understood symbolically, that is, to mean "while the covenant-maker is still ritually alive, not yet having undergone the death represented by the sacrificial animals."

Hebrews 9:18–22, which speaks of the sprinkling of blood at the establishment of the first covenant at Sinai, follows naturally from Hebrews 9:16–17 (ὅθεν, "hence"). Hebrews 9:16–17 states that a covenant requires the ritual death of the covenant-maker; Hebrews 9:18–22 points out that in fact the first covenant was established in this way, with the blood of the representative animals being sprinkled over the people and all the implements of the covenant cult.

2.2.3 Difficulties in the Case for διαθήκη as Covenant

In many respects the case for διαθήκη-as-covenant in Hebrews 9:16–17, as it has been argued to date, is appealing. It retains continuity with the author's Jewish, cultic understanding of the nature of "covenant," and produces a logically sound reading of Hebrews 9:15–18. However, there are at least two serious objections to the view as outlined above.

First, covenants were not always ratified by the ritual slaughter of animals. William Lane goes so far as to say, "The formulation [Heb. 9:17, ἐπεὶ μήποτε ἰσχύει ὅτε ζῇ ὁ διαθέμενος] accurately reflects the legal situation that a covenant is *never* secured until the ratifier has bound himself to his oath by means of a representative death" (italics added).[53] While it is true that many covenants were solemnized in this way, one cannot assert that a "representative death" was *always* necessary.[54] There was no monolithic form for covenant-making in the Bible or the ancient Near East. Moreover, it was the oath rather than the sacrifices that sufficed to establish a covenant, as Hugenberger and others have demonstrated.[55]

Second, it does not seem plausible that the two phrases θάνατον ἀνάγκη φέρεσθαι τοῦ διαθεμένου, "it is necessary for the death of the covenant-maker to be borne," and ὅτε ζῇ ὁ διαθέμενος, "while the covenant-maker is alive," are

---

53 Lane, *Hebrews*, 243.

54 Brown, *Hebrews*, 415: "Far less have we evidence that the death of the sacrificial victim was necessary to the validity of every arrangement to which the word rendered 'covenant' may be applied"; Attridge, *Hebrews*, 254: "There are covenants recorded in scripture where no inaugural sacrifice is mentioned."

55 Hugenberger, *Marriage as Covenant*, 196–197, and Weinfeld, G. J. Botterweck et al. (eds.), *Theological Dictionary of the Old Testament* 2:256 and scripture references cited therein.

intended in a figurative sense. The author *does* appear to be speaking of the actual death of the covenant-maker.[56]

These two objections suggest that, although the reading of διαθήκη as "covenant" may be an improvement over the alternative "testament," a better case must be made for it.

2.3 A New Proposal: The Broken Covenant and the Curse-of-Death

An interpretation of Hebrews 9:16–17 that renders the text intelligible and coheres with the theological system expressed in the rest of the epistle is possible, if one recognizes that the particular covenant occupying the author's thought in Hebrews 9:15–22 is the first or Sinai covenant, seen as a *broken* covenant. It is not covenants in general, but the broken Sinai covenant that forms the context within which Hebrews 9:16–17 should be understood. In what follows I will offer my exegesis of Hebrews 9:16–17 phrase by phrase.

2.3.1 Ὅπου γὰρ διαθήκη (Heb. 9:16a)

Hebrews 9:16–17 is a parenthetical explanation of the genitive absolute construction in Hebrews 9:15, θανάτου γενομένου εἰς ἀπολύτρωσιν τῶν ἐπὶ τῇ πρώτῃ διαθήκῃ παραβάσεων, "a death having occurred for the remission of transgressions *under the first covenant*" (italics added). The purpose of Hebrews 9:16–17 is to explain *why a death was necessary*, given the predicament of the broken first covenant.

In Hebrews 9:16, when the author says "For where there is a covenant," the reader must also incorporate from Hebrews 9:15 the concept παραβάσεων γενομένων, "transgressions having taken place." In other circumstances—for example, if there were no covenant in place, or if a different kind of relationship was in place (for example, a trade contract)—transgressions would not result in death, or would simply not be of concern. However, the author of Hebrews emphasizes, ὅπου γὰρ διαθήκη, θάνατον ἀνάγκη φέρεσθαι τοῦ διαθεμένου, "*where there is a covenant, it is necessary for the death of the covenant-maker to be endured* [when transgressions have taken place]." The fact that a covenant is in force renders the situation of transgression deadly. The author's point becomes clearer when ὅπου is taken causally, that is, not as "where" but as "whereas" or "since."[57] Verse 16 could be rendered, "*Since there is a covenant, it is necessary for the death of the covenant-*

---

56   Robert P. Gordon, *Hebrews* (Sheffield: Sheffield Academic Press, 2000), 103–104: "V. 16b refers unmistakably to the death of the ratifier of the will/covenant as being essential for its implementation. . . . Interpreting this as the symbolic death of the ratifier . . . requires a lot of reading between the lines in v. 16b and even more so in v. 17"; see also Vos, *Hebrews*, 39.

57   See W. Bauer, W. F. Arndt, and F. W. Gingrich (3d ed.; rev. by F. W. Danker), *Greek-English Lexicon of the NT* 576a (def. 2b); Louw-Nida *Lexicon of the NT* 782a (§89.35); Liddell-Scott-Jones, *Greek-English Lexicon* 1242a (def. II.2). Ὅπου is clearly causal in 1 Cor. 3:3, 4 Macc. 14:11, 14, 19; possibly also in 4 Macc. 2:14 and 6:34. Ὅπου occurs in Heb. 6:20; 9:16 and 10:18. In both Heb. 9:16 and 10:18 the causal meaning ("whereas, since") seems to provide a better reading than the usual rendering.

maker to be borne." Under different circumstances, the fact that there had been transgressions (παραβάσεις) may have been inconsequential or given rise to some lesser punishment, but "since there is a covenant"—particularly one that has been ratified by a bloody *Drohritus* (Heb. 9:18–22), that is, which entails a curse-of-death for violations—"the death of the covenant-maker must be borne."

2.3.2 θάνατον ἀνάγκη φέρεσθαι τοῦ διαθεμένου (*Heb.* 9:16b)

A broken covenant of this kind demands the curse-of-death. The biblical and extra-biblical examples of death as the sanction for covenant-breaking (see above) support the author's assertion. Some commentators have voiced the opinion that "covenants or contracts, of whatever sort, simply do not require the death of one of the parties,"[58] but in the understanding of the author of Hebrews, covenants of this sort (ratified by sacrifice) certainly *do* require the death of one of the parties when broken.

An explanation of the circumlocution θάνατον ἀνάγκη φέρεσθαι τοῦ διαθεμένου is in order. Φέρω should be taken in its common meaning "to bear, to endure,"[59] rather than the otherwise-unattested meanings most modern versions and lexicons provide here for the phrase θάνατον φέρεσθαι.[60] The phrase διαθέμενον ἀνάγκη ἀποθανεῖν, "it is necessary for the covenant-maker to die," would be more succinct, but the difference in emphasis between "the covenant-maker must die" and "the death of the covenant-maker must be borne" is significant, if subtle. In the first formulation, the subject of the verbal idea is the *covenant-maker*, in the second, it is the *death*. The second formulation does not actually specify who must die, only that the covenant-maker's death must be endured. The author leaves open the possibility that the death of the covenant-maker might be borne by a designated representative, for example, the high-priest Jesus. He only stresses that, because of transgression (Heb. 9:15), *someone* must bear the curse-of-death, without specifying whom. In the view of the author, ultimately Christ endures the curse-of-death on behalf of the *actual* covenant-makers, that is, those under the first covenant (Heb. 9:15).

The concept of someone "bearing" (φέρω) the death of the covenant-maker in Hebrews 9:16, like the "bearing (ἀναφέρω) the sins of many" in Hebrews 9:28, may be shaped by the use of φέρω in Isaiah 53 LXX, where (ἀνα)φέρω is consistently used in the sense "bear something for another."[61] Hebrews 9:28 (τὸ πολλῶν ἀνενεγκεῖν ἁμαρτίας) is a clear reference to Isaiah 53:12 LXX (καὶ αὐτὸς ἁμαρτίας πολλῶν ἀνήνεγκεν), which suffices to show that Isaiah 53 is in the mind of the

---

58 Attridge, *Hebrews*, 256.

59 W. Bauer, W. F. Arndt, and F. W. Gingrich (3d ed.; rev. by F. W. Danker), *Greek-English Lexicon of the NT* 855a (def. 1c); Louw-Nida *Lexicon of the NT* 807a (§90.64); Liddell-Scott-Jones, *Greek-English Lexicon* 1923a (def. A.III). In Heb. 13:13 φέρω is used in this sense (τόν ὀνειδισμόν αὐτοῦ φέροντες). See also Heb. 12:20 (οὐκ ἔφερον γάρ τό διαστελλόμενον); Isa. 53:4 LXX (οὗτος τὰς ἁμαρτίας ἡμῶν φέρει); Jer. 51:22 LXX; Ezek. 34:29, 36:6 LXX.

60 See discussion above, especially n. 25.

61 See Isa. 53:3, 4, 11, 12.

author in Hebrews 9. Thus, it may well be that the use of φέρω in the sense of "bear on another's behalf" in Isaiah 53:3–4 elucidates the use of φέρω in Hebrews 9:16.

2.3.3 διαθήκη γὰρ ἐπὶ νεκροῖς βεβαία (Heb. 9:17a)

The sense of Hebrews 9:17a ("a [broken] covenant is confirmed upon dead [bodies]") is that, after a covenant has been broken (the situation under the first covenant), the only means of enforcing the covenant is to actualize the covenant curses, which ultimately result in the death of the covenant-maker-turned-covenant-breaker.[62]

The use of the plural ἐπὶ νεκροῖς, "dead bodies"—problematic under the testamentary reading—is not unexpected under the reading proposed here. The situation the author envisions is the first covenant, made by the people. Ὁ διαθέμενος and ἐπὶ νεκροῖς refer to the people of Israel in the collective singular and the plural form respectively. The grammatically-singular "people" (see Heb. 9:19, λαός) is the "covenant-maker" (ὁ διαθέμενος) at Sinai; yet "dead bodies" (νεκροί, see Deut. 28:26 LXX) would result if the curse-of-death was actualized upon them.

2.3.4 ἐπεὶ μήποτε ἰσχύει ὅτε ζῇ ὁ διαθέμενος (Heb. 9:17b)

The bold statement of Hebrews 9:17b, "since it certainly is not in force while the covenant-maker lives,"[63] expresses the following principle: for the covenant-maker(s) to remain alive after violating the covenant indicates that the covenant has no binding force (μήποτε ἰσχύει). It is useful to recall the rhetorical question of Ezek. 17:15: "But he rebelled against him. . . . Will he succeed? Can a man escape who does such things? Can he break the covenant and yet escape?" (RSV). For the author of Hebrews, as well as for Ezekiel, the answer is an emphatic "No!" (see Heb. 12:25!). The survival of the covenant-maker after the violation of his sworn commitment demonstrates the impotence of the covenant and the powerlessness of the oath-curse. A covenant is not *in force* if it is not *enforced*.

2.3.5 ὅθεν οὐδὲ ἡ πρώτη χωρὶς αἵματος ἐγκεκαίνισται (Heb. 9:18)

Hebrews 9:18–22 explicitly concerns the first Sinaitic covenant, strengthening the case that this broken covenant is the assumed context of Hebrews 9:16–17. The sense of Hebrews 9:18, ὅθεν οὐδὲ ἡ πρώτη χωρὶς αἵματος ἐγκεκαίνισται, may be "hence, neither was the first covenant inaugurated without blood," the emphasis being on the fact that, at its very inauguration, the first covenant liturgically pre-enacted the death of the covenant-maker should the covenant be transgressed.[64] Thus, the reader should not doubt that the Sinaitic covenant was one that entailed

---

62   See Lev. 26:14–39, especially v. 30, but also vv. 16, 22, 25, 38; Deut. 28:15–68, especially vv. 20, 22, 24, 26, 48, 51, 61. As was noted above for the ancient Near Eastern oath-curses, although not all the curses of Lev. 26 and Deut. 28 are *immediate* death, virtually all the curses are *means* of death: plague, disease, enemy attack, wild animals, siege, famine, etc.

63   For μήποτε as a strong negative ("certainly not") see Ellingworth, *Hebrews*, 464.

64   See Vanhoye, *New Priest*, 203.

the curse-of-death. The flow of thought from Hebrews 9:16–17 to 9:18–22 could be paraphrased as follows: "A broken covenant requires the death of the covenant-maker (Heb. 9:16–17); hence, the first covenant liturgically portrayed the death of the covenant-maker by bloody sacrifice (Heb. 9:18–21). Nearly everything about the first covenant was covered in blood, representing the necessity of death for the forgiveness of transgressions of the covenant (Heb. 9:22, see 9:15)."

3. Conclusion and an Avenue for Further Study

At the beginning of this essay, we discussed the close integration of the legal and liturgical aspects of the covenant in the thought-world of Hebrews. However, Hebrews 9:15–18 appeared to be counter-evidence for this integration. In Hebrews 9:16–17, the author appears to use διαθήκη in a sense quite different from his customary usage, stepping outside Israelite-Jewish cultic categories in order to draw an analogy from Greco-Roman law, whose relevance is anything but clear.

I have argued that the solution to the puzzle of Hebrews 9:16–17 is not to abandon the cultic-covenantal framework of the author's thought, with its close relationship between liturgy and law, but to enter into that framework more deeply. If it is understood that the context for the statements of Hebrews 9:16–17 is the broken first covenant mentioned in Hebrews 9:15, one can see that the author is drawing out the *legal* implications of the *liturgical* ritual (that is, bloody sacrifices) that established the first covenant: a broken covenant demands the death of the covenant-maker (Hebrews 9:16), and it is not being enforced while the offending covenant-maker lives (Hebrews 9:17).

Therefore, Hebrews 9:16–17 does not involve an abrupt, unmarked switch in context (from Jewish to Greco-Roman), nor does the author argue for a strained analogy between a "covenant" and a "testament." Verses 16–17 simply restate a theological principle summarized in the verse they seek to explicate (Heb. 9:15): the first covenant entailed the curse-of-death for those who broke it (Heb. 2:2; 10:28), which Christ takes upon himself as Israel's corporate representative (Heb. 2:9, 14; 9:28), thus freeing those under the first covenant from the curse-of-death (Heb. 2:15; 10:14) and providing for them a new and better covenant (Heb. 9:28; 10:15–17; 12:22–24).

If I have been correct in my exegesis of Hebrews 9:16–17, then the statement of v. 17b certainly opens up an avenue for further study: ἐπεὶ μήποτε ἰσχύει ὅτε ζῇ ὁ διαθέμενος, "since [the covenant] is certainly not in force while the covenant-maker lives." According to my paradigm, the author is speaking about the broken Sinaitic covenant: having been broken (at the golden calf apostasy), it is not in force (or being enforced) until the covenant curse (that is, death) is actualized upon the covenant-maker (Israel). The covenant-curse of death is only finally visited upon Israel when Christ dies as their representative (Heb. 9:15). But this implies that, in the author's view, there is an extended hiatus in Israel's history between the violation of the first covenant (Exod. 32:1–14) and the death of Christ, during which the first covenant was, in a sense, not "strong" or "in force" (μήποτε ἰσχύει), held in abeyance, its curses not being actualized. It is as if, after the golden calf, a verdict is reached, the sentence handed down, but the execution suspended indefinitely. What justified this suspension?

The answer is to be found in the narrative of Exodus 32. After the covenant has been broken God threatens to enforce it: "Now let me alone, so that my wrath may burn hot against them and I may consume them; and of you I will make a great nation" (Exod. 32:10 NRSV). But Moses pleads with God to relent, based on the divine oath to the Patriarchs: "Remember Abraham, Isaac, and Israel, your servants, how you swore to them by your own self" (Exod. 32:13 NRSV). Moses is referring to God's oath at the Aqedah (Gen. 22:15–18), the only record of God swearing by himself to the Patriarchs. On Mt. Moriah, after the near-sacrifice of Isaac, God spoke to Abraham:

> By Myself I swear, the LORD declares: Because you have done this and have not withheld your son, your favored one, I will bestow My blessing upon you and make your descendants as numerous as the stars of heaven and the sands on the seashore; and your descendants shall seize the gates of their foes. All the nations of the earth shall bless themselves by your descendants, because you have obeyed My command. (Gen. 22:16–18 NJPS)

In Exodus 32:13, Moses appeals to this oath, making the following argument to God: "You cannot annihilate Israel for violating their covenant-oath, for if you do, you would violate your own self-sworn oath to bless and multiply Abraham's descendants." In other words, the covenant *curses* of Sinai could not be enforced upon the people of Israel because of God's prior oath to Abraham to *bless* his descendants (that is, Israel).

The Levitical priesthood, according to the narrative of the Pentateuch, is established in response to the golden calf apostasy (Exod. 32:29). The author of Hebrews notes that "on the basis of [the Levitical priesthood] the law was given to the people" (Heb. 7:11). This would refer to the fact that the bulk of the sacrificial system (Lev. 1–7, 16), as well as the Deuteronomic Code, was given to Israel subsequent to the golden calf episode and the elevation of the Levites. The author of Hebrews may have held the view that this Levitical cultic system was "weak and useless" (Heb. 7:18) because it was only a symbolic or pedagogical apparatus designed to remind Israel of her covenant violations (Heb. 10:3) until one could come who was capable of bearing the curse-of-death of the (broken) covenant on behalf of the whole nation (Heb. 2:9; 9:15), thus enabling God to enforce the first covenant without undermining his self-sworn oath to bless the "seed of Abraham" (Gen. 22:15–18; Heb. 6:13–20).

The author of Hebrews places considerable weight on divine oaths in general,[65] and devotes particular attention to this divine oath at the Aqedah (Gen. 22:15–18) in Hebrews 6:13–20. He mentions the Aqedah again in Hebrews 11:17–19. Dunnill remarks:

> The story of the "Binding of Isaac" [is] a theme which has vastly greater significance, not only for this chapter but for the theology of the letter as a whole, than its rather brief appearance ([Heb.] 11:17f) would suggest. [It is of] fundamental importance for the letter's Christology. . . . It acts as the organizing centre of Hebrews 11 and as a "foundation sacrifice" for the faith-covenant established through Jesus.[66]

In Jewish tradition, the Aqedah took place on the Day of Atonement, and the rituals of the Day of Atonement were interpreted as a yearly anamnesis of Isaac's "sacrifice."[67] Thus, the author's theology of the Day of Atonement, articulated throughout Hebrews 9:1–28, may have an integral relation to the significance he sees in the Aqedah and the divine oath given there (Heb. 6:13–20; 11:17–19).

In sum, it may be that the author of Hebrews regards the divine oath to Abraham at the Aqedah as a foundational act for Israel, which is renewed in Christ. The divine oath of the Aqedah is an expression of God's providential mercy, inasmuch as it prevents the full enforcement of the curses of the first covenant (Exod. 32:13–14) until the coming of the Christ, who can bear the curse-of-death on behalf of all (Heb. 2:9; 9:15) and restore for Israel the Abrahamic blessing (Heb. 6:13–20; Gen. 22:15–18). Christ's death is simultaneously the legal execution of the curses of the old covenant and the liturgical ritual of sacrifice which establishes the new. Hebrews' theology on this point would be strikingly similar to Paul's in Galatians 3:6–25, which is unsurprising given the numerous connections between Galatians and Hebrews already noted by other scholars.[68] In any event, the complex of issues surrounding the divine oath at the Aqedah, the "weakness" of the Sinaitic covenant rituals, and the author's bold statement in Hebrews 9:17b certainly merits further study.[69]

---

65 Dunnill, *Covenant and Sacrifice*, 249: "Oaths and the finality they confer are deeply important in Hebrews, especially the unique status and revolutionary consequences of divine oaths." The author discusses the divine oath of Num. 14:20–23 (through Ps. 95:7–11) in Heb. 3:7–4:11 and that of Ps. 110:4 in Heb. 7:20–22. For an expanded treatment, see Hahn, *Kinship by Covenant*, 278–331.

66 Dunnill, *Covenant and Sacrifice*, 173.

67 See Dunnill, *Covenant and Sacrifice*, 174–175.

68 For example, Ben Witherington III, "The Influence of Galatians on Hebrews," *New Testament Studies* 37 (1991): 146–152.

69 See Hahn, *Kinship by Covenant*, 101–175; 278–331. This article is a revision of an article that appeared in *Hebrews: Contemporary Methods—New Insights*, ed. Gabriella Gelardini (Leiden: Brill, 2005), 66–88, under the title, "Covenant, Cult, and the Curse-of-Death: Διαθήκη in Heb 9:15–22."

Letter & Spirit 8 (2013): 35-54

Jesus, the Messianic Wedding Banquet, and the Restoration of Israel

~: Brant Pitre :~
Notre Dame Seminary

Introduction

If there are any issues about which historical scholarship is in widespread agreement, they are that Jesus' preaching of the Kingdom of God was a central aspect of his message and mission, and that he used parables to teach about the mystery of the kingdom. For example, the comments of James D. G. Dunn regarding the kingdom of God are representative:

> The centrality of the kingdom of God (*basileia tou theou*) in Jesus' preaching is one of the least disputable, or disputed, facts about Jesus.[1]

With regard to the role of the parables, Craig S. Keener expresses the remarkable confidence of contemporary scholarship on Jesus when he writes:

> By normal historical standards, then, we should give special attention to parables in the Gospels as among the least debatable, most securely authentic elements of the Jesus tradition.[2]

In short, although many areas of Jesus research are characterized by competing hypotheses and contradictory claims, these two conclusions—that Jesus taught about the Kingdom of God and that he used parables to do so—are accepted by almost all modern scholars.[3]

---

1   James D. G. Dunn, *Jesus Remembered* (Grand Rapids: Eerdmans, 2003), 383.

2   Craig S. Keener, *The Historical Jesus of the Gospels* (Grand Rapids: Eerdmans, 2009), 188.

3   On the centrality of the kingdom, see also John P. Meier, *A Marginal Jew* (3 vols.; Anchor Bible Reference Library; New York: Doubleday, 1991, 1994, 2001), 2:237; E. P. Sanders, *Jesus and Judaism* (Philadelphia: Fortress, 1985), 307; Norman Perrin, *Rediscovering the Teaching of Jesus* (New York: Harper & Row, 1967), 54; Joachim Jeremias, *New Testament Theology: the Proclamation of Jesus*, trans. John Bowden (London: SCM, 1971), 96; Rudolf Bultmann, *Theology of the New Testament* (2 vols.; London: SCM, 1952), 1:4. On the importance of parables, see also Craig S. Keener, *The Historical Jesus of the Gospels* (Grand Rapids: Eerdmans, 2009), 188–189; Gerd Theissen and Annette Merz, *The Historical Jesus: A Comprehensive Guide*, trans. John Bowden (Minneapolis: Fortress, 1998), 316–317, 337–339; Jürgen Becker, *Jesus of Nazareth*, trans. James E. Crouch (New York and Berlin: Walter de Gruyter, 1998), 143–144; C. H. Dodd, *The Parables of the Kingdom* (New York: Charles Scribner's Sons, 1961), viii; Joachim Jeremias, *The Parables of Jesus*, 2nd rev. ed. (New York: Charles Scribner's Sons, 1963), 11.

However, where scholars do disagree—and disagree quite strongly—is in the *interpretation* of the parables of Jesus. In recent years a host of volumes on the parables of Jesus have appeared, offering quite divergent interpretations, from the counter-cultural aphorisms of a Cynic-like sage stringing his pearls of wisdom across the Galilean countryside, to the stories of a Jewish rabbi anticipating the teaching methods and traditions later preserved in the Midrash and the Talmuds.[4]

In this article, I would like to suggest that in order to unlock the meaning the parables would have had for Jesus' disciples in a first-century Jewish context, one must focus attention above all on *their Old Testament background*. To be sure, recourse to other sources besides Jewish Scripture, such as the Dead Sea Scrolls, the Pseudepigrapha, and rabbinic parables is extremely helpful in shedding light on these often enigmatic statements of Jesus. However, given the popular character of the parables and Jesus' use of them in his public teaching, there seems to be a good *prima facie* argument in favor of focusing first on the common background of *Jewish Scripture* in the attempt to unpack their (often mysterious) meaning.[5] In order to illustrate this approach, we will select one of Jesus' most memorable and difficult parables in the Gospels: the parable of the Royal Wedding Feast (Matt. 22:1–14). As I hope to show, by giving proper attention to the biblical backdrop of Jesus' startling tale, one can throw an extraordinary amount of light both on the meaning of this parable in particular and on the heart of Jesus' wider message: the mystery of the kingdom of God.

The Parable of the Royal Wedding Feast[6]

Although the basic contours of this parable are well known, it is worth citing it in its entirety before we turn to its exegesis:

---

4   On the one hand, John Dominic Crossan, *In Parables: The Challenge of the Historical Jesus* (repr. Polebridge, 1992), and on the other, Brad H. Young, *Jesus and His Jewish Parables: Rediscovering the Roots of Jesus' Teaching* (Mahwah: Paulist, 1989).

5   In this regard, see especially Klyne R. Snodgrass, *Stories with Intent: A Comprehensive Guide to the Parables of Jesus* (Grand Rapids: Eerdmans, 2008), who makes ample use of Jewish Scripture in his exegesis. See also Arland J. Hultgren, *The Parables of Jesus* (Grand Rapids: Eerdmans, 2000).

6   On this parable, see especially Snodgrass, *Stories with Intent*, 299–325; Peter-Ben Smit, *Fellowship and Food in the Kingdom: Eschatological Meals and Scenes of Utopian Abundance in the New Testament*, Wissenschaftliche Untersuchungen zum Neuen Testament 2:234 (Tübingen: Mohr-Siebeck, 2008), 229–236; R. T. France, *The Gospel of Matthew* (Grand Rapids: Eerdmans, 2007), 820–828; Marianne Blickenstaff, "While the Bridegroom is with Them": Marriage, Family, Gender and Violence in the Gospel of Matthew Journal for the Study of the New Testament Suppplement Series 292 (London: T & T Clark: 2005), 46–77; Dunn, *Jesus Remembered*, 427; Hultgren, *The Parables of Jesus*, 341–351; Craig S. Keener, *A Commentary on the Gospel of Matthew*, (Grand Rapids: Eerdmans, 1999), 517–522; Jürgen Becker, *Jesus of Nazareth*, trans. James E. Crouch (New York/Berlin: Walter de Gruyter, 1998), 163–165; Gerd Theissen and Annette Merz, *The Historical Jesus: An Introduction*, trans. John Bowden (Minneapolis: Fortress, 1998) 266–267; W. D. Davies and Dale C. Allison, Jr., *A Critical and Exegetical Commentary on the Gospel According to Saint Matthew*, 3 vols. (Edinburgh: T. & T. Clark, 1988, 1991, 1997),

And again Jesus spoke to them in parables, saying, "The kingdom of heaven may be compared to a king who gave a marriage feast for his son, and sent his servants to call those who were invited to the marriage feast; but they would not come. Again he sent other servants, saying, 'Tell those who are invited, Behold, I have made ready my dinner, my oxen and my fat calves are killed, and everything is ready; come to the marriage feast.' But they made light of it and went off, one to his farm, another to his business, while the rest seized his servants, treated them shamefully, and killed them. The king was angry, and he sent his troops and destroyed those murderers and burned their city. Then he said to those servants, 'The wedding is ready, but those invited were not worthy. Go therefore to the streets and invite to the marriage feast as many as you find.' And those servants went out into the streets and gathered all whom they found, both bad and good; so the wedding hall was filled with guests. But when the king came in to look at the guests, he saw there a man who had no wedding garment; and he said to him, 'Friend, how did you get in here without a wedding garment?' And he was speechless. Then the king said to the attendants, 'Bind him hand and foot, and cast him into the outer darkness, where there will be weeping and gnashing of teeth.' For many are called, but few are chosen." (Matt. 22:1-14)[7]

Several exegetical questions swirl around this text: (1) Does the comparison of the kingdom with the royal wedding feast (Matt. 22:1–10) belong with the account of the king's examination of the guests (Matt. 22:11–14), or are these two separate parables? (2) What is the background of this parable? Are there any stories of royal banquets from the Old Testament or ancient Judaism that might shed light on the meaning Jesus' words? (3) What is the significance of identifying the kingdom of

---

3:193–209; Marius Reiser, *Jesus and Judgment: The Eschatological Proclamation in its Jewish Context*, trans. Linda M. Maloney (Minneapolis: Fortress, 1997), 241-45; Richard Bauckham, "The Parable of the Royal Wedding Feast (Matthew 22:1–14) and the Parable of the Lame Man and the Blind Man (*Apocryphon of Ezekiel*)," *Journal of Biblical Literature* 115 (1996): 471–488; Robert W. Funk, Roy Hoover, and the Jesus Seminar, *The Five Gospels: The Search for the Authentic Words of Jesus* (New York: Macmillan, 1993), 234–235; Geza Vermes, *The Religion of Jesus the Jew*, 113; Crossan, *The Historical Jesus*, 261–262; G. R. Beasley-Murray, *Jesus and the Kingdom of God* (Grand Rapids: Eerdmans, 1985), 119–122; Crossan, *In Parables*, 70–73; Norman Perrin, *Rediscovering the Teaching of Jesus* (New York: Harper & Row, 1967), 110–114; Jeremias, *The Parables of Jesus*, 67–70, 176–180, 187–189; Dodd, *The Parables of the Kingdom*, 93–94; T. W. Manson, *The Sayings of Jesus* (London: SCM, 1949), 128–130; Johannes Behm, "*deipnon*," *Theological Dictionary of the New Testament* 2:34–35; Rudolf Bultmann, *History of the Synoptic Tradition*, rev. ed., trans. John Marsh (Oxford: Basil Blackwell, 1963), 175, 197–198.

7   All translations are from the RSV unless otherwise noted.

heaven with not just any banquet, but a "wedding" banquet for the king's "son"? (4) What is the meaning of the king's inspection of the guests? In particular, what is "the wedding garment," and why is lacking one so grave as to merit being cast out of the wedding feast and into "the outer darkness"? (5) What is the overall thrust of the parable? What is the meaning of the final declaration: "many are called, but few are chosen"? (6) Finally, once the parable has been interpreted, what does its overall message reveal about the nature of the "the kingdom of heaven"?

The Unity of the Parable of the Royal Wedding Feast

The first issue is whether the parable of the Royal Wedding Feast is one parable, comparing the kingdom of heaven to a banquet that climaxes with the advent of the king (Matt 22:1–14), or two separate parables—one focusing on the similitude of the kingdom (Matt 22:1–10) and another separate story of a king inspecting his guests (Matt 22:11–14).

Interpreters are divided on this point. On the one hand, some commentators insist that these are two entirely separate parables.[8] Inevitably, scholars who hold this position do so because they view the Parable of the Royal Wedding Feast (Matt. 22:1–10) and the Parable of the Great Banquet (Luke 14:15–24) as two "versions" of the same hypothetical "original" parable. From this perspective, the inspection of the wedding garments is a separate parable primarily because it is absent from the other version of the parable found in the Gospel of Luke.[9]

On the other hand, other scholars hold that the text consists of a single parable, with two parts.[10] In favor of this conclusion is the connection between the royal "wedding feast" (*gamos*) of the first half (Matt. 22:2–3) and the "king's" inspection of the "wedding garment" (*enduma gamou*) in the second half (Matt. 22:11). Moreover, in terms of form, a unified view of the Royal Wedding Feast coheres with other two-part parables of Jesus. For example, the Parable of the Wicked Tenants consists of an initial narrative of the vineyard (Mark 12:1–9) followed by the concluding riddle of the "stone" rejected by the builders (Mark 12:10–12). Along the same lines, the parable of the Prodigal Son consists of the initial narrative of the son's return (Luke 15:11–24), followed by the account of the elder brother's reaction (Luke 15:25–32). Likewise, the parable of the Dishonest Steward has a quite distinct opening narrative (Luke 16:1–9) followed by a concluding application (Luke 16:10–13). As Joachim Jeremias comments: "[I]n all the double-edged parables the emphasis lies on the second point."[11]

---

8   See, for example, Jeremias, *The Parables of Jesus*, 64–66; Dodd, *The Parables of Jesus*, 94; see Hultgren, *The Parables of Jesus*, 346, n. 23 for further examples.

9   As well as the later *Gospel of Thomas* 64. So Jeremias, *The Parables of Jesus*, 65.

10   See, for example, Snodgrass, *Stories with Intent*, 320; Hultgren, *The Parables of Jesus*, 333; Davies and Allison, *Saint Matthew*, 3:194.

11   Jeremias, *The Parables of Jesus*, 38, though he does not follow the logic of his own insight when he separates the Royal Wedding Feast into two parables.

In light of such considerations, it is reasonable to treat the parable of the "Royal Wedding Feast" (Matt 22:1–14) as a single, unified narrative, with two parts. With this in mind, we can now ask the question: What does the parable mean? How do we interpret it in a first-century Jewish context?

The Eschatological Wedding Banquet

The first aspect of this parable that strikes the reader is that of the royal "wedding banquet" (*gamos*), given by a "king" (*basileus*) for his "son" (*huios*) (Matt. 22:2). On the one hand, the basic meaning of this analogy is easily identified. As many commentators recognize, this is yet another example of Jesus' use of the image of a feast to describe the eschatological banquet of the kingdom (cf. Matt 8:11–12; Luke 13:28–29).[12] Moreover, in this case, the specifically messianic character of the banquet seems particularly manifest, insofar as the king who hosts the banquet represents God, while the son for whom the banquet is celebrated is none other than the royal "son of God"—a title ascribed to the Davidic king of old, and later applied to the coming messiah.[13]

On the other hand, the depiction of the messianic banquet as a *wedding* banquet is distinctive, if not completely unique. According to W. D. Davies and Dale C. Allison, although the messianic banquet is a common *topos* in ancient Jewish literature, this parable of Jesus is unique in depicting the messianic feast as a wedding.[14] The significance of this identification can be found both by briefly exploring the character of such a wedding banquet in a Jewish context, and then connecting this context to Jewish eschatology.

In ancient Jewish literature, although there are multiple references to wedding banquets, we unfortunately lack any detailed descriptions of these feasts. We are forced to paste together somewhat skeletal sketches of what the customs might have entailed from sources spanning a wide range of time and place.[15] Such

---

12   See Snodgrass, *Stories with Intent*, 311; Reiser, *Jesus and Judgment*, 242; Theissen and Merz, *The Historical Jesus*, 267; Davies and Allison, *Saint Matthew*, 3:199.

13   Hultgren, *The Parables of Jesus*, 343; Ben-Smit, *Fellowship and Food in the Kingdom*, 230–231, who points out that "while the *Title* Son of God is not used, ... the concept seems to be implied." For a full-length recent study, see Adela Yarbro Collins and John J. Collins, *King and Messiah as Son of God: Divine, Human, and Angelic Figures in Biblical and Related Literature* (Grand Rapids: Eerdmans, 2008).

14   Davies and Allison, *Saint Matthew*, 3:199, n. 27.

15   See David Instone-Brewer, "Marriage and Divorce," in *The Eerdmans Dictionary of Early Judaism* (Grand Rapids: Eerdmans, 2010), 916–917; Michael Satlow, *Jewish Marriage in Antiquity* (Princeton: Princeton University Press, 2001); John J. Collins, "Marriage, Divorce, and Family in Second Temple Judaism," *Families in Ancient Israel*, ed. L. G. Perdue et al. (Louisville: Westminster John Knox, 1997), 104–162; Victor P. Hamilton, "Marriage (OT and ANE)," in *Anchor Bible Dictionary* 4:559-69; Raymond F. Collins, "Marriage (NT)," in *Anchor Bible Dictionary* 4:569–72; Ethelbert Stauffer, "*gameo, gamos*," *Theological Dictionary of the New Testament* 1:648–657; Joachim Jeremias, "*numphe, numphios*," *Theological Dictionary of the New Testament* 4:1099–1106.

evidence suggests that an ancient Jewish wedding celebration ordinarily consisted of seven days of festivities (Gen. 29:22–27; Judg. 14:12; *Jos. Asen.* 21:8; *b. Ket.* 4b). If the parable of the Ten Virgins is any indicator, then it appears that the wedding feast proper took place late in the evening and that it consisted of some manner of procession of select young women to the celebration of the marriage (Matt 25:1-13). As one might expect, such a feast would be a time of great happiness, when the "voice of the bridegroom" and the "voice of the bride" would be lifted up in song and joyful celebration (Jer. 33:11).[16]

In light of such background, it is significant that Jewish Scripture utilizes the image of a wedding as a way of describing the everlasting joy that would be experienced at the eschatological restoration of Israel.[17] For example, the prophet Hosea declares that when the ingathering of "the people of Judah" (the two tribes) and "the people of Israel" (the ten tribes) under a future king takes place, God will wed himself to Israel his bride "as at the time when she came out of the land of Egypt" (Hos. 1:10–11; 2:14–23).[18] In similar fashion, Jeremiah describes the restoration of Israel under a future Davidic king in terms of an "everlasting love" with which God loves the "virgin Israel" (Jer. 31:3–4). Perhaps most important of all for the Parable of the Royal Wedding Feast, the prophet Isaiah not only speaks of this eschatological wedding, but on several occasions ties this hope to the celebration of a great eschatological banquet.[19] Consider, for example, the following texts:

> Sing, O barren one, who did not bear; break forth into singing and cry aloud, you who have not had labor pains! … *For your Maker is your husband, the* LORD *of hosts is his name* … For the LORD has called you like a wife forsaken and grieved in spirit, like a wife of youth when she is cast off, says your God. For a brief moment I forsook you, but with great compassion *I will gather you. … Ho, every one who thirsts, come to the waters; and he who has no money, come, buy and eat!* Come, buy wine and milk without money and without price. Why do you spend your money for that which is not bread, and your labor for that which does not satisfy? Listen diligently to me, and eat what is good, and delight yourselves in rich food. Incline your ear, and come

---

16   For numerous references in Greek literature to the sumptuous nature of ancient wedding feasts, see Blickenstaff, *"While the Bridegroom is With Them,"* 57–58, n. 40.

17   See Ben-Smit, *Fellowship and Food in the Kingdom,* 25–26. In contrast to those who analyze them separately, scholars who tend to treat the Royal Wedding Feast and the Great Supper as two versions of an "original" parable tend to overlook the significance of the nuptial imagery. Compare Hultgren, *The Parables of Jesus,* 344, with Snodgrass, *Stories with Intent,* 318–321, the latter of whom does nothing with the eschatological wedding imagery in Isaiah.

18   Both these events are referred to as the day of "Jezreel," meaning "God sows," for he will sow his people "in the land" (Hos. 1:11; 2:23).

19   Dennis Smith, "Messianic Banquet," *Anchor Bible Dictionary* 4:788–791.

to me; hear, that your soul may live; and I will make with you an everlasting covenant, my steadfast, merciful love for David ... Behold, you shall call nations that you know not, and nations that knew you not shall run to you. (Isa. 54:1, 5–7; 55:1–5)

For Zion's sake I will not keep silent, and for Jerusalem's sake I will not rest, until her vindication goes forth as brightness, and her salvation as a burning torch. The nations shall see your vindication, and all the kings your glory; and you shall be called by a new name which the mouth of the LORD will give. You shall be a crown of beauty in the hand of the LORD, and a royal diadem in the hand of your God. You shall no more be termed Forsaken, and your land shall not be termed Desolate; but you shall be called "My Delight is in her," and your land "Married;" for the LORD delights in you, and *your land shall be married ... As the bridegroom rejoices over the bride, so shall your God rejoice over you ...* The LORD has sworn by his right hand and by his mighty arm: "I will not again give your grain to be food for your enemies, and foreigners shall not drink your wine for which you have labored; but *those who garner it shall eat it and praise the LORD, and those who gather it shall drink it in the courts of my sanctuary."* (Isa. 62:1–5, 8–9)

Two aspects of these oracles stand out. First, in both prophecies, the restoration of Israel is described in terms of a wedding between God and Israel. In the first of the two oracles (Isa. 55:3), this nuptial covenant is explicitly identified as an "everlasting covenant" that is rooted in God's "love for David" (compare with Psalm 89). This Davidic dimension is important, for it suggests that the future wedding is not merely *eschatological*; it is Davidic, and therefore *messianic* in character. Second, in both oracles, the eschatological wedding of God and Israel is tied to a banquet of great joy.[20] As Dennis Smith notes, in Isaiah, "the theme of a *divine marriage* (54:5) is combined with *a joyful feast* which is characterized by an abundance of food (55:1–2), vindication of the righteous (54:6–17), and the pilgrimage of the nations (55:5)."[21]

When the Parable of the Royal Wedding Feast is interpreted in light of this background in Jewish Scripture, Jesus' use of the image of a "royal wedding feast" suddenly appears as more than simply an image of happiness drawn from daily life; even more, it is an allusion to the oracles of the biblical prophets regarding

---

20 In the second oracle, Isaiah explicitly describes the banquet as taking place in the Temple ("the courts of my sanctuary"). In other words, this eschatological feast of "grain" (for making bread) and "wine" will not be any ordinary meal, but a cultic feast (Isa. 62:9).

21 Dennis Smith, "Messianic Banquet," *Anchor Bible Dictionary* 4:788–791, at 790 (my emphasis).

the eschatological restoration of Israel. In the future age of salvation, the twelve tribes and the nations will not only be gathered to the restored Jerusalem, but God will wed himself to Israel in an everlasting nuptial covenant, in a wedding celebrated—as are all weddings—with a great banquet.

This nuptial dimension of the Old Testament background helps explain another strange part of Jesus' parable of the Royal Wedding Feast. Some commentators have been puzzled by the severity of the punishment for rejecting the invitation to a wedding, which is usually a voluntary festive celebration.[22] However, when Jesus' parable is interpreted against the backdrop of the eschatological wedding of God and Israel, then the gravity of failing to attend the wedding becomes clear. Jesus' message is one of warning: this is no ordinary wedding feast. It is the feast of the eschatological restoration of Israel and the renewal of the Davidic kingdom covenant (see 2 Sam. 7). Hence, the rejection of the invitation to this wedding banquet means rejecting the "everlasting covenant" that God will make with Israel and "the nations" in the age of "salvation" (Isa. 54:4–5; 62:1–2).

King Hezekiah's Rejected Banquet and the Restoration of Israel

Once this background of the eschatological wedding feast is firmly in place, we can now make sense of a second important element in the parable: the invitations sent out by the king and the various responses they engender. First, the king sends his servants to call those who had been invited to the feast, but the invitees refuse to come. Next, the king sends "other servants" to tell those invited that the banquet is "ready" and that they should "come to the marriage feast." In this instance, the invitees not only make light of the invitation; some of them even persecute and kill the king's "servants," eliciting a military reaction from the king, who sends his troops to destroy "those murderers" and burn "their city." In the wake of this destruction, the king declares the original invitees "unworthy" and commands a third and final invitation to go out to "as many" as possible, "both bad and good," so that the wedding hall might be filled with guests (Matt. 22:3–10).

What are we to make of this seemingly bizarre series of actions and reactions?[23] As several scholars have suggested, their hyperbolic and even unrealistic character seem to be signs of an allegorical meaning.[24] What might such meaning have been in an ancient Jewish context?

Once again, the answer seems to lie in the Old Testament background of the parable. If scholars are correct, and the Royal Wedding Feast is a retelling of the

---

22 See Jan Lambrecht, *Out of the Treasure: The Parables in the Gospel of Matthew* (Louvain: Peeters, 1991), 128.

23 For a plethora of interpretations, see Blickenstaff, *"While the Bridegroom is With Them,"* 55, n. 30.

24 See, for example, Davies and Allison, *Saint Matthew,* 3:196–197.

history of Israel in a new key,[25] then it is surely significant that this parable of Jesus is not the first story of a royal banquet to which many were invited and refused, and so were replaced by others.[26] Indeed, a remarkably similar story can be found in 2 Chronicles, when one of the greatest Davidic kings, King Hezekiah, sends out invitations to the northern tribes to come to the Passover feast in Jerusalem—only to have his invitations rejected. The author of Chronicles evidently regarded the event as pivotal and of great moment, in that it is recounted in conspicuous detail in his otherwise concise narrative:

> *Hezekiah sent to all Israel and Judah, and wrote letters also to Ephraim and Manasseh that they should come to the house of the* Lord *at Jerusalem, to keep the Passover to the* Lord *the God of Israel.* ... So they decreed to make a proclamation throughout all Israel, from Beer-sheba to Dan, that the people should come and keep the Passover to the Lord the God of Israel, at Jerusalem; for they had not kept it in great numbers as prescribed. *So couriers went throughout all Israel and Judah with letters from the king and his princes, as the king had commanded, saying, "O people of Israel, return to the* Lord, *the God of Abraham, Isaac, and Israel, that he may turn again to the remnant of you who have escaped from the hand of the kings of Assyria. Do not be like your fathers and your brethren, who were faithless to the* Lord *God of their fathers, so that he made them a desolation, as you see. Do not now be stiff-necked as your fathers were, but yield yourselves to the* Lord, *and come to his sanctuary, which he has sanctified forever, and worship the* Lord *your God, that his fierce anger may turn away from you. For if you return to the* Lord, *your brethren and your children will find compassion with their captors, and return to this land. For the* Lord *your God is gracious and merciful, and will not turn away his face from you, if you return to him." So the couriers went from city to city through the country of Ephraim and Manasseh, and as far as Zebulun; but they laughed them to scorn, and mocked them. Only a few men of Asher, of Manasseh, and of Zebulun humbled themselves and came to Jerusalem.* The hand of God was also upon Judah to give them one heart to do what the king and the princes commanded by the

---

25 For example, Joachim Jeremias identifies the parable as "an outline of the history of the plan of redemption." Jeremias, *The Parables of Jesus*, 69. Likewise, Klyne Snodgrass concludes that it "uses language of Israel's history ... to warn of the consequences of rejecting God's messengers." Snodgrass, *Stories with Intent*, 319.

26 See Snodgrass, *Stories with Intent*, 302; France, *The Gospel of Matthew*, 824, n. 12; Blickenstaff, "While the Bridegroom is with Them," 61, all of whom mention Hezekiah's banquet in passing but do not draw out the significance of the parallel for Jesus' parable.

word of the LORD. And many people came together in Jerusalem
to keep the feast of Unleavened Bread, in the second month, a
very great assembly. ... Then the whole assembly agreed together
to keep the feast another seven days; so they kept it for another
seven days with gladness. ... *The whole assembly of Judah, and
the priests and the Levites, and the whole assembly that came out of
Israel, and the sojourners who came out of the land of Israel, and the
sojourners who dwelt in Judah, rejoiced.* So there was great joy in
Jerusalem, for since the time of Solomon the son of David king
of Israel there had been nothing like this in Jerusalem. (2 Chron.
30:1, 5–13, 23, 25–26)[27]

Here we see several potentially significant parallels with Jesus' parable of the Royal
Wedding Banquet.

First, we have the story of a king who invites many of his subjects to a royal
feast. Although the feast is obviously not a marriage feast, it is intriguing that it
lasts for "seven days," which is also the customary length of a wedding feast (Gen.
29:22–27; Judg. 14:12; *Jos. Asen.* 21:8; *b. Ket.* 4b). Despite this difference, the
parallel still intrigues, especially when we note that the invitees are identified as
the twelve tribes of Israel: both "Israel" (the northern kingdom) and "Judah" (the
southern kingdom). The obvious implication of this pan-Israelite invitation is that
King Hezekiah has as his goal the *cultic* restoration of Israel and the reunification
of the twelve tribes *by means of the Passover banquet.* In the words of Scott Hahn:

> The Chronicler presents Hezekiah's Passover as a kind of
> sacrament of the united kingdom intended by God. It is a sign
> of the unity of all the tribes under the Davidic king as well as
> the efficacious means or instrument by which that unity is
> brought about ...[28]

According to the messengers, by accepting the king's invitation to celebrate the
Passover feast, the invitees will somehow not only preserve Israel from future
"desolation," but will ultimately bring about the ingathering of the Assyrian exiles,
enabling them to "return to this land" (2 Chron. 30:9).

Second, King Hezekiah sends out "couriers" or messengers, presumably
his servants, to invite the twelve tribes, but his invitations are rejected ("laughed
to scorn") and even "mocked" by those who, according to covenant made with
David, should have been his loyal subjects (see 2 Sam. 5:1–5). Indeed, although
many were invited, "only a few" from among the northern tribes of Israel actually

---

27 RSV, slightly altered.

28 Scott W. Hahn, *The Kingdom of God as Liturgical Empire: A Theological Commentary on 1–2
Chronicles* (Grand Rapids: Baker Academic, 2012), 181.

came to the Passover feast in Jerusalem (2 Chron. 30:11). Again, the story differs from Jesus' parable insofar as the servants are not put to death. Nevertheless, the consequences of rejection are severe: if the Israelites refuse to come, they will face the "fierce anger" of God (2 Chron. 30:8).

Third—and this is significant—the refusal of King Hezekiah's invitations by the northern tribes did *not* mean that no one attended the Passover banquet or that the city of Jerusalem was not filled with people. Strikingly, in response to the refusal of the invitation by the northern tribes, the Chronicler reports that although the original invitees refused to attend, there were non-Israelites who accepted the invitation! At the Passover were Gentile "sojourners" or "foreigners" (Hebrew *gerim*) who came out of the land of both Israel and Judah to participate in the feast (2 Chron. 30:25; compare Exod. 12:19).[29] In other words, despite the widespread refusal by the northern tribes of King Hezekiah's invitations to the Passover, his plans of a celebratory feast are ultimately not foiled, for Jerusalem is filled with a "remnant" of the twelve tribes of Israel alongside certain Gentiles, whose piety ironically exceeds that of the Israelites who refused to attend (see 2 Chron. 30:6). In light of this remarkable turn of events, it is no wonder that Hezekiah's banquet was deemed unforgettable: according to the Chronicler, "Since the time of Solomon the son of David king of Israel there had been nothing like this in Jerusalem" (2 Chron. 30:26).

To my mind, these parallels with the parable of the Royal Wedding Feast are too striking to be coincidental. Instead, it seems more likely that Jesus' teaching is modeled in part on the famous story of King Hezekiah's Passover banquet, with the Passover banquet of Hezekiah functioning in Chronicles the same way the messianic banquet functions in the parable. Lest there be any doubt about this, it is remarkable to note that extra-biblical Jewish reflection on Hezekiah's Passover also provides us with a striking parallel to Jesus' parable.[30] In his *Antiquities of the Jews*, Josephus elaborates on the biblical account of Hezekiah's banquet and adds that not only did the king's "messengers" invite the northern tribes to come to the feast, but "the prophets" did so as well. And what was the result? Not only did the northern tribes reject the invitations, they also persecuted and killed the prophets:

> Then the king [Hezekiah] sent messengers throughout his realm, summoning the people to Jerusalem to celebrate the festival of Unleavened Bread, which had for a long time been allowed to lapse through the lawless action of the kings previously mentioned. He also sent messengers to the Israelites, exhorting

---

29 For examples of "sojourner" as a reference to non-Israelites see also Lev. 24:16; Num. 15:30; Jos. 8:33; "*ger*," in Francis Brown, S. R. Driver, and C. A. Briggs, *A Hebrew and English Lexicon of the Old Testament* (Oxford: Clarendon, 1907), 158. See also Hahn, *The Kingdom of God as Liturgical Empire*, 182.

30 Davies and Allison, *Saint Matthew*, 3:201; Keener, *The Gospel of Matthew*, 520–521.

them to give up their present manner of life and return to their ancient custom and reverence God, for he said he would permit them to come and celebrate the festival of Unleavened Bread and join in their festal assembly ... *However, when the envoys came and brought them this message from their king, the Israelites were not only not persuaded, but even laughed at his envoys as fools; and when their prophets exhorted them in like manner and foretold what they would suffer if they did not alter their course to one of piety toward God, they spat upon them and finally seized and killed them. And not stopping even at these acts of lawlessness, they devised things still worse than those mentioned, and did not leave off until God punished them for their impiety by making them subject to their enemies.* But of these things we shall write farther on. However, many of the tribes of Manasseh, Zabulon, and Isaachar heeded the prophets' exhortations and were converted to piety. And all these flocked to Jerusalem to Hezekiah that they might worship God. (Josephus, *Antiquities* 9:263–67; [my emphasis])[31]

From an ancient Jewish perspective, the refusal of Hezekiah's invitations to the Passover feast in Jerusalem was no minor incident. Rather, for both the Chronicler and Josephus—and, presumably, for Jews who regarded Chronicles as Scripture— it was an *irreparably* tragic and consequential moment in the history of Israel. Never before in the Davidic Monarchy had an invitation to a feast caused so much to hang in the balance.

In the case of the northern tribes, the ultimate result of their rejection of Hezekiah's invitation was the dissolution of the Davidic kingdom, the dispersion of ten of the twelve tribes of Israel, and the intermingling of the remnants of the northern tribes with the Gentile nations. In other words, *for Josephus, the overthrow of Samaria and the Assyrian exile of the ten northern tribes in 722 B.C. was a direct result of their refusal to repent and come to Hezekiah's Passover banquet.* Because of the "impiety" of the northern tribes, God "brought them under their enemies," by allowing the capital city of Samaria to be overthrown by King Shalmaneser. The vast majority of the northern tribes were then scattered among the nations (see *Antiquities* 9:267, 277–291).

In short, when both Jewish Scripture and Jewish literature outside the Bible are taken into account, the parable of the Royal Wedding Feast appears to be deeply rooted in ancient Jewish history as well as eschatology, in such a way that both its similarities and its differences with Hezekiah's Passover shed light on its possible meaning. On the one hand, Jesus' image of the refusal of invitations to a king's banquet hearkens directly back to the refusal of the northern tribes to come

---

31   Translation by Ralph Marcus, *Josephus, Jewish Antiquities, Books IX–XI* (Loeb Classical Library 326; Cambridge: Harvard University Press, 1937), 139–143.

to the Passover banquet of Hezekiah. Moreover, Jesus' image of the initial invitees being punished with the destruction of their city likewise hearkens back to the destruction of Samaria by the Assyrians in the Assyrian exile (2 Kings 17:24–41). On the other hand, the banquet of which Jesus speaks is no mere annual Passover meal, but rather the eschatological wedding feast that the prophets had said would coincide with the restoration of Israel (Isa. 54:1–7; 55:1–5; 62:1–9). Whereas with Hezekiah's banquet it was primarily the wicked northern tribes who refused to repent and accept the invitation of the heir to the Davidic throne, in the parable of Jesus it is his contemporaries—and, in context, the chief priests and Pharisees in Jerusalem (Matt. 21:45–46, 22:15)—who refuse to come to the banquet of the kingdom of God.

Finally, but by no means least significant, whereas in Hezekiah's day it was the city of *Samaria* that was destroyed because of the northern tribes refusal to repent and come to the Passover, in the parable of Jesus, it is the unidentified "city" of those who reject the invitation to the messianic banquet that ends up destroyed and "burned" (Matt. 22:7). It is not surprising that interpreters have almost unanimously identified this unnamed city as the capital of the southern kingdom, the city of *Jerusalem*.[32]

If this is correct, and the parable is in fact about the messianic banquet, then the overall message of Jesus in this parable can be summed up in a warning: "Do not reject my invitation to the messianic banquet, which is now ready, or your fate will be worse than that of the lost tribes of the northern kingdom. You too will be cast out—not from the earthly promised land, but from the banquet of the kingdom of God."

The Messianic Wedding Garment

The third and final part of the parable is the king's arrival at the banquet and his inspection of the wedding guests (Matt. 22:12–13). As we saw above, upon seeing a man who had no "wedding garment," the king immediately questions him: "Friend, how did you get in here without a wedding garment?" But the man is speechless. As a result, the king orders his servants to bind him hand and foot and "cast him into the outer darkness, where there will be weeping and gnashing of teeth." What is the meaning of this mysterious and troubling ending? In particular, what is signified by the wedding garment? What does the ending of this parable reveal about the nature of the kingdom of God?

The overall meaning of the conclusion revolves almost entirely around how one identifies the "wedding garment" (*enduma gamou*) (Matt. 22:11–12).[33] Among

---

32 Although many commentators regard the implicit warning of Jerusalem's destruction as a prophecy that has been attributed to Jesus *after* the Roman destruction of Jerusalem in A.D. 70, a case can be made that Jesus is using the destruction of Samaria as a warning for an unspecified future destruction of Jerusalem. See Snodgrass, *Stories with Intent*, 318.

33 See Hultgren, *The Parables of Jesus*, 347–348. For a helpful survey of ancient and medieval

the interpretations proposed by scholars focused on what the garment might have signified in Jesus' first-century Jewish context, three proposals stand out:

1. The garment signifies *deeds of righteousness*.[34] This view is supported by Jewish parallels in which the metaphor of clothing is used to signify the good works or "the robe of righteousness" (Isa. 61:10; Bar. 5:1–4; Sir. 27:8; Wis. 5:18).

2. The garment signifies *divine favor and salvation*.[35] This view is supported by Jewish parallels which speak of a "garment of salvation" (Isa. 61:10; compare Isa. 52:1; Ezek. 16:10–13; 1 En. 62:16).[36]

3. The garment signifies *the glory of heavenly beings*.[37] This view is supported by Jewish parallels in which heavenly beings such as God or the angels are depicted as wearing special garments of light (Ps. 104:1–2; 1 En. 62:13–16; T. Mos. 20:1–3; Apoc. Zeph. 8:3–4).[38]

Although these are sometimes pitted against one another, a closer examination reveals that none of them are mutually exclusive: good deeds and divine favor go hand in hand, and can result in the righteous being exalted into heaven to share in the heavenly glory of God and his angels (see Dan. 12:1–2). Moreover, given Jesus' emphasis in the parable on the fact that the messengers of the king gathered both "bad and good" (Matt. 22:10), some kind of moral symbolism of the garment lies "close at hand."[39] Finally, two of the three meanings listed above have in common the oracle regarding the "anointed one" in Isaiah 61. Indeed, as Joachim Jeremias convincingly suggests, Isaiah 61 stands out as the most likely background for Jesus' imagery of the eschatological wedding garment:[40]

---

interpretations, see Blickenstaff, "*While the Bridegroom is with Them*," 70–71, n. 89.

34 Smit, *Fellowship and Food in the Kingdom*, 235; Funk and Miller, *The Five Gospels*, 235.

35 Jeremias, *The Parables of Jesus*, 189.

36 Intriguingly, this imagery is frequently linked to priestly vestments (Isa. 61:10; Ps. 132:15; 2 Chron. 6:41). See Blickenstaff, "*While the Bridegroom is with Them*," 72, n. 92.

37 Davies and Allison, *Saint Matthew*, 3:204.

38 This imagery seems to suggest that by means of the garment of glory God restores to the righteous what Adam had lost in the fall. See *1 En.* 62:15–16; *Asc. Isa.* 7:22; 8:14, 26; 9:9, 24–26; 11:40; *L.A.B.* 20:1–3; Davies and Allison, *Saint Matthew*, 3:204, n.55.

39 Hultgren, *The Parables of Jesus*, 347.

40 See Jeremias, *The Parables of Jesus*, 188–189.

> The Spirit of the Lord GOD is upon me,
> because *the LORD has anointed me* to bring good news to
>   the afflicted ...
> I will greatly rejoice in the LORD, my soul shall exult in
>   my God;
> for he has clothed me with *the garments of salvation*,
> he has covered me with *the robe of righteousness*,
> as a *bridegroom* decks himself with a garland,
> and as a *bride* adorns herself with jewels. (Isa. 61:1, 10)

The explanatory power of this oracle in Isaiah as background for the image of the wedding garment in the parable of the Royal Wedding Feast is manifold.

First, Isaiah not only uses the imagery of wedding "garments"; it does so in the context of an oracle describing the future marriage of the LORD and Israel (Isa. 62:1–5). This strengthens our suggestion above that the parable of the Royal Wedding Feast is about the eschatological wedding of God and his chosen people.

Second, in Isaiah 61 the wedding represents the renewal of the covenant between God and Israel; hence, the wedding garment symbolizes both the righteousness of the elect and the salvation won for them by God. Assuming that Jesus had this Isaianic background in mind, a similar meaning for the wedding garment in the parable is likely: the garment represents the righteousness of those who answer the invitation to the banquet, as well as the salvation given them by God.

Third and finally, the oracle in Isaiah 61 is not merely eschatological; it is demonstrably messianic. Not only is the word "messiah" (*mashiah*) utilized (Isa. 61:1), but the passage was consistently interpreted in messianic terms in ancient Jewish literature (see *11QMelchizedek* 2:4–20; *4QMessianic Apocalypse* [521] 2:12).[41] This is important because in Isaiah, the anointed figure is compared to "a bridegroom," just as the son of the king in Jesus' parable is a bridegroom. If the king signifies God, then his son, like the figure in Isaiah 61, is both bridegroom and messiah.[42]

Once again, the Old Testament illuminates Jesus' parable, strongly suggesting that the Royal Wedding Feast is not only about the eschatological wedding of God and Israel, but about the messianic banquet of the kingdom. In support of this suggestion, it is worth noting that the imagery of eschatological garments of salvation finds support in two ancient descriptions of the messianic banquet, one indisputably Jewish in character and one arguably Jewish, though thought by some scholars to be Christian.[43] Compare the following texts:

---

41   See Craig Evans, "Jesus and the Messianic Texts from Qumran," in *Jesus and His Contemporaries* (Leiden: Brill, 1995), 83–154, at 118–120; M. P. Miller, "The Function of Isa 61:1–2 in 11QMelchizedek," *Journal of Biblical Literature* 88 (1969): 467–469.

42   See further Brant Pitre, *Jesus the Bridegroom: Seeing Christ and the Cross through Ancient Jewish Eyes* (forthcoming; New York: Image, 2014).

43   See J. Priest, "A Note on the Messianic banquet," in *The Messiah: Developments in Earliest*

And the righteous and the chosen will be saved on that day; and the faces of the sinners and the unrighteous they will henceforth not see. And the Lord of Spirits will abide over them, and *with that Son of Man they will eat*, and they will lie down and rise up forever and ever. *And the righteous and the chosen will have arisen from the earth*, and have ceased to cast down their faces, *and have put on the garment of glory*. And this will be your garment, *the garment of life* from the Lord of Spirits; and *your garments will not wear out*, and your glory will not fade in the presence of the Lord of Spirits. (*1 Enoch* 62:13–16)[44]

Receive what the Lord has entrusted to you and be joyful, giving thanks to him who has called you to *heavenly kingdoms*. Rise and stand, and see at *the feast of the Lord* the number of those who have been sealed. Those who have departed from the shadow of this age have received *glorious garments* from the Lord. Take again your full number, O Zion, and conclude the list of your people who are clothed in white, who have fulfilled the law of the Lord ... I, Ezra, saw on Mount Zion a great multitude, which I could not number. ... Then I asked an angel, "Who are these, my lord?" He answered and said to me, "These are they who have put off mortal clothing and put on the immortal, and they have confessed the name of God; now they are being crowned, and receive palms." (*4 Ezra* 2:37–42, 44)

Whatever we make of the provenance of the latter text, the first text provides us with a striking parallel to Jesus' imagery of a garment that symbolizes the eschatological salvation given to the righteous at the messianic banquet. Further, in both *1 Enoch* and *4 Ezra* the kingdom is not only eschatological but a *heavenly* kingdom. This heavenly kingdom has been prepared for all eternity and will be revealed for the righteous at the banquet (see *4 Ezra* 2:10–14, 33–35). The righteous ascend to this glorious banquet, so that they are in "the presence" of God in heaven (*1 En.* 62:16).

In light of such parallels, it seems safe to conclude with Jeremias that in the parable of the Royal Wedding Feast, "the white robe, or the garment of Life and Glory, is a symbol of the righteousness awarded by God (see especially Isa. 61.10), and to be clothed with this garment is a symbol of membership in the redeemed community."[45] To this I would only add that the community in question is nothing less than *the messianic kingdom* that will be manifested at the eschatological wedding banquet of Israel's restoration. To this banquet, "many" are called (meaning

---

Judaism and Christianity, ed. James H. Charlesworth (Minneapolis: Fortress, 1992), 224–225.

44   See Jeremias, *The Parables of Jesus*, 189.

45   Jeremias, *The Parables of Jesus*, 189.

"everyone"), but "few" are chosen (meaning, "not everyone").[46] Those who either reject the invitation or refuse to wear the garments of righteousness and salvation will not be allowed to enter into the joy of the kingdom.

The Nature of the Kingdom

With these various aspects of the Old Testament background in mind, we can now step back from the details of the parable's narrative and ask the broader question about its message as a whole. Given that the parables of Jesus are intended to teach something about the nature of the kingdom of God, what kind of kingdom does the parable of the Royal Wedding Feast describe? In light of our analysis, several significant implications emerge.

First, the kingdom envisaged is a *messianic* kingdom.[47] Although it is true that the parable does not develop the character of the king's son, to the extent that the king represents God, his son is by clear implication the "son of God"—an identity regularly associated with the Davidic king of Israel, both in his historical and eschatological roles (2 Sam. 7; Ps. 2; *Psalms of Solomon* 17). Moreover, if, as I suggested above, King Hezekiah's famous Passover banquet and the northern tribes' refusal to come to the feast lies in the background of Jesus' parable (2 Chron. 30), then the Davidic (and therefore messianic) nature of the kingdom Jesus is describing is strengthened. Indeed, given this Old Testament background, the parable seems to suggest that the broken kingdom of David, which Hezekiah himself failed to fully restore through his Passover banquet, will finally be restored *via* the messianic banquet hosted by God himself.

Second, the kingdom is also a *universal* kingdom.[48] Although there is a clear chronological distinction in the parable between "those who are invited" first and the "many" who are invited subsequently (Matt. 22: 3–4, 8–9), in the final analysis, everyone is invited. Although the parable itself does not give the exact identity of the original invitees vs. the later guests,[49] to the extent that the story echoes the Passover banquet of King Hezekiah, Jesus may be suggesting a distinction between those Israelites who fail to respond to his message and those who accept it, the later group including both responsive Israelites and Gentiles (see 2 Chron. 30:25). Admittedly, however, the emphasis in Jesus' parable is not on ethnicity but on receptivity and righteousness.

Third, the kingdom is an *imminent* kingdom.[50] This is very important to stress. The king notifies the invitees because the dinner is *ready*. Twice this is

---

46　See Ben F. Meyer, "Many (=All) Are Called, But Few (=Not All) Are Chosen," *New Testament Studies* 36 (1990): 89–97.

47　Jeremias, *The Parables of Jesus*, 177–178.

48　See Davies and Allison, *Saint Matthew*, 3:202.

49　Snodgrass, *Stories with Intent*, 321.

50　Beasley-Murray, *Jesus and the Kingdom of God*, 120–121.

emphasized: "Tell those who are invited, Behold, I have made ready (*hetoimaka*) my dinner ... everything is ready (*hetoima*)" (Matt. 22:4). Given that Isaiah's oracle of the eschatological feast was centuries old, this message of imminence in Jesus' parable would have been particularly arresting in a first-century Jewish context. The long-awaited eschatological banquet is coming soon. The question is no longer when the kingdom will come but how people will respond. Will they prefer the things of this world—a "farm," a "business" (Matt. 22:5)? Or will they even reject the messengers of the king and put them to death (Matt. 22:6)? To the extent that those invited refuse, they will miss participating in the kingdom itself.

Fourth, although the kingdom is in some way *present*, it is not yet *fully realized*. This is evident in that both "bad and good" are allowed into the kingdom—at least for a time (Matt 22:10). When the king finally comes to the banquet, however, there will be a separation.[51] The kingdom is now a *corpus permixtum* (mixed body); but at the arrival of the king it will be purified of those who have failed to put on the proper "wedding garment" (Matt. 22:11–14). This distinction is important because it suggests some kind of interim period between being *gathered* into the kingdom banquet and the final *separation*. The kingdom is currently in "the process of gathering" but awaits a final sifting that will take place at the eschatological judgment.[52] The parable thus envisions, in the words of Jeremias, "*an eschatology that is in the process of realization.*"[53]

Fifth and finally, the kingdom is not merely eschatological, but *heavenly*.[54] When the king throws the man without a wedding garment out of the banquet (=the kingdom), he is cast into "the outer darkness" where there is a "weeping and gnashing of teeth" (Matt. 22:13). Although "outer darkness" imagery does not appear in the Old Testament itself, it is a standard early Jewish way of describing the realm of the damned, sometimes called Gehenna.[55] Consider the following parallels:

> Indeed, I will bring forth in shining light those who loved my
> holy name, and I will set each one on the throne of his honor ...

51   France, *The Gospel of Matthew*, 828.

52   Snodgrass, *Stories with Intent*, 320–321.

53   Jeremias, *The Parables of Jesus*, 230 (my emphasis).

54   See Allison, *Constructing Jesus*, 172, n. 613: "It is understandable that in Christian sources 'the kingdom (of God)' sometimes means 'heaven.' ... In like fashion, 'the world to come' can, in Jewish sources, mean 'the other world'." See also Perrin, *Rediscovering the Teaching of Jesus*, 113, who equates the marriage feast with "the life of the age to come" in accordance with "the regular Jewish use of these symbols." As we have seen elsewhere, the World to Come is, in Jewish thought, a heavenly realm that will appear in its fullness in the eschaton. See, for example, *1 En.* 39:4; 61:8–12; 71:15; *4 Ezra* 8:52; *2 Baruch* 51:7–8, 10–13, 14; *2 Enoch* [J] 42:3–5; *m. Aboth* 4:16; *Midrash on Psalms* 31:6; cf. *y. Yeb.* 15:14d; *b. Ber.* 28b; *Sifra* on Lev 85d; see Allison, *Constructing Jesus*, 198.

55   See, for example, France, *The Gospel of Matthew*, 319.

And the righteous, as they shine, will see those who were born in darkness *cast into darkness*; the sinners will cry out and see them shining, and they, for their part, will depart to where days and times are written for them. (*1 Enoch* 108:12, 14–15)

Rabbi Nehemiah said: It came from the darkness of Gehinnom [=Gehenna], for it says, "A land of thick darkness, as darkness itself; a land of the shadow of death, without any order" (Job 10:22) ... Rabbi Judah ben Rabbi said: *With what are the wicked covered in Gehinnom? With darkness.* (*Exodus Rabbah* 14:2)

The upshot of such parallels is simple: in the Royal Wedding Feast, the messianic kingdom envisaged is no mere earthly reality. Rather, *the kingdom stands in direct contrast to Gehenna, the spiritual realm of the damned.* Both realms—the kingdom and Gehenna—are not earthly in character. In sum, the kingdom spoken of by Jesus is not merely prefigured in the history of Israel (as in the allusions to Hezekiah's Passover); nor can it be reduced to the mere invitation to and gathering of the invited to the wedding banquet. Rather, the kingdom consists of a heavenly realm, which is contrasted with its opposite: the supernatural (but abysmal) realm of the damned.

Conclusion

The basic conclusion to our study can be summed up as follows: although at first glance the parable of the Royal Wedding Feast has struck many commentators as difficult and even bizarre, upon closer inspection of its Old Testament background each of its images becomes remarkably clear. For example, the gravity of one's response to the Wedding Banquet invitation is because this is no ordinary banquet. It is the messianic banquet of salvation spoken of by the prophets. Likewise, the severity of the king's reaction to those who reject his invitations is understandable against the backdrop of the mockery and rejection of King Hezekiah's invitations to the Passover feast in the book of Chronicles. As this Old Testament background reveals, the banquet in question is not just the eschatological feast of the messiah; it is the banquet of the restoration of the twelve tribes of Israel. To despise and reject an invitation to this feast is no less egregious than was the rejection of King Hezekiah's attempts to restore Israel by means of the Passover feast. Indeed, the situation is even more serious, for rejecting the invitation to the messianic feast is tantamount to rejecting God's repeatedly stated plan to gather and restore the twelve tribes of Israel. Further, the image of a man being cast out of this messianic banquet of restoration and salvation because he had no "wedding garment" can be illuminated by recourse to the prophecies of Isaiah, who speaks about the "garments of salvation" with which God will clothe his people in the eschatological age of salvation.

If these basic observations are correct, then at least three important implications stand out.

First and foremost, if the other parables of Jesus are anything like that of the Royal Wedding Banquet, then close attention needs to be paid to possible backgrounds in *Jewish Scripture* as a tool for unlocking the meaning that the parable would have had in a first-century Jewish context. In particular, the Old Testament background of this parable strongly suggests that Jesus spoke about the coming of the kingdom of God in ways that were deliberately evocative of the history of Israel, especially the famous story of King Hezekiah's rejected invitations to the Passover feast in Jerusalem.

Second, if this suggestion is correct, then a strong case could be made that Jesus is comparing himself to the Davidide Hezekiah, who sought to unite the northern and southern kingdoms, and the twelve tribes of Israel, not through military or personal might, but through the celebration of the Passover feast. In other words, Jesus, like Hezekiah before him, is attempting to bring about *the liturgical restoration of Israel*, through the banquet at which he will act as host and to which he is inviting his contemporaries. If this is correct, then a case can be made that the Last Supper—as a Passover meal celebrated by Jesus with the Twelve disciples (Matt. 26:26–28; Mark 14:24–25; Luke 22:19–30; 1 Cor. 11:23–25)—is nothing less than a prophetic sign which will both signify and set in motion the liturgical restoration of Israel and the inauguration of the Kingdom of God.

Third and finally, and by no means least significantly, the parable of the Royal Wedding Feast provides an important corrective for the way in which scholars imagine Jesus' vision of the restoration of Israel. Some interpreters are inclined to interpret Jesus' vision of the restoration of the twelve tribes as a this-worldly ingathering to the earthly promised land.[56] The parable of the Royal Wedding Feast, however, unequivocally states that whoever is cast out of the wedding feast of the kingdom will not just be cast out of the land of Canaan, but into the "outer darkness" of the spiritual realm of Gehenna. In other words, how one responds to the invitation to this banquet of the messiah is not ultimately a question of geographical restoration or dislocation, but a matter of *eternal life and death*. For the kingdom envisaged in this parable is no earthly kingdom, but the eschatological kingdom of heaven.

---

56 See, for example, Karen J. Wenell, *Jesus and Land: Sacred and Social Space in Second Temple Judaism*, Library of New Testament Studies 334 (London: T. &. T. Clark, 2007).

Letter & Spirit 8 (2013): 55-76

MATTHEW AS EXEGETE
The Unity and Function of the Formula Citations in Matthew 1:1–4:16

~: Jeremy Holmes :~

Wyoming Catholic College

Introduction

When scholars approach the subject of Matthew as an interpreter of Old Testament Scripture, most of their attention goes to a feature unique to Matthew among the synoptics, the so-called "formula citations." In some fourteen places, Matthew pauses his story to state explicitly that these events happened to fulfill certain prophecies. Since these prophetic citations offer the narrator's reflection on the meaning of his story, they are often called *Reflexionszitate* (reflection citations), but among English-speaking scholars they are usually dubbed "formula citations" because of the set formula Matthew uses to introduce them.[1] Of the fourteen, only one is shared by the other synoptic gospels. So the formula citations present an approach to the Old Testament that is distinctively Matthean, both in form and content.

However, there is very little agreement about what Matthew is doing in his formula citations. Raymond Brown comments:

> In finding this fulfillment, Matthew makes no attempt to in-
> terpret what we might consider the full or contextual meaning
> of the OT text that he cites; rather he concentrates on features
> of the text wherein there is a resemblance to Jesus or the NT
> event. His method of quoting the prophet directly rather than
> weaving an allusion into the wording of the Matthean narrative
> is an indication of a Christian effort to supply the story of Jesus
> with OT background and support.[2]

---

1   For a discussion of opinions on how many formula citations Matthew presents, see George M. Soares Prabhu, *The Formula Quotations in the Infancy Narrative of Matthew: An Enquiry into the Tradition History of Mt 1–2*, Analecta biblica 63 (Rome: Pontifical Biblical Institute, 1976), 24–25. For an older but classic treatment of the same question see Krister Stendahl, *The School of St. Matthew and Its Use of the Old Testament*, 2d ed. (Philadelphia: Fortress Press, 1968), 97–127, at 97.

2   Raymond Brown, *The Birth of the Messiah: A Commentary on the Infancy Narratives in the Gospels of Matthew and Luke*, rev. ed. (New York: Doubleday, 1993), 97.

Brown seems to be echoing the opinion of Barnabas Lindars, who argues that Matthew looks for Old Testament texts that bear a pictorial resemblance to the life of Jesus, and that he deploys these texts for apologetical purposes.[3] S. V. McCasland sums up this apologetic approach to Matthew's exegesis in the title of his article, "Matthew Twists the Scriptures."[4] By contrast, R. T. France argues that beyond the surface meaning of Matthew's citations—the pictorial resemblance accessible by any reader—there is a deeper meaning. What precisely that deeper meaning may be can be difficult to assess, but France concedes that the basic motive for the citations is apologetical.[5] Donald Hagner understands the formula citations as appealing to a *sensus plenior*, a meaning of the Old Testament beyond that which the original author could have known, and flatly denies that they are meant to serve as apologetical arguments. Rather, he says, they interpret Jesus Christ for those who already believe.[6] This lack of agreement among scholars suggests that we need to rethink Matthew's use of the Old Testament.

The focus of this article will be on what Matthew is doing with the formula citations in a small section of his Gospel, namely 1:1–4:16, the entire portion of the story that takes place before Jesus' public preaching begins. Many scholars take chapters 1–2 as the first major division of Matthew's Gospel, but, for reasons that will become clear later, I will follow Jack Dean Kingsbury and others who have seen the phrase "from that time Jesus began" in 4:17 as significant for the structure of the Gospel.[7] The advantages of taking 1:1–4:16 as a unit will emerge as we proceed. For the moment, let me simply point out that 4:16 offers the last of seven formula citations in this section—a number suggestive of unity and completion.

---

3   Lindars, *New Testament Apologetic: The Doctrinal Significance of the Old Testament Quotations* (Philadelphia: Westminster, 1961), 259–260.

4   S. Vernon McCasland, "Matthew Twists the Scriptures," *Journal of Biblical Literature* 80 (1961): 143–48. Such negative comments about Matthew's awareness of context could be multiplied: see, for example, Howard Clark Kee, Franklin L. Young, and Karlfreid Froehlich, *Understanding the New Testament*, 3rd ed. (Engelwood Cliffs, NJ: Prentice-Hall, 1973), 321–323.

5   R. T. France, "The Formula-Quotations of Matthew 2 and the Problem of Communication," in G. K. Beale, ed., *The Right Doctrine from the Wrong Texts? Essays on the Use of the Old Testament in the New* (Grand Rapids, MI: Baker Books, 1994), 114–134; reprinted from *New Testament Studies* 27 (1981): 233–251.

6   See Donald A. Hagner, *Matthew 14–28*, Word Biblical Commentary Series 33B (Dallas: Word, 1995), lv–lvi and 20–21. Raymond Brown also suggests this position in "The *Sensus Plenior* of Sacred Scripture" (Ph.D. diss., St. Mary's University, 1955), 102 and 143, classifying it as the "prophetical sensus plenior." Later in his career, Brown moved away from the *sensus plenior* in favor of a purer historical-critical approach. For the evolution of his thought, see his article "The *Sensus Plenior* in the Last Ten Years," *Catholic Biblical Quarterly* 25 (1963): 262–285, and his article on "more-than-literal senses" in *The New Jerome Biblical Commentary*, ed. Raymond E. Brown, S.S., Joseph A. Fitzmyer, S.J., Roland E. Murphy, O. Carm. (Englewood Cliffs, NJ: Prentice Hall, 1990): 71:31–77. In his later work, Brown puts some distance between himself and those who interpret Matthew's citation of Isa. 7:14 in this way (*Birth*, 146, fn. 9 and 149–150, esp. 150, fn. 53).

7   Jack D. Kingsbury, *Matthew: Structure, Christology, Kingdom* (Philadelphia: Fortress, 1975).

Exodus Typology in Matthew 1–4

However, one cannot discuss the formula citations in isolation. Donald Senior has rightly pointed out that Matthew's use of the Old Testament is all too often reduced to the formula citations, as though he did not use the Old Testament in any other way. He calls this "the lure of the formula citations."[8] The prophetic citations do not stand alone, but have to be appreciated within the context of Matthew's more allusive use of Scripture in the surrounding narrative. While it would be impossible in the present article to cover all of Matthew's allusions in detail, fortunately one can discuss most of Matthew's biblical allusions under one rubric: the Exodus. Most scholars are convinced of a Moses typology in Matthew 1–2, and many favor a more extended Exodus typology stretching as far as chapter 7. Before taking up the formula citations in 1:1–4:16, therefore, let me walk quickly through the Exodus typology surrounding them. Here I am particularly indebted to Dale Allison's *The New Moses: A Matthean Typology.*[9]

Jesus is born in chapter 1 of Matthew. In chapter 2, Jesus, like Moses, is threatened by an attempt to destroy all the children in his region; like Moses, he is forced to flee into exile; like Moses, he returns only when those persecuting him have died. When extra-biblical traditions are taken into account, the parallelism is more detailed. Jewish tradition portrays Amram, who will be the father of Moses, concerned because of the Pharaoh's edict against male children and considering a divorce with his bride-to-be. He is told in a dream that the child resulting from his marriage will be the deliverer of Israel, so he proceeds with the marriage. The parallel to Joseph's situation is apparent.[10] Other traditions, which retain the dream of Amram without the preceding concern about Pharaoh's edict, show Pharaoh being told of the coming deliverer through a dream which is subsequently interpreted for him by scribes and magicians. This parallels the magi's obscure announcement to Herod of the deliverer's coming, which must then be interpreted by scribes. In both cases, the result of the prediction is fear on the ruler's part and an edict decreeing the death of all the male children.[11]

Matthew concludes this part of his story with the angel's command that Joseph return with his family from exile: "Arise, take the child and his mother and

---

8   Donald Senior, "The Lure of the Formula Quotations: Re-assessing Matthew's Use of the Old Testament with the Passion Narrative as Test Case," in *The Scriptures in the Gospels*, ed. C. M. Tuckett, Bibliotheca ephemeridum theologicarum lovaniensium 131 (Louvain: Louvain University Press, 1997), 89–115. Many years previously, Robert H. Gundry made the same point at length in *The Use of the Old Testament in St. Matthew's Gospel with Special Reference to the Messianic Hope*, Novum Testamentum Supplement 18 (Leiden: Brill, 1967).

9   Dale Allison, *The New Moses: A Matthean Typology* (Minneapolis: Fortress, 1993). For an extensive review of "New Moses" typology in the work of previous scholars, see Allison, *New Moses*, 293–328; for further bibliography see Allison, *New Moses*, 140, n. 3. See also Allison, *New Moses*, 161–162 for a glance at ancient authors who detected the same typology.

10   Allison, *New Moses*, 144 and 159–160.

11   Allison, *New Moses*, 145 and 156–157.

return to the land of Israel, for those seeking the life of the child have died."[12] This parallels the command given to Moses in Exodus: "Go, depart into Egypt, for all those seeking your life have died."[13] The last clause is particularly impressive with regard to the parallel between Matthew's Greek and the Septuagint.[14] If we see Jesus as a type of Moses, then like Moses he is returning to his home after an exile. If Jesus can also be seen as a type of the nation of Israel, as will be argued below, then, unlike Moses, he is leaving Egypt, the place of bondage. Moses' exile from and return to Egypt foreshadows in its own way the bondage and release of the nation to which he was sent.

Matthew's story goes on in chapter 3 to describe Jesus' baptism in the river Jordan. Because this story comes immediately after a typological re-play of the Exodus, we are prepared to see Jesus' baptism as re-presenting the crossing of the Red Sea. Three factors favor this view. First, Paul states that baptism was foreshadowed by the crossing of the Red Sea, indicating that this understanding of the Red Sea event existed previous to Matthew's writing.[15] Second, the Jordan is most notable in the Old Testament for Joshua's crossing of the Jordan, which is undoubtedly portrayed in the book of Joshua as a re-enactment of the crossing of the Red Sea—accomplished in fact by one who shares Jesus' Hebrew name. Third, an argument can be made that John the Baptist should be understood in light of the angel who went before Israel in the Exodus.[16]

Immediately after Jesus' baptism, Matthew describes how he went out into the wilderness where he fasted "forty days and forty nights" and was tempted by the devil. This fits quite well with the Moses theme, because immediately after crossing the Red Sea Moses led Israel into the desert, whereupon he went up on a mountain and did not eat for forty days and forty nights. The parallel accounts in

---

12   Matt. 2:19.

13   Exod. 4:19.

14   Allison, *New Moses*, 142–143.

15   1 Cor. 10:1–2; see Allison, *New Moses*, 195, especially n. 131.

16   Matthew quotes Isa. 40:3 as applying to John: "The voice of one crying in the wilderness, prepare the way of the Lord." Only two places in the Masoretic Text speak of "preparing" the "way" of the Lord: Isa. 40:3 and Mal. 3:1. Mark 1:2–3 conflates the two verses in applying them to John, while Matthew quotes Isa. 40:3 alone in 3:3 and Mal. 3:1 alone in 11:10. Malachi 3:1 is closely related to Exod. 23:20 inasmuch as the phrase "behold I will send my messenger [angel]" appears only in these two passages in the Masoretic Text or the Septuagint, and all three synoptics conflate these two passages to some degree. Malachi 3:1 is closely related in context to the prophecy in Mal. 4:5 that "I will send you Elijah the prophet before the great and terrible day of the LORD comes." This seems to identify the "messenger" or "angel" of Mal. 3:1/Exod. 23:20 with "Elijah." If Matthew 3:3 pursues the connections from the "voice" of Isa. 40:3 through the "angel" of Mal. 3:1 and Exod. 23:20 to "Elijah" of Mal. 4:5, then this explains the description of John's clothing in Matt 3:4, which alludes to the description of Elijah in 2 Kings 1:8 (compare the description of John as "Elijah who is to come" in Matt. 11:14). From the same set of connections, John is implicitly cast as the angel of Exod. 23:20 who went before Israel in the Exodus as John now goes before Jesus.

Mark and Luke mention the "forty days," but do not add "and forty nights," a small but significant addition, since "forty days and forty nights" is a phrase associated in the Old Testament almost exclusively with Moses and Elijah (who is portrayed as a Moses-figure in this respect).[17] Moreover, a Rabbinic tradition, which perhaps predates Matthew, states that the golden calf incident happened because the devil tempted Israel and then accused them before God, but Moses stood in the breach and overcame the devil's accusations.[18] Jesus, like Moses, is tempted by the devil. Further, in the last temptation in Matthew's Gospel, the devil takes Jesus up on a high mountain to show him all the kingdoms of the world. This is paralleled in Jewish traditions (developing Numbers 27) by the portrayal of Moses on the mountain receiving a cosmic vision of the whole world.[19]

In this desert scene, Jesus is portrayed not only as a new Moses, but as a new and faithful Israel. Just as the Lord says in Exodus that Israel is his "first-born son," so he proclaims Jesus as his "beloved son" at the baptism in the Jordan, and Satan begins his temptation of Jesus with the challenge, "If you are the son of God. . . ."[20] Jesus draws each of his responses to Satan from a short section of Deuteronomy in which Moses is repeating for Israel the lessons they should have learned from their experiences in the desert—each one an area in which they had failed. Jesus is the faithful son of God, who heeds his father's commands. Jesus is the antitype not only of Moses, but of the nation as well.[21]

From the wilderness scene, Matthew moves into the beginning of Jesus' ministry, and then quickly into the Sermon on the Mount in chapter 5. Given that we have seen Jesus re-live the Exodus, the passage through the sea, and the time in the wilderness, it is hardly surprising that he next goes up on a mountain and gives a law. In fact, he explicitly points to the parallel between himself and Moses, clarifying that his project is not one of abandonment, but of fulfillment (5:17). Then, rather than interpreting the law as one of the scribes would, Jesus adds to the law as an authoritative law-giver—as a Moses figure.[22]

The Exodus typology in the early chapters of Matthew could be developed at much greater length. For the purpose of interpreting the formula citations, though, I would like to draw attention to three main elements of this typology. First, it is about the Exodus. Second, it is typology: Moses or Israel stand as the types, and Jesus as the antitype. Third, this Exodus typology is sustained and coherent: rather than a collage of varying or competing typologies, Matthew presents us with a

---

17   Compare Mark 1:13 and Luke 4:2 with Matt. 4:2. See Allison, *New Moses*, 166–168. The phrase "forty days and forty nights" also occurs in connection with Noah in Gen. 7:4, 12.

18   Allison, *New Moses*, 169. Allison adds a caution here about the dating of such Rabbinic sayings.

19   Allison, *New Moses*, 169–172.

20   Exod. 4:22; Matt. 3:17; 4:3.

21   Allison, *New Moses*, 165–166.

22   Matt. 7:28–29; see Allison, *New Moses*, 182–190.

typological narrative extending over several chapters. This will be important to keep in mind as we turn to see how the formula citations, like jewels, are placed in this golden setting.

The Formula Citations

As mentioned above, Matthew puts seven formula citations in the first four chapters of his Gospel: (1) when Jesus is born of a virgin mother, Matthew adds, "All this took place to fulfill what the Lord had spoken by the prophet: 'Behold, a virgin shall conceive and bear a son, and his name shall be called Emmanuel' (which means, God with us)";[23] (2) when Herod inquires of the scribes where the Messiah will be born, they reply, "In Bethlehem of Judea; for so it is written by the prophet: 'And you, O Bethlehem, in the land of Judah, are by no means least among the rulers of Judah; for from you shall come a ruler who will govern my people Israel'";[24] (3) when Herod slaughters the infants of Bethlehem as Jesus flees into Egypt, Matthew comments, "Then was fulfilled what was spoken by the prophet Jeremiah: 'A voice was heard in Ramah, wailing and loud lamentation, Rachel weeping for her children; she refused to be consoled, because they were no more'";[25] (4) when Jesus (with Mary and Joseph) came back from Egypt: "This was to fulfill what the Lord had spoken by the prophet, 'Out of Egypt have I called my son;'"[26] (5) when Joseph returns to Israel and finds that he must settle in the north, in Nazareth, Matthew says, "And he went and dwelt in a city called Nazareth, that what was spoken by the prophets might be fulfilled, 'He shall be called a Nazarene'";[27] (6) when, thirty years later, Matthew introduces John the Baptist with the comment, "For this is he who was spoken of by the prophet Isaiah when he said, 'The voice of one crying in the wilderness: Prepare the way of the Lord, make his paths straight'";[28] and (7) when Jesus, after his baptism and temptation, goes to Capernaum in Galilee to begin his ministry, Matthew states that the move was so "that what was spoken by the prophet Isaiah might be fulfilled: 'The land of Zebulun and the land of Naphtali, toward the sea, across the Jordan, Galilee of the Gentiles—the people who sat in darkness have seen a great light, and for those who sat in the region and shadow of death light has dawned.'"[29]

---

23   Matt. 1:22–23.

24   Matt. 2:5–6.

25   Matt. 2:17–18.

26   Matt. 2:15.

27   Matt. 2:23.

28   Matt. 3:3.

29   Matt. 4:14–15.

Thematic Unity in the Formula Citations

Is there any unifying theme or structure to these seven citations, taken from various prophets? Do they relate in any definite way to the Exodus typology Matthew develops at the level of biblical allusion?

As a springboard into these questions, I would like to start with Matthew 1:17, which seems to be a quasi-formula citation in the way it presents Matthew's authorial reflection on the meaning of his genealogy: "So all the generations from Abraham to David were fourteen generations, and from David to the deportation to Babylon fourteen generations, and from the deportation to Babylon to the Christ fourteen generations." Matthew has structured his genealogy into three sets of fourteen, even leaving out certain names to achieve this effect, in order to highlight four very significant events in the history of Israel: the covenant with Abraham, the covenant with David, the Babylonian exile, and the coming of the Christ.

These four moments form a coherent picture: the covenant with Abraham was in part fulfilled by the glory of the Davidic monarchy; the promises made to Abraham and to David seem to have been destroyed by the Babylonian exile; the Christ comes to restore the kingdom and the promises. In other words, Matthew uses his genealogy to highlight Jesus' role as the one who will restore Israel after the exile.

Jesus' role as *restorer* is a very important idea for Matthew: all seven of the formula citations in Matthew 1:1–4:16 are drawn from contexts that speak about the restoration of Israel. But there is more. All seven are drawn from passages that portray the restoration of Israel as a *new Exodus*. As of old God rescued Israel from Egyptian bondage and made them into a nation, so now he will rescue them from exile and re-form them as a nation. Outside of Second Isaiah, which is rife with Exodus imagery, I have found the new Exodus theme only in the following prophetic texts: several points within Isaiah 2–12; in Isaiah 19:19–25 (although this is very different from other new Exodus passages); possibly in Isaiah 26:20–27:1; in Jeremiah 16:14 (= 23:7), and 30–31; in Hosea 1–3, 8–9, and 11; in Micah 7; and in Zechariah 10:11.[30]

In other words, there are only a limited number of new Exodus passages in the prophets—between ten and fifteen, depending on how one counts them—and Matthew has drawn all seven of his formula citations from these passages. His interest in the Exodus—evinced by his copious use of Mosaic typology (see above)—is apparently paralleled by an interest in the New Exodus. He does not always cite the particular verses that manifest the New Exodus theme, but it is there in the background for those who know the surrounding contexts of his citations.

---

30 Helpful overviews of the use of Exodus themes in the OT can be found in David Daube, *The Exodus Pattern in the Bible* (London: Faber and Faber, 1963), and—covering more ground in less space—Michael Fishbane, *Text and Texture* (New York: Schocken, 1979), 121–140.

Textual Links between Formula Citations

The seven formula citations share more than a common theme: they are also united by an important theme and textual proximity.[31] Three of Matthew's citations are drawn from the same oracle within Isaiah: Matthew 1:23 cites Isaiah 7:14, Matthew 2:23 cites Isaiah 11:1 (probably), and Matthew 4:15–16 cites Isaiah 9:1–2. These are not only within the same oracle (Isaiah 2–12), but are drawn from the three points within that oracle where Isaiah speaks of a divinely given child. Micah 5:2, cited in Matthew 2:6, can be attached to this group. It too speaks of a divinely given child, and in vocabulary so reminiscent of Isaiah 7:14 that some have seen Micah 5:2 as a literary reference to the prophecy in Isaiah.[32] This group of four citations is bound together by proximity in context and by shared vocabulary and themes.

The passages Matthew cites from within Isaiah 2–12 are tightly bound to Second Isaiah (chapters 40–55 of canonical Isaiah), so much so that scholars dispute among themselves whether Isaiah of Jerusalem is responsible for all of Isaiah 9 and 11, or whether his later followers added to these passages on the model of Second Isaiah. It is not surprising, therefore, to find that Matthew 3:3 cites Isaiah 40:3, from the opening of Second Isaiah—especially since Second Isaiah is the primary Old Testament locus for the new Exodus theme.

Second Isaiah is a highly allusive text, weaving in allusions to many other prophets and biblical texts, but the source singled out by scholars as most important for Second Isaiah is Jeremiah, with Jeremiah 30–31 (the so-called "Book of Consolation") being the richest source of allusions.[33] In fact, Isaiah 40:10, a few verses away from the text cited in Matthew 3:3 (Isa. 40:3—see preceding paragraph) alludes to Jeremiah 31:16; it is not surprising to find that Matthew cites Jeremiah 31:15. Jeremiah 31 in turn is heavily dependent on Hosea 11, and so again we are not surprised to find that Matthew cites Hosea 11:1.[34] These three

---

31   Carol Stockhausen pioneered the exploration of key-word links in her work on St. Paul. She bases her work on the rabbinical technique of *gezera sheva*, "an analogy which rests on a similarity of *verbal expression* in two separate texts, which on the basis of this verbal similarity are linked and used to explain, clarify or amplify one another." See Stockhausen, *Moses' Veil and the Glory of the New Covenant: The Exegetical Substructure of II Cor. 3,1–4,6*, Analecta biblica 116 (Rome: Pontifical Biblical Institute, 1989), 26–27.

32   See Hans Walter Wolff, *Micah: A Commentary*, trans. Gary Stansell (Minneapolis: Augsburg, 1990), 136.

33   See Benjamin D. Sommer, *A Prophet Reads Scripture: Allusion in Isaiah 40–66* (Standford, CA: Stanford University Press, 1998), 315–325. Sommer finds Jer. 30:10–11 alluded to in Isa. 41:8–13, 43:1–6, and 44:1–2, Jer. 31:16 in Isa. 40:8–10, Jer. 31:31–36 in Isa. 42:5–9, Jer. 31:7–9 in Isa. 42:10–16, Jer. 31:1–8 in Isa. 43:6–9, Jer. 30:14 in Isa. 47:9, Jer. 33:3 in Isa. 48:6, Jer. 31:32 in Isa. 51:7, Jer. 31:35 in Isa. 51:14, Jer. 31:33–35 in Isa. 54:10–13, and Jer. 31:8 in Isa. 55:12. See also the treatment in Shalom Paul, "Literary and Ideological Echoes of Jeremiah in Deutero-Isaiah," in *Proceedings of the 5th World Congress of Jewish Studies* (Jerusalem: Hebrew University Press, 1969), 104–110.

34   For Jeremiah's dependence on Hosea, see Lindars, "Rachel, Weeping for Her Children—Jer-

texts cited by Matthew—Isaiah 40, Jeremiah 31, and Hosea 11—are connected by shared vocabulary and themes that lead modern scholars to posit a chain of literary dependencies; the same shared vocabulary and themes may have led Matthew to see a connection between them.

Typology in the Formula Citations

To sum up what we have done so far: we have seen that Matthew uses biblical allusions to construct a sustained typological narrative in which Jesus re-enacts the Exodus. We have seen further that Matthew's explicit prophetic citations betray an interest in the restoration of Israel seen as a new Exodus. Lastly, we have seen that Matthew's citations are connected one to another not only by the common theme of "new Exodus," but also by more particular themes and shared vocabulary. The unified Exodus typology that scholars have unearthed in the early chapters of Matthew serves as a background for a unified set of new Exodus citations. If the Exodus theme in Matthew's narrative corresponds to a new Exodus theme in his citations, and if the unity of Matthew's Exodus allusions is matched in some way by a unity among his citations, one may well ask whether the typology he employs in his Exodus allusions corresponds to any typology in the citations.

Two of Matthew's citations are commonly interpreted as typological. When Jesus is forced to stay some time in Egypt, Matthew says, "This was to fulfill what the Lord had spoken by the prophet, 'Out of Egypt have I called my son.'"[35] In its original context in Hosea 11, this is not a prophecy of a future event but a statement about what happened in the past, namely, that God brought Israel out of Egypt. But since we have seen that Matthew portrays Jesus typologically in the wilderness scene as a new Israel, the faithful son of God, it makes sense to suppose that the same typology is at work here. While Hosea speaks of Israel as God's son and complains of his infidelity in the wilderness, Matthew sees in this description a type of Christ the faithful son of God. As Israel came out of Egyptian bondage, so Jesus will return from his forced Egyptian exile. Further, Hosea's words apply even more dramatically to Jesus than to their original referent, because Jesus is the "son of God" beyond all others. This view of Matthew's intention is all the more plausible because Hosea 11 itself takes the original Exodus as a type of a future event, a future "Exodus" that Israel must accomplish after the exile.

Similarly, when Herod has the infants of Bethlehem slaughtered, Matthew comments, "Then was fulfilled what was spoken by the prophet Jeremiah: 'A voice was heard in Ramah, wailing and loud lamentation, Rachel weeping for her children;

---

emiah 31:15–22," *Journal for the Study of the Old Testament* 12 (1979): 47–62, at 47.

35 Matt. 2:15. For the view that Matthew is interpreting Hosea typologically see, for example, Brown, *Birth*, 214–215; W. D. Davies and Dale C. Allison, *A Critical and Exegetical Commentary on the Gospel According to Saint Matthew*, 3 vols., International Critical Commentary (Edinburgh: T&T Clark, 1988), 1:263; John P. Meier, *Matthew*, New Testament Message 3 (Wilmington, DE: Michael Glazier, 1980), 13–14.

she refused to be consoled, because they were no more.'"[36] In its original context, this saying of Jeremiah is not a prophecy of a future event but a statement about a past event, when the southern kingdom of Israel was taken into captivity. Rachel's tomb was supposed to be somewhere near Ramah, where the captives were held in preparation for transport to Babylon. The statement that her children "were no more" means that the inhabitants of the kingdom of Judah were taken away into exile. Jeremiah employs the phrase "were no more" to use death as a metaphor for exile while Matthew cites it as pointing to the slaughter of the infants in Bethlehem—a case of literal rather than figurative death—but Jesus himself does go into exile as would be indicated by the original metaphorical meaning of Jeremiah's phrase. Given the typology of Jesus as Israel, Matthew sees the forced exile of Jesus and the slaughter of the infants as foreshadowed by the Babylonian captivity.

W. D. Davies and Dale Allison have this to say about these two citations from Hosea and Jeremiah:

> There is in 2.13–23 a Jesus/Israel typology, a typology which will be taken up once again in chapters 3 and 4 (where Jesus passes through the waters of baptism and then enters into the desert). In 2.15, for instance, the "son" of Hos 11.1, originally Israel, becomes Jesus. And behind the quotation of Jer. 31.15 in 2.18 there apparently lies, as argued, a typological equation of Jesus with Israel: in Jeremiah's prophecy of return for the exiles Matthew discerns a cipher for the Messiah's return to Israel. We may say, then, that while Jesus culminates Israel's history in chapter 1, in chapter 2 he repeats it.[37]

Many of Matthew's other formula citations are to be understood as similarly typological. Indeed, Matthew uses his formula citations to interpret the events of Jesus' pre-ministry period as a unified story in which Jesus relives the history of the exile and then symbolically returns from exile to inaugurate Israel's own return. Like the Suffering Servant of Second Isaiah, Jesus first takes on himself the punishment of Israel and then comes bearing the light of God's salvation.

This approach unlocks some problems that have puzzled scholars for centuries. For example, Matthew's citation of Isaiah 7:14 (referencing a "young woman" or "virgin" bearing a son) has been a source of controversy since the patristic era. Almost every thesis imaginable has been proposed to explain his intentions. The many views can be arranged under four general headings: (1) until the modern era, most interpreters took Matthew as saying that the words of Isaiah apply at

---

36 For the view that Matthew is interpreting Jeremiah typologically here, see Brown, *Birth*, 216–217; Davies and Allison, *Matthew*, 1:267–268.

37 Davies and Allison, *Matthew*, 1:282.

the literal level to the birth of Christ;[38] (2) some have argued that Matthew took Isaiah's words to be partially fulfilled in Isaiah's own time but completely fulfilled only at the birth of Christ;[39] (3) others have argued that Matthew took Isaiah to be speaking of an event in his own times, but that Matthew's confidence in the divine authorship of Scripture led him to see further significance in Isaiah's choice of words;[40] (4) still others believe that Matthew lifted the text completely out of context and interpreted it without regard for its original significance—this seems to be the majority view today.[41]

The problem is that, in context, the child is supposed to know how to "refuse the evil and choose the good" before Assyria devastates Syria and Israel, while Matthew cites Isaiah's words as pointing to an event long after the demise of the Assyrian empire itself. Exegetes have debated endlessly about whether or not the word used for the child's mother means "young woman" or "virgin." In the end it does not make a difference: all that "virgin" would have to mean in context is that the woman in question was a virgin at the time of Isaiah's prophecy, not that she was a virgin even after conception.[42]

But the view that Matthew interprets Isaiah 7:14 *typologically* solves the questions posed by all of the above views. To begin with, it fits well with the context of Matthew's citation. Isaiah says of himself and his own child Mahershalalhashbaz that "I and the children whom the Lord has given me are signs and portents in Israel from the Lord of Hosts,"[43] meaning here not "proofs" but "signifiers." Since the child of Isaiah 7:14 is also given as a "sign," it is natural to take him not as a proof but as a signifier, and so the question becomes: What does this child signify? It is a response to Ahaz's concern about an attempt by Syria and Israel to remove

---

38 For a summary of the patristic tradition, see D. A. Carson, *Matthew*, ed. Frank E. Gaebelein, Expositor's Bible Commentary 8 (Grand Rapids, MI: Zondervan, 1984), 77–81. See also M. -J. Lagrange, *Évangile selon Saint Matthieu* [The Gospel According to Saint Matthew] (Paris: J. Gabalda, 1948), 16–17.

39 See, for example, Robert H. Gundry, *Matthew: A Commentary on His Handbook for a Mixed Church Under Persecution*, 2d ed. (Grand Rapids: Eerdmans, 1994), 24–25; Craig L. Blomberg, "Interpreting Old Testament Prophetic Literature in Matthew: Double Fulfillment," *Trinity Journal* 23 (2002): 17–33; Walter C. Kaiser, "The Promise of Isaiah 7:14 and the Single-Meaning Hermeneutic," *Evangelical Journal* 6 (1988): 55–70.

40 See Hagner, *Matthew*, lv–lvi and 20–21, and Brown, *"Sensus Plenior,"* 102 and 143.

41 In addition to the scholars cited above, see C. D. F. Moule, *The Origin of Christology* (Cambridge: Cambridge University Press, 1977), 128: "Ignoring the context and doing violence to the original meaning, the Evangelist fits the ancient words by force into a contemporary, Christian meaning. ..."

42 As Joseph Blenkensopp comments, "Neither the context nor biblical usage in general provides much help in establishing the identity of either the prospective mother or her child, with the result that by now the scholarly debate on the designation of the woman and the name of the child practically defies documentation. ..." See Blenkensopp, *Isaiah 1–39*, Anchor Bible 19 (New York: Doubleday, 2000), 232–233.

43 Isa. 8:18.

him from the throne of Judah, and so in a general way "Emmanuel" must signify the divinely guaranteed continuance of the Davidic kingship even in the face of hostile plots.

But more specifically, the child's significance is brought out by the contextual parallel between Emmanuel and the Davidic scion of Isaiah 9:6–7 and 11:1–12:6. The child of 9:6–7 is also divinely "given to us," and his names, which include "Mighty God," recall the name "Emmanuel" or "God-with-us." So it seems reasonable to conclude, even before looking to Matthew, that the child "Emmanuel" is a sign of the Davidic messiah.[44]

At the same time, we saw that in both of Matthew's commonly recognized typological interpretations (namely Hos. 11:1 and Jer. 31:15), Matthew found texts whose wording applies better to Matthew's use of them than to their original situation. The same is true here. The word used to designate the child's mother can be taken to mean a virgin, and was so taken by the Septuagint translators. But the phrase "the virgin shall conceive" takes on a startling depth of meaning when we see that the savior signified by Emmanuel was born of one who remained a virgin after conception. The name "God with us" applies to the child Emmanuel because he signifies one who will bring God's salvation, while Jesus not only is that one but makes God present in a unique way.

Consequently, we can affirm the strengths of all the views concerning Matthew's intentions: (1) Matthew understood and interacted with the literal meaning of Isaiah's words; (2) he saw the literal meaning as fulfilled in a child born in Isaiah's day, but he saw the meaning of that child himself as fulfilled only at Christ's birth; (3) as he does elsewhere, he finds a divine depth of meaning in the words that fit the typological meaning even more closely than the literal; and (4) his dependence on the original literal and contextual meaning of the words for his typological interpretation shows that it would be a mistake to take that meaning as Christ's birth straightaway.

Typological Narrative in the Formula Citations

We began by seeing how Matthew constructs a detailed and sustained typological story of the Exodus in the early chapters of his Gospel. Then we found that all of the formula citations in those chapters are connected by a new Exodus theme and by key-words. Next we discovered that Matthew's formula citations interpret the Old Testament typologically. It would be reasonable therefore to ask whether Matthew's formula citations offer a sustained typological narrative to match the typological Exodus story of their surrounding context in Matthew's Gospel.

---

44 For a similar argument, see Craig L. Blomberg, "Interpreting Old Testament Prophetic Literature in Matthew: Double Fulfillment," *Trinity Journal* 23 (2002): 17–33, at 20–21; Brevard S. Childs, *Isaiah* (Louisville, KY: Westminster John Knox, 2001), 66, 73, 80–81; compare Childs, *The Struggle to Understand Isaiah as Christian Scripture* (Grand Rapids, MI: Eerdman's, 2004), 9–11.

If the formula citations are taken as telling a *story*, the resulting picture of Matthew's use of the Old Testament is neither purely literal nor purely typological. Most of the citations in 1:1–4:16 should be taken as typological, but as Jesus' typological re-living of Israel's history brings him closer to the time of his ministry, he begins to carry Israel's history forward: Israel's history finds its continuation in Jesus. Thus we find that certain of the citations, specifically those about a Davidic Messiah who will restore Israel, are interpreted as applying literally to Jesus. The constant in Matthew's citations turns out to be not a textual theory, whether typological or literal, but the conviction that Jesus bears the identity of Israel.

The following analysis will summarize the *story* of Matthew's citations.

(1) Isaiah 7:14

Isaiah 7:14 (cited in Matt. 1:23) refers to a child born during the 8th century B.C., just before the exile of the northern kingdom. Seeing this child as a type of Christ, we can understand Jesus' birth as symbolically re-enacting this period before the exile.

(2) Jeremiah 31:15

Jeremiah 31:15 (cited in Matt. 2:18) speaks of the time just after the last stage of the deportation of Israel, when Judah was taken away to Babylon. Understanding these events typologically, we see Jesus, as a *Judean*, take part in the exile of the southern kingdom.

(3) Hosea 11:1

Hosea 11:1 (cited in Matt. 2:15) speaks of Israel coming out of Egypt, but this event, as the context in Hosea implies, should be understood as a foreshadowing of the return from exile; by applying this text to Jesus, Matthew portrays him as Israel returning from exile.

(4) Isaiah 11:1 / 4:3

The next prophecy cited in Matthew 2:23, that "He shall be called a Nazorean," is hard to pin down, but most scholars identify the primary referent as either Isaiah 11:1 or Isaiah 4:3. This identification is based on a word play between "Nazorean" and the Hebrew words for "branch" or "holy."[45] Isaiah 11:1 describes a "branch" springing up from the root of Jesse, while Isaiah 4:3 states that the one who survives after the devastation of Israel shall be called "holy." Applied to Jesus, either text would name Jesus as a survivor of the exile. In the typological *story* of the

---

45 See Brown, *Messiah*, 207–213 and 223–225; Davies and Allison, *Matthew*, 1:276–281; Stuart Chepey, *Nazirites in Late Second Temple Judaism: A Survey of Ancient Jewish Writings, the New Testament, Archaeological Evidence, and Other Writings from Late Antiquity*, Ancient Judaism and Early Christianity 60 (Leiden: Brill, 2005), 151–155.

formula citations, therefore, Jesus is born before the very beginnings of the exile, suffers exile with Judah, returns from exile, and is named as a survivor of the exile.

(5) Isaiah 40:3

A shift occurs in the story at this point. Jesus has re-lived the history of Israel all the way up to the present, and has experienced in himself the restoration he must bring to the nation. This brings us to Matthew chapter 3, where John is identified as the "voice" that cries out in Isaiah 40:3, the beginning of Second Isaiah.[46]

This chapter in Isaiah begins with a command from God: "Comfort, comfort my people, says your God. Speak tenderly to Jerusalem, and cry to her that her warfare is ended, that her iniquity is pardoned, that she has received from the LORD's hand double for all her sins." In response to God's command,

> A voice cries: "In the wilderness prepare the way of the LORD, make straight in the desert a highway for our God. Every valley shall be lifted up, and every mountain and hill be made low; the uneven ground shall become level, and the rough places a plain. And the glory of the LORD shall be revealed, and all flesh shall see it together, for the mouth of the LORD has spoken."

What the "voice" announces is a summary of the whole message of Second Isaiah. As we read on through chapters 40–55, it becomes clear that the preparation required for the way of the Lord is repentance and conversion of heart. When the hearts of the people of Israel return to God, he will bring them through the wilderness in a new Exodus. The glory of the Lord will be revealed to all flesh when all mankind sees the salvation God brings for his people.

Further, regarding Matthew's use of Isaiah 40:3—again, a text connected to all of Isaiah 40–55—it is of crucial importance to note that the key figure in this new Exodus is the so-called "Suffering Servant." The Suffering Servant bears the identity of Israel in himself, to the point that his suffering and death are counted as Israel's suffering and death: he himself bears the punishment of the people.[47] John the Baptist is the "voice" who cries out that the time of the new Exodus is at hand, and that the Suffering Servant is coming—Jesus, who carries the identity of Israel.

(6) Isaiah 42:1

When Jesus is baptized by John, the Holy Spirit descends upon him and God's voice says, "This is my beloved son, in whom I am well pleased,"—an allusion to the description of the Servant in Isaiah 42:1.[48]

---

46   Matt. 3:3.

47   Isa. 53.

48   Matt. 3:17.

(7) Isaiah 8:23–9:1

Jesus then goes out into the wilderness, endures the time of temptation, and moves his residence to Capernaum. This, Matthew tells us, happened "that what was spoken by the prophet Isaiah might be fulfilled: 'The land of Zebulun and the land of Naphtali, toward the sea, across the Jordan, Galilee of the Gentiles—the people who sat in darkness have seen a great light, and for those who sat in the region and shadow of death light has dawned.'"[49] The region of Zebulun and Naphtali is at the very northernmost part of Northern Israel, and was the first part of Israel to suffer exile, right about the time of Emmanuel's birth. The typological story has come full circle: born just before the beginning of the exile, Jesus suffers the exile himself, returns from exile, is named as a survivor of the exile, and comes as the Suffering Servant to bring restoration to Israel. He then begins his ministry in the very place where the exile began, in the region of Zebulun and Naphtali.[50]

Matthew's narrative operates on three levels at once: (1) it is the story of Jesus' pre-ministry period, (2) it reenacts the history of the exile, and (3) it reenacts the Exodus from Egypt. Since Matthew sees the restoration of Israel as a new Exodus, these levels of story line are not independent but mutually supportive. The relationship among these three levels of the story can be put in chart form as follows:

	Matt. 1:23 / Isa. 7:14	Matt. 2:18 / Jer. 31:15	Matt. 2:15 / Hos. 11:1	Matt. 2:23 / Isa. 11:1 / Isa. 4:3	Matt. 3:1 / Isa. 40:3	Matt. 4:15–16 / Isa. 8:23–9:1
1 Pre-ministry Story of Jesus	Jesus is born	Jesus flees to Egypt / death of Bethlehem infants	Jesus returns to Israel	Jesus becomes a Nazarean	The preaching of John	Jesus moves to Capernaum
2 History of the Exile Reenacted	Emmanuel is born	Exile of Israel	[No corresponding event]	The names to be given the future remnant	The messenger of Isa. 40:3	The place where the exile began
3 History of the Exodus Reenacted	Moses is born	Death of Hebrew infants / flight of Moses	Exodus from Egypt	[No corresponding event]	Angel of the Lord goes before Israel	[No corresponding event]

---

49 Matt. 4:14–16.

50 Because it is placed on the mouths of characters within the story, the citation of Mic. 5:2 in Matt. 2:6 regarding the Messiah's birth-place speaks about *the present arrival* of the Messiah instead of his *typological reenactment* of a past event. With this exception, all of the citations attach to Matthew's narrative in the order of their place within the typological story.

Note that when Jesus reenacts the return of Israel from exile, there is no historical return from exile that Matthew can interpret typologically (see column 3, position 2). As a result, he cites a text that describes the original Exodus instead of a text concerning the history of the exile (see column 3, position 3).

This multi-level, unified interpretation of the formula citations in Matthew 1:1–4:16 is supported by three considerations:

(1) First, the typological story of exile and restoration lines up perfectly with the Exodus typology we find in Matthew's use of the Old Testament outside of his formula citations. The Exodus story we find in Matthew's biblical allusions matches the new Exodus story of his biblical citations. As Jesus bears the identity of Israel in re-living the captivity in Egypt and the Exodus, so he bears the identity of Israel in re-living the exile and pre-living the restoration.

(2) Second, Matthew has chosen all of his citations in 1:1–4:16 from passages describing the restoration of Israel in imagery borrowed from the Exodus. Further, his citations are all interconnected by key-words and particular themes. These two observations suggest that Matthew's use of these citations are unified in some way. One would expect that the commonly held typological interpretations of Jeremiah 31:15 (Jesus going down into Egypt) and Hosea 11:1 (Jesus coming out of Egypt) are connected to Matthew's understanding of the surrounding formula citations.

(3) That the formula citations fall into the narrative outlined above—when placed in their order as Matthew has attached them to the events of Christ's life—is an argument in its own favor. It seems improbable that such order could appear by chance. Micah 5:2 is the only one out of order, and it is also the only one spoken by characters within Matthew's narrative; the exception thus proves the rule.

The Proleptic Function of the Formula Citations

It should be clear by now why I have chosen to treat Matthew 1:1–4:16 as a unit rather than introducing a major break after chapter 2. Having made an argument for Matthew 1:1–4:16 as a unit, I would further argue that this unit has an identifiable function within the larger context of Matthew's Gospel.

This function becomes apparent in the story of the slaughter of the infants of Bethlehem. Matthew finds a text in Jeremiah 31:15 that not only advances his typological narrative about Jesus but uses wording more applicable to the slaughtered infants than to its original referent. However, the neat applicability of Jeremiah's wording to the infants of Bethlehem highlights the difference between their fate and Jesus' successful escape. While they literally died and thus "were no more," Jesus went into exile like the original subjects of Jeremiah's text. Considered in its original sense as a metaphor, Jeremiah 31:15 might indeed be more applicable to Jesus than to the infants, but Matthew has applied it to the victims who suffer death in the literal sense. Commentators note that Jesus' flight into Egypt and the massacre of the innocents both fall under an exile typology, but Jean Miler points out that the difference between the two raises an important question: what is the relationship between the infants' death and Jesus' escape?[51]

To answer the question, we have to see that Matthew has crafted this portion of his infancy narrative to foreshadow the passion account. Herod is said to assemble "all the chief priests and scribes of the people" in Matthew 2:4. Elsewhere in Matthew, the phrase "chief priests and scribes" occurs only in connection with Jesus' final rejection and passion in Jerusalem.[52] In Matthew 2:4 the "chief priests and scribes" are consulted about the birth-place of the "king of the Jews," a title that appears elsewhere in Matthew only in the passion narrative. As Raymond Brown has noted, Matthew 1–2 follows the sequence of revelation, proclamation, and two-fold reaction, giving the infancy narrative the shape of a "gospel in miniature."[53]

This foreshadowing makes sense inasmuch as the climax of Jesus' redemptive action, and therefore of Matthew's Gospel, is not in the infancy narrative but in the paschal mystery. Although Jesus appears in the infancy narrative as the one who bears Israel's identity, takes on himself the punishment of Israel, and returns from exile, still, Matthew knows that it was on the cross that Jesus offered his blood for the forgiveness of sins.[54] The flight into Egypt is not his final salvific work. The time will come when Jesus will indeed share the fate of the innocents by dying at the hands of a foreign ruler, but that time is not yet. The discrepancy between Jesus' fate and that of the infants of Bethlehem hints already at what Jesus must ultimately do in order to bear the punishment of Israel. In the meantime, his solidarity with the infants is expressed by suffering at the level of metaphor what they suffer literally.

---

51 Jean Miler, *Les Citations d'accomplissement dans l'évangile de Matthieu: Quand Dieu se rend présent en toute humanité* [The Accomplishment Citations in the Gospel of Matthew: When God Makes Himself Present in All Humanity], Analecta biblica 140 (Rome: Pontifical Biblical Institute, 1999), 60.

52 See, for example, Matt. 16:21, "From that time Jesus began to show his disciples that he must go to Jerusalem and suffer many things from the elders and chief priests and scribes, and be killed, and on the third day be raised." The other occurrences of the phrase are similar: 20:18, 21:15, and 27:41.

53 For commentary on the parallels between this scene and the Passion see Brown, *Birth*, 183.

54 Matt. 26:28.

If the infants' death looks forward to the end of the Gospel, it is also true that the end of the Gospel sheds light on the infants' fate. Jeremiah 31:15 says that Rachel refuses to be consoled for her children "because they are no more." However, Jeremiah 31:16–17 continues:

> Thus says the LORD: Keep your voice from weeping, and your eyes from tears; for your work shall be rewarded, says the LORD, and they shall come back from the land of the enemy. There is hope for your future, says the LORD, and your children shall come back to their own country.

One might think that Matthew's awareness of the context has failed here. While the exiles may have come back from Babylon, the infants of Bethlehem are dead, and for them there will be no return. But when Jesus comes to share in their fate by dying, his death is in fact followed by a restoration. Matthew and his readers knew that there is a return from death, and for them there would be no problem in applying Jeremiah 31:16–17 to the Jewish infants. Richard J. Erickson's remarks are apt:

> The death of the Innocents, like the death of the male Hebrew babies in Egypt, is a harbinger of the coming New Exodus. Tragic though the massacre in Bethlehem may be, it is in the end no more tragic than the death of any single human being in the history of the human race. The one who escaped at Bethlehem comes back to endure it all himself, *and to reverse it!* Therefore, says Matthew by implication, weep no more![55]

That Matthew lines up the exile with the death of the infants of Bethlehem, and ultimately with Jesus' death, gives us new ground for examining Matthew's understanding of the exile, which we have seen to be so dominant a theme in this first part of his Gospel. In some way, the exile is death, and the promised restoration is resurrection from the dead.[56]

While commentators have seen that the slaughter of the infants has a proleptic function in Matthew's Gospel, Matthew 4:16–17 (about Jesus beginning his ministry in the northern parts of Galilee) and its citation of Isaiah 8:23–9:1 appear to foreshadow later events in Matthew's story. According to most commentators, the reason Matthew cites Isaiah 8:23–9:1 is his interest in the mission to the Gentiles. Ulrich Luz lays out the majority position clearly, and his comments are worth citing at length:

---

55   Richard J. Erickson, "Divine Injustice?: Matthew's Narrative Strategy and the Slaughter of the Innocents (Matthew 2.13-23)," *Journal for the Study of the New Testament* 64 (1996): 5–27, at 26 (my emphasis).

56   Compare Ezek. 37:1–14.

> In the quotation, the phrase "Galilee of the Gentiles" ... is most important to Matthew. With that it is clear that he does not mean that Galilee is settled by Gentiles or that Jesus' ministry had taken place entirely or partly among Gentiles. Matthew in his Gospel makes it clear that Jesus was the Messiah of Israel, ministered in Israel's synagogues, and forbade his disciples to work outside of Israel (10:5f.). ... Thus the designation "Galilee of the Gentiles" has a fictive character. With this Old Testament designation Matthew intends to point on a second level to that which the sending of Jesus has started in the history of salvation: the way of salvation to the Gentiles. In Galilee, the risen Lord will give the disciples the command to make disciples of all Gentiles (28:16–20). Under the future perspective of salvation which is to come to the Gentiles and precisely in agreement with God's plan, Jesus in v. 17 begins his proclamation to Israel. Matthew wants to point to a perspective which applies to the entire ministry of Jesus in Israelite Galilee.[57]

Luz goes on to explain that the motivation behind the quotation is polemical, inasmuch as Matthew wants to claim the Hebrew Bible for Christianity against the Jews. Davies and Allison add that Matthew was trying "to make an asset out of a liability," that is, to counteract the negative image associated with Galilee by citing this from the prophet Isaiah.[58] These latter commentators argue that this is the *only* function of the citation, and that Galilee does not have any theological significance for Matthew beyond the need to offer an apologetic for the geographical details of Jesus' life.[59] Similarly, Luz remarks that "it is very difficult to judge how far the evangelist has interpreted the other statements of the quotation aside from 'Galilee of the Gentiles.'" Indeed, Luz does not succeed in finding anything but dissonance between the rest of the citation and Matthew's use of it.[60]

I have already responded to the view that would reduce Matthew's interest in Galilee to the keyword "Gentiles" by arguing that, in the context of his new-Exodus typological story, Matthew wants to emphasize that Jesus begins his ministry of light in the very region where the darkness of exile began for Israel.[61] But Luz is

---

57 Luz, *Matthew 1–7: A Commentary*, trans. Wilhelm C. Linss (Minneapolis: Augsburg, 1989), 194–195. He is followed by Davies and Allison (*Matthew*, 1:383–4), and Gundry (*Matthew*, 60).

58 Davies and Allison, *Matthew*, 1:379 and 383.

59 Davies and Allison, *Matthew*, 1:379–380.

60 Luz, *Matthew 1–7*, 196.

61 St. Jerome offers the following comment: "The Hebrews who believe in Christ explain this passage thus: In former times, these two tribes of Zebulun and Naphtali were taken captive by the Assyrians and led away to an enemy land, and Galilee was deserted; but the prophet says here that it has been relieved, because [Christ] would bear the people's sins. And later not only

right to point out that Matthew has a special interest in Galilee: in addition to citing the text from Isaiah, Matthew emphasizes Jesus' residence in Galilee more than the other synoptics do.

Matthew's emphasis on Galilee becomes clearer when compared to the other synoptic gospels. Mark 1:14 reports that "Jesus came into Galilee, preaching the gospel of God," but Matthew 4:13 says specifically that Jesus went and lived in Capernaum, which Mark says later in 2:1 only implicitly. Similarly, Luke 4:14 says that Jesus returned from the wilderness to Galilee, and in 4:41 he says that Jesus went to Capernaum, but he does not say that Jesus actually dwelt in Capernaum. From this point on, Matthew and Mark are substantially the same with regard to where Jesus traveled. One or the other sometimes includes an additional name for the same region, but Matthew only includes one place name which Mark does not, a reference to Capernaum in the story of the temple tax, and Mark does not have any place names which Matthew does not.[62]

However, there are interesting differences between the synoptics in how they handle the transition from Galilee to Judea. Luke goes his own way entirely, using the journey to Jerusalem as an opportunity to insert many of Jesus' sayings. His account of the journey begins at 9:51, but he does not have Jesus arrive at Jerusalem until 19:45. In Matthew and Mark, the journey is described in one verse: with regard to the departure from Galilee, Mark says simply, "He left there," while Matthew specifies that he "went away from Galilee." Mark's version seems to place the region of Judea as one more destination among many, while Matthew's version stresses that the journey to Judea is the end of the Galilean scene.[63] From this point to the end of the synoptic story, Matthew and Mark are almost interchangeable with regard to place-names, as before.

---

the two tribes but all the rest, who were dwelling beyond the Jordan and in Samaria, were led into captivity. And, [the Hebrew Christians] say, Scripture asserts here that the region whose people were first led into captivity and began to serve the Babylonians, and which first dwelt in the darkness of error, that same region would first see the light of Christ preaching, and from that region the gospel would be sown among all the nations." See Jerome, *Commentariorum in Esaiam libri I–XI*, Corpus Christianorum Series Latina 73 (Turnhout: Typographi Brepols Editores Pontifici, 1963), 123. Davies and Allison (*Matthew*, 1:381) and Luz (*Matthew 1–7*, 197) pass on this early Christian interpretation, but do not seem impressed by it.

62   See Matt. 17:24.

63   Sean Freyne points out Matthew's emphasis on this point in *Galilee, Jesus and the Gospels: Literary Approaches and Historical Investigations* (Philadelphia: Fortress, 1988), 76 and 89, but he does not see any particular emphasis on Galilee in Matthew as compared with Mark. Guido Tisera, borrowing from Freyne, also points out that Matthew is clearer on the Galilee-Judea transition than Mark, in *Universalism According to the Gospel of Matthew* (Berlin: Peter Lang, 1993), 293–294. Tisera goes beyond Freyne in pointing out connections in the meetings between the resurrected Jesus and others in Matthew 28, but the connection he sees is rather general.

This brings us to the resurrection account. In Matthew and Mark, an angel tells the women who come to the tomb to tell the disciples that Jesus will go before them to Galilee.[64] The women in Matthew then see Jesus, who repeats the instruction to tell the disciples that he is going before them to Galilee.[65] Mark never shows us the disciples arriving at Galilee. Luke has the disciples meet Jesus in Jerusalem. In Matthew's account, the disciples not only receive admonitions to go to Galilee, but they actually go there and see Jesus, and they do not see him before they see him there.[66] Once again, at an important juncture in the story, Matthew places emphasis on Galilee.

All of these observations can be summed up as follows. Matthew and Mark are very close to one another in describing where Jesus went, but Matthew puts more emphasis on Galilee at three important points: the beginning of Jesus' ministry in Galilee, the transition from Galilee to Judea, and the end of the gospel story. At the beginning of Jesus' ministry he gives Galilee a theological interpretation based on Isaiah 8:23–9:1. At the transition from Galilee to Judea he emphasizes that Jesus is no longer working in Galilee. At the end of the story he makes Galilee the actual and only meeting place between the disciples and the resurrected Jesus.

Given Matthew's sustained interest in Galilee, it seems reasonable to conclude with Luz that Matthew's citation in 4:15–16 of Isaiah 8:23–9:1 should be interpreted in light of Jesus' sending the disciples out to the nations from Galilee. Just as the slaughter of the infants and the flight into Egypt looks forward to Christ's death, and just as his return from Egypt looks forward to his resurrection, so the beginning of his preaching in Galilee looks forward to the beginning of the apostles' preaching at the end of the Gospel.

We can, therefore, add a fourth layer to the story of Matthew 1–4: as the story of the Exodus underlies the story of the exile, and the story of the exile underlies the infancy narrative, so the infancy narrative looks forward to the climactic events of Matthew's Gospel.

The story of Matthew 1:1–4:16 thus turns out to have an intermediate role: by having Jesus simultaneously recapitulate Israel's history and foreshadow his saving ministry, Matthew uses the infancy narrative as something like a lens to focus the light of Israel's history onto the coming ministry of Jesus. It can thus be compared to the prologue in John, which announces the major theological themes of his Gospel.

---

64 Matt. 28:7 and Mark 16:7. Luke refers to Galilee, but does not say that Jesus will go there.

65 Matt. 28:10.

66 Matt. 28:16.

Matthew as Exegete

At the beginning of this article, I suggested that the formula citations shed some light on how Matthew approaches the interpretation of Scripture. Having dealt with the formula citations at some length, I would like to make a few general observations about Matthew the exegete.

Contrary to some trends in scholarship, Matthew does not seek to construct an argument based on the Old Testament to convince or refute non-Christians. His intentions are not apologetic. Rather, he presumes a belief that Christ bears the identity of Israel, and on the basis of this belief he uses Old Testament citations to illuminate the mystery of Christ's life, death, and resurrection.

However, this does not mean that "ignoring the context and doing violence to the original meaning, the Evangelist fits the ancient words by force into a contemporary, Christian meaning."[67] Matthew sees his citations as parts of larger contexts, and he weaves these contexts together by way of keyword and thematic links to form a unified textual network with a meaning. In a wonderful way, he finds texts whose wording applies better to the story of Christ than to the original contexts, but the key to his interpretation of these same texts lies not in the words of the Old Testament but in the persons and events described by the words: he attends to the words but focuses on the realities behind the words. To use traditional Christian terms, Matthew seeks to bring out the spiritual sense of the Old Testament, a spiritual sense which he understands as grounded in the literal sense and, indeed, is unavailable without it.

Matthew's use of the Old Testament to illuminate the mystery of Christ reveals his conviction that the mystery of Christ unlocks the Old Testament, and this conviction itself leads him to a serious engagement with the Old Testament in the light of Christ. The result is a compelling, symphonic story in which the reader sees several layers of history converge in the death and resurrection of the Messiah. We have much to learn from Matthew about the relationship between the Old and New Testaments.

---

67   Moule, *Origin*, 128.

Letter & Spirit 8 (2013): 77-99

THE TRADITION OF CHRISTIAN ALLEGORY YESTERDAY AND TODAY

~: Leroy A. Huizenga :~
University of Mary

Allegory and Its Cultured Despisers

Many modern readers of the Bible disdain allegory, whether practicing Christians or academics, regarding it as a relic of a fanciful, unscientific Catholic past, an arbitrary way of imposing foreign meanings onto texts which has been fully superseded by modern ways of reading and interpreting rooted in common sense. In his brilliant essay on allegory, Andrew Louth writes, "There seems to be a fundamental distaste for, or even revulsion against, the whole business of allegory."[1] Why? Louth continues:

> Basically, I think because we feel that there is something *dishonest* about allegory. If you interpret a text by allegorizing it, you seem to be saying that it means something which it patently does not. It is irrelevant, arbitrary: by allegory, it is said, you can make any text mean anything you like.

The root of this judgment is the conviction that texts have one, simple, plain sense:[2]

> Behind this, perhaps, lies a feeling that there is something relatively unproblematic about the meaning of a literary passage: roughly, the meaning is what the author of the passage meant when he wrote it.[3]

R. C. P. Hanson's words are representative of the attitude Louth describes:

> Origen's use of allegory, with the exception of those few cases where he is confusing allegory with simple metaphor, is today widely regarded as wholly indefensible and as merely a process which caused Origen to mislead himself and others. At the best we may describe it as quaint and somewhat poetical; at the worst it is a device for obscuring the meaning of the Bible from

---

1   Andrew Louth, "Return to Allegory," in *Discerning the Mystery: An Essay on the Nature of Theology* (Clarendon Press: Oxford, 1983), 97.

2   Louth, "Return to Allegory," 97.

3   Louth, "Return to Allegory," 97.

> its readers. ... This is a conception which, since the arrival of
> historical criticism, has had to be entirely abandoned and is, as
> far as one can prophesy, never again likely to be revived.[4]

Louth's article is entitled "Return to Allegory" for a reason, and since its publication thirty years ago, theologians and ecclesially-minded exegetes have developed a
renewed appreciation for the historical practice of allegorical reading (allegoresis)
and the possibilities it may afford for the present as they have ever more endeavored
to reclaim the Bible as the Church's Scripture and develop substantive theological
exegesis for the present day.[5] The reasons largely concern both postmodern and
postliberal turns in the humanities and theology, after which modern disdain for
the past is considered a conceit and social location within a tradition taken as tru-
ism, as well as the failure of the so-called historical-critical method to deliver much
of relevance or substance for the contemporary Christian life.[6]

My thesis is as follows: Reading for the spiritual senses of Scripture, commonly called "allegory," is a natural and normal way to read religious texts, is seen
in the biblical texts themselves as well as premodern tradition, and is for Catholics
affirmed by contemporary authorities from the Second Vatican Council to the
present. Before discussing particular biblical texts and the tradition of spiritual
interpretation in detail, two preliminary questions require attention. What, really,
is "allegory"? And further, why has the Church engaged in it since its earliest days?

What Allegory Is—and Isn't

Allegory is not the questionable or illegitimate substitution of one thing for another,
as many have defined it, nor wanton eisegesis in which interpreters read things into
texts that simply are not there, but rather the practice of the disciplined, religious,
spiritual interpretation of sacred, authoritative texts motivated by their inspired,
inherent dynamism for the nurturing of the life of the community.

---

4   R. P. C. Hanson, *Allegory and Event: A Study of the Sources and Significance of Origen's
Interpretation of Scripture* (London: SCM Press, 1959; repr., Lousiville: Westminster John
Knox, 2002), 367.

5   See, for instance, the cautious remarks of Brian E. Daley, S.J., in "Is Patristic Exegesis Still
Usable? Reflections on Early Christian Interpretations of the Psalms," *Communio* 29 (2002):
185–216.

6   The most bracing critique of the so-called historical-critical method remains Walter Wink's
"The Bankruptcy of the Biblical Critical Paradigm," in *The Bible in Human Transformation:
Toward a New Paradigm in Bible Study* (Philadelphia: Fortress, 1973; repr., 2010), 1–12. For
a critique from an orthodox Christian perspective, see Joseph Cardinal Ratzinger, "Biblical
Interpretation in Conflict: The Question of the Basic Principles and Path of Exegesis Today,"
in *God's Word: Scripture, Tradition, Office*, trans. Henry Taylor (San Francisco: Ignatius Press,
2008), 91–126. This essay was first delivered orally on January 27, 1988, at Saint Peter's Church,
New York, N.Y., as the Erasmus Lecture, sponsored by the Institute on Religion and Public
Life, publisher of *First Things*.

Clarification of terms is in order. "Allegory" is generally used to refer to the three spiritual senses of Scripture, the other sense being the literal. The Western, Catholic tradition came to divide the spiritual sense further into the more narrow allegorical sense proper, the moral (or tropological) sense, and the anagogical sense (which concerns the pilgrimage to heaven). Now "allegory" is often misunderstood, as if Origen's brand thereof were definitive, but the Western, Catholic tradition delimits its proper scope. The Western Fathers and medievals generally use the term "allegory" to describe what most today call "typology." But premodern interpreters made no such distinction, and in fact the Latin word *typologia* did not appear until 1840, nor the English "typology" until 1844.[7] What premoderns called "allegory" resembles what moderns call "typology." For instance, for St. Thomas Aquinas, the "allegorical sense" (*sensus allegoricus*) concerns the Christological fulfillment of Old Testament events and figures. He writes, "so far as the things of the Old Law signify the things of the New Law, there is the allegorical sense."[8] Like him and before him, St. Augustine rooted all the spiritual senses in the letter and asserted that one does constructive theology from the literal sense alone. And before him St. Irenaeus saw in Scripture a record of the divine economy of salvation, with the Church's rule of faith serving as the hypothesis that revealed its mosaic unity, a unity centered on the risen Jesus Christ, a unity requiring spiritual exegesis. In our age the *Catechism of the Catholic Church* has codified this longstanding understanding of the fourfold sense of Scripture and its interpretation in Christian tradition,[9] and teaches that allegory proper concerns the significance of Old Testament events in Christ.[10] Far from being a license for enthusiastic speculation, then, the Western tradition has understood "allegory" as that which concerns typological relationships between the Testaments as well as the other spiritual senses as rooted in and constrained by the literal sense.

Why Allegory Was, and Is, and Will Be

But why did the tradition of the fourfold sense evolve? Jesus and the Church engaged in spiritual exegesis (allegory in the broader sense) of the Bible because it is a natural and normal way to read sacred, authoritative texts, common to pagans and Jews as well as Christians, regardless of any particular philosophical undergirding. In general, spiritual interpretation in paganism, Judaism, and Christianity trades on several common assumptions and concerns. First, it is assumed the text is a

---

7   Louth, "Return to Allegory," 118, citing Alan C. Charity, *Events and Their Afterlife: The Dialectics of Christian Typology in the Bible and Dante* (Cambridge: Cambridge University Press, 1966), 171.

8   Thomas Aquinas, *Summa Theologica* [The Summa Theologica of St. Thomas Aquinas], pt. 1a, q. 1, art. 10, resp. (London: Burns, Oates, and Washburne, 1920).

9   *Catechism of the Catholic Church*, 2d. ed. (Vatican City: Libreria Editrice Vaticana, 1997), nos. 109–119.

10 *Catechism*, no. 117 § 1.

coherent unity, the product of one ultimate mind that also reflects the reality of a coherent cosmos. Here allegory becomes a tool to reconcile myriad texts into a harmonious whole through some key so that they cohere with the divine and created reality. Second, ancient pagans, Jews, and Christians had developed substantive moral instincts and convictions based on reason, nature, and convention, and so the sacred text needed to be seen to conform with the claims of good morals. Third, most cultures have assumed an invisible world behind and above the visible, whether the ancient Greeks or animists today; in many ways Plato merely codified commonsense convictions about the nature of reality. Fourth, the desire to use authoritative texts for positive purposes in the present necessitates creative application.

It is not only premodern pagans, Jews, and Christians who read allegorically, however. Because allegory, broadly speaking, concerns the art of interpreting the Scriptures for their perpetual relevance and applying them to the life of the community in the present, many contemporary Christians, especially evangelical Protestants, who would reject the validity of allegorical interpretation if asked directly, regularly engage in it unwittingly in preaching, teaching, and Bible study. Any time one perceives and presents Biblical "typology" between the Testaments, at which Reformed Christians in particular excel, one is engaging in what Aquinas called allegory. Whenever one reads Christ as an example for the Christian life, even along the lines of something as simple and popular as the former "What Would Jesus Do?" phenomenon, one is engaging in what the tradition came to call tropology, the moral sense. And anytime a practicing Christian uses Scripture to learn about heaven or indeed to shape one's faith and life so that one might by God's grace achieve heaven, one is engaging in anagogy.

Sacred texts simply function in these dynamic ways in religious communities, and contemporary theologians and exegetes are ever more coming to this realization as theory catches up with practice. In the wake of the poststructuralist turn in literary and cultural studies, church historian David Steinmetz wrote a broadside entitled "The Superiority of Pre-critical Exegesis," in which he stated bluntly:

> The defenders of the single meaning theory usually concede that the medieval approach to the Bible met the religious needs of the Christian community, but it did so at the unacceptable price of doing violence to the biblical text. ... I should like to suggest an alternative hypothesis. The medieval theory of levels of meaning in the biblical text, with all its undoubted defects, flourished because it is true, while the modern theory of a single meaning, with all its demonstrable virtues, is false.[11]

---

11   David C. Steinmetz, "The Superiority of Pre-critical Exegesis," *Theology Today* 37 (1980): 38.

Steinmetz does not root his claim in any particular conception of God or meta-physics but rather in an appreciation for the dynamic nature of the process of inter-pretation as texts interact with readers. This is not to say premodern interpreters were wrong, but that they were fundamentally right: reading for the fourfold sense is a natural way to read the Christian Bible, as the four senses cover the totality of the normative function of sacred Scripture. The practice of Christian allegoresis precedes the theoretical, philosophical undergirding that Augustine and Aquinas (among others) would give it; it does not depend on it. Much Jewish exegesis (with the exception of Philo) operated in ways similar to early Christian allegoresis but without any sustained, reflective metaphysical undergirding. Christian theology (and exegesis) has always appropriated structures, concepts, and tools from the realm of philosophy to provide theoretical undergirding for theological conviction and Christian practice. In our own day, it may indeed be possible for spiritual exegesis to thrive without a particularly Platonic or Aristotelian metaphysics, or in accord with the theological and philosophical program provided by the *ressourcement* school in its drive to recover the riches of patristic resources for the present day, particularly as embodied in the work of Henri de Lubac.[12] As the four senses are so bound up with the story of the economy of salvation from creation to eschaton as inscripturated in the Biblical story, one suspects that the narrative theology of recent decades could also do much to reinvigorate spiritual exegesis, especially when done in a Catholic context, as it has already done so much for the postcritical retrieval of authentic Christian tradition in the face of theology's and exegesis' captivity to a withering modernity.

But let us now return to the past to examine spiritual exegesis in the Bible and then the work of the three seminal figures of the Western Catholic tradition mentioned above regarding the unity and interpretation of Scripture, so as to reveal the fundamental coherence of that tradition as it began with Jesus and the apostles and continued through the early and medieval Church.

Allegory in the New Testament

The modernity to which the Reformation gave birth[13] assumed the Reformation's rejection of allegory in favor of the "plain sense" of Scripture, and so many today regard allegory as something foreign to the Scriptures, something imposed upon them by the corrupting influence of Greek metaphysics. In recent decades, how-ever, the significant interest in the use of the Old Testament by New Testament

---

12 See Henri de Lubac, "Spiritual Understanding," trans. Luke O'Neill, in *The Theological Interpretation of Scripture*, ed. Stephen E. Fowl, (Cambridge, MA: Blackwell, 1997), 3–25; and Henri de Lubac, *Medieval Exegesis: The Four Senses of Scripture*, 3 vols. (Grand Rapids: Eerdmans, 1998–2009).

13 See Brad S. Gregory, *The Unintended Reformation: How A Religious Revolution Secularized Society* (Cambridge, MA: Belknap Press of Harvard University Press, 2012).

writers[14] has shown, I believe, that early Christians stand in fundamental continuity with Jewish interpreters of sacred Scripture before them and the Fathers
and the medievals after them, reading the Old Testament allegorically. Precision
is required when examining how a particular figure appropriates and interprets
Scripture, whether (say) the Dead Sea community, Hillel, St. Paul, Augustine, or
Aquinas, but, broadly speaking, Jewish authorities, the New Testament writers,
the Fathers, and the medievals all engaged in spiritual exegesis.

Galatians 4:21–31 presents the classic case. Therein St. Paul presents what
he terms "allegories" (*hatina estin allēgoroumena* ["this is an allegory"], Gal. 4:24);
he compares Abraham's slave-born son Ishmael to the Judaizing, enslaving earthly
Jerusalem, his mother Hagar representing Mt. Sinai in Arabia, bearing children
for slavery, while on the other hand he compares Abraham's free-born son Isaac
to the free Jerusalem above, the Galatians' true mother. The passage is a radical
spiritual interpretation of the Genesis accounts concerning Ishmael and Isaac, and
thus constitutes an embarrassment for those dedicated to the ideology of reading
for the plain sense alone. Either the rejoinder is made that Paul here is really doing
typology,[15] or that Paul's "allegories" are driven by his opponents' use of texts Paul
himself would not have chosen.[16] But claiming that Paul is doing typology while
using the term allegory has no force, for the distinction is not made until many
centuries later. The idea that Paul is interpreting Ishmael and Isaac ironically fails
as well, for Paul makes his rhetorical point skillfully. Most importantly, Paul engages in similar radical acts of exegesis in Galatians (for instance, in Gal. 3:1–14) as
well as in contexts involving less passion, such as 1 Corinthians 10; Paul's hermeneutical maneuvers in Galatians 4:21–31 are not an idiosyncratic, isolated instance.

The most important passage for biblical allegory, however, is Luke 24:13–35,
the story of the two disciples who encounter the risen Jesus on the road to Emmaus.

14   See C. H. Dodd, *According to the Scriptures: The Sub-structure of New Testament Theology*
      (London: Nisbet & Co., Ltd., 1952); Donald H. Juel, *Messianic Exegesis: Christological
      Interpretation of the New Testament in Early Christianity* (Minneapolis: Augsburg Fortress,
      1998); Richard B. Hays, *Echoes of Scripture in the Letters of Paul* (New Haven: Yale University
      Press, 1993); Richard B. Hays, Stefan Alkier, and Leroy A. Huizenga, eds., *Reading the Bible
      Intertextually* (Waco: Baylor University Press, 2009). Indeed, given the sheer size and depth
      and history of composition of the Hebrew Bible, it is not surprising to find Israelite and Jewish
      tradents engaging in the phenomenon that Michael Fishbane calls "inner-biblical exegesis"
      within the broad bounds of the Hebrew Bible itself. See Fishbane, *Biblical Interpretation in
      Ancient Israel* (New York: Oxford University Press, 1989).

15   See Gregory K. Beale, "Positive Answer to the Question Did Jesus and His Followers Preach
      the Right Doctrine from the Wrong Texts?" in *The Right Doctrine from the Wrong Texts? Essays
      on the Use of the Old Testament in the New* (Grand Rapids, MI: Baker Academic, 1994, repr.
      2007), 387–403.

16   See C. K. Barrett, "The Allegory of Abraham, Sarah and Hagar in the Argument of Galatians,"
      in *Essays on Paul* (London: SPCK, 1982), 154–168; Ronald Y. K. Fung, *The Epistle to the
      Galatians*, The New International Commentary on the New Testament (Grand Rapids: Wm.
      B. Eerdmans, 1988), 219; Richard N. Longenecker, *Galatians*, Word Biblical Commentary 41
      (Nashville, TN: Thomas Nelson, 1990), 210.

After Jesus' passion, two disciples are walking to Emmaus discussing "the things that have happened."[17] The risen Jesus draws near and walks with them, but "their eyes were kept from recognizing him."[18] Luke employs the divine passive here: God is keeping them from recognizing the risen Jesus, and will reveal him to them at a moment of particular significance. Jesus inquires about the substance of their discussion, and in an instance of intense irony they proceed to relate to the risen Jesus much of what has just happened to Jesus.[19] What they relate lacks coherence; they tell of events—Jesus' mighty prophetic ministry, his unjust execution, reports of visions of angels and the empty tomb—and their dashed hopes that he might have been "the one to redeem Israel,"[20] but they can make no sense of the data.

But the risen Jesus can and does make sense of it for them,[21] and here Luke's story teaches both that the Old Testament is the necessary matrix for understanding Jesus while it takes the risen Jesus to bring coherence to the Old Testament: "And beginning with Moses and all the prophets, he interpreted to them in all the scriptures the things concerning himself."[22] Here lies the root of the fundamental Christian claim that the death and resurrection of Jesus Christ provides the hermeneutical key to the Scriptures, that he is the lens that brings them into focus.

But Luke is not finished, as if Scriptural interpretation were merely a matter of drawing the proper connections between Old Testament types and New Testament antitypes on an intellectual level. The two disciples compel Jesus to remain with them, for it is "evening."[23] They sit down for supper, and the risen Jesus—still unknown to them—"took the bread and blessed, and broke it, and gave it to them."[24] Luke's language is patently eucharistic, recalling the institution of the Lord's Supper in Luke 22:14–23. And it is precisely when the risen Jesus begins to celebrate the Eucharist that "their eyes were opened and they recognized him" and he then "vanished out of their sight."[25] If it takes the risen Jesus to reveal the ultimate coherence of the Scriptures, it then takes the Eucharist to reveal Jesus (something Luke reinforces in Luke 24:35 as the two disciples relate "how he was made known to them in the breaking of the bread").[26] Further, his vanishing suggests he has not

---

17   Luke 24:13–14.

18   Luke 24:15–16.

19   Luke 24:17–24.

20   Luke 24:21.

21   Luke 24:25–27.

22   Luke 24:27.

23   Luke 24:29.

24   Luke 24:30.

25   Luke 24:31.

26   In *Verbum Domini* [The Word of the Lord], Pope Benedict observes, "The Eucharist opens us to an understanding of Scripture, just as Scripture for its part illumines and explains the mystery of the Eucharist. Unless we acknowledge the Lord's real presence in the Eucharist, our

departed, but that going forward he remains present in the Eucharist. And here, then, we see that Scriptural interpretation goes beyond intellectual construals; Scriptural interpretation comes to full fruition in the liturgy, at the center of which stands the Eucharist. Emmaus implies mystagogy, to which we must later return.

Scripture and Allegory in the Western Tradition

St. Irenaeus

St. Irenaeus explicitly describes much of what Luke's Emmaus story suggests and implies about the Christological unity of Scripture and reading for the spiritual sense. For Irenaeus, there is one authoritative Church beginning with Jesus himself marked out by apostolic succession from Jesus, with one monotheist, Trinitarian rule of faith, and the Church rightly possesses the proper interpretive key for construing the mosaic of the Scriptures, Christ himself, the same Christ who founded and vivifies that same Church.

Irenaeus engaged in mortal struggle with the heresy of "Gnosticism," a term of art used to group together various diverse movements nevertheless related by certain family resemblances.[27] In general, the Gnostics filtered the Christian faith through an extreme Platonic lens with the result that that which was invisible and spiritual was considered good but that which was material, including the human body, was evil. This necessitated a minimum of two gods, one responsible for evil creation and another, the god of the New Testament, the Father of the Lord Jesus Christ. In some gnostic systems many gods or aeons mediate between true divinity and the material order. Salvation concerns the liberation of the spirit from the body and is attained through knowledge ("*gnōsis*," hence "Gnosticism"): knowledge that the illusory material order is evil, knowledge that one is a member of the elect, and knowledge of a secret key. Gnosticism is hierarchal and elitist: those elites who have spirits (*pneuma*) may attain salvation by knowledge, while those who have souls (*psuchē*) may attain some enlightenment if not salvation, while the vast majority of humanity belongs to those who have only bodies, the hylics (*hūlē*, "matter"), who can be neither enlightened nor saved.

In general, Gnostic doctrine and practice (such as contraception, abortion, extreme abstinence from sex and food or, conversely, extreme indulgence) flow from a rejection of the goodness of creation. Traditional, orthodox Christianity, being fundamentally Jewish, affirms the goodness of creation, both before and after the Fall, and from this traditional Christian doctrine and practice flow. Indeed, all of Christian doctrine and practice can be conceived of in terms of creation:

---

understanding of Scripture remains imperfect" (*The Word of the Lord: Verbum Domini: Post-Synodal Apostolic Exhortation* [Washington, D.C.: USCCB, 2011], at 55).

27   For an examination of the diversity of these movements, see Michael Allen Williams, *Rethinking "Gnosticism": An Argument for Dismantling a Dubious Category* (Princeton: Princeton University Press, 1999).

God is the triune Creator, creation is damaged in the Fall, and the entire story of redemption culminating in the eschaton is the story of the triune God redeeming and transforming creation. For traditional Christianity, then, there is one God responsible for both creation and redemption, the Creator and the Father of the Lord Jesus Christ. The material world is good, if fallen, and so salvation consists in the redemption of human bodies (as well as spirits or souls or both, depending on one's anthropology) made possible by Christ's bodily incarnation, life, crucifixion, resurrection, ascension, and (ultimately) return. Further, in principle all can be saved, not merely some elite, and salvation is achieved not by some secret knowledge but by saving, personal faith in a loving, personal God who gives the Church the sacraments as means to participation in his divine life, a salvation made known by a public gospel.

For Irenaeus, there is one Church founded by Jesus, a visible Church marked out by bishops who stand in apostolic succession going back to the apostles themselves and who bear forth the teaching of Jesus throughout the ages. In his famous work *Against Heresies*, he writes:

> It is possible, then, for everyone in every church, who may wish to know the truth, to contemplate the tradition of the apostles which has been made known to us throughout the whole world. And we are in a position to enumerate those who were instituted bishops by the apostles and their successors down to our own times, men who neither knew nor taught anything like what these heretics rave about.[28]

Later he will remind his readers, "The true knowledge [*gnōsis*] is the doctrine of the apostles, and the ancient organization of the Church throughout the whole world, and the manifestation of the body of Christ according to the succession of bishops, by which succession the bishops have handed down the Church which is found everywhere."[29]

It is fashionable nowadays to speak not of the early Christianity but of "Christianities," and to claim that the idea that there was one Church was the anachronistic revision of history on the part of the religious victors. True, many claimed to be "Christians" in antiquity, and there were many bodies claiming Christian status proclaiming various doctrines (as Irenaeus himself describes). But to say that this means we must speak of "Christianities" is to smuggle in a value judgment under the guise of objective sociological description, for even though there were many groups claiming the name Christian, is does not follow

---

28 St. Irenaeus, *Against Heresies*, in the *Ante-Nicene Fathers*, 10 vols., eds. Alexander Roberts and James Donaldson (Peabody, MA: Hendrickson, 2004 [reprint]), vol. 1., 3.3.1; cf. 3.3.2, 3.3.4.

29 Irenaeus, *Against Heresies*, 4.33.8; see 3.4.1.

that they were all entitled to it. The question concerning what counts as authentic Christianity cannot be decided on sociological or historical grounds.

Irenaeus' answer, as we have seen, is that authentic Christianity is found in the Church Jesus founded. The bishops of this visible Church guard and proclaim Christian doctrine according to what many in the early Church call the *regula fidei*, the "rule of faith," or sometimes other phrases such as the "rule of the Church," or the "rule of truth;" Irenaeus will employ the phrase "the canon of truth."[30] Versions of the Rule as given by various early tradents are rudimentary monotheistic and Trinitarian statements not unlike the Apostles' Creed with which modern Christians are familiar. Irenaeus describes it as follows:

> The Church ... has received from the apostles and their disciples this faith: [She believes] in one God, the Father Almighty, Maker of heaven, and earth, and the sea, and all things that are in them; and in one Christ Jesus, the Son of God, who became incarnate for our salvation; and in the Holy Spirit, who proclaimed through the prophets the dispensations of God, and the advents, and the birth from a virgin, and the passion, and the resurrection from the dead, and the ascension into heaven in the flesh of the beloved Christ Jesus, our Lord, and His [future] manifestation from heaven in the glory of the Father. . . .[31]

Irenaeus, then, operates with a hermeneutics of authority. The Bible is the Church's book which, being outside the visible Church and lacking its rule, heretics have no right to interpret. The Church founded by Jesus has the rule of faith given by that same Jesus, and the Scriptures may not and cannot be interpreted contrary to it.

Here we see subtly an idea found repeatedly in the Fathers and medievals: any spiritual, allegorical readings are constrained by the rule of faith, for the rule is a summary of the Faith that Scripture itself presumes and presents. Indeed, Irenaeus will anticipate Augustine and Aquinas by his insistence on the clarity of the letter of Scripture such that the doctrinal contents of the Faith presented in the rule "are such as fall under our observation, and are clearly and unambiguously in express terms set forth in the sacred Scriptures."[32]

For Irenaeus, then, the monotheist, Trinitarian rule of faith functions as the "hypothesis" of the Christian Bible, the plot, the narrative, the story of Scripture.[33] For Irenaeus, "the rule is the principle or logic of scripture itself. It is the right rule

---

30   Irenaeus, *Against Heresies*, 3.2.1.

31   Irenaeus, *Against Heresies*, 1.10.1.

32   Irenaeus, *Against Heresies*, 2.27.1.

33   Irenaeus, *Against Heresies*, 1.9–10.

to use because it articulates the divine order within Scripture. It is the right plan because it describes that actual architecture of the Bible."[34]

The rule is necessary because Scripture can appear to us as bits and pieces. And so Irenaeus speaks of it as a mosaic that must follow a particular pattern if it is to remain coherent:

> [The heretics'] manner of acting is just as if one, when a beautiful image of a king has been constructed by some skillful artist out of precious jewels, should then take this likeness of the man all to pieces, should rearrange the gems, and so fit them together as to make them into the form of a dog or of a fox, and even that but poorly executed; and should then maintain and declare that *this* was the beautiful image of the king which the skillful artist constructed, pointing to the jewels which had been admirably fitted together by the first artist to form the image of the king, but have been with bad effect transferred by the latter one to the shape of a dog, and by thus exhibiting the jewels, should deceive the ignorant who had no conception what a king's form was like, and persuade them that that miserable likeness of the fox was, in fact, the beautiful image of the king.[35]

It is the rule of faith given by Jesus to the Church he founded, then, that provides the hypothesis, the proper key for organizing the mosaic of the Church's canonical Scriptures. Crucial here are the concepts of economy and recapitulation, as they require spiritual exegesis or allegoresis. *Oikonomia* (economy) in the ancient world meant orderly arrangement, particularly with reference to literature, and so for Irenaeus, the divine economy means that God works in an orderly way in creation and history and thus Scripture, with Christ as the center, as the goal of sacred history. In Christ, then, all things in heaven and earth are "recapitulated" in Christ: "from David's belly the King eternal is raised up, who [recapitulates] all things in Himself, and has gathered into Himself the ancient formation [of man] ... recapitulating Adam in himself."[36] For Irenaeus, then, the divine economy in which Christ recapitulates all things enables not only allegorical (typological) relationships between the Testaments but their continuation in mystagogy, as the risen Christ is not merely textual but real, ascended into heaven.

One is here reminded of the encounter of the despairing disciples on the road to Emmaus: they were not able to organize the data of their experiences into

---

34 John J. O'Keefe and R. R. Reno, *Sanctified Vision: An Introduction to Early Christian Interpretation of the Bible* (Baltimore: The Johns Hopkins University Press, 2005), 120.

35 Irenaeus, *Against Heresies*, 1.8.1.

36 Irenaeus, *Against Heresies*, 3.21.9.

any coherent image. But the risen Jesus—who, in Luke's presentation[37] and according to the ancient Christian concept of *Christus Totus* is the Church—was able to provide the key, even himself, which brought coherence to the Scriptures and their experiences as he explained he was the center of both. For Irenaeus, then, like the risen Jesus on the road to Emmaus, there is an allegorical relationship between the Testaments seen clearly when one reads spiritually according to the rule of faith.

St. Augustine

St. Augustine has much to say about biblical interpretation. Indeed, whereas for Augustine the Scriptures' perceived crudity proved an obstacle to his conversion, St. Ambrose's allegorical homilies opened them up for Augustine in a way that made his eventual conversion possible. And so the mature Augustine presents a sophisticated understanding of Scripture and its interpretation that allows for disciplined allegory.

Augustine operates with a fundamental neoplatonic worldview; visible things, including words, are signs of invisible, intelligible things. Like many others in antiquity, then, whose allegorical interpretation was rooted in a fundamental conviction that reality was both visible and invisible, for Augustine reading for the spiritual sense was natural, for it accorded with the nature of reality. One reads the visible words of Scripture, then, to discern and learn the invisible, intelligible doctrines of the Christian faith. But this is not a raw intellectual exercise; it is also a matter of existential involvement as biblical interpretation is meant to increase the interpreter's faith, hope, and (especially) charity, for God is love and Scripture functions to cultivate love of God and love of neighbor.

De doctrina christiana ("On the transmission of Christian culture," or, more simply, "Teaching Christianity") is Augustine's treatise training teachers how the canon cultivates Christian culture. He means to empower readers by giving them rules to solve obscurities and get at hidden meanings of passages.[38] For Augustine, everything—his theology, his conception of the Trinity, Scriptural interpretation—comes down to love, for God himself is love. Augustine informs his readers that "the fulfillment and the end of the law and of all the divine Scriptures is love,"[39] and this love is twofold: "love of the thing which is to be enjoyed" (God), and "of the thing which is able to enjoy that thing together with us" (neighbor). Thus, Augustine argues, Scriptural interpretation must edify in love: "So if it seems to you that you have understood the divine Scriptures, or any part of them, in such a way that by this understanding you do not build up this twin love of God and

---

37   See Acts 9:4–5: "Saul, Saul, why do you persecute me ... I am Jesus, whom you are persecuting."

38   *De doctrina christiana*, Prol. 9. Quotations of *De doctrina christiana* are from the translation in *Teaching Christianity*, trans. Edmund Hill, O.P., The Works of Saint Augustine: A Translation for the 21st Century (Hyde Park, NY: New City Press, 1996).

39   Augustine, *Teaching Christianity*, Bk. 1, Chap. 39, alluding to Rom. 13:8 and 1 Tim. 1:5.

neighbor, then you have not understood them."[40] For Augustine, unlike most modern biblical interpreters, interpretation is self-involving, not merely descriptive or objective but something that requires embodiment and transformation.

Ultimately, as Augustine reads Paul's words regarding the three theological virtues in 1 Corinthians 13, the goal of interpretation is eschatological blessedness: "all knowledge and all prophecy are into service" for the sake of "faith, hope, charity," but in the end "faith gives way to sight, and hope gives way to bliss itself, which we are going to arrive at, while charity will actually grow when these other two fade out."[41] Indeed, Augustine here speaks of the instrumental nature of the Scriptures in a way perhaps shocking to those who have been trained to revere them: "And so people supported by faith, hope and charity, and retaining a firm grip on them, have no need of the Scriptures except for instructing others."[42]

But the beginning of the path to such lofty spiritual stature begins with the letter of Scripture. Having developed familiarity with the Scriptures to the point of memorizing them, the teacher is to master "those things put clearly in them," for "in the passages that are put plainly in scripture is to be found everything that touches upon faith, and good morals, that is to say hope and charity." Only then can one use the clear passages to understand the unclear: "instances from the plainer passages are used to cast light on the more obscure utterances, and the testimony of some undoubted judgments is used to remove uncertainties from those that are more doubtful."[43] Later Augustine will assert that one must phrase and pronounce the written Scriptures (which at that time were written in *lectio continua*, that is, continually, with no spaces between words or punctuation) and thus interpret them in accord with the *regula fidei*, the rule of faith, "which you have received from the plainer passages of Scripture and from the authority of the Church."[44] Augustine assumes the Church's rule and the "plainer passages" of Scripture itself do not contradict each other; Christian Scripture and tradition both come from the one Word of God. Further, we also see how important the rule of faith is, for Augustine adverts to it first before context; only if the rule and the plainer passages fail to resolve questions about interpretation in pronunciation does one then refer to the wider literary context.

---

40 Augustine, *Teaching Christianity*, Bk. 1, Chap. 40.

41 Augustine, *Teaching Christianity*, Bk. 1, Chap. 41–42.

42 Augustine, *Teaching Christianity*, Bk. 1, Chap. 43.

43 Augustine, *Teaching Christianity*, Bk. 2, Chap. 14.

44 Augustine, *Teaching Christianity*, Bk. 3, Chap. 2. St. Augustine provides an example: *In principio erat Verbum et Verbum erat apud Deum et Deus erat* ("In the beginning was the Word and the Word was with God and God was") is a heretical reading of John 1:1, as severing it from what follows, *Verbum hoc erat in principio apud Deum* ("This Word was in the beginning with God") "is a refusal to confess that the Word is God. But this is to be refuted by the rule of faith, which prescribes for us the equality of the three divine persons" (*Teaching Christianity*, Bk. 3, Chap. 3).

Augustine now begins to discuss "metaphorical" signs. Signs (here, words) are either proper or metaphorical. Knowledge of proper signs (words) is necessary for the letter, and securing that knowledge involves learning Latin, Hebrew, and Greek.[45] Metaphorical signs for Augustine function allegorically, and he employs the classic example from 1 Corinthians 9:9, "You shall not muzzle the ox that threshes the corn." The word "ox" signifies the animal "ox," but the thing that is the bovine creature signified by the verbal sign can in turn function as a further signifier and signify what Paul means in his metaphorical point: "the Lord commanded that those who proclaim the gospel should get their living by the gospel."[46]

But again, for Augustine, spiritual exegesis is not merely a matter of apostolic example. Rather, it is rooted in the nature of that twofold reality of visible and invisible which Scripture itself describes. If one remains in the realm of the letter and fails "to refer what is signified in this proper sense to the signification of something else," one suffers "the wretched slavery of the spirit, treating signs as things, and thus being unable to lift up the eyes of the mind above bodily creatures, to drink in the eternal light."[47] The examples Augustine uses, however, reveal that he is thinking of what moderns might call typology: "sabbath" should point beyond one of the seven days of the week, presumably to the eschaton,[48] while "sacrifice" should point beyond animal and grain offerings, presumably to Christ.

But how does one determine when something is meant "metaphorically" or allegorically? Augustine writes, "And here, quite simply, is the one and only method: anything in the divine writings that cannot be referred either to good, honest morals, or to the truth of the faith, you must know is said figuratively. Good honest morals belong to loving God and one's neighbor, the truth of the faith to knowing God and one's neighbor."[49]

St. Thomas Aquinas

St. Thomas Aquinas discusses the question of whether Scripture has multiple senses in the *Summa* at 1.1.10. Although appropriating an Aristotelian framework rather than Augustine's neo-Platonism, Aquinas saw himself as an Augustinian and saw himself as a servant of the Christian tradition. Thus we see in Aquinas much of the substance we have surveyed regarding Augustine. Aquinas asserts that God is the author of Scripture, and thus it is in his divine power "to signify His meaning, not by words only (as man can also do), but also by things themselves."[50]

---

45   Augustine, *Teaching Christianity*, Bk. 2, Chap. 16.

46   1 Cor. 9:14, even though Paul says he has not made use of that right in 1 Cor. 12b and 15.

47   Augustine, *Teaching Christianity*, Bk. 3, Chap. 9.

48   See Augustine, *Confessiones* [Confessions] Bk. 13, Chap. 50–53, in *Confessions*, trans. Henry Chadwick, Oxford's World Classics (New York: Oxford University Press, 2009), 304–305.

49   Augustine, *Teaching Christianity*, Bk. 3, Chap. 14.

50   Aquinas, *Summa*, pt. 1a, q. 1, art. 10, resp.

In theological science, then, "things signified by the words have themselves also a signification."[51] For Aquinas, as for Augustine, this double signification explains the relationship between the literal and the spiritual senses: "That signification whereby things signified by words have themselves also a signification is called the spiritual sense, which is based on the literal, and presupposes it."[52] Note well the import of this claim: the spiritual sense is logically and theologically secondary to the literal sense, which therefore functions as a constraint.

Aquinas then divides the spiritual sense into three divisions, echoing the codification of the tradition that had been achieved by his time. First, the "allegorical sense" (*sensus allegoricus*) is found when "the things of the Old Law signify the things of the New Law."[53] Aquinas mentions Hebrews 10:1 as Scriptural support, which teaches that the law is a shadow of further realities, not the realities themselves. This means that "allegory" for Aquinas was not speculation born of monastic practice or spiritual enthusiasm, but was what moderns call typology, something demanded by the structure of Scripture itself and defended with apostolic warrant. Second, Aquinas says that insofar as things which Christ does or which signify him are concerned with what we ought to do, there we encounter the moral sense (*sensus moralis*), or tropology, for in the New Law "whatever our head [Christ] has done is a type of what we ought to do."[54] Finally, that which signifies "eternal glory" concerns "the anagogical sense" (*sensus anagogicus*), drawing on (pseudo-) Dionysius, who says, "The New Law itself is a figure of future glory,"[55] which implies mystagogy, as liturgical and sacramental life is a participation of heaven in time.

Aquinas then roots the coherence of the four senses in the divine author, claiming that God comprehends the multiple senses of Scripture in his intellect while intending the literal sense. Further, God does not generate those senses by pure divine will; it is also in the nature of Scripture's words. Aquinas says that the multiplicity of senses does not depend on words having multiple meanings but "because the things signified by the words can be themselves types of other things."[56] In what follows, we see the classic Western constraint of spiritual exegesis by the literal sense:

---

51 Aquinas, *Summa*, pt. 1a, q. 1, art. 10, resp. We are here reminded of Augustine's discussion of 1 Cor. 9:9.

52 Aquinas, *Summa*, pt. 1a, q. 1, art. 10, resp.

53 Aquinas, *Summa*, pt. 1a, q. 1, art. 10, resp.

54 Aquinas, *Summa*, pt. 1a, q. 1, art. 10, resp.

55 Aquinas, *Summa*, pt. 1a, q. 1, art. 10, resp., quoting Pseudo-Dionysius, *De caelesti hierarchia* [*The Celestial Hierarchy*] 1, in Pseudo-Dionysius, *The Complete Works*, trans. Colm Luibheid; Classics of Western Spirituality (New York: Paulist, 1987), 147.

56 Aquinas, *Summa*, pt. 1a, q. 1, art. 10, rep. obj. 1.

> Thus in Holy Writ no confusion results, for all the senses
> are founded on one—the literal—from which alone can any
> argument be drawn, and not from those intended in allegory,
> as Augustine says. Nevertheless, nothing of Holy Scripture
> perishes on account of this, since nothing necessary to faith is
> contained under the spiritual sense which is not elsewhere put
> forward by the Scripture in its literal sense.[57]

For the West, then, the spiritual sense of Scripture was rooted in the nature and
will of God and the twofold structure of reality. Further, God, Scripture in all
its senses, and reality formed a coherent unity understood by the Church and
fundamentally articulated by the Church's rule of faith, whose story proclaimed
God as creator and consummator with Christ at the center. For the west, "allegory"
is somewhat narrow, concerning typological and mystagogical relationships in the
economy of salvation, while all the three spiritual senses are rooted in the letter,
which, in turn, constrains spiritual exegesis.[58]

Allegory and Mystagogy

Let us return to Emmaus, in which the risen Jesus provides dominical warrant and
example for the practice of allegory consummated in mystagogy. But given that we
are dealing here with the risen Jesus, who is soon to ascend into heaven,[59] allegory
in this strict sense is not merely one salutary practice among many or simply a good
idea. Much more than that, Luke's Christology of the risen and ascended Jesus
suggests allegory is inherent in the structure and function of Scripture, and indeed
not just Scripture but the entire cosmos, since, as Paul puts it, "in him all things
hold together,"[60] the same Risen One who was revealed to the disciples on the road
to Emmaus. We encounter this risen Jesus supremely in the eucharistic liturgy,
which the Second Vatican Council taught is "the summit toward which the activity

---

57   Aquinas, *Summa*, pt. 1a, q. 1, art. 10, rep. obj. 1.

58   If allegory is as reasonable and defensible as the tradition claims, why did the Reformation
reject spiritual exegesis? First, not all exegetes were as cautious as Augustine and Aquinas would
have them be; some interpreters do worse than their theory. Second, the tradition buttressed
the spiritual senses with a metaphysical worldview the Reformers (being voluntarists and
nominalists) rejected. Third, the Reformers were trained in rhetoric, and throughout Church
history, those trained in rhetoric, which concerns the human use of words in concrete situations
on the ground, were skeptical about the philosophical commitments undergirding allegory
(such as the Antiochene Fathers, who had plenty to say against Alexandrian allegory). Finally,
our late formal distinction between "typology" and "allegory" owes itself to the Reformation.
On the one hand, the Reformation rejected allegory in its desire to pursue the "plain sense" of
Scripture through the grammatico-historical method, but, on the other hand, could not reject
the obvious correspondences between the Testaments. The material distinction between what
would later be called typology and allegory is perhaps first seen in William Tyndale.

59   Luke 24:51.

60   Col. 1:17.

of the Church is directed; at the same time it is the font from which all her power flows."[61] The Mass is indeed heaven breaking into earth, with architecture, art, music, and *ars celebrandi* (the "art of celebration") all ideally functioning to point us to the eschatological moment which even now breaks in, as it did on the road to Emmaus. As Scott Hahn writes, "[E]very eucharistic liturgy conforms to the pattern established at Emmaus: the opening of the scriptures followed by the breaking of the bread, the liturgy of the word followed by the liturgy of the eucharist. The Mass, then, is the place par excellence of the scriptures' faithful reception."[62]

The linking of Scriptural word and liturgical eucharistic sacrament in the Emmaus story points to a truth largely forgotten. In our individualistic, post-Gutenberg age, in which Bibles are readily available and literacy widespread, most Christians read Scripture as individuals and as members of small groups. For this reason, many are unaware that both historically and theologically the Bible's natural habitat is the liturgy. Indeed, in the biblical story itself what would become the original Scriptures of Israel—the Ten Commandments and the broader Torah—were given to Moses in the midst of an encounter with the Lord God on Sinai,[63] and the covenant with Israel is sealed with sacrificial liturgy,[64] after which Moses receives many detailed instructions concerning Israel's sacred sacrificial liturgy going forward.[65] From the outset, the first Scriptures were received in and with liturgy, concerned liturgy, and were handed down in liturgy. Later Christian questions concerning the contents of the canon of the New Testament were also driven by liturgical concerns. The question was, "Which documents could be read, chanted, and proclaimed in liturgy, and which were forbidden?" For early Christians and Jews before them, then, the Bible was learned and experienced in the context of the liturgy. The Scriptures were read or chanted and preached in synagogues and churches. Most of the young learned the Jewish or Christian faith not by reading scrolls or codices they did not possess, given their great expense, and could not read, given near-universal illiteracy, but from their parents and in liturgy.

But the liturgical habitat of Scripture is not merely a function of ancient social conditions in which scrolls were scarce, codices uncommon, and readers rare. Rather, Scripture's home in the liturgy is a function of theology. In fact, it is more than that, more than an intellectual datum; it is a function of Catholic

---

61　Second Vatican Council, *Sacrosanctum Concilium* [This Sacred Council], Constitution on the Sacred Liturgy (December 4, 1963), 10, in *Vatican Council II: Volume 1: The Conciliar and Post Conciliar Documents*, ed. and trans. Austin Flannery, O.P. (rev. ed.; Northport, New York: Costello, 2004), 1–36, at 6.

62　Scott Hahn, *Letter and Spirit: From Written Text to Living Word in the Liturgy* (NY: Doubleday, 2005), 29.

63　Exod. 19–20.

64　Exod. 24.

65　Exod. 25–31, 35–40

culture (which the Catholic liturgical cultus cultivates). As the Pontifical Biblical Commission put it:

> From the earliest days of the Church, the reading of Scripture has been an integral part of the Christian liturgy, an inheritance to some extent from the liturgy of the synagogue. Today, too, it is above all through the liturgy that Christians come into contact with Scripture, particularly during the Sunday celebration of the Eucharist. In principle, the liturgy, and especially the sacramental liturgy, the high point of which is the Eucharistic celebration, brings about the most perfect actualization of the biblical texts, for the liturgy places the proclamation in the midst of the community of believers, gathered around Christ so as to draw near to God. Christ is then "present in his word, because it is he himself who speaks when sacred Scripture is read in the Church" (*Sacrosanctum Concilium*, 7). Written text thus becomes living word.[66]

There is an organic relationship among the economy of salvation in history, its inscripturation in the Bible, and mystagogy, which is salvation history continuing in our present. As Jean Daniélou writes:

> The sacraments are conceived in relation to the acts of God in the Old Testament and the New. God acts in the world; His actions are the *mirabilia*, the deeds that are his alone. God creates, judges, makes a covenant, is present, makes holy, delivers. These same acts are carried out in the different phases of the history of salvation. There is, then, a fundamental analogy between these actions. The sacraments are simply the continuation in the era of the Church of God's acts in the Old Testament and the New. This is the proper significance of the relationship between the Bible and the liturgy. The bible is a sacred history; the liturgy is a sacred history.[67]

A purely intellectual conception of Christian faith would content itself with examining the typological relationships between the Testaments as they present the economy of salvation culminating in Jesus Christ. But salvation history does not

---

66 Pontifical Biblical Commission, *The Interpretation of the Bible in the Church* (April 15, 1993), IV.C.1, in *The Scripture Documents: An Anthology of Official Catholic Teachings*, ed. Dean P. Béchard, S.J. (Collegeville, MN: Liturgical Press, 2002), 244–316, at 308.

67 Jean Cardinal Daniélou, S.J., "The Sacraments and the History of Salvation," *Letter & Spirit* 2 (2006): 210.

stop with Jesus Christ or the effective closing of the New Testament canon (if we could indeed put a firm date on it). Daniélou continues:

> But did sacred history stop with Jesus Christ? This is, indeed, what we usually seem to ask. And this is because we do not place the sacraments in the perspective of sacred history. We forget that, although Jesus Christ is the goal of sacred history, his coming into the world is only the inauguration of his mysteries. In the Apostles' Creed, after the mysteries of the past, we speak of a mystery still to come: *inde ventúrus est* ("he will come again"). But between the two there is a mystery of the present: *sedet ad déxteram patris* ("he is seated at the right hand of the Father").[68]

Daniélou was a leader of the *ressourcement* school leading up to and during the Second Vatican Council, and the influence of this movement proved decisive in the substance of the conciliar documents and later fruits of the Council such as the *Catechism of the Catholic Church*. As mystagogy is the sacramental completion of typological allegory, this official affirmation of mystagogy is part and parcel of the official affirmation of allegory one finds in *Dei Verbum* and the *Catechism*. Therefore we should not be surprised to find mystagogy codified therein: "The mysteries of Christ's life are the foundations of what he would henceforth dispense in the sacraments, through the ministers of his Church, for 'what was visible in our Savior has passed over into his mysteries.'"[69]

Return to Allegory

Unfortunately, the intellectual and existential riches of this approach are often neglected as many Catholic biblical scholars have opted for a sterile historicism, finding in documents such as *Divino Afflante Spiritu* ("inspired by the divine spirit") and *Dei Verbum* little more than official approbation of the historical-critical method. For instance, the Jesuit scholar John Donahue claims that *Dei Verbum* gave the historical-critical method "the highest stamp of ecclesiastical approval."[70] But far from codifying historical criticism as the method par excellence for approaching the Scriptures, *Dei Verbum* subtly affirms the traditional fourfold sense of Scripture.

Dei Verbum 12 is crucial but controverted, with assumptions about conciliar desires to crown historical criticism as the queen of all methods driving faulty translations. *Dei Verbum* 12 falls naturally into three paragraphs, the first instructing interpreters to investigate the intentions of both the human authors of scripture

---

68   Daniélou, "Sacraments," 213.

69   *Catechism*, no. 1115, quoting St. Leo the Great, *Sermo* 74,2.

70   John R. Donahue, S.J., "Scripture: A Roman Catholic Perspective," *Review & Expositor* 79 (1982): 233–234.

and also God as divine author, the second then dealing with the human authors, and the third with God as divine author. But mistranslation of a crucial line obscures this. The end of the first paragraph of section 12 reads *attente investigare debet quid hagiographi reapse significare intenderint et eorum verbis manifestare Deo placuerit.* As Avery Cardinal Dulles contends, many translations of this line reduce divine intention to the literal sense.[71] In Austin Flannery's edition, for instance, the phrase reads, "[the interpreter] should carefully search out the meaning which the sacred writers really had in mind, that meaning which God has thought well to manifest through the medium of their words."[72] The translation conflates the human and divine authors and eliminates the spiritual sense by eliding the Latin *et*. Better is the translation on the Vatican website, which reads, "the interpreter of Sacred Scripture ... should carefully investigate what meaning the sacred writers really intended, and what God wanted to manifest by means of their words."[73] This translation permits God to intend spiritual senses beyond any literal (or spiritual!) senses intended by the human author in the way Aquinas suggests.

It is clear, then, that both the literal and spiritual senses are in view. Indeed, *Dei Verbum* here appropriates the distinction Pius XII made in *Divino Afflante Spiritu* 26[a]:

> For what was said and done in the Old Testament was ordained and disposed by God with such consummate wisdom, that things past prefigured in a spiritual way those that were to come under the new dispensation of grace. Wherefore the exegete, just as he must search out and expound the literal meaning of the words, intended and expressed by the sacred writer, so also must he do likewise for the spiritual sense, provided it is clearly intended by God.[74]

For its part, the *Catechism* receives and interprets *Dei Verbum* 12 in a striking way, making explicit its implications about the fourfold sense. Paragraphs 109–119 are entitled "The Holy Spirit, Interpreter of Scripture," in which it presents and in-

---

71 For what follows, see Avery Cardinal Dulles, "Vatican II on the Interpretation of Scripture," *Letter & Spirit* 2 (2006): 18–19.

72 Second Vatican Council, *Dei Verbum* [The Word of God], Dogmatic Constitution on Divine Revelation (November 18, 1965), 12, in *Vatican Council II: Volume 1: The Conciliar and Post Conciliar Documents*, ed. and trans. Austin Flannery, O.P. (rev. ed.; Northport, NY: Costello, 2004), 1–36, at 6.

73 http://www.vatican.va/archive/hist_councils/ii_vatican_council/documents/vat-ii_const_19651118_dei-verbum_en.html. Béchard's own translation in *SD* reads, "the interpreter of Sacred Scripture ... should carefully search out what the sacred writers truly intended to express and what God thought well to manifest by their words" (24), thus bringing out the force of the Latin and preserving both literal and spiritual senses.

74 Pope Pius XII, *Divino afflante Spiritu* [Inspired by the Divine Spirit, Encyclical Letter Promoting Biblical Studies], September 30, 1943, 26, in *SD*, 115–139, at 126.

terprets *Dei Verbum* 12. First, no. 109 reads, "To interpret Scripture correctly, the reader must be attentive to what the human authors truly wanted to affirm and to what God wanted to reveal to us by their words," thus translating the crucial Latin phrase in *Dei Verbum* 12 correctly in a way recognizing the fourfold sense. Then the next two paragraphs discuss the sacred author's intention (no. 110) and the divine intention of the Holy Spirit (no. 111), echoing the structure of *Dei Verbum* 12. Then, nos. 112–114 follow *Dei Verbum* 12's "three criteria for interpreting Scripture in accordance with the Spirit who inspired it": attention "to the content and unity of the whole Scripture," reading Scripture within "the living Tradition of the whole Church," and attention to the analogy of faith. Then in the midst of this presentation of *Dei Verbum* 12, the *Catechism* in nos. 115–118 explicitly affirms the classic Western approach to Scripture: there are two fundamental senses of Scripture, the literal and spiritual, and spiritual is divided into the allegorical, moral, and anagogical senses. This section of the *Catechism* then closes in no. 119 with a direct quote from *Dei Verbum* 12 § 3:

> It is the task of exegetes to work, according to these rules, toward a better understanding and explanation of the meaning of Sacred Scripture in order that their research may help the Church to form a firmer judgment. For, of course, all that has been said about the manner of interpreting Scripture is ultimately subject to the judgment of the Church which exercises the divinely conferred commission and ministry of watching over and interpreting the Word of God.

The *Catechism* is an authoritative document for Catholics, one of the greatest fruits of the Second Vatican Council, and in this section it has made explicit what the text of *Dei Verbum* 12 implies: that the classical fourfold sense of Scripture abides. Far from giving the historical-critical method pride of place, *Dei Verbum* 12 preserves the tradition of the fourfold sense.

Of course, *Dei Verbum* (as well as the *Catechism*) does demand the use of proper philological, historical, and literary tools, but this is not new; Augustine requires as much in *De doctrina christiana*. It must here also be remembered that the historical-critical method engages in the impossibility of objective neutrality, even while it is not; its assumptions are rooted in a reductionist rationalism that John Paul II and Benedict XVI did so much to counter. At best, the historical-critical method brackets God and the community of faith, regarding them as afterthoughts, treating the Bible as an accidental collection of ancient artifacts, not sacred Scripture inspired by the one Holy Spirit of God. For this reason, Pope Benedict writes in *Verbum Domini*, "It is important that the criteria indicated in Number 12 of the Dogmatic Constitution *Dei Verbum* receive real attention and become the object of deeper study. A notion of scholarly research that would consider itself neutral with regard to Scripture should not be encouraged."[75]

But the letter is Scripture too, and as *Dei Verbum* 12 affirms, modern tools help us in our quest for it. Yet attention to the Scriptural letter is required not merely because the letter belongs to human history as human speech but because the letter is human speech inspired by God. We have theological reasons, not just anthropological reasons, for investigating the letter. And so, in *Verbum Domini* Pope Benedict roots the validity of modern methods of interpretation in the Incarnation:

> Before all else, we need to acknowledge the benefits that his-torical-critical exegesis and other recently-developed methods of textual analysis have brought to the life of the Church. For the Catholic understanding of sacred Scripture, attention to such methods is indispensable, linked as it is to the realism of the Incarnation: "This necessity is a consequence of the Christian principle formulated in the Gospel of John 1:14: *Verbum caro factum est*. The historical fact is a constitutive dimension of the Christian faith. The history of salvation is not mythology, but a true history, and it should thus be studied with the methods of serious historical research."[76]

Therefore, the Catholic warrant for the study of the letter is not historical-critical curiosity or a passion for facts inferred from textual artifacts but rather the Incarnation. Christian theology can have it no other way, for the Word is the Creator of the cosmos, in whom all things in heaven and on earth hold together.[77] History must be God's story, for Christ is the key to all creation. History is theo-logical; history is Christological.

Thus, in *Verbum Domini* Benedict calls for more real theological interpretation:

> While today's academic exegesis, including that of Catholic scholars, is highly competent in the field of historical-critical methodology and its latest developments, it must be said that comparable attention needs to be paid to the theological di-mension of the biblical texts, so that they can be more deeply understood in accordance with the three elements indicated by the Dogmatic Constitution *Dei Verbum*.[78]

---

75   *Verbum Domini*, 47.

76   *Verbum Domini*, 32.

77   See John 1:1ff; Col. 1:16–17.

78   *Verbum Domini*, 34.

Heeding the tradition culminating in *Dei Verbum*, the *Catechism*, and *Verbum Domini* by studying the Bible as sacred Scripture under the aegis of the Holy Spirit need not be constraining. Rather, given the richness of the tradition and the indispensable interdisciplinary work involved in such an endeavor as one engages in fields such as patristics, philosophy, literary theory, historical theology, as well as all the varied tools and methods of the contemporary guild, Catholic scholars ought to find reclaiming proper theological interpretation liberating and intellectually satisfying as they engage in the discipline of biblical studies under the joyful discipline of prayer and the gracious discipline of the Church.

Letter & Spirit 8 (2013): 101-124

The New Temple, the New Priesthood, and the New Cult in Luke-Acts

~: Michael Patrick Barber :~

John Paul the Great Catholic University

I. Introduction

More than perhaps any other New Testament writer, Luke stresses the theme of prophecy and fulfillment.[1] This motif occurs in the very first verse of the Gospel of Luke, which speaks of "the things *fulfilled* [*peplērophorēmenōn*] among us" (Luke 1:1). Likewise, at the end of his Gospel we find the Risen Lord explaining to the disciples how he has brought fulfillment to all the Scriptures: "And beginning with Moses and all the prophets, *he interpreted to them in all the scriptures the things concerning himself*" (Luke 24:27). This theme is continued in the Acts of the Apostles (see, for example, Acts 1:16; 3:18).

Yet, one aspect of the prophetic hope is often overlooked. Scholars have shown little interest in the way Luke interacts with the prophets' announcement of a coming new priesthood and cult. While some scholars have explored Luke's interest in expectations for a new temple (see Luke 19:46 = Isa. 56:7),[2] many have simply neglected the way he envisions the realization of related hopes for a new priesthood and cult.[3]

In fact, cultic imagery seems to frame Luke's Gospel. The narrative opens with an angelic announcement to a priest serving in the Temple (Luke 1:7–11) and ends with the apostles returning to the Temple to praise God after the ascension of Jesus (Luke 24:53). Cultic concerns are picked up again in Acts 1 where Luke underscores that the apostles' journey back to Jerusalem following the ascension complied with Sabbath regulations (Acts 1:12). While contemporary scholars may downplay the significance of such elements in his presentation,[4] Luke's emphasis

---

1   Luke Timothy Johnson, *The Acts of the Apostles* (SP; Collegeville: The Liturgical Press, 1992), 12: "… Luke's use of 'prophecy and fulfillment' goes far beyond that found in any other NT writing."

2   See, for example, the excellent treatment in Nicholas Perrin, *Jesus the Temple* (Grand Rapids: Baker Academic, 2010), 59–64.

3   See Darrell Bock, *Acts*, Baker Exegetical Commentary on The New Testament (Grand Rapids: Baker Academic, 2007), 75–76.

4   Two notable exceptions are Rick Strelan, *Luke the Priest: The Authority of the Third Gospel* (Aldershot: Ashgate, 2008); and Crispin H. T. Fletcher-Louis, "Jesus Inspects His Priestly War Party (Luke 14:25–33)," in *The Old Testament in the New Testament. Essays in Honour of J.L. North*, Journal for the Study of the New Testament Supplement Series 189; ed. S. Moyise (Sheffield: Sheffield Academic Press, 2000), 126–143.

on such matters was not lost on the early Church fathers. Irenaeus, Ambrose, Jerome, and Augustine all identified his Gospel with the symbol of the ox precisely because of the evangelist's perceived focus on cultic imagery.[5]

Contemporary scholarship's lack of interest in these features is not hard to explain. Because of certain longstanding biases, the cultic dimension of Israel's faith has long been perceived as unpalatable. Such prejudices can be traced back to the pioneers of the historical-critical methods.[6] For many Protestant scholars, the priestly and cultic elements of the Old Testament represented the degeneration of Israel's religion in the post-exilic era and the very antithesis of the Gospel proclaimed by Jesus.[7]

Such biases have led scholars to overlook the role of the cult in Luke-Acts. In this paper, we shall begin by examining how the threefold hope for a new temple, a new priesthood, and a new cult was proclaimed by the prophets and how such hopes continued into Jesus' day. As we shall see, the three ideas were inextricably linked together for ancient Jews. We shall then identify ways that Luke describes their fulfillment in the New Covenant established by Christ. Specifically, as we shall show, Luke describes Jesus and the Church as the new temple, Jesus and the apostles as the new priests, and the celebration of the Lord's Supper as the new cult.

II. The Restoration of Israel and the Eschatological Cult in Ancient Judaism

1. Jewish Hopes for an Eschatological Temple and Cult

In the past, the importance of the cult in prophetic literature was downplayed due to a prevailing tendency that equated the prophetic critique of the Temple with a wholesale rejection of it, an attitude that was no doubt shaped by Protestant theological biases.[8] The trend in recent research, however, has shifted. It is now generally accepted that while the prophetic literature condemns corruption in the priesthood, it was not radically opposed to the temple cult in and of itself, recognizing it as a divine institution.[9]

---

5   See Irenaeus, *Adversus haereses* 3.11.8; Ambrose *Expositio Evangelii secundum Lucam*, Prologue; Jerome, *Commentariorum in Ezechielem libri XVI*, 1.1.10; Augustine, *De Consensu Evangelistarum*, 1.6.9; 4.10.11; *Tractatus in Joannis Evangelium*, 36.5.

6   See, for example, Jonathan Klawans, *Purity, Sacrifice, and the Temple: Symbolism and Supersessionism in the Study of Ancient Judaism* (Oxford: Oxford University Press, 2006), especially 3–10.

7   See, for example, Crispin H. T. Fletcher-Louis, "Jesus as the High Priestly Messiah: Part 1," *Journal for the Study of the Historical Jesus* 4/2 (2006): 156.

8   See Peter Berger, "Charisma and Religious Innovation: The Social Location of Israelite Prophecy," *American Sociological Review* 28/6 (1963): 940–950 at 942.

9   See also James Swetnam, "Malachi 1,11: An Interpretation," *Catholic Biblical Quarterly* 31/2 (1969): 200–209 at 207; Klawans, *Purity, Sacrifice and the Temple*, 75–100; Anderson, "Sacrifice and Sacrificial Offerings (OT)," *Anchor Bible Dictionary*, 5:881. See also Marvin A. Sweeney,

Indeed, in numerous places the scriptures of Israel link the hope for the restoration of Israel to the Temple. Specifically, the Temple is understood as the future site of the ingathering of Israel in the messianic age. This hope is powerfully attested in Isaiah 2:

> [2] It shall come to pass in the latter days that *the mountain of the house of the* Lord shall be established as the highest of the mountains, and shall be raised above the hills; and *all the nations shall flow to it,* [3] and many peoples shall come, and say: "Come, let us go up *to the mountain of the* Lord, *to the house of the God of Jacob;* that he may teach us his ways and that we may walk in his paths (Isa. 2:2–3; see Mic. 4:1–2).[10]

A host of other biblical texts could also be cited.[11] That such hopes continued into the Second Temple period and beyond is also clear.[12]

Frequently overlooked, however, is that hopes for a new Temple were inextricably linked to another expectation: the coming of a *new cult.* The two ideas—new temple and new cult—were inseparable. For ancient Israel, the temple was understood as the place of sacrificial worship.[13] It is no surprise then that many prophetic texts that anticipate the coming of a new temple describe cultic worship taking place there. Malachi describes how the eschatological age will involve the Lord coming to his temple (Mal. 3:1) and the purification of the sons of Levi, who will present "right offerings" (Mal. 3:3). Ezekiel supplies an exhaustive account of what this new cult will look like, detailing the specific offerings that will be made in the new temple (see, for example, Ezek. 42:13; 43:18–27; 44:11, 15–16, 29–30; 45:13–25; 46). A number of texts also link the idea of the restoration with the offering of sacrifice (see, for example, Zeph. 3:10; Ps. 51:18–19; 69:30–36; 107:22).

"The Priesthood and the Proto-Apocalyptic Reading of Prophetic and Pentateuchal Texts," in *Knowing the End from the Beginning: The Prophetic, the Apocalyptic and their Relationships,* Journal for the Study of the Pseudepigrapha, Supplement Series 46; eds. L. L. Grabbe and R. D. Haak (London: T & T Clark, 2003), 167–178.

10 Among other passages, see Isa. 60:3–7; Neh. 1:8–9 (see Deut. 12:10–11); Ezek. 37:21–28.

11 In addition to the passages below, see also Ezek. 37:21–28.

12 See Tob. 14:5–7; Sir. 36:11–14; 2 Macc. 1:27–29; 4Q448 (*Apocryphal Psalm and Prayer*) A, 8–10; 11Q19 (*11QTempleᵃ*) XLVII, 1–18; 2 Bar. 68:4–7; T. Ben. 9:2–3; Jub. 1:15–18; Tg. on Isa. 53:15; Tg. on Zech 6:12; Gen. Rab. 2:5; 56:2; Exod. Rab. 31:10. The same hope is found in the Dead Sea Scrolls, see 4Q174 (*4QFlorilegium*) frags. 1 col. i, 21, 2:2–7; 1Q28 (*1QRule of the Community*) V, 1–7; VI, 2–5; VIII, 4–10; IX, 4–5; 4Q171 III, 11; 1Q33 (*1QWar Scroll*) II, 1–6; 4QpPs XXXVII, III, 1–11; see 5QNJ; 11Q19 (*11QTempleᵃ*). Even in those cases where an explicit reference to the temple's role in the eschatological ingathering is absent, the restoration is virtually always linked with *Jerusalem* or *Mt. Zion,* the site of the Temple (see, for example, Ps. 87:5–6). See R. J. McKelvey, *The New Temple: The Church in the New Testament* (London: Oxford University Press, 1969), 11, n. 2: "The descriptions of the New Zion presuppose a new temple, for no good Israelite could think of one without the other."

13 E. P. Sanders, *Jesus and Judaism* (Philadelphia: Fortress Press, 1985), 47–54.

From Second Temple sources such as the Dead Sea Scrolls we know these hopes were still maintained in Jesus' day.[14]

Some depictions of the future cult go beyond what even the Mosaic Law would seem to allow. For example, though Deuteronomy insists that all sacrifices must be brought to the central sanctuary, i.e., the Temple (Deut. 12:13–14), Isaiah asserts that Gentiles will offer sacrifices to the Lord in Egypt: "In that day there shall be an altar to the LORD in the midst of the land of Egypt … and the Egyptians will know the Lord in that day and worship with *sacrifice* and *burnt offering* [minḥâ]…" (Isa. 19:19a, 21).[15] This closely resembles Malachi 1:10–12:

> [10] I have no pleasure in you, says the LORD of hosts, and I will not accept an *offering* [minḥâ] from your hand. [11] For from the rising of the sun to its setting my name is great among the nations, and in every place incense is offered to my name, and a pure *offering* [minḥâ]; for my name is great among the nations, says the LORD of hosts. [12] But you profane it when you say that the LORD's table is polluted, and the food for it may be despised.

This prophecy has been read by some as contrasting the polluted sacrifices of the corrupt cult with the pure sacrifices of the eschatological age.[16]

One particular sacrifice that is frequently associated with the restoration of Israel is the *tôdâ*, the thanksgiving sacrifice. The *tôdâ* was a kind of peace offering.[17] Specifically, the *tôdâ* was linked to the idea of deliverance. The LXX identifies it as a *thysias sōtēriou*, a "sacrifice of salvation/deliverance" (see LXX Lev. 7:11). Given this rendering it is probably no wonder that it was associated with the redeemed in

---

14   See, for example, 2Q24 [*2QNew Jerusalem ar*] IV; 11Q18 [*11QNew Jerusalem*]; see also 1Q28b [*1QRule of Benedictions*] III, 1–3; 4Q504 [*4QDibHam*] IV, 9–11; CD–A [*Damascus Document*ᵃ] XI, 17–12:2; 16:13–19; 1Q33 [*1QWar Scroll*] II, 1–6.

15   See John D. Watts, *Isaiah 1–33*, Word Biblical Commentary 24; rev. ed. (Dallas: Thomas Nelson, 2005), 315. The passage goes on to describe how the Assyrians will join with the Egyptians in worshipping the Lord (Isa. 19:23).

16   That an eschatological view is likely present is suggested by the similarity of language to the eschatological visions of other prophets contained in the collection of the "Book of the Twelve". See Donald K. Berry, "Malachi's Dual Design: The Close of the Canon and What Comes Afterward," in *Forming Prophetic Literature: Essays on Isaiah and the Twelve in Honor of D. W. Watts*, eds. J. W. Watts, J. D. W. Watts, P. R. House (Sheffield: Sheffield Academic Press, 1996), 277–278; Peter Verhoef, *The Books of Haggai and Malachi*, New International Commentary on the Old Testament (Grand Rapids: Eerdmans, 1987), 228.

17   The principle prescriptions for this sacrifice are laid out in Lev. 7:12–15. In addition, the *tôdâ* likely served as the life-setting for many of the psalms. For further discussion see David E. Stern, "Remembering and Redemption," in *Rediscovering the Eucharist: Ecumenical Conversations*, ed. R. Keresztky (New York: Paulist Press, 2003), 11–12; Hartmut Gese, *Zur biblischen Theologie*, 117–122; Patrick D. Miller, *They Cried to the Lord: The Form and Theology of Biblical Prayer* (Minneapolis: Fortress, 1994), 197–198; Herman Gunkel, *Einleitung in die Psalmen: Die Gattungen der religiösen Lyrik Israels* (Göttingen: Vandenhoeck & Ruprecht, 1933), 265–292.

the eschatological age. For example, Psalm 107:22 describes those returning from exile, saying, "let them offer *sacrifices of thanksgiving*, and tell of his deeds in songs of joy!"[18] In addition, Jeremiah, looking forward to the future restoration of Israel, announces:

> [10] Thus says the LORD: In this place of which you say, "It is a waste without man or beast," in the cities of Judah and the streets of Jerusalem that are desolate, without man or inhabitant or beast, there shall be heard again [11] the voice of mirth and the voice of gladness, the voice of the bridegroom and the voice of the bride, the voices of those who sing, *as they bring thank offerings to the house of the LORD:* "Give thanks to the LORD of hosts, for the LORD is good, for his steadfast love endures forever!" For I will restore the fortunes of the land as at first, says the LORD. (Jer. 33:10–11; see also Jer. 17:26)

Citing this passage, later rabbinic tradition explained: "In time to come all offerings will come to an end, but the thanksgiving-offering will never come to an end" (*Pesiq. Rab.* 9:12).[19]

2. The Restoration of Israel and the New Priesthood

Closely associated with the idea of the new cult in Jewish sources is the expectation of a new priesthood. A key element of the future age described by Ezekiel is the installment of the sons of Zadok as the priests in the Temple, a belief also present in the Dead Sea Scrolls.[20] As mentioned above, Malachi also links the eschatological age with the purification of the priesthood (Mal. 3:3). By Jesus' day it even seems that at least some Jews were anticipating the coming of a priestly messiah.[21]

---

18 That the term *tôdâ* in such contexts refers to actual cultic sacrificial offerings and not simply to a spiritual sacrifice is clear. See Norman Whybray, *Reading the Psalms as a Book*, Journal for the Study of the Old Testament Supplement Series 222 (Sheffield: Sheffield Academic Press, 1996), 113.

19 Cited from Jacob Neusner, trans., *Pesiqta deRab Kahana: An Analytical Translation*, Brown Judaic Studies 122; 2 vols. (Atlanta: Scholars Press, 1987), 1:151. See also *Leviticus Rabbah* 9:7.

20 The concern to preserve the Zadokite priesthood is also evidenced in the Dead Sea Scrolls (for example, see 1Q28b III, 22; CD–A [*Damascus Document*[a]] IV, 3–4).

21 The Dead Sea Scrolls refer to the "the Messiah(s) of Aaron and Israel" (CD–A [*Damascus Document*[a]] XII, 23–13:1; XIV, 19 [=4Q266 (4QDamascus Document[a]) X, 1:12]; XIX, 10–11; XX, 1; 1Q28 [*1QRule of the Community*] IX, 11). Many scholars think that these references, particularly the one in the passage from 1Q28, indicate a hope for two distinct figures, one Davidic (a royal figure) and one Aaronic (a priestly figure). For recent discussions see Eric Mason, *'You are a Priest Forever': Second Temple Jewish Messianism and the Priestly Christology of the Epistle to the Hebrews* (Leiden: Brill, 2008) 87–93; Joseph Angel, *Otherworldly and Eschatological Priesthood in the Dead Sea Scrolls*, Studies on the Texts of the Deserts of Judah 86 (Leiden: Brill, 2010), 171–208.

Moreover, just as some passages in the prophets suggest a vision for the future cult that transcends the Mosaic Law, so there are passages that seem to suggest something similar regarding the priesthood. For example, as the book of Isaiah envisioned Egyptians worshipping the Lord at an altar in Egypt, something apparently at odds with Deuteronomy, it also suggests that non-Levites will be allowed to serve as priests:

> [6] And the foreigners who join themselves to the LORD, to *minister* [šārat] *to him, to love the name of the* LORD, *and to be his servants, everyone who keeps the Sabbath, and does not profane it, and holds fast my covenant—* [7] *these I will bring to my holy mountain, and make them joyful in my house of prayer; their burnt offerings and their sacrifices will be accepted on my altar; for my house shall be called a house of prayer for all peoples.* (Isa. 56:6–7)

> [20] And they shall bring all your brethren from all the nations *as an offering to the* LORD, *upon horses, and in chariots, and in litters, and upon mules, and upon dromedaries, to my holy mountain Jerusalem, says the* LORD, *just as the Israelites bring their cereal offering in a clean vessel to the house of the* LORD. [21] And *some of them also I will take for priests and for Levites,* says the LORD. (Isa. 66:20–21)

The expectation that foreigners will *"minister"* [šārat] to the Lord in Isaiah 56 is striking. The terminology employed (šārat) is used to describe priestly activity throughout the Old Testament.[22] Stunningly, this passage is omitted from the text of the book of Isaiah found in the Dead Sea Scrolls. As scholars recognize, its absence is likely due to discomfort with the suggestion that Gentiles will somehow serve as priests.[23] The announcement that God will "take" some "for priests and Levites" in Isaiah 66 also suggests the bestowal of sacerdotal responsibilities on those who otherwise would not be entrusted with them.

That such ideas could be drawn from Isaiah 56 might be concluded from the *Testament of Levi*:

---

22 See, for example, Exod. 28:35; Num. 3:6; 8:26; 18:2; Deut. 10:8; 17:12; 1 Kings 8:11; 2 Chron. 5:14; Jer. 33:21. For the cultic implication of šārat see F. Brown, S. R. Driver, and C. A. Briggs, *Hebrew and English Lexicon of the Old Testament*, 1058, which links Isa. 56:7 to the idea "of foreigners admitted to priesthood." Likewise, see Gregory K. Beale, *The Temple and the Church's Mission: A Biblical Theology of the Dwelling Place of God* (Downers Grove: Inter-Varsity Press, 2004), 262 n. 29: "Is. 56:6 even says that Gentiles will 'minister' to the Lord in the temple as priests, which Is. 66:18–21 makes clearer."

23 See Dwight W. Van Winkle, "An Inclusive Authoritative Text in Exclusive Communities," in *Writing and Reading the Scroll of Isaiah*, eds. C. C. Broyles and C. A. Evans (Leiden: Brill, 1997), 425.

> Levi, your posterity shall be divided into *three offices* as a sign of the glory of the Lord who is coming. The first lot shall be great; no other shall be greater than it. The second shall be in the priestly role. But the third shall be granted a new name, because from Judah a king will arise and shall found *a new priesthood in accord with the gentile model and for all nations.* His presence is beloved, as a prophet of the Most High, a descendant of Abraham, our father. (*T. Levi* 8:11–15)[24]

Three priesthoods are mentioned in this text: (1) the high priesthood given to the descendants of Aaron; (2) the order of the Levites; and (3) a priesthood established by a coming king, likely the Davidic messiah ("from Judah"), which is linked with Gentiles. Although this schematization could easily be seen as betraying the hand of a Christian editor, it should be pointed out that the association of Gentiles with the priesthood may also simply reflect what is found in the passages above that seem to link the Gentiles with priestly activity in the eschatological age. Its apparent association of the priesthood with the Davidic Messiah is also not entirely inexplicable, as we explain below.

3. The Priestly Davidic Messiah

In some texts the Davidic messiah is explicitly described as having a cultic role. Jeremiah 30:21 explains, "Their prince shall be one of themselves, their ruler shall come forth from their midst; I will make him *draw near* and *he shall approach* me, for who would dare of himself to approach me? says the LORD." The word translated, "I will make him draw near" (*qārab*), is frequently used in cultic settings (see Exod. 29:4, 8; 40:12, 14; Lev. 3:6; 7:35; 8:6, 13, 24; Num. 8:9, 10; 16:5, 9, 10), as is the word for "*he shall approach*" (*nāgaš*—see Exod. 28:43; 30:20; Lev. 21:23; Ezek. 44:13). Used together, these terms unavoidably convey the notion that the future Davidic king will have cultic responsibilities.[25]

The Davidic figure of the eschatological era in Ezekiel is also associated with cultic responsibilities. He is given the unique privilege of entering the eastern gate and is able to "eat bread before the Lord" (Ezek. 44:3). Here it seems that the Davidic king is associated with the Bread of the Presence, food reserved for the priests. In addition, he is said to provide the sacrificial offerings (Ezek. 45:17, 22–25; 46:6–15).

---

24 See J. H. Charlesworth (ed.), *The Old Testament Psudepigrapha* 1:791.

25 See Walter Kaiser, *The Messiah in the Old Testament,* Studies In Old Testament Biblical Theology (Grand Rapids: Zondervan, 1995), 190–191 who writes: "Most surprising of all is the fact that this king will also be a priest, for verse 21c specifically declares God's promise, 'I will bring him near and he will come close to me.' To 'come near' or 'approach' God means to engage in the work of the priest (see Ex 24:2; Nu 16:5) ... Thus, the picture is of a 'Glorious Ruler-Priest' who performs both political and priestly duties—a well-known concept in the ancient Near East."

Ezekiel's description of the future Davidic king's cultic role seems to have influenced the author of *Psalms of Solomon*, a work dating to the Second Temple period. Scholars recognize allusions to Ezekiel in the description of the Davidic Messiah in *Psalms of Solomon* 17 (compare *Ps. Sol.* 17:21 with Ezek. 34:23 and *Ps. Sol.* 17:32 with Ezek. 37:24). Here the Davidic king is presented as carrying out responsibilities otherwise associated with the priests.[26]

Recognizing a priestly role for the Davidic figure in the eschatological age would not be entirely unprecedented. Psalm 110, a passage that was interpreted eschatologically in later Jewish sources,[27] describes the Davidic king as "a priest forever in the order of Melchizedek" (Ps. 110:4). Even more striking, David's sons are said to be "priests" (*kōhenim*) in 2 Samuel 8:18.

Numerous other texts could be mentioned.[28] For example, David himself is described as having priestly prerogatives: he wears the ephod (the priestly garment—see 2 Sam. 6:14; 1 Chron. 15:27; compare Exod. 28:4), erects the tabernacle for the ark (2 Sam. 6:17; 1 Chron. 15:1; 16:1; compare Num. 1:51; 4:1–33), offers sacrifices (2 Sam. 6:17; 1 Chron. 16:2; compare Num. 3:6–8, 14–38; 4:47; 6:16–17; 8:14–26), and blesses the people (2 Sam. 6:18; compare Num. 6:22–27). Given this background, it is not at all surprising to find sources describing the eschatological Davidic figure as enjoying priestly prerogatives.

III. *The New Temple in Luke-Acts*

1. *Jesus' Condemnation of the Jerusalem Temple and the Messianic "House of Prayer"*

That new temple hopes play a role in Luke's portrayal of Jesus' mission of fulfillment is clear from his description of Jesus' action in the Temple. Luke writes, "And he entered the temple and began to drive out those who sold, saying to them, 'It is written, '*My house shall be a house of prayer*'; but you have made it *a den of robbers*'

---

26 See Fletcher-Louis, "Jesus as High Priestly Messiah," 1:163 n. 28; Jostein Ådna, *Jesu Stellung zum Tempel: Die Templaktion und das Tempelwort als Ausdruck seiner messianischen Sendung*, Wissenschaftliche Untersuchungen zum Neuen Testament 2/119 (Tübingen: Mohr-Siebeck, 2000), 65–70; P. N. Franklyn, "The Cultic and Pious Climax of Eschatology in the Psalms of Solomon," *Journal for the Study of Judaism in the Persian, Hellenistic, and Roman Periods* 18 (1987): 1–17.

27 The messianic interpretation of this psalm is found in *b. Sanh.* 38b; *Midr. Ps* 18.29; *Tg.* on Ps 110. It also appears to be applied to eschatological figures in 4Q491 and the *Similitudes of 1 Enoch*. See Rikk Watts, "The Psalms in Mark," in *The Psalms in the New Testament*, eds. S. Moyise and M. J. Menken (London: T & T Clark, 2004), 38.

28 For a fuller treatment of David's priestly connections, see Scott W. Hahn, *Kinship by Covenant: A Canonical Approach to the Fulfillment of God's Saving Promises*, Anchor Yale Bible Reference Library (New Haven / London: Yale University Press, 2009), 187–194; Scott W. Hahn, *The Kingdom of God as Liturgical Empire: A Theological Commentary on 1–2 Chronicles* (Grand Rapids: Baker Academic, 2012), 44–45, 50–64, 73–77, 90–95, 105–137.

(Luke 19:45–46). Jesus' action evokes Zechariah 14:21, which explains that in the eschatological age "there shall no longer be a trader in the house of the Lord ..."

Moreover, Luke's quotation of Jesus' words draws on two Old Testament passages. The first (*"My house shall be a house of prayer"*) is taken from the vision of the eschatological temple found in Isaiah 56, which we have already examined above. By drawing from this prophecy, Jesus is presented as endorsing its vision for a future temple.

The second quote, however, is taken from the condemnation of the Temple in Jeremiah 7, which links the Jerusalem Temple to the defunct sanctuary at Shiloh. As the sanctuary at Shiloh was destroyed on account of the people's sin, so too, the prophet explains, God's judgment is about to come upon the Temple in Jerusalem:

> [11] Has this house, which is called by my name, *become a den of robbers* in your eyes? Behold, I myself have seen it, says the LORD. [12] Go now to my place that was in Shiloh, where I made my name dwell at first, and *see what I did to it for the wickedness of my people Israel*... [14] therefore *I will do to the house which is called by my name, and in which you trust, and to the place which I gave to you and to your fathers, as I did to Shiloh.* (Jer. 7:11–14)

In citing this text Jesus is doing more than merely critiquing the *status quo*. Jesus specifically targets a prophecy of the destruction of Solomon's Temple to signal the coming destruction of the Herodian Temple. That Luke understood this episode along these lines is clear from the context: immediately before the account of Jesus' temple action we read about Jesus' prediction of the destruction of Jerusalem (Luke 19:41–44),[29] a prophecy Jesus reiterates in Luke 21:5–6.

Yet this raises an important question. If the Jerusalem Temple is not the temple of the messianic age and if Jesus has come as the Messiah, what for him would constitute the promised temple of Isaiah 56? Moreover, if Jesus affirmed Isaiah's prophecy of a coming eschatological temple, how did he envision the realization of the expectations of a new priesthood and new cult related in that passage?

2. The Parable of the Vineyard and Jesus' Identity as the "Cornerstone"

A critical clue in answering these questions is found in the Parable of the Vineyard and the cornerstone saying that accompanies it (Luke 20:9–18). The imagery of the parable comes from Isaiah 5.[30] In Luke 20, as in Isaiah 5, Israel is described

---

29 Scholars have detected numerous allusions to Jeremiah within these verses, many of which occur in the near context of the prophecy from Jeremiah 7:11 cited by Jesus in the temple episode. See John Nolland, *Luke*, 3 vols., Word Biblical Commentary 35 (Dallas: Word Books, 1993), 3:923; Lloyd Gaston, *No Stone on Another: Studies in the Significance of the Fall of Jerusalem in the Synoptic Gospels*, Novum Testamentum Supplements 23 (Leiden: Brill, 1970), 359.

30 For a list of scholars who take this view see Green, *Luke*, 704 n. 21. There are a number of similarities between Jesus' parable and Isaiah 5: (1) a vineyard is used as a symbol of the "house

as a vineyard, an image used elsewhere in Jewish literature to symbolize God's people.[31] As scholars note, the owner of the vineyard in Luke's parable is therefore an image of the Lord. The "servants" sent by the owner and rejected by the tenants are widely recognized as representing the prophets.[32] Finally, the son who is killed by the tenants in the parable clearly symbolizes Jesus.

Jesus closes the parable by citing Psalm 118: "The very stone which the builders rejected (*apodokimazō*) has become the cornerstone" (literally, "head of the corner" [*kephalēn gōnias*], see Luke 20:17; compare Ps. 118:22). As with the figure of the son who is killed in the parable, Jesus' use of the psalm's imagery clearly anticipates his passion and exaltation.[33] The language closely mirrors Jesus' passion prediction in Luke 9:22: "the Son of Man must suffer ... and be *rejected* (*apodokimazō*)."

That Jesus moves from a story about a "son" to imagery of a "stone" may at first appear strange. However, the transition would not have seemed odd to a Jewish audience. A word-play on the Hebrew words for "stone" (*'eben*) and "son" (*ben*) was well established in ancient Israel (compare Exod. 28:9).[34]

While the sudden introduction of "stone" imagery is therefore not difficult to account for, the exact terminology used by Jesus—the "cornerstone"—is not insignificant. As other scholars have noted, the appearance of "cornerstone" language is likely related to cultic imagery embedded in the parable. The "cornerstone" is almost certainly a reference to the architecture of the Temple.[35] Psalm 118, the source of the saying, was clearly envisioned as a song sung in the Temple (Ps.

---

of Israel"; (2) righteousness is symbolized by "fruits"; and (3) the passage ends with judgment on the wicked, which is symbolized by coming destruction. Green also points out verbal parallels: *ton agapēton* (Luke 20:13; Isa. 5:1); *ti oun poiēsei* (Luke 20:15; Isa. 5:4–5); and *ho kurious tou ampelōnos* (Luke 20:15; Isa. 5:7).

31 For example, see Isa. 1:8; 3:13; 27:2–7 [37:30–32; 65:21]; Jer. 12:10–11; Ezek. 19:10. See also *L.A.B.* 12:9; 28.4; 4Q500 1; *Midr. Tanh.* B. *Qedošin* § 6; *Exod. Rab.* 30.17 [on Exod. 21:18]; *Midr. Prov.* 19:21.

32 The imagery of the prophets as "messengers" is particularly evocative of 2 Chron. 36:15–16. Moreover, in many of passages the prophets are identified as "servants" of the Lord (see, for example, Jer. 7:25–26; 25:3–4; 26:2–6). See Klyne R. Snodgrass, *Stories with Intent: A Comprehensive Guide to the Parables of Jesus* (Grand Rapids: Eerdmans, 2008), 288, 682 n. 133.

33 See, for example, Fitzmyer, *Luke*, 2:1282; Nolland, *Luke*, 3:955.

34 Many scholars accept that the wordplay explains Jesus' language. Especially insightful is the approach taken in Seyoon Kim, "Jesus—The Son of God, the Stone, the Son of Man, and the Servant," 134–148, who makes a plausible case for Jesus' combination of various texts.

35 See Michael Giesler, "The Rejected Stone and the Living Stones: Psalm 118:22–23 in New Testament Christology and Ecclesiology," *Letter & Spirit* (2008): 98; Beale, *Temple and the Church's Mission*, 184; Joel Marcus, *The Way of the Lord: Christological Exegesis of the Old Testament in the Gospel of Mark* (Louisville: Westminster/John Knox Press, 1992), 121; Timothy Gray, *The Temple in the Gospel of Mark*, Wissenschaftliche Untersuchungen zum Neuen Testament II/242 (Tübingen: Mohr-Siebeck, 2008), 76.

118:26: "We bless you from the *house of the LORD*").[36] The language of the psalm also appears in the temple-building scene of Ezra 3 (see Ps. 118:29 and Ezra 3:11).[37] Moreover, the psalm was closely associated with the feast of Tabernacles (*m. Sukk.* 4.5), a feast closely associated with hopes for an eschatological temple (compare Ezek. 40:1–2; Zech. 14:16–21; Hag. 2:1–9). In sum, the "cornerstone" mentioned by the psalmist seems best read as an allusion to temple traditions. It is simply impossible to imagine an ancient Jew thinking that any *other* building is in view.

In fact, "stone" imagery is frequently linked with temples and sacred sites in the Old Testament (see, for example, Gen. 28:10–22; Isa. 8:14–15; 28:16; Zech. 4:7–9) and Jewish literature (*m. Yoma* 5.2; *b. Yoma* 54a–b; *Lev. Rab.* 20.4; *Bet ha-Midr.* 5.63; *Num. Rab.* 12.4), as well as in 1 Peter (1 Pet. 2:4–8). Significantly, Jesus connects "stone" language to the Temple in the very next chapter of Luke (Luke 21:5–6).[38]

Noteworthy in this discussion is *Testament of Solomon* 23:6–8. Here "cornerstone" imagery is used in connection with the building of the Temple. If the passage is pre-Christian it can be included with other Old Testament and Jewish sources that closely link stone imagery to the Temple. If not, it can be cited with 1 Peter as evidence that Christians linked the psalm's cornerstone language to the sanctuary.[39]

That the "cornerstone" is to be identified with the Temple is also reinforced by its association with the parable. As Evans and others have shown, that Jesus would close the Parable of the Vineyard by alluding to temple imagery makes sense.[40] Isaiah 5, the most probable quarry of the story's vineyard symbolism, was itself closely linked to the Temple. The "tower" the Lord is said to have built in his vineyard (Isa. 5:2) was identified with the Temple in the Enochic literature, the

---

36   That the psalm was linked to the temple worship in the Mishna and later Jewish literature simply confirms the cultic connections already present in the psalm itself (see, for example, *m. Pesaø.* 5.5–7, 10.6–7; *m. Sukkah.* 3.9; 4.5; *t. Pesaø* 4.10–11; *b. Pesaø* 95b).

37   For a fuller discussion on the background of the psalm, see the excellent treatment in Gray, *Temple in the Gospel of Mark*, 72–77.

38   See Marcus, *Way of the Lord*, 120–121.

39   For a fuller discussion, see, for example, Dennis C. Duling, "Testament of Solomon," in *Old Testament Pseudepigrapha: A New Translation and Introduction*, ed. James H. Charlesworth, 2 Vols. (New York: Yale University press, 1983), 1:943–944; Dennis C. Duling, "Solomon, Testament of," *Anchor Bible Dictionary*, ed. David Noel Freedman, 6 vols. (New York: Doubleday, 1992), 6:111–117; Michael E. Stone, *The Literature of the Jewish People in the Period of the Second Temple and the Talmud: Jewish Writings of the Second Temple Period*, Compendia Rerum Iudaicarum ad Novum Testamentum, Section 2 (Assen: Van Gorcum, 1978), 327; Ian K. Smith, *Heavenly Perspective: A Study of the Apostle Paul's Response to a Jewish Mystical Movement at Colossae* (London: T & T Clark, 2006), 83.

40   For what follows see Craig A. Evans, *Mark 8:27–16:20* (Nashville: Thomas Nelson Publishers, 2001), 226–227; Craig A. Evans, *Jesus and His Contemporaries: Comparative Studies*, Arbeiten zur Geschichte des antiken Judentums und des Urchristentums (Leiden: Brill, 1995), 397–401; Gray, *Temple in the Gospel of Mark*, 70–77.

Dead Sea Scrolls, as well as in rabbinic tradition (see *1 En.* 89:56–73; 4Q500[41]; *t. Meil.* 1.16; *t. Sukkah* 3.15). Moreover, the "winepress" of the vineyard in Isaiah 5:2 was linked to the altar in the Targum of Isaiah 5 and in the Tosephta (see *t. Meil.* 1.16; *t. Sukkah* 3.15). The temple-vineyard connection may have also been reinforced by the Herodian Temple's architecture. Josephus relates that a giant golden vine was prominently displayed above the main entrance of the Temple (*A.J.* 15.395).

While some might insist that the temple connections of Isaiah 5 are merely coincidental and are unrelated to Jesus' parable, what weighs heavily against such a view is the context: Jesus offers the parable and identifies himself with the cornerstone of Psalm 118 while teaching *in the Temple* (Luke 20:1). Indeed, the parable comes as a response to questions about his authority to act so imperiously (driving out the merchants) and to teach in the Temple (Luke 19:45–20:2). In light of this, it can hardly be an accident that Jesus responds to the Jewish leaders' question about his authority with a story and a saying both containing imagery ("vineyard" and "cornerstone") closely connected to the Temple.

Further support for the idea that temple imagery is in play may be found in the saying that immediately follows the quotation of Psalm 118: "Everyone *who falls on that stone* will be *broken to pieces*; but when it falls on any one *it will crush him*" (Luke 20:18). Here Jesus appears to employ the Jewish hermeneutic of *gezerah shavah*, which connects passages based on common words.[42] Specifically, Jesus appears to link the "stone" of Psalm 118 with two prophetic texts, both of which also seem linked to eschatological temple imagery: Isaiah 8:14–15 and Daniel 2:44–45.[43] Let us look briefly at these texts.

First, scholars recognize that Jesus' description in Luke 20:18 of a "stone" that many will "fall upon" and thereby be "broken" draws from Isaiah 8:14–15:"[*The Lord*] *will become a sanctuary*, and a stone of offense, and a rock of stumbling to both houses of Israel …[15] And many shall stumble thereon; *they shall fall and be broken*; they shall be snared and taken." It is important to point out that the stone in the Isaianic prophecy is closely related to temple imagery. The prophecy, cited

---

41   4Q500 I is poorly preserved, however, it is clear that it links the vineyard with "the gate of the holy height," a term linked with the Temple (see Ezek. 20:40), and has points of contact with the Targum on Isaiah 5, which connects the vineyard with the sanctuary. See, among others, Evans, *Mark*, 232; Evans, *Jesus and His Contemporaries*, 400–401; George J. Brooke, "4Q500 1 and the Use of Scripture in the Parable of the Vineyard," *Dead Sea Discoveries* 2 (1995): 268–294.

42   For further discussion see, David Instone Brewer, *Techniques and Assumptions in Jewish Exegesis before 70 c.e.*, Texte und Studien zum antiken Judentum 30 (Tübingen: Mohr-Siebeck, 1992), 17–18.

43   These allusions are recognized by many scholars. See, for example, Nolland, *Luke*, 3:953; Fitzmyer, *Luke*, 2:1282; John S. Kloppenborg, *The Tenants in the Vineyard: Ideology, Economics, and Agrarian Conflict in Jewish Palestine* (Tübingen: Mohr-Siebeck, 2006), 213; Snodgrass, *Stories with Intent*, 67–68.

by Jesus in the parable, anticipates a future day when the Lord will *himself* become a sanctuary (see also Isa. 28:16).

The second prophetic text alluded to in Jesus' saying is found in Daniel 2. Here Daniel relates and interprets a dream of Nebuchadnezzar. He explains that it involved a statue composed of four parts, which he explains represents four wicked Gentile powers (Dan. 2:31–45). He goes on to explain that the king had seen a "stone" that was "cut out by no human hand," which destroys the statue, causing it to be "broken in pieces" (Dan. 2:34–34). This passage is likely the source of Jesus' teaching that, "Everyone who *falls on that stone*"—in context, the cornerstone of Psalm 118:22—"will be *broken to pieces*." It also informs his warning that "when it falls on any one *it will crush him*."

Once again Jesus appears to target a passage with temple associations. In particular, Zion imagery may be detected in the vision's description of the stone that "became a great mountain and filled the whole earth" (Dan. 2:35). The vision of a growing "great mountain" would have naturally evoked traditions regarding the eschatological temple in Zion (see Isa. 2:2; Mic. 4:1). As mentioned above, stone imagery was frequently linked to the sanctuary or other sacred sites in Jewish literature.

Furthermore, the likelihood that such traditions are in play in Daniel 2 is further reinforced by the fact that the imagery of a mountain growing from a stone is used in connection with descriptions of temples in other ancient Near Eastern texts, such as the Sumerian Cylinders of Gudea.[44] It is also worth mentioning that 4 Ezra 13:36 explicitly links the stone of Daniel 2 with the eschatological Zion. Given that hopes for the eschatological Zion were inextricably linked to hopes for a new temple,[45] this offers strong confirmation that Jewish readers linked the stone imagery to temple traditions.

All of this confirms the idea that the "cornerstone" saying involves temple imagery. In addition, by alluding to Isaiah 8 and Daniel 2 Jesus specifically evokes passages relating to the *eschatological* age. In some way, then, it seems that he identifies *himself* with the eschatological temple. The prophecy of Isaiah 8:14 is fulfilled: in Christ, the Lord has become a temple.

It should also be pointed out that the language chosen by Jesus—his being the "cornerstone" of the Temple—seems to imply that the new temple would involve something more than merely himself. In Acts 2, the Spirit appears as "tongues of fire" over the heads of the members of the Christian community (Acts 2:3). As Beale and Perrin note, the language may well have evoked the imagery of the heavenly temple, which is described as being composed of tongues of fire in

---

44   See Cyl. A 12.1–9; 18:24–25; 19:13–14, 17–20; 21:19–23; B 23.25; 1.1–10. For a discussion, see Beale, *Temple and the Church's Mission*, 149–151.

45   See n. 12 above.

ancient Jewish sources (see *1 En.* 14:8–25; 71:5; 4Q204 VI, 19–29).[46] That Acts 2 has numerous similarities with the theophany at Sinai[47] further strengthens the possible temple imagery, since Sinai was closely linked to the sanctuary.[48] Jesus is therefore portrayed as the cornerstone of the new temple, but, as 1 Peter also indicates, believers are incorporated into this structure as well, which, by virtue of the ascension, is ultimately a heavenly reality. All of this illuminates the meaning of Stephen's speech in Acts 7: as he insisted before the Jewish leaders, the true temple is not "made with hands" (Acts 7:48).

IV. The New Priesthood and the New Cult in Luke-Acts

1. The Parable of the Wicked Tenants and Hopes for a New Priesthood

Some have interpreted the Parable of the Vineyard as a lesson communicating God's rejection of Israel in favor of the Church or the Gentiles. This view, however, misses a key element in the parable: it is the *tenants*, not the vineyard itself, which are judged.[49] As many scholars recognize, since the parable is specifically directed at the Jewish leaders, the wicked tenants are best seen as a reference to them.[50] Jesus' mention of the "builders" who reject the cornerstone in Psalm 118 further reinforces such a reading. In Second Temple and rabbinic Judaism the terminology of "builders" was frequently used as a term for the Jewish leaders.[51]

It is significant, therefore, that the tenants (= Jewish leaders) are punished by having the vineyard taken away from them. This raises the question: what does it mean for the vineyard to be given to *others*? It seems that the parable's message is not simply that God will judge the leaders but that he is also going to appoint *new* ones.[52] Moreover, given the cultic overtones of the context discussed above, it seems probable that what is in view is the institution of new *temple officials*, in essence, new *priests*. Who would these new priestly leaders be?

---

46   Beale, *Temple and the Church's Mission*, 63; Perrin, *Jesus the Temple*, 63.

47   On the Sinaitic imagery in Acts 2 see Alan Thompson, *One Lord, One People: The Unity of the Church in Acts in Its Literary Setting*, Library of New Testament Studies (London: T & T Clark, 2008), 85–88.

48   See John Davies, *A Royal Priesthood: Literary and Intertextual Perspectives on an Image of Israel in Exodus 19:6*, Journal for the Study of the Old Testament Supplement Series 395 (London: T & T Clark, 2004), 137.

49   Against the view that the parable teaches that Jesus has rejected Israel, Evans points out that the identity of the vineyard remains constant, it is the *tenants*—likely the Jewish "leadership" which changes hands. See Evans, *Mark*, 223.

50   See, for example, Snodgrass, *Parable of the Wicked Tenants*, 77; Evans, *Mark 8:27–16:20*, 239; Bock, *Luke*, 2:1605; Fitzmyer, *Luke*, 2:1287; Nolland, *Luke*, 3:949.

51   See 1QIsa^a LIV, 13; CD IV, 19; VIII, 12; *b. Šabb.* 114a; *b. Ber.* 64a; *Song Rab.* 1.5 §3; *Exod. Rab.* 33.10; *Tg. Ps.* 118:22–28; see also Acts 4:11.

52   See Morna Hooker, *The Gospel According to St. Mark*, Black's New Testament Commentaries (Peabody, MA: Hendrickson, 1991, 276; Arland J. Hultgren, *The Parables of Jesus: A Commentary* (Grand Rapids: Eerdmans, 2000), 360; Evans, *Mark 8:27–16:20*, 237.

2. Jesus as the Davidic Priestly Messiah and Suffering Servant

Scholars have long noted priestly hues in Luke's portrait of Jesus' ascension.[53] Luke tells us, "Then he led them out as far as Bethany, and *lifting up his hands he blessed them*" (Luke 24:50). By "lifting up his hands" while giving a blessing, Jesus performs an unmistakably priestly gesture. In Leviticus 9:22 we read, "Aaron lifted up his hands toward the people and blessed them." Likewise, Sirach 50 relates how the high priest Simon, "*lifted up* his hands over the whole congregation of the sons of Israel, to pronounce the blessing of the Lord with his lips, and to glory in his name" (Sir. 50:20). Thus, just as Luke's narrative begins with the priest Zechariah (Luke 1:8–23), it concludes with the image of another priestly figure, Jesus.

The sacerdotal identity of Jesus in Luke 24 coheres well with other imagery connected with him in Luke-Acts. In particular, Luke identifies Jesus with two figures associated with priestly roles: the royal-priestly figure of Psalm 110 and the Suffering Servant of Isaiah 52:7–53:12. The priestly roles identified with these figures should not be overlooked, especially given Luke's portrayal of the ascension.

First, Jesus is associated with Psalm 110, which declares that the Davidic king is "a priest forever in the order of Melchizedek" (Ps. 110:4). In Luke 20:41–44, Jesus explains that this psalm describes the Messiah. Luke makes it clear that Jesus is the Messiah, leaving no doubt that the psalm applies to him. Moreover, the psalm is directly tied to Jesus' resurrection and ascension in Acts (Acts 2:29–36; 5:31; 7:55–56). Since Luke uses this psalm to describe Jesus' ascension, his depiction of Jesus blessing the disciples as a priest immediately before he is taken up in Luke 24:51 makes sense. Furthermore, that Luke would identify Jesus as a priestly figure should hardly seem surprising: as we have already seen, aside from Psalm 110, there are numerous texts that link the Davidide to priestly activity.

Second, Luke-Acts clearly links Jesus with the Suffering Servant. In Acts 8:29–35, Philip explains to the Ethiopian eunuch that Jesus is the Suffering Servant of Isaiah 52:7–53:12. Other descriptions of Jesus in Acts also seem influenced by this passage. For example, Stuhlmacher points out that passages in Acts 3 and 4 which portray Jesus as the anointed "servant" (*pais*) of the Lord who is put to death according to the will of God and exalted (Acts 3:13, 26; 4:27, 30) are undoubtedly influenced by Isaiah 61:1–2 and the Suffering Servant Song. That Jesus is identified in Acts 3 as the "Righteous One" confirms the presence of Suffering Servant imagery (compare Acts 3:14 with Isa. 53:11).[54]

---

53 See K. M. Kapic, "Receiving Christ's Priestly Benediction: A Biblical, Historical, and Theological Exploration of Luke 24:50–53," *Westminster Theological Journal* 67 (2005): 247–260; Nolland, *Luke*, 3:1227; J. Ernst, *Das Evangelium nach Lukas*, Regensburger Neues Testament (Regensburg: Pustet, 1977), 672.

54 Peter Stuhlmacher, "Isaiah 53 in the Gospels and Acts," in *The Suffering Servant: Isaiah 53 in Jewish and Christian Sources*, eds. B. Janowski and P. Stuhlmacher (Grand Rapids: Eerdmans, 2004), 156.

It is important to underscore that the Suffering Servant is presented as a *priestly* figure. This is evident in a number of ways. First, he offers a *sacrifice* for sin—himself (see Isa. 53:10). Second, Isaiah relates that the Servant "bore" (*nāśā'*) the sins of many (see Isa. 53:12). The same term is used in the description of the Day of Atonement in Leviticus 16; the scapegoat is said to "bear" (*nāśā'*) the sin of the people (Lev. 16:22). The term is also applied to the high priest in Exodus 28:30: "Aaron shall *bear* (*nāśā'*) the judgment of the people of Israel upon his heart before the LORD continually." Leviticus 10 even speaks of bearing sins as a priestly function, explaining that the priests must consume the sin offering so that they can "bear [*nāśā'*] the iniquity of the congregation" (Lev. 10:17). Given the sacrificial imagery present in Isaiah 53:10, it seems likely that such cultic connotations are in play in the description of the Servant.

In addition, Adams argues for a connection with the cult in the description of the servant as being "afflicted" (ânâ') (Isa. 53:4), language also linked with the Day of Atonement (Lev. 16:29).[55] Finally, whatever one makes of these specific cultic echoes in Isaiah 53, it seems hard to deny that, at least in some way, ancient readers identified the Servant as a priestly figure since its imagery appears to be used in the description of the eschatological priest in *4QApocryphon of Levi*[b].[56]

3. The Eucharistic Words and Jesus' Sacrificial Death

Jesus, then, like the Suffering Servant, is portrayed as a priestly figure that offers his own life as a sacrifice. This idea is especially emphasized in the Eucharistic words of Jesus at the Last Supper. For the moment, let us bypass Jesus' words and actions over the bread, which are somewhat more ambiguous than those associated with the cup, and consider the cup-saying[57]: "This cup which is poured out for you is the new covenant in my blood" (Luke 22:20).

As scholars note, since "blood" and "life" were closely linked in Judaism (see Lev. 17:11–13; 11Q19 LIII, 6), by *giving* the cup associated with his blood to the disciples Jesus conveys the idea of giving his life.[58] Contextually, it is clear that Jesus' death is in view. Jesus links "cup" imagery to his death immediately after the Last Supper in his prayer in Gethsemane (Luke 22:42). Moreover, Jesus speaks of

55 See the treatment in Jim W. Adams, *The Performative Nature and Function of Isaiah 40–55* (New York: T & T Clark, 2006), 203–206.

56 Émile Puech, "Fragments d'um apocryphe de Lévi et le personnage eschatologique: 4QTestLévi^{c-d}(?) et 4QAJa," in *The Madrid Qumran Congress: Proceedings of the International Congress on the Dead Sea Scrolls, Madrid 18–21 March, 1991*; eds. J. T. Berrera and L. V. Montaner (Leiden: Brill, 1992), 467–470.

57 In this we follow the approach of Kim Huat Tan, *The Zion Traditions and the Aims of Jesus*, Society for New Testament Study Monograph Series 91 (Cambridge: Cambridge University Press, 1997), 200–201.

58 See, for example, I. Howard Marshall, *Last Supper and Lord's Supper* (Exeter: Paternoster, 1980), 91.

the cup, identified with his blood, being "poured out" (*ekchynnomai*), terminology often linked with the depictions of a violent death.[59]

Yet Jesus' cup-saying not only anticipates his death, it describes it as a *sacrifice*. Not only is the language of Jesus' blood being "poured out" (*ekchynnomai*) a reference to his violent death, the terminology evokes the imagery of cultic sacrifice; the terminology used in depictions of cultic offerings (see, for example, Lev. 4:7, 18, 25, 30, 34; 4Q220 I, 3; 11Q19 LII, 11).[60]

That the sacrificial connotation of "poured out" is intended is clear from the fact that Jesus explicitly links the term to the language of a "new covenant."[61] For ancient Israelites, covenants were sealed by sacrifice. The psalmist thus explains, "Gather to me my faithful ones, who made a covenant with me by *sacrifice!*" (Ps. 50:5).[62] The sacrificial dimension of covenant making is particularly evident in the covenant ratification ceremony related in Exodus 24, where Moses seals the covenant between God and Israel through cultic offerings made on Mt. Sinai (Exod. 24:3–8).

The importance of Exodus 24 for understanding the Eucharistic words can hardly be overstated. By speaking of the cup of "the new covenant in my blood" Jesus evokes the words spoken by Moses at the close of the covenant ceremony: "Behold, *the blood of the covenant* which the LORD has made with you ..." (Exod. 24:8). While the Lukan formulation of the cup-saying bears less resemblance to this declaration than its Matthean and Markan parallels (Matt. 26:28; Mark 14:24), it is hard to deny that a connection to Moses' words is present.[63] Though Luke's version of the cup-saying, which has Jesus speak of the "the cup of the new covenant in my blood," clearly evokes the new covenant prophecy of Jeremiah 31, such an allusion does not mute the echoes of Exodus 24.[64] For one thing, as many have noted, Jeremiah 31 itself draws upon Exodus 24. The allusion of the cup-

---

59 See LXX Gen. 9:6; Judg. 9:25; Isa. 59:7; Ezek. 18:10; 22:13; 4Q201 1 IV, 7; 4Q219 II, 18. See also, for example, Green, *Luke*, 762.

60 The majority of interpreters recognize this connotation. See, for example, Adela Yarbro Collins, "Finding Meaning in the Death of Jesus," *Journal of Religion* 78 /2 (1998): 174; Fitzmyer, *Luke*, 2:1391, 1402–1403; Green, *Luke*, 763.

61 Evans describes the use of covenant language as the "major interpretive issue" in understanding the Institution Narrative (*Mark 8:27–16:20*, 386).

62 For further discussions see Dennis J. McCarthy, *Treaty and Covenant* (Rome: Biblical Institute Press, 1981), 91–92.

63 Against Beasley-Murray's attempt to pit an allusion to Exodus 24 in Matthew and Mark against a reference to Jeremiah 31 in Luke and Paul (*Jesus and the Kingdom of God* [Grand Rapids: Eerdmans, 1986], 264–265), see the discussion in Tan, *Zion Traditions and the Aims of Jesus*, 204–205. Indeed, most commentators recognize the allusion to Exodus 24 in the cup saying. See Fitzmyer, *Luke*, 2:1391; Green, *Luke*, 763.

64 See Tan, *Zion Traditions and the Aims of Jesus*, 215; Marshall, *Last Supper and the Lord's Supper*, 92.

saying to Exodus 24 is therefore reinforced, not diminished.[65] Moreover, it is hard to figure out how Jeremiah 31 alone explains the connection drawn between blood and covenant language: nowhere does Jeremiah link covenant to blood.

The appearance of "blood" with "covenant" is not the only parallel between Exodus 24 and Luke's account of the Last Supper. The Septuagintal version of Exodus 24:8 explicitly states that the sacrificial blood is *poured out* (*enecheen*) by Moses. This mirrors the terminology used by Jesus, further reinforcing the link with Exodus 24. In addition, that Luke has Jesus linking his blood to the motif of covenant while celebrating a *meal* mirrors not only Moses' words concerning the "blood of the covenant" but also the sacred *feast* that culminates Exodus 24 (see Exod. 24:8–11). Moreover, just as Exodus 24:4 highlights the way God's covenant is established with the *twelve tribes*, the *twelve apostles* are prominent in Luke's Last Supper scene (Luke 22:14, 30). Taken individually, each of these parallels are only suggestive of a connection between Jesus' words and Exodus 24. Taken together, however, these points of contact are too strong and numerous to be written off as mere coincidence. All of this leads us to concur with the conclusion drawn by Protestant scholar I. Howard Marshall: the idea of sacrifice in the Eucharistic words is "inescapable."[66]

The clear presence of cultic language in the cup-saying throws into relief the sacrificial imagery associated with Jesus' words and actions over the bread. Jesus explains, "This is my body which is *given for you*" (*touto estin sōma mou to hyper humōn didomenon*) (Luke 22:19). While the idea of "giving one's life" need not have sacrificial implications, its close connection to the cup-saying's cultic allusions suggests that such a meaning is intended here as well. Moreover, Jesus' language also evokes Isaiah 53:12, a passage we have seen Luke use elsewhere in connection with Jesus. As we have seen, Isaiah 53 identifies the Suffering Servant as a *sacrificial* offering.[67] We might also observe that elsewhere in the New Testament the term *hyper* ("for") is employed to describe the atoning nature of Jesus' death (1 Cor. 15:3; Rom. 5:6, 8). Finally, it should be noted that Jesus' actions with the bread also appear to compliment his words. Jesus has *broken* the bread, and *given* it to the disciples, a symbolic action that seems to suggest that his "body" is to be broken (=death) and *given* away for others.[68]

---

65   For an especially detailed look at the intertextual echoes between Exodus 24 and Jeremiah 31 see A. van der Wal, "Themes from Exodus in Jeremiah 30–31," in *Studies in the Book of Exodus: Redaction, Reception, Interpretation*, Bibliotheca Ephemeridum theologicarum Lovaniensium 126; ed. M Vervenne (Louven: Leuven University Press, 1996), 564.

66   Marshall, *Lord's Supper and Last Supper*, 91. See also Nolland, *Matthew*, 1079.

67   See Stuhlmacher, "Isaiah 53 in the Gospels and Acts," 152, who stresses this point.

68   Some have denied that this symbolic meaning is intended, insisting that breaking the bread was merely an action necessary for its distribution (see, for example, Marshall, *Last Supper and Lord's Supper*, 86; Evans, *Mark 8:27–16:20*, 389–390). However, to insist that simply because the breaking of the bread had a *practical* function it was therefore not infused also with *symbolic* meaning is unconvincing. Indeed, it is striking that many of the same scholars who deny the

4. The Eucharistic Rite as Cultic Act

Yet Jesus does not simply speak of his *death* in cultic terms; such language is also used for the Eucharistic rite *itself*. This is most evident in Jesus' instructions to the apostles that they must repeat what he has done: "Do this in *remembrance* (*anamnēsin*) of me" (Luke 22:19b). The language of "remembrance" or "memorial" (*anamnēsis*) was closely linked to Israel's cultic life.[69] To give a few examples:

> On the day of your gladness also, and at your appointed feasts, and at the beginnings of your months, you shall blow the trumpets over your burnt offerings and over the sacrifices of your peace offerings; they shall serve you for *remembrance* (LXX: *anamnēsis*) before your God: I am the LORD your God. (LXX Num. 10:10)

> And you shall put pure frankincense with each row, that it may go with the bread as a memorial (LXX: *anamnēsin*) portion to be offered by fire to the LORD. (LXX Lev. 24:7)

> A Psalm of David for remembrance (*anamnēsin*) concerning the Sabbath. (Superscription of LXX Ps. 37).

The cultic connotation is reinforced by Jesus' command to "do" (*poieō*) the rite, terminology that scholars also recognize as closely associated with Israel's liturgy (see, for example, LXX Exod. 29:35; LXX Num. 15:11–13).[70] Specifically, Luke's presentation of the Eucharistic rite seems to evoke three particular offerings: the bread of the presence, the Passover, and the *tôdâ* (thank offering).

Before proceeding, the reader should be aware that these three sacrificial offerings are not to be understood as hermetically sealed categories. An allusion to one does not necessarily rule out the likelihood that imagery from another is in play. For ancient Jews, these three sacrifices were easily linked together. Thus

---

symbolic meaning of Jesus' act of *breaking* the bread go on to find symbolic meaning in his *giving* it to the disciples (see Marshall, *Last Supper and Lord's Supper*, 84; Evans, *Mark 8:27–16:20*, 389–390).

69   See, for example, David E. Garland, *1 Corinthians*, Baker Exegetical Commentary on The New Testament (Grand Rapids: Baker Academic, 2003), 548, who, writing on the appearance of the same terminology in 1 Corinthians 11, explains: "The memorial requires that Christians reenact ritually what Christ did at his last meal to betoken his death and to explain its significance. The repeated imperative, 'do this unto my remembrance,' then, commands ritual remembrance of this foundational saving event (see Exod. 12:14; Ps 77:12–12; 105:5). It is related to Jewish liturgical remembrance that praises and proclaims the mighty acts of God."

70   Marshall (*Luke*, 804) points out that the verb *poieō* ("do") "is used of repeating rites" (see Exod. 29:35; Num. 15:11–13; Deut. 25:9; 1QS II, 19; 1Q28a 2:21). See also Otfried Hofius, "The Lord's Supper and the Lord's Supper Tradition," in *One Loaf, One Cup: Ecumenical Studies of 1 Cor. 11 and other Eucharistic Texts*, The Cambridge Conference on the Eucharist August 1988; NGS 6; ed. B. F. Meyer (Macon: Mercer, 1993), 101, 106–111.

Passover and the tôdâ were often closely linked. In the Jerusalem Talmud, regulations for the tôdâ are laid out in the tractate on Passover (see *y. Pesaḥ* 27d). Given the similarities between the Passover and the tôdâ the two sacrifices could easily be linked. Both involved a *sacred meal* in which the worshipper ate of the sacrifice and of the unleavened bread (Exod. 12:8; Lev. 7:12). The rabbis even state that the specific regulations for the tôdâ were derived directly from the ordinances relating to the Passover (see *m. Menaḥ* 7:6). Furthermore, as we stated earlier, the tôdâ was also linked to praising God for deliverance. In this the tôdâ was also very similar to the Passover. It is no wonder that Philo describes Passover as "a reminder and thank-offering" (*Spec.* 2:146). Notably, Philo also links the unleavened bread of Passover to the bread of the presence (see *Spec.* 2:158–161). Suffice it to say that Luke can be seen highlighting connections between all three offerings simultaneously in his presentation of the Eucharistic words and deeds of Jesus.

First, Jesus' use of the word *anamnēsis* in connection with bread, wine, and covenant imagery likely alludes to the Bread of the Presence. The Bread of the Presence offering was directly linked to the motif of the covenant (Lev. 24:8), to drink-offerings (Exod. 25:29), and to "memorial" (*anamnēsis*) language (Lev. 24:7).[71] This connection is anticipated earlier in Luke's narrative when Jesus compares himself and his disciples to David and his men who were given access to this sacred bread (Luke 6:1–5).

Second, given the Passover context of Jesus' meal in Luke, it hardly seems coincidental that the word *anamnēsis* closely resembles the term used for the Passover, *mnēmosynon* (see Exod. 12:14).[72] The two terms are synonymous, meaning "memorial" or "remembrance." Jesus' choice of a Passover meal as the context for his command to repeat the Eucharistic rite as a "memorial" (Luke 22:15, 19) manifestly draws on the imagery of the feast itself. That Jesus alludes to Jeremiah's new covenant prophecy in his Eucharistic words may also reinforce the Passover imagery; Jeremiah's vision of the new covenant age is explicitly linked to the Passover in the Septuagint (LXX Jer. 38:8).

The Passover imagery also makes sense of why both Jesus' death and the Eucharistic meal are described in cultic terms. In light of the paschal connection, Jesus' act of giving the bread (=his body) to the disciples to be *consumed* is the natural corollary of his role as the sacrificial victim; the Passover lamb was not only sacrificed but also *eaten*. Indeed, eating the lamb was a *necessary* part of the cultic celebration. Thus Jesus is presented as the *paschal* sacrifice that must be consumed.

---

71 For further discussion see Mary Douglas, "The Eucharist: Its Continuity with the Bread Sacrifice of Leviticus," *Modern Theology* 15/2 [1999]: 209–224.

72 See also Nolland, *Luke*, 3:1057; Green, *Luke*, 762.

As Fitzmyer explains, "[Jesus'] own body and blood will replace the Passover lamb ..."[73]

Third, and finally, scholars have argued that the Eucharistic rite seems to evoke the thanksgiving sacrifice (*tôdâ*). Luke's Last Supper narrative emphasizes Jesus' act of giving *thanks* over the bread (Luke 22:19).[74] By itself the language of giving thanks need not point to the *tôdâ*. Other observations, however, incline the reader to make the connection.

First, as we have seen, Jesus alludes to Jeremiah's new covenant prophecy. It can hardly be dismissed as irrelevant that this prophecy is followed by a vision of the messianic age in which the returned exiles offer *tôdâ* sacrifices (see Jer. 33:11). In this light, if Jesus is being presented as instituting a cultic rite in connection with the new covenant, the appearance of "thanksgiving" imagery seems fitting, if not even expected.[75] Second, the *tôdâ* was closely linked to language of "remembrance," a motif that is obviously also found in the Eucharistic words. Third, the rest of the passion narrative is especially linked with psalms that were closely linked with the *tôdâ* offering, for example, Psalm 22. Finally, like the Passover connection, such an allusion would make sense of why the Eucharistic meal itself, and not simply Jesus' death, would be identified with cultic language: in the *tôdâ*, the meal is of a piece with the offering of the animal—the worshipper partakes of the sacrificial victim.

5. The Eucharistic Words and the Priesthood of the Apostles

If the Eucharist is described as a cultic rite, and if Jesus is assuming a priestly role in the rite, then his instructions to the apostles to repeat it would seem to imply a priestly role for them as well. Indeed, the language Jesus employs, "*Do* [*poieō*] this," evokes the language used for the priests' performance of the cultic rites of the Old Testament (LXX Lev. 4:20; LXX Num. 15:11–13). In fact, in the immediate

---

73 Fitzmyer, *Luke*, 2:1392.

74 For what follows, see, in particular, Hartmut Gese, *Essays in Biblical Theology*, trans. K. Crim (Minneapolis: Augsburg, 1981), 128–140. Other scholars have also noted the connection. See Richard H. Bell, *Deliver Us from Evil*, Wissenschaftliche Untersuchungen zum Neuen Testament 216 (Tübingen: Mohr-Siebeck, 2007), 274–277; Jerome Kodell, *The Eucharist in the New Testament* (Collegeville: Michael Glazier, 1988), 48–50; D. R. Lindsay, "Todah and Eucharist: The Celebration of the Lord's Supper as a 'Thank Offering' in the Early Church," *Restoration Quarterly* 39 (1997): 83–100; James Swetnam, "The Crux at Hebrews 5,7–8," *Biblica* 81 (2000): 347–361.

75 Here we might also note the objection of Paul F. Bradshaw that the *tôdâ* fails to explain the eschatological significance of the meal (*The Search for the Origins of Christian Worship* [Oxford: Oxford University Press, 1992], 65). What Bradshaw fails to recognize is the eschatological associations made with the *tôdâ* in passages such as those outlined above. See also Lindsay, "Todah and Eucharist," 89: "There is an eschatological dimension to the thank offering. This becomes obvious in Isa. 25:1–10 where a song of thanksgiving transforms the eschatological feast into a thank offering of the entire spiritual community of God."

context of the Last Supper narrative Jesus applies other language to the apostles that would have appeared to suggest a priestly role for them.

Shortly after the Institution Narrative, Jesus tells the twelve that they will "sit on thrones judging the twelve tribes of Israel" (Luke 22:30). The priestly implications here are often missed. According to the Old Testament, "judging" the twelve tribes was primarily a *priestly* task (see Deut. 17:9; 2 Chron. 19:8–11). Such a task was viewed as a priestly responsibility in Jesus' day. Josephus assigns the task of judging *solely* to the priests, omitting the secondary role of lay elders elsewhere mentioned by the Law (see *A.J.* 2.165; 4.304).[76] Grossberg writes, "In Hellenistic times the high priest replaced the king as the principle judge..."[77] "Judgment" was also linked to the high priest,[78] the president of the Sanhedrin (see 1 Macc. 14:44; Acts 5:17; Josephus, *C. Ap.* 2.194; *A.J.* 20.200, 251).[79]

Furthermore, judging the twelve tribes in the *eschatological* age was particularly associated with priests. Ezekiel explains that priests will be the judges in the future age (Ezek. 44:23). According to the Dead Sea Scrolls, even the Messiah will defer to the priests' juridical authority (see 4QpIsaᵃ 8-10:24–25). Therefore, when Jesus assigns special juridical power over the twelve tribes—clearly envisioning their eschatological restoration—it strongly suggests that the apostles would be functioning as priests.

The priestly nature of the apostolic ministry is also supported by other passages in Luke-Acts. In Acts 1, Luke describes how the apostles chose a replacement for Judas. Specifically, Luke explains that this was accomplished by the casting of lots (Acts 1:26). While the practice was associated with games of chance (see Matt. 27:35; Mark 15:24), such does not appear to be its purpose in Acts 1. According to the Old Testament, lot-casting was a sacred rite. Significantly, the duties of the priests were assigned by the casting of lots (1 Chron. 24:31). In choosing the man to "share in this ministry" (Acts 1:17), the apostles' make recourse to the practice used for determining priestly responsibilities.

That the Old Testament rite of lot-casting is in the background of Acts 1:26 is reinforced when one recognizes that Luke begins his Gospel narrative by

---

76 See Sanders, *Judaism: Practice & Belief*, 171: "In summarizing Deut. 31, in which Moses consigns the law to the priests and the elders, Josephus left out the elders" (*A.J.* 4.304).

77 Daniel Grossberg, "Judges," in *Eerdmans Dictionary of the Bible*, eds. D. N. Freedman, A. C. Myers, and A. B. Beck (Grand Rapids: Eerdmans, 2000), 752. In addition, see Sanders, *Judaism: Practice and Belief*, 171.

78 The high priest's task of judging is particularly underscored in his association with the Urim and Thummim. While their exact nature is unclear, we do know that they were related to judgment (see Exod. 28:30; Num. 27:21; Sir. 45:10; see also Lev. 8:8; Ezra 2:63; Neh. 7:65).

79 See G. H. Twelftree, "Sanhedrin," in *Dictionary of Jesus and the Gospels*, eds. J. B. Green, S. McKnight, and I. H. Marshall (Downers Grove: InterVarsity Press, 1992), 730.

highlighting the priestly associations of the practice. Introducing Zechariah, the evangelist tells us, "Now while he was serving as priest before God when his division was on duty, *according to the custom of the priesthood, it fell to him by lot* to enter the temple of the Lord and burn incense" (Luke 1:8–9).

The placement of the two scenes of lot-casting in Luke-Acts seems intentional: Luke begins the narrative of both his Gospel and Acts with a scene involving the practice. This is hardly accidental. Scholars have long noted the way the material in Acts mirrors the flow of the narrative of the Gospel.[80] To name a few of the parallels:

- Both works begin with a prologue to Theophilus (Luke 1:1–4; Acts 1:1–2).

- The commencement of Christ's ministry in Luke and the apostles' ministry in Acts is described in similar ways. Both begin with an account of the descent of the Spirit in visible form: the dove at the Baptism of Jesus (Luke 3:21–22) and the tongues of fire at Pentecost (Acts 2:1–3 [described as "baptism" in Acts 1:5]).

- Just as in Luke Jesus begins his ministry with a speech in the Jewish place of worship, the synagogue (Luke 4:16–27), Peter launches the apostles' ministry in Acts with a speech likely delivered in the Temple (Acts 2:14–40).

- Jesus performs a miracle involving the healing of a man who is unable to walk (Luke 5:17–26). Peter's first miracle involves the healing of a lame man (Acts 3:1–10).

- In Luke 7:1–10 a centurion who is well respected by the Jews sends men to Jesus to ask him to come to his house. In Acts 10:1–48 a centurion, also well-spoken of by the Jews, sends men to ask Peter to come to his house.

These parallels run through the entirety of Luke-Acts. That Paul stands accused before rulers *four* times at the end of Acts (Acts 23: Sanhedrin; Acts 24: Felix; Acts 25: Festus; Acts 26: Agrippa) is hardly a coincidence for Luke—Jesus also ap-

---

80 See, for example, Charles H. Talbert, *Literary Patterns, Theological Themes and the Genre of Luke-Acts*, Society for Biblical Literature Monograph Series 20 (Missoula, MT: Scholars Press, 1974).

peared before rulers on *four* occasions (Luke 22:54: the high priest and the council; Luke 23:1: Pilate; Luke 23:9: Herod; Luke 23:11: Pilate).

Given this parallel structuring of Luke-Acts it hardly seems coincidental that both books begin with a scene of lot casting. In addition, given the cultic associations of the Eucharist, which Jesus commands the apostles to perform, and the priestly connotations of "judging" the twelve tribes at the Last Supper, it is unlikely an accident that Luke describes the selection of Judas' successor by means of a process he elsewhere explicitly links to the priesthood.

V. Conclusion

Luke-Acts presents Jesus as bringing about the fulfillment of the Scriptures of Israel. This includes the realization of messianic hopes rooted in the prophets. Yet Luke also reveals Jesus as the one who brings about the realization of expectations for a new temple, a new priesthood, and a new cult. God's people would be restored at the new temple as the prophets envisioned—yet this new temple would not be a building. Christ is the cornerstone of this new temple, which believers are incorporated into by virtue of their union with him. Since Christ is now ascended into heaven, the members of the Church are identified with tongues of fire, an image associated with the heavenly temple.

Likewise, the coming new priesthood is identified with Christ and the apostles. Jesus is the priest who offers his life as a sacrificial oblation like the Servant of Isaiah. Jesus is also the fulfillment of the figure related in Psalm 110, the priest in the order of Melchizedek. Notably, just as Melchizedek's priesthood was associated with bread and wine (Gen. 14:10), Jesus identifies his priestly self-offering with the Eucharistic bread and wine.

Furthermore, as the Parable of the Vineyard suggests, Jesus installs a new priestly leadership over God's people. The apostles are described as priests inasmuch as they are tasked with repeating the Eucharistic rite that forms one piece with Christ's sacrificial death on the cross. They are also established as the eschatological priestly judges, who are to be replaced by successors. As prophets such as Isaiah suggested, the eschatological age would transcend the limitations of the Law. Presumably, not all of the apostles are Levites—nor would they need to be, as Isaiah suggests.

Likewise, as Isaiah announces, right offerings are no longer bound geographically to Jerusalem. Luke reveals that the restoration of Israel is essentially a *sacramental* reality. Expectations for a new cult are realized in the Eucharistic celebration, the true Paschal celebration, "the *tôdâ* of the Risen One,"[81] and true bread of the presence. As the people of God gather around the Eucharistic body of Christ, they are restored at the true eschatological temple.

---

81 Joseph Cardinal Ratzinger [Pope Benedict], *Feast of Faith*, trans. G. Harrison (San Francisco: Ignatius Press, 1986), 59.

Letter & Spirit 8 (2013): 125-143

New Approaches to Marian Typology in Luke 1
Mary as Daughter Zion and Queen Mother

❖ Edward Sri ❖

Augustine Institute

In a little-known 1953 article called "The Scriptural Basis for Mary's Queenship," Eustace Smith makes a subtle but very important point about evaluating possible Marian types in the Old Testament. He argues that in order to build the strongest case for Marian typology, one must demonstrate that the typological connections are made by the New Testament writers themselves. According to Smith, Marian typologies based on, for example, Esther, the woman of Psalm 44 (45), and the "Lady Wisdom" figure, have been established by what he calls "extra-Scriptural agents" (such as the liturgy, the saints, or the Church Fathers) and are not developed within the Scriptures themselves. Smith comments:

> Types or figures foreshadowing the Blessed Virgin undoubtedly exist in the Old Testament. Difficulty with the typical sense in this regard is had in the fact that persons, events, and things have been employed as symbols by *extra scriptural agents*. ... A mariological type must conform to all the requirements of a messianic type and above all, that it *be revealed as such in Scripture*."[1]

Smith's comment, that a mariological type *be revealed as such in Scripture*, raises an important issue. There seems to be a distinction between types and figures that are developed by "extra scriptural agents" (the Church Fathers, the liturgy, magisterial teaching) and those that are developed in the New Testament itself. Raymond Brown[2] and the Pontifical Biblical Commission (PBC)[3] have made similar distinctions.

For example, the Pontifical Biblical Commission's 1993 document *The Interpretation of the Bible in the Church* makes this point when discussing the *sensus plenior* of Scripture. Without intending to engage the discussion in Biblical schol-

---

1   E. Smith, "The Scriptural Basis for Mary's Queenship," *Marian Studies* 4 (1953): 114 (my emphasis).

2   R. Brown, *Introduction to the New Testament* (New York: Doubleday, 1997), 41; R. Brown, "Hermeneutics," in R. Brown, et. al., eds., *The Jerome Biblical Commentary* (London: Geoffrey Chapman, 1968), 616–19; R. Brown, "Hermeneutics" in R. Brown, et al., eds., *The New Jerome Biblical Commentary* (Englewood Cliffs, New Jersey: Prentice Hall,1990), 1157.

3   Pontifical Biblical Commission (PBC), *The Interpretation of the Bible in the Church*, II, B, 2–3 in J. Fitzmyer, *The Biblical Commission's Document "The Interpretation of the Bible in the Church"*: *Text and Commentary* (Rome: Editrice Pontificio Istituto Biblico, 1995).

arship surrounding the notion of *sensus plenior*, I simply wish to highlight how the PBC makes a distinction between a level of *sensus plenior* that comes to be known when Scripture is read in light of "authentic doctrinal tradition or conciliar definition" and a level of *sensus plenior* that is found in "the meaning that a subsequent biblical author attributes to an earlier biblical text, taking it up in a context which confers on it a new literal sense."[4] In this latter case, the fuller sense is found not in an extra-Biblical agent (such as a Church Father or a magisterial pronouncement), but in the literal sense of the New Testament itself.[5]

The PBC makes a similar point when it specifically discusses Biblical typology. The document states that an authentic typological sense of Scripture is found in the connections made by the New Testament writers: "The connection involved in typology is ordinarily based on the way in which *Scripture* describes the ancient reality. ... Consequently, in such a case one can speak of *a meaning that is truly Scriptural*."[6] Once again, with the strongest cases for Biblical typology, the connection between the Old Testament type and the New Testament reality is not based simply on the way extra-Biblical sources such as the Church Fathers or Church councils reflected on Old Testament people, places, and events. Rather, it is based on the way subsequent *Scriptural texts* describe those ancient realities. Hence, the PBC gives special attention to Scripture as the criterion for determining an authentic typological sense.[7]

The main difference between the two kinds of typology examined here is this: "Extra-biblical typology" involves the creative discernment of the theologian who perceives connections between the Old Testament, the New Testament, and the Christian faith; whereas, what one might call "inter-biblical typology" can be observed in the New Testament writer's interpretation of the Old Testament. In the latter case, it is the New Testament itself that points out how a particular Old Testament figure foreshadows a reality in the New.

Both extra-biblical and inter-biblical typology can contribute positively to one's understanding of God's revelation through Scripture. Both have been used

---

4   PBC, *Interpretation of the Bible in the Church*, II, B, 3.

5   Brown makes a similar distinction when discussing the criteria by which one can determine an authentic *sensus plenior*. He notes how the "fuller sense" is grounded either in "the use of the OT in the NT" or "the use of the Bible in the post-Biblical church practice and preaching." See R. Brown, *An Introduction to the New Testament*, 41. See also his earlier treatment of this topic in R. Brown, "Hermeneutics" (1968), 616–617.

6   PBC, *Interpretation of the Bible in the Church*, II, B, 2, (my emphasis).

7   Similar to the PBC, Brown draws attention to the "types that have been pointed out by the NT" and "already existing scriptural patterns" as criteria for recognizing an authentic typical sense (see R. Brown, "Hermeneutics," [1968], 619). See also R. Brown, *An Introduction to the New Testament*, 41. As we will see below, Brown is also open to the possibility of extra-Biblical typologies (those which are established not by the New Testament) provided they are found in a consensus of the Fathers, the liturgy, or Church doctrine. Although he recognizes these as authentic typologies, Brown still gives a certain primacy to those types that are supported by the Scriptures themselves.

in the Church throughout the centuries and both should continue to be employed in Catholic Scriptural interpretation. But extra-biblical typology is distinguished from the inter-biblical typology that the New Testament writers themselves actually develop. As Raymond Brown has noted, "Advocates of typical exegesis have been more persuasive when the types they proposed could be related to patterns already supported in the Scriptures, e.g., Davidic typology of Jesus, exodus typology for elements of the Christian salvific mysteries."[8] For our purposes of considering possible Marian typologies, one should note that extra-biblical typology, while valuable, remains a step removed from the literal sense of the New Testament and its narrative presentation of Mary.

This article will consider two Marian types that have been noted by some scholars as appearing in the first chapter of Luke's Gospel: Mary as "Daughter Zion" and Mary as "queen mother." The study will serve as an example of how some Marian typology can be credibly supported not just from "extra-Scriptural agents," but in and through the literal sense of the New Testament itself. By examining Mary within the context of salvation history, within the narrative structures of Luke's annunciation and visitation scenes—and in light of the Old Testament themes that the annunciation and visitation scenes evoke—we will see that Luke's Gospel portrays Mary in ways that recall the Old Testament prophetic figure "Daughter Zion" as well as the royal maternal office in the Davidic kingdom known as the "queen mother."

Daughter Zion

The thesis that Luke 1:26–38 intends to portray Mary as the Daughter Zion figure of the Old Testament prophets is one that has been supported by numerous commentators.[9] Central to this interpretation is the angel Gabriel's first word to greet Mary in Luke 1:28, *chaire*. "*Chaire*" is the singular imperative form of the verb *chairein*, which literally means "to rejoice." This word, some argue, echoes the

---

8   R. Brown, "Hermeneutics" (1990), 1157.

9   See, for example, L. Deiss, *Mary Daughter of Sion* (Collegeville: Liturgical Press, 1972), 54; I. De La Potterie, *Mary in the Mystery of the Covenant*, 14–17; Joel Green, *The Gospel of Luke* (Grand Rapids: Eerdmans, 1997), 87; L. T. Johnson, *Luke*, 37; Arthur Just, *Luke 1:1-9:50* (St. Louis: Concordia House, 1996), 61, 66; S. Lyonnet, "Χαιρε, χεχαριτωμένη" *Biblica* 20 (1939): 131–141; J. McHugh, *The Mother of Jesus in the New Testament* (London: Darton, Longman & Todd, 1975), 38; John Nolland *Luke 1–9:20* (Waco: Word Publishing, 1989), 49–50; E. G. Mori, "Annunciazione del Signore" in *Nuovo Dizionario di Mariologia* (Milan: Edizioni San Paolo, 1986), 73; J. McHugh, *The Mother of Jesus in the New Testament*, 38; J. Paredes, *Mary and the Kingdom of God* (Middlegreen: St. Paul Publications, 1991), 67–68; Joseph Ratzinger, *Jesus of Nazareth: The Infancy Narratives* (New York: Image, 2012), 26–27; *Daughter Zion* (San Francisco: Ignatius Press,1983), 42–44; "'Hail, Full of Grace': Elements of Marian Piety according to the Bible" in Hans Urs von Balthasar & Jospeh Ratzinger, *Mary: The Church at the Source* (San Francisco: Ignatius Press, 2005), 64; Alberto Valentini, *Maria secondo le Scritture* (Bologna: Edizioni Dehoniane Bologna, 2007), 93; R. Tannehill, *Luke* (Nashville: Abingdon Press, 1996), 48.

prophetic call for Daughter Zion to rejoice over the saving work of God (Zeph. 3:14–15; Zech. 9:9; Joel 2:21). Thus, Luke associates Mary with the Daughter Zion symbolism in this verse.

Others, however, interpret *chaire* in Luke 1:28 not as an invitation to rejoice, but as a simple, conventional greeting and one that does not recall these prophetic texts and does not associate Mary with Daughter Zion.[10] It is pointed out that, although the literal meaning of the verb *chairein* is "rejoice," the imperative of this verb was ordinarily used simply to hail someone in classical Greek, in the other three Gospels[11] and elsewhere in the New Testament.[12] Would the original readers of the Third Gospel have seen in this word, which ordinarily meant "hello," anything more than an ordinary salutation? This was Raymond Brown's objection:

> Luke's readers would hear [the word *chaire*] used every day of their lives with the meaning "Hail, hello." If a modern English writer used "Goodbye" in a farewell without any interpretive comment, would his readers recognize that he was giving it its ancient religious value as "God be with you"?[13]

Brown's question is a good one. There are, however, several cogent exegetical reasons for concluding that Mary is, in fact, being greeted with an extraordinary call to rejoice over the coming of the long-awaited king—reminiscent of the way the Old Testament figure of Daughter Zion, the personification of the faithful remnant of Israel, was called to rejoice over the advent of Israel's king. Though *chaire* could mean simply "hello," there are several indications in Luke's narrative which suggest that Luke did intend something more than an ordinary greeting when using this word in 1:28. This article will show how those signs in the text support the interpretation that Mary is, indeed, being greeted by the angel Gabriel in ways that recall Daughter Zion symbolism from the Old Testament.

Chaire: *More Than a Hello?*

Though *chaire* ordinarily is used as a secular salutation in classical Greek and elsewhere in the New Testament, we must consider the way in which Luke expresses a simple greeting. This is key. Whenever Luke intends to express a conventional greeting in a *Semitic* context, he always uses the Semitic word "peace" (*eirene* =

---

10   See Brown, *Birth of the Messiah* (New York: Doubleday, 1993), 320–321, 639–640; *Mary in the New Testament*, eds. Raymond Brown, et. al. (New York: Paulist Press, 1978), 128–132; Joseph Fitzmyer, *The Gospel According to Luke: I–IX* (New York: Doubleday, 1979), 344–345; Beverly Gaventa, *Glimpses of Mary* (Columbia, SC: University of South Carolina Press, 1995), 52; Darrel Bock, *Luke 1:1–9:50* (Grand Rapids: Baker, 1994), 109.

11   Matt. 26:49, 27:29; 28:9; Mark 15:18; John 19:19.

12   See James 1:1; Phil. 3:1; 4:4 where it is used as a greeting in the opening or closing of a letter.

13   R. Brown, *Birth of the Messiah*, 324.

Hebrew *shalom*; see Luke 10:5; 24:36). The only two occasions in the entirety of Luke-Acts when the verb *chaire* is employed as a secular greeting come in a non-Jewish context for openings to letters intended for a Greek audience.[14] For Luke-Acts, therefore, the word "peace" (*eirene*)—not *chaire*—is used to express an ordinary salutation in a Semitic context. It is therefore striking when Gabriel uses the word *chaire* instead of the more Semitic greeting *eirene* to address Mary in Luke 1:28.[15] Paredes, for example, asks, "Why was a Greek salute used in a Jewish milieu? It would have been more normal to attribute to the angel the Hebrew greeting *shalom* (Greek = *eirene*)."[16] He continues:

> The Greek greeting *chaire* appears several times in the first three Gospels (compare Matt. 26:49; 27:29; Mark 15:18; John 19:3). However, whenever Luke's Gospel refers to a greeting, except in the annunciation, the greeting is always the Hebrew word *shalom*. (Luke 10:5; 24:36)[17]

The unusual use of *chaire* in Luke 1:28 has led some interpreters to conclude that the word was not meant to be taken merely as an *ordinary greeting*, but as an *invitation to rejoice*. McHugh, for example, states: "Now if Luke's only concern in 1:28 was to express a conventional greeting from Gabriel to Mary, why did he choose to write this greeting in the Greek, not the Semitic, form? Why did Luke not write 'Peace unto thee!', since he was so visibly striving to imitate a Semitic style and to imprint on the reader's mind a lively picture of a thoroughly Jewish world?"[18]

Moreover, interpreting *chaire* in Luke 1:28 not as a simple salutation but as a call to rejoice fits the theme of joy throughout Luke's Gospel and specifically in the infancy narrative (1:14, 47, 58; 2:10).[19] Very important to this discussion is the phenomenon that the other two birth announcements in Luke's Gospel—the annunciations to Zechariah and to the shepherds in Bethlehem—prominently include the theme of joy (1:14; 2:10). If *chaire* in Luke 1:28 is viewed merely as an

---

14   See Acts 15:23; 23:26.

15   W. Harrington comments: "The occurrence, in such a Semitically colored narrative, of the Greek greeting formula *chaire* ("Hail") instead of the Semitic "Peace!" is so surprising that one hesitates to accept it at its face value." See W. Harrington, *The Gospel of Luke* (Westminster, MD: Newman Press, 1967), 45.

16   J. Paredes, *Mary and the Kingdom of God* (Middlegreen: St. Paul Publications, 1991), 67.

17   Paredes, *Mary and the Kingdom of God*, 79–80, n. 16.

18   J. McHugh, *The Mother of Jesus in the New Testament* (London: Darton, Longman & Todd, 1975), 38. See also Lyonnet, "Χαιρε, χεχαριτωμένη," 131–41; Joel Green, *The Gospel of Luke* (Grand Rapids: Eerdmans, 1997), 87; Arthur Just, *Luke 1:1–9:50* (St. Louis: Concordia House, 1996), 61, 66.

19   See Klemens Stock, *Maria, la Madre del Signore nel Nuovo Testamento* (Rome: Edizioni ADP, 1997), 51.

ordinary greeting and not as a call to rejoice, the annunciation to Mary would be the only birth announcement in Luke 1–2 without the theme of joy.

Once it becomes plausible that the angel is doing more than simply greeting Mary—that he is, rather, *inviting her to rejoice*—other features in Luke 1:28 help shed light on the *kind* of rejoicing to which Mary is being called.

Luke's Use of Chaire in the Imperative

Luke's use of the imperative *chaire* is significant. In the Septuagint, the imperative form of *chairein* is always used in a context related to Zion being invited to share in the future joy that will come when God rescues his people (Joel 2:21–23; Zeph. 3:14; Zech. 9:9; cf. Lam. 4:21).[20] In two of these occurrences, the exact form of greeting used for Gabriel's address to Mary in Luke 1:28 (*chaire*) is used to address "Daughter Zion" when she is being called to rejoice over the coming messianic age.

Zephaniah 3:14 LXX uses the imperative *chaire* to call on God's people to rejoice in the Lord, the King, coming in their midst to take away their judgment and free them from their enemies:

> Sing aloud, O daughter of Zion;
>> Shout, O Israel!
> Rejoice [*chaire*] and exult with all your heart,
>> O daughter of Jerusalem!
> The Lord has taken away the judgments against you,
>> He has cast out your enemies.
> The King of Israel, the Lord is in your midst,
>> You shall fear evil no more.

Similarly, Zechariah 9:9–10 uses the imperative *chaire* to direct God's people to rejoice over the king coming to Jerusalem to bring "peace to the nations" and his dominion "to the ends of the earth":

> Rejoice [*chaire*] greatly, O daughter of Zion
>> Shout aloud, O daughter of Jerusalem!
> Lo, your king comes to you;
>> triumphant and victorious is he,
> humble and riding on an ass,
>> on a colt, the foal of an ass.

---

20 In Lam. 4:21, *chaire* is used ironically in a parody of this theme as Edom is told to rejoice while the Daughter of Zion is told in the next verse that God will bring an end to her suffering in exile and punish the "daughter of Edom" (4:22). Arthur Just notes, "Therefore all the occurrences in the LXX of this form of the imperative are at least in proximity to the theme of the daughter of Zion." See Arthur Just, *Luke 1:1–9:50* (St. Louis: Concordia Publishing House, 1996), 66. See De La Potterie, *Mary in the Mystery of the Covenant*, 14; McHugh, *Mother of Jesus*, 39.

I will cut off the chariot from Ephraim
and the war horse from Jerusalem.
And the battle bow shall be cut off,
And he shall command peace to the nations;
His dominion shall be from sea to sea,
and from the River to the ends of the earth.

The Threefold Pattern of the Daughter of Zion Texts

In addition to Luke's unique use of the imperative *chaire*, there are other connections between Luke 1:28 and these same prophetic texts (see immediately above) calling on Zion to rejoice. As Nolland and Green have pointed out, the words the angel uses to address Mary follow the same three-fold formulaic pattern found in these same Daughter Zion texts.[21]

First, there is the call to rejoice. The call to rejoice is followed by an address taking the form of a title: "*kecharitomene*" in Luke 1:28; "daughter of Zion" in Zephaniah 3:14 and Zechariah 9:9; "sons of Zion" in Joel 2:23; and "daughter of Edom" in Lamentations 4:21. Third and finally, a divine attitude or action is mentioned as the reason for rejoicing.

In Zephaniah 3:15–16, the basis for rejoicing is that the Lord, the King, is in their midst, coming to remove their judgment and cast out their enemies. In Zechariah 9:10, the reason for rejoicing is that their king is coming to them to bring peace to the nations and establish his reign to the ends of the earth. In Joel 2:23–24, the reason for rejoicing is that the Lord is vindicating his people, ending the curse of drought and famine while blessing the people with rain and a great harvest.[22] Similarly, Gabriel calls Mary to rejoice because "the Lord is with you" (Luke 1:28).

Therefore, it is not only the imperative *chaire* that links Luke 1:28 with these OT prophetic texts calling Zion to rejoice. The three-fold pattern of *chaire* + address + divine action as the cause of joy in Luke 1:28 is also found specifically in the only OT passages where the imperative *chaire* is found—passages in which *chaire* clearly serves as more than a simple greeting, for these passages invite God's people to rejoice in His saving action.

Mary is not being given an ordinary salutation. She is being addressed in a way that recalls the invitation for Zion to rejoice over God's work of salvation and in particular, over the coming of the King as in Zephaniah 3:14–15 and Zechariah 9:9. Nolland states, "Mary here is greeted with a mini-oracle of salvation."[23] De La Potterie goes further by arguing that Luke links Mary with Daughter Zion of old.

---

21 Green, *The Gospel of Luke*, 87; Nolland, *Luke 1–9:20*, 49–50.

22 In Lam. 4:21, where this three-fold pattern is used in a parody to mock Edom, the cause for this ironic rejoicing is the cup of judgment that is about to fall upon Edom.

23 Noland, *Luke 1–9:20*, 50.

He notes how in these OT texts, Daughter Zion was given the command to rejoice over the future saving work of God. Now, Mary is being given this command in Luke 1:28: "The joy which was announced by the prophets in the Old Testament to the people of Israel—the Woman Zion—diffuses itself and comes to be focused on one particular woman, Mary, who unites in her person, so to speak, the desires and the hopes of all the people of Israel."[24] Such a view would fit well with how Mary serves as a representative figure in the Magnificat where the celebrated blessings bestowed on her (1:46–50) are commonly seen as anticipating the blessings God desires to bestow on all of Israel (1:51–55).[25] Since the woman Zion figure of the OT represented the faithful Israelites, Mary's association with Daughter Zion in Luke 1:28 could be seen as laying a foundation for Luke's further development of Mary embodying the hopes of Israel.

Coherence with the Royal Messianic Themes in Luke 1–2

Seeing *chaire* in Luke 1:28 as a call to rejoice that is reminiscent of the Daughter Zion oracles fits the royal messianic themes in Luke 1–2 and specifically in the annunciation scene in 1:26–38. As the angel's message to Mary unfolds, Luke underscores how Mary's child will be the long-awaited messiah-king. The angel announces that the child will be given "the throne of his father David" (1:32)—an image that presents Jesus as fulfilling Nathan's promise for the Davidic dynasty in which God would establish "the throne of his kingdom forever" (2 Sam. 7:13).[26] Furthermore, Gabriel pronounces how the child will "reign over the house of Jacob forever"[27] and says "of his kingdom there will be no end" (1:33). Gabriel's words elucidate even more clearly Jesus' royal status in terms of the hopes surrounding the Davidic covenant (2 Sam. 7:13; Ps. 89:36f.; Isa. 9:6f.).[28]

---

24 De La Potterie, *Mary in the Mystery of the Covenant*, 16.

25 See Brown, *Mary in the New Testament*, 141–143; Joel Green, *The Gospel of Luke*, 98–105; Tannenhill, *Luke* (Nashville: Abingdon Press, 1995), 55.

26 According to Evans, the child being given "the throne of his father David" by God could be "an extension of Jesus' title 'Son of the Most High' expressed in terms of the Davidic king who was called God's Son (Ps. 2:7)." See Craig Evans, *Saint Luke* (London: SCM Press, 1990),162. See also J. Fitzmyer, *Luke*, 348. See also Ellis who notes how 4QFlor intertwines the messianic "Son of God" with a never-ending kingship by using the same passage 2 Sam. 7:10–14 (E. Ellis, *The Gospel of Luke* [London: Nelson, 1966], 71).

27 "Jacob" was an ancient designation for Israel (Gen. 46:27; Exod. 19:3; Isa. 8:17). Thus, these words refer to the child being king over all of Israel. See Johnson, *Luke*, 37. With this background, the child reigning "over the house of Jacob" probably recalls how David was the king who ruled over all of Israel. As Deiss explains, "Like David Jesus possesses the throne of Jerusalem and at the same time is king over the house of Jacob. The unification of the North and the South achieved under David was thus a prophetic foreshadowing of the spiritual unification that Jesus would accomplish, a thousand years later, in the messianic kingdom." L. Deiss, *Mary: Daughter of Zion*, 39.

28 Fitzmyer (*Luke*, 348) comments: "Possibly Luke alludes here to Isa. 9:6 (LXX) or to Daniel 7:14, where promise of an everlasting kingdom is made. The endless character of this kingship is thus

The clear parallels between Luke 1:32–33 and the Davidic covenant promises described in 2 Sam. 7:9–16 are often noted.[29] Brown, for example, shows how Gabriel's words are a "free interpretation" of Nathan's oracle which became the foundation for Jewish messianic hopes (see more on this below).[30] Clearly, one of the main messages given to Mary in Luke's annunciation scene is that she will be the mother of the messiah-king.

Interpreting the angel's opening word *chaire* in 1:28 as recalling the prophetic call to rejoice in the coming of the king (Zeph. 3:14–15; Zech. 9:9) would prepare the reader (and Mary as a character in Luke's narrative) for Gabriel's explicit announcement of the coming of the king.

Queen Mother

Our second consideration of Marian typology in Luke 1 focuses on Mary as queen mother. In this section, we will first examine the role of the queen mother in the Old Testament. Second, we will look at how Luke chapter 1 portrays Mary in ways that recall this royal maternal office in the Davidic kingdom.

The Queen Mother in the Davidic Kingdom

The king's mother played an important role in many ancient near eastern kingdoms. She was known to have influenced political, military, economic, and cultic affairs in the royal court and played a key part in the process of dynastic succession. In fact, it was generally the king's *mother* who ruled as queen, not the king's wife. We see this in Hittite, Ugaritic, Egyptian, and Assyrian kingdoms, as well as in ancient Israel.[31]

---

one of the qualities of the messianic kingdom. At this point in the Lukan Gospel the kingship should be understood in terms of the OT theme of kingdom (e.g. as in Ps. 45:7). Jesus in some sense is to be anointed descendant of David and restorer of ancient kingship (Amos 9:11)."

29 Numerous scholars have discussed these parallels. For example: E. Schillebeeckx, *Mary, Mother of the Redemption* (New York: Sheed and Ward, 1964), 9; J. Fitzmyer, *Luke*, 338–339; J. Green, *The Gospel of Luke*, 88; L. Deiss, *Mary: Daughter of Zion*, 38–39; R. Brown, *Birth of the Messiah*, 310–311; R. Nelson, "David: A Model for Mary in Luke?" *Biblical Theology Bulletin* 18 (Oct. 1988): 139; A. Valentini, "Editoriale: L'Annuncio a Maria," *Theotokos* 4 (1996): 286.

30 R. Brown, *Birth of the Messiah*, 310–311. Brown shows how Gabriel quotes that promise from 2 Samuel 7 "in a slightly rephrased manner" (which he notes was customary at the time, as is seen in the Dead Sea Scrolls). R. Brown, "The Annunciation to Mary, the Visitation, and the Magnificat," 253.

31 See Ted Sri, *Queen Mother: A Biblical Theology of Mary's Queenship* (Steubenville, Ohio: Emmaus Road Publishing, 2005), 45–53; "Queen Mother: A Biblical Theology of Mary's Queenship" in *Marian Studies* 56 (2005): 123–154. See also: N. Andreasen, "The Role of the queen Mother in Israelite Society" *Catholic Biblical Quarterly* 45 (1983): 179–194; L. Schearing, "Queen" in D. Freedman, ed., *The Anchor Bible Dictionary*, 6 vols. (New York: Doubleday, 1992), 5:583–588; R. De Vaux, *Ancient Israel* (New York: McGraw-Hill, 1961), 115–119; G. Kirwin, *The Nature of the Queenship of Mary* (Ann Arbor, Michigan: UMI Dissertation Services, 1973), 297–312.

The importance of the monarch's mother may seem strange to some modern readers, but one must recall that most ancient near eastern kings practiced polygamy and had large harems. Although the king may have had many wives, he only had one mother, and the queenship was given to her. This is what one finds in ancient Israel, where the king's mother was given preeminence over all the women in the kingdom of Judah, even over the king's wives. She was given the title *Gebirah*—or "Great Lady"—and reigned as queen in her son's kingdom.

The queen mother's *importance* is expressed in many Old Testament passages. For example, the succession narratives of 1 and 2 Kings present the mother of the king as having such importance that almost every time a new Davidic king is introduced in the Kingdom of Judah, the *mother's* name also is mentioned, but the wife's name is not. Thus, at the crucial transition points of dynastic succession, the narrative consistently highlights the queen mother's important place alongside the new king. As one commentator has explained, "On the throne the queen mother represented the king's continuity with the past, the visible affirmation of God's ongoing plan for his people, the channel through which the Lord's dynastic promise to David was fulfilled."[32]

Second, the Old Testament shows how the queen mother held an *official position in the kingdom of Judah*. She wears a crown (Jer. 13:18) and sits on a throne (1 Kings 2:19; cf., Jer. 13:18). In 2 Kings 24, the queen mother is listed among the members of the royal court whom King Jehoiachin surrenders to the king of Babylon. In this passage, the queen mother is the first of the king's royal court listed as being given over to Babylon to go into exile (2 Kings 24:12-15). Miguens notes how this highlights the queen mother's preeminence in the royal court:

> ... she is mentioned *before* the "wives of the king" (2 Kings 24:15) and before the ministers, dignitaries, and officers (2 Kings 24:12, 15; Jer. 29:2). Significantly, these biblical passages say that the *gevirah* is the second, only to the king, in the list of prominent official persons brought into captivity. This detail speaks very highly of the political significance of the mother of the king.[33]

Third, the queen mother had real *royal authority*, participating in her son's reign. She did not merely hold an honorary "figure head" position. For example, consider the following prophecy, which the prophet Jeremiah addresses both to the king and to the queen mother:

---

32 G. Montague, *Companion God: A Cross-Cultural Commentary on the Gospel of Matthew* (New York: Paulist Press, 1989), 92.

33 Manuel Miguens, *Mary "The Servant of the Lord": An Ecumenical Proposal* (Boston: St. Paul Editions, 1978), 65.

> Say to the king and the queen mother: "Take a lowly seat, for
> your beautiful crown has come down from your head ... Lift up
> your eyes and see those who come from the north. Where is the
> flock that was given you, your beautiful flock?" (Jer. 13:18,20)

In this passage God tells the prophet to address both the king and the queen
mother. The prophecy thus recognizes the queen mother's important royal office.
In ominous imagery, the king and queen mother are told to "take a lowly seat"—
symbolizing how both had thrones, but would lose them soon. Moreover, both are
told that they will lose their crowns—also foreshadowing their political downfall.
Most of all, both king and queen are described as having the responsibility to shepherd the flock of the people of Judah, a flock that is about to be taken away from
them: "Where is the flock that was given you, your beautiful flock?" The important
point for our purposes is to note how this prophecy portrays the queen mother as
participating in the king's reign: she has a throne and a crown with the king, and
she shares in the king's mission of shepherding the people.[34]

The best example of the queen mother's royal authority can be seen in 1
Kings 1–2. Here we can observe the stark contrast between Bathsheba's role in the
kingdom when she was the *wife* of the king compared to her role when she became
the *mother* of the king. In 1 Kings 1, her husband David, the king, is still alive, so
she is just the king's wife. When she wants to enter the royal chamber to meet him,
she bows before her husband and pays him homage (1 Kings 1:16). As she leaves
she honors the king, saying, "May David live forever!" (1 Kings 1:31).

In 1 Kings 2, however, David has died and Bathsheba's son Solomon has
ascended the throne, making her queen mother. When she enters the royal chamber this time as *mother* of the king, she is treated much differently than when she
was just the *wife* of the king. The narrative tells not of Bathsheba bowing before
the king, but of King Solomon rising and bowing down before *her*. Then Solomon
has a throne brought in for her, symbolizing her royal status. Even more striking
is the place where Solomon places Bathsheba's royal seat: at his right hand. The
queen mother being seated at the king's right hand has great significance, for in the
Bible, the right is a position of authority and supreme honor.[35] As Gray observes,

---

34   T. Gray, "God's Word and Mary's Royal Office," *Miles Immaculatae* 13 (1995): 378–79. See also:
L. Schearing, "Queen," 585; M. Miguens, *Mary, Servant of the Lord*, 64–65.

35   Andreasen comments: "She was seated at his right, the place offered to the king by God (Ps
110:1), i.e., she took precedence above all others." See Andreasen, "The Role of the Queen
Mother in Israelite Society," 189, n. 59. This is seen in particular in Psalm 110 ("Sit at my right
hand until I make your enemies your footstool"). In fact, the New Testament refers to the "right
hand" imagery of Psalm 110 to express Christ's reign with the Father over the whole universe.
For example, the author of Hebrews cites this verse from Psalm 110 to show how Christ is above
all the angels since he sits at the right hand of the Father, sharing in his Father's dominion over
all creation (Heb. 1:13; compare Heb. 1:3).

"Nowhere else in the Bible does the king honor someone as Solomon does the Gebirah."[36]

Fourth, the queen mother often *served as a counselor to the king*.[37] We have some evidence of this in the Old Testament. For example, in Proverbs 31, a queen mother gives wise counsel to her son about how to serve the poor, rule the people with justice, avoid too much alcohol, and choose a good wife. Although not always quite so positive in nature, the queen mother's counsel seems to have had the ability to greatly influence affairs in the kingdom. 2 Chronicles 22:3, for example, tells how King Ahaziah "walked in the ways of the house of Ahab [an evil king], for his mother was his counselor in doing wickedly." This shows how at least this particular queen mother's counsel was so influential that it led the king into wickedness.

Fifth, the Gebirah also served as an *advocate for the people in ancient Israel*.[38] She played an intercessory role, taking petitions from the people and presenting them to the king. Her intercessory function can be seen in the passage from 1 Kings 2 when Bathsheba went to meet her royal son Solomon. In the context, Solomon has been crowned king and Bathsheba has thus become queen mother. Her new intercessory power is immediately recognized when a man named Adonijah asks Bathsheba to bring a petition of his to the king. Adonijah expresses great confidence in her intercessory role, saying "Pray ask King Solomon—he will not refuse you" (1 Kings 2:17). Bathsheba agrees and then goes to the king. After she is welcomed by the king, who bows before her and gives her a throne at his right hand, Bathsehba tells Solomon she has a small request to bring to him. Solomon responds by saying "Make your request my mother, for I will not refuse you." Indeed, Solomon's words reveal the king's ordinary commitment to the queen mother's petitions.[39]

---

36 T. Gray, "God's Word and Mary's Royal Office," 377.

37 P. De Boer, "The Counselor," *Vetus Testamentum Supplements* 3 (Leiden: Brill, 1955): 54; Andreasen, "The Role of the Queen Mother in Israelite Society," 190–191.

38 P. De Boer, "The Counselor," 60–61; Andreasen, "The Role of the Queen Mother in Israelite Society," 194.

39 See F. Rossier, *L'intercession Entre les Hommes dans la Bible Hébraique*, Orbis Biblicus et Orientalis 152 (Gottingen: Vandenhoeck & Ruprecht, 1996), 189, who states: "On a même vu en elle, dans cette perspective, quelqu'un susceptible de représenter les intérêts du peuple à la cour. Dans de telles circonstances, Adoniah n'aurait pu choisir meilleure avocate ou meilleur intercesseur. Le fait que la reine-mère jouit de l'autorité sur toutes les femmes de la maison royale a son importance pour Adoniah vu que sa requête a justement une de ces femmes pour object." Also, see Gray's important note ("God's Word and Mary's Royal Office," 381, n. 16): "The fact that Solomon denies the request in no way discredits the influence of the Gebirah. Adonijah wanted Abishag the Shunammite for the treacherous purpose of taking over the kingdom from Solomon." Taking the king's concubine was a sign of usurping the throne in the ancient Near East. For example, see how Absalom (Adonijah's older brother), in his attempt to take the throne from David, took his concubines (2 Sam. 16:20–23). Gray continues ("God's Word and Mary's Royal Office," 381, n. 16): "Thus *the wickedness of Adonijah's intention is the reason for denial, which in no way reflects negatively upon the Gebirah's power to intercede. The narrative bears out the fact that the king normally accepted the Gebirah's request, thus Solomon*

The Emmanuel Prophecy in Isaiah 7:14

So far, we have seen the role of the queen mother in the Davidic kingdom. She held an official position in the royal court, sharing in the shepherding responsibilities of the king and serving as a counselor for the king and as an advocate for the people. But the importance of the queen mother also is seen in Israel's prophetic tradition, particularly in the Emmanuel prophecy of Isaiah 7:14. This passage, filled with strong Davidic overtones, is important for our study because it later was related specifically to Mary and Jesus in the New Testament (Matt. 1:23). However, this passage must first be examined in its original context.

The prophecy is portrayed as coming during a period of dynastic crisis. Syria and the Northern Kingdom of Israel threaten to invade the Kingdom of Judah. Ahaz, the king of Judah, fears that the dynasty may be coming to an end with him (Isa. 7:1–6). Isaiah is sent by God to assure a doubting Ahaz that the kingdom will survive this foreign threat and to challenge him to entrust his throne to the Lord. Isaiah then gives a sign to the house of David that will serve as a confirmation of Yahweh's protection of the Davidic dynasty:

> Here then O house of David! Is it too little for you to weary men,
> that you weary my God also? Therefore the Lord himself will
> give you a sign. Behold, a young woman [*almah*] shall conceive
> and bear a son and shall call his name Immanuel. (Isa. 7:13-14)

The child most likely represents an heir to the Davidic throne.[40] Such a view best demonstrates how this sign for the house of David relates to the immediate context of the dynastic crisis at hand. Not only is the Davidic line in danger of expiring (Isaiah 7:6) but as a result, God's faithfulness to the Davidic dynasty is called into question (see 2 Sam. 7:11–14). It is within this setting that Isaiah specifically addressed "the house of David" with this oracle announcing the Immanuel child in 7:14. Given this context, it is likely that the child represents some type of dynastic sign guaranteeing the succession of the endangered Davidic line.

This view finds further support in that the child's name ("God with us") is bound up with the idea of the preservation of the Davidic dynasty. Since God promised to be "with" the sons of David in a special way (2 Sam. 7:9; 1 Kings 1:37;

---

says, 'Ask, I will not refuse you.' To say then that this illustrates the weakness of the Gebirah's ability to intercede would be to miss the whole point of the narrative, which tells how Adonijah uses the queen mother's position in an attempt to become king" (my emphasis). For more on the political symbolism of usurping a member of a king's harem, see Roland De Vaux, *Ancient Israel* (New York: McGraw-Hill, 1961), 116.

40 R. Clements, *Prophecy and Covenant* (Naperville, Illinois: Alec R. Alleson, 1965), 51, n. 51; S. Mowinckel, *He That Commeth* (New York: Abingdon, 1954), 117; J. McKenzie, "Royal Messianism," *Catholic Biblical Quarterly* 19 (1957): 41, 43; R. Brown, "God's Future Plans for His People," in R. Brown, et. al., eds., *The New Jerome Biblical Commentary* (London: Geoffrey Chapman, 1989), 1311; H. Wildberger, *Isaiah 1–12* (Minneapolis: Fortress, 1991), 311–312.

Ps. 89:22, 25; 1 Kings 11:38), the sign of a child named "Immanuel" gives assurance that God will remain faithful to his promise to the Davidic dynasty: God will still be with his people even through this crisis in which the House of David appears to be crumbling.[41] All this strongly supports an understanding of the child as a successor to the Davidic throne—an heir to King Ahaz who would continue the dynasty.

Once it is established that the Immanuel child would have been viewed as a future Davidic king, one can see how the *almah* would have been understood as the mother of the king. Furthermore, in this oracle addressed specifically to the Davidic household (Isa. 7:13), the young woman bearing the royal son, an heir to the throne, would have been understood as a queen mother.[42] With Isaiah's overriding concern for dynastic succession in the house of David, it is fitting that this prophecy links the royal son with his queen mother, who played an important role in dynastic succession and in the royal court.

The Annunciation to Mary (Luke 1:26–38)

The Third Gospel evokes many Davidic kingdom themes in its infancy narrative.[43] In the annunciation scene, Luke presents Mary's vocation as mother of the messiah within a Davidic kingdom framework. She is introduced in the narrative as being betrothed to a man who is "of the house of David" (Luke 1:26). Luke mentions this detail of Joseph's heritage in order to prepare the reader for understanding Jesus as a Davidic heir.[44]

The angel's announcement to her in Luke 1:32–33 highlights that her child will be the son of David, fulfilling the promises God made to David in 2 Samuel 7.

---

41   H. Wildberger, *Isaiah 1–12*, 311–312. See also, F. Moriarty, "Isaiah 1–39" in R. Brown, et. al., eds., *The Jerome Biblical Commentary* (Englewood Cliffs, New Jersey: Prentice Hall, 1968), 271: "The child about to be born, therefore, may be the young Hezekiah in whose birth Judah would see the continuing presence of God among his people and another renewal of the promise made to David."

42   A. Serra, "Bibbia," in S. De Fiores and S. Meo, eds., *Nuovo Dizionari di Mariologia* (Milan: Edizioni San Paolo, 1996), 219; G. Montague, *Companion God*, 93–94; C. Stuhlmueller, "The Mother of Emmanuel (Is. 7:14)," *Marian Studies* 12 (1961): 185–192; H. Cazelles, "La Mère du Roi-Messie dans L'Ancien Testament," in *Mater et Ecclesia*, vol. 5 (Congressus Mariologicus Lourdes, 1958), 51–52.

43   See M. Strauss, *The Davidic Messiah in Luke-Acts: The Promise and its Fullfillment in Lukan Christology*, Journal for the Study of the New Testament Supplement Series 110 (Sheffield: Sheffield Academic Press, 1995), 75–125; D. Bock, *Proclamation from Prophecy and Pattern: Lukan Old Testament Christology*, Journal for the Study of the New Testament Supplement Series 12 (Sheffield: Sheffield Academic Press, 1987), 55–90.

44   J. Green comments: "Joseph—who has scarcely any role in Luke 1–2 and is only mentioned otherwise in 3:23—receives more of an introduction than Mary, the primary character in the birth narrative. Why? Luke is interested in his royal ancestry. He is 'of the house of David' (v. 27), and this prepares for the identification of his (albeit adopted) son as a Davidide." See J. Green, *The Gospel of Luke* (Grand Rapids: Eerdmans, 1997), 84–85.

First, she is told by Gabriel that her son will be called "Son of the Most High" (1:32). Since "Most High" was a title for God in the Old Testament and a common divine title in Luke as well,[45] the description of Jesus as "Son of the Most High" would refer to him as son of God. This expression also could be understood in light of the Old Testament designation of the Davidic king as God's son. Thus, Jesus as "Son of the Most High" likely recalls Nathan's oracle (2 Sam. 7:14) and the royal Psalms (Ps. 2:7; 89:26–27; compare Ps. 110:1)—which describe the Davidic king as having a special filial relationship with God.

That this is the primary meaning of the child's divine sonship in 1:32 is made clearer in the following verses, which include even more direct allusions to the Davidic covenant and thus bring Jesus' kingship into sharper focus. The angel goes on to tell Mary that her child will be given "the throne of his father David" (Luke 1:32), showing Jesus as fulfilling Nathan's promise for the Davidic dynasty in which God would establish "the throne of his kingdom forever" (2 Sam. 7:13). When the angel describes how the child will "reign over the house of Jacob forever" and says "of his kingdom there will be no end" (Luke 1:33), these words further explicate Jesus' kingship in terms of the hopes surrounding the Davidic dynasty (2 Sam. 7:13; Ps. 89:36f; Is. 9:6f).

Further, the following appear to be clear parallels between Luke 1:32–33 and the promises God made to David in 2 Sam. 7:9–16: both passages involve a great name, a throne, divine sonship, house, and kingdom. Indeed, Gabriel's words draw upon Nathan's oracle, a foundational Old Testament passage for Jewish messianic hopes.[46] Brown sums up the parallels in the following chart:

Luke 1:

32a: He will be great and will be called Son of the Most High.

32b: And the Lord God will give him the throne of his father David,

33a: and he will be king over the House of Jacob forever,

33b: and there will be no end to his kingdom.

---

45   Fitzmyer notes how Luke uses this title for God more than any other New Testament author: Luke 1:35, 76; 6:35; 8:28; Acts 7:48; 16:17. See J. Fitzmyer, *The Gospel According to Luke* (Garden City, New York: Doubleday, 1981), at 348.

46   R. Brown, *Birth of the Messiah* (New York: Doubleday, 1993), 310–311.

2 Samuel 7:

> 9:   I shall make for you a *great* name ...
> 13: I shall establish *the throne of his kingdom forever*.
> 14: I shall be his father, and he will be *my* son ...
> 16: And your *house* and your *kingdom* will be made sure *forever*.[47]

With these words of Gabriel, Jesus is clearly identified as the Davidic messiah. Therefore, the narrative shows that Mary is given the vocation of being mother of the king.

This obvious Davidic background is the reason why some have suggested that the queen mother tradition may be in the background of the annunciation scene.[48] Indeed, this passage portrays Mary as a mother linked with the house of David and giving birth to a Davidic son. Especially since Luke places this scene in the context of the Davidic kingdom, it seems that Mary's role should be understood in light of that Davidic tradition as well. In that context, Mary, as mother of the Davidic king, could be seen as queen mother of her royal son. So concludes Susan Ackerman: "If Jesus is characterized as the royal messiah, Israel's new king, then Mary, at least figuratively, is depicted as queen mother."[49]

In summary, we have attempted to understand Mary in light of the Davidic kingdom tradition which Luke's narrative strongly evokes. Viewing Mary within this context leads us to conclude that, as the mother of the king, she could be seen as queen mother. Along these lines, Cazelles has pointed out that while the angel's words speak of Jesus as the messiah-king, they also provide a basis for Mary's royal maternity:

> One could not more explicitly announce the birth of the messiah who was waited for and announced by the prophets. However, by speaking directly to the mother of the messiah, the angel implicitly evoked the woman who was the mother of the king,

---

47 Brown, *Birth of the Messiah*, 310.

48 S. De Fiores, "Regina: Approfondimento Teologico Attualizzato," in S. De Fiores and S. Meo, eds., *Nuovo Dizionario di Mariologia* (Milan: Edizioni San Paolo, 1996), 1080–1081; A. Serra, "Regina," 1073–1074; J. Ibáñez and F. Mendoza, *La Madre del Redentor* (Madrid: Ediciones Palabra, 1988), 290; S. Ackerman, "The Queen Mother and the Cult of the Ancient Near East," in K. King, ed., *Women and Goddess Traditions* (Minneapolis: Fortress, 1997), 196; G. Del Moral, "Santa María, La Guebiráh Messiánica," *Communio* (Spanish Edition) 13 (1980): 82–108; Timothy Gray, "God's Word and Mary's Royal Office," 384; H. Cazelles, "La Mère du Roi-Messie," 55–56; A. Valentini, "Lc 1, 39–45: Primi Inizi di Venerazione delle Madre del Signore," *Marianum* 58 (1996): 348.

49 Ackerman, "The Queen Mother and the Cult of the Ancient Near East," 196.

linked to her son. It is thus that these words contain a theology of the queenship of Mary.[50]

The Visitation (Luke 1:39–45)

Luke's account of Mary's visit to Elizabeth offers further support for viewing Mary in light of the Old Testament queen mother traditions. Elizabeth's greeting to Mary using the title "the mother of my Lord" (Luke 1:43) is charged with great royal significance that points to Mary as the mother of the king, the queen mother.

This is the first time Jesus is called "Lord" in Luke-Acts. While *kurios* (LXX translation of the Hebrew *adonai*) was used often in the Old Testament as a circumlocution for avoiding the Tetragrammaton (*Yahweh*), it also referred to the Davidic king (2 Sam. 24:21; 1 Kings 1:13–47) and the royal messiah (Ps. 110:1). As the narrative of Luke-Acts progresses, the title "Lord" eventually comes to refer to Jesus' total authority and places him on par with Yahweh (Acts 2 and 10).[51] However, at this point in the narrative (Luke 1:43), its use is not as clear. Bock explains that its use by Elizabeth is "a prophetic foreshadowing" of Jesus' full identity to be revealed later in the narrative.[52] But in this first use of the title "Lord," "it could be seen to signify simply the Lordship of the Messiah (Luke 20.41–44)."[53]

Precision and clarity might be found in Elizabeth's words to Mary, "And why is this granted me, that the mother of my Lord should come to me?" (Luke 1:43). These words echo 2 Samuel 24:21 where the phrase "my Lord" is used as a royal title honoring King David. Araunah greets David, saying: "Why has my lord the king come to his servant?" (2 Sam. 24:21). If Luke has this OT background in mind, Elizabeth's words in 1:43 would have regal connotations that further present Jesus as a Davidic king.[54]

---

50   H. Cazelles, "La Mère du Roi-Messie," 6.

51   Bock, *Proclamation from Prophecy and Pattern*, 69–70.

52   Bock comments: "Luke's readers may well have understood this fuller sense of κύριος, but the choice of Luke to postpone the defining of this term is still a significant literary point to note." See Bock, *Proclamation from Prophecy and Pattern*, 300, n. 61.

53   Bock continues: "... but in view of Luke's later development of this term, clearly something more is in mind here, though this deeper intention is *not clear by this text alone*. It only emerges from later Lucan usage." See Bock, *Proclamation from Prophecy and Pattern*, 70. While Strauss agrees that "the significance of *kurios* in Lukan theology as a whole must be considered in interpreting this reference," he also stresses that "it is of even greater importance to follow Luke's narrative development and not read ideas into a passage which Luke has not yet presented or clarified." Thus, Strauss also argues that "Lord" here in 1:43 is primarily to be understood in a royal messianic sense. See M. Strauss, *The Davidic Messiah in Luke-Acts*, 96.

54   F. Fearghail comments, "If Elizabeth's inspired words in 1,43 echo Ps. 110, 1 or 2 Sam 24, 21, then the title has a royal connotation here." See F. Fearghail, *The Introduction to Luke-Acts: A Study of the Role of Lk 1,1–4,44 in the Composition of Luke's Two-Volume Work* (Rome: Editrice Pontificio Istituto Biblico, 1991), 134. See also Strauss, *The Davidic Messiah in Luke-Acts*, 95–96; R. Brown, *Birth of the Messiah*, 345.

It could also be significant that the title in 1:43 is not used in an absolute sense, but stands alongside the first person possessive, "*my* Lord." This could further signify its royal messianic meaning, since this expression ("Lord" + first person possessive pronoun) was used in the Old Testament to denote the king and the future messiah.[55] Brown observed, "Both in the Gospel (20:41-44) and in Acts (2:34) Luke uses Ps. 110:1, 'the Lord said to *my Lord*,' to show that Jesus is the Messiah and Son of God; and Elizabeth is recognizing Mary as the mother of 'my Lord' i.e., of the Messiah."[56]

Thus, when Elizabeth calls Mary "the mother of my Lord," these words not only point to Jesus as the messiah, but they also tell us something important about Mary.[57] While recognizing the messianic lordship of Mary's child, Elizabeth, at the same time, acknowledges Mary as the mother of her king. Here it should be pointed out that in the New Testament Mary often is referred to as the "mother of Jesus" or "his mother," but nowhere is she called the "mother of my Lord" except here in 1:43.[58] Thus, this unique title for Mary seems to draw attention to her position not just as mother of Jesus in a general way, but as mother of Jesus specifically in his role as messianic Lord. In other words, Elizabeth, in greeting Mary as "the mother of my Lord," refers to her as *mother of the messiah-king*.[59]

This is why some have seen the words "the mother of my Lord" as pointing to Mary as a queen mother figure.[60] It has been pointed out that in the royal court

---

55 Nolland notes how "my Lord" was a royal court expression which also reflected messianic use in Ps 110:1. See Nolland, *Luke 1–9:20*, 67, 75. Miguens explains that Luke 20:41 and Mark 12:36ff. provide evidence that in New Testament times, "Yahweh said to *my* Lord" (Ps. 110:1) was interpreted messianically. After noting how the phrase "my Lord" was used in Old Testament times to address the king himself and the messiah, he concludes that "my Lord" is "a respectful and courtly description of the Messiah; it is, in practical terms, a messianic title related to the royal dignity of 'the son of David' to whom the 'throne' of David is given, who will 'be king over the house of Jacob,' and whose 'kingdom' will have no end." See Miguens, *Mary: Servant of the Lord*, 61.

56 Brown, *Birth of the Messiah*, 344.

57 "Elisabetta riconosce al tempo stesso l'identità di Maria (la Madre) e di Gesú (il mio Signore)." B. Maggioni, "Esegesi di Lc 1,39–45," *Theotokos* 5 (1997): 19.

58 Miguens, *Mary: Servant of the Lord*, 61.

59 Strauss notes how the context surrounding the narrative of the visitation supports a messianic interpretation for Elizabeth's words "mother of my Lord." Following the description of Jesus as the Davidic messiah in 1:32–33, mother of my Lord in 1:43 "suggests that *kurios* has a 'messianic' sense somewhat equivalent to 'the mother of *my king*.' Strauss, *The Davidic Messiah in Luke-Acts*, 96.

60 X. Pikaza, "La Madre de mi Señor (Lc 1,43)," *Ephemerides Mariologicae* 46 (1996): 421–426; G. Perez, "La Visitacion: El Arca Nuevamente en Camino," *Ephemerides Mariologicae* 43 (1993): 201; B. Ahern, "The Mother of the Messiah," *Marian Studies* 12 (1961): 27–48 at 46–48; A. Feuillet, *Jesus and His Mother* (Still River, Massachusetts: St. Bede's, 1984), 13; A. Valentini, "Lc 1, 39–45," 341–342; M. Miguens, *Mary: Servant of the Lord*, 60–61; G. Kirwin, *The Nature of the Queenship of Mary*, 27–32; D. Bertetto, *Maria La Serva del Signore* (Napoli: Edizioni Dehoniane, 1988), 349–350; M. Cuellar, *María, Madre del Redentor y Madre de la Iglesia* (Barcelona: Editorial Herder, 1990), 108; G. Del Moral, "La Realeza de María segun la Sagrada

language of the ancient near east, the title "Mother of my Lord" would have been used to address the queen-mother of the reigning king (who himself was addressed as "my Lord"; see 2 Sam. 24:21).[61] Thus, within the strong Davidic context of Luke's infancy narrative, Elizabeth addressing Mary with this royal title provides a basis for viewing her in light of the queen mother tradition of the Old Testament.

Conclusion

The methodological approach used in this article to support Mary as Daughter Zion and as queen mother has focused on an examination of Mary in the context of salvation history and on the narrative presentation of Mary in Luke 1. While reference to "extra-Scriptural agents," such as the Church Fathers, the liturgy, or magisterial teaching could be made, this article aimed to explore how much Luke 1 could support these typologies in the literal sense. In other words, are interpretations of Mary as Daughter Zion and Queen just the result of later theological reflection of the Church's councils, theologians, saints, and liturgy? Or can these typological connections developed in the Church's tradition be seen as grounded, at least in part, in the New Testament writer's own presentation of Mary? It was demonstrated that the angel's greeting to Mary in Luke 1:28 presents her in ways that recall the prophecies about lady Zion in the Old Testament. This seems to be a part of Luke's own portrayal of Mary.

It was also shown that Luke's accounts of the annunciation to Mary and her visit to Elizabeth invite us to view Mary in light of the Davidic kingdom traditions which those passages evoke. Here we saw how considering Mary against that Davidic kingdom backdrop could at least shed some important Biblical light on why we should see Mary, the mother of the Davidic king, as the queen mother. Considering Mary more along these lines of what we have called "inter-Biblical typology" can help strengthen the case for these and other typological connections involving Mary in the New Testament.

Escritura," *Ephemerides Mariologicae* 12 (1962): 176; J. Bastero de Eleizalde, "Fundamentos Cristológicos de la Realeza de María," *Estudios Marianos* 51 (1986): 201–211 at 209; T. Gray, "God's Word and Mary's Royal Office," 384–385; A. Serra, "Regina," 1074.

61   Ahern, "The Mother of the Messiah," 28; G. Kirwin, *The Nature of the Queenship of Mary*, 29, n. 72; G. Del Moral, "La Realeza de María segun la Sagrada Escritura," 176; Miguens, *Mary: Servant of the Lord*, 60–62.

Letter & Spirit 8 (2013): 145-159

Qumran and the Concept of
Pan-Israelite Restoration

~: John S. Bergsma :~

Franciscan University of Steubenville

In their so-called "sectarian" documents, the members of the Qumran community show a marked preference for identifying themselves either as "Israel" or "Israelites" (Hebrew: *b'nê yisra'el*, lit. "sons of Israel") rather than as "Judah" or "Judahites" (Hebrew: *yehûdîm*, "Judahites"). This curious phenomenon contrasts sharply with other Second Temple texts (such as the works of Josephus and 1–2 Maccabees).

In this paper, I will first discuss terminology, in order to establish that "Israel" and "Judah," and their respective gentilic formations, are not necessarily synonymous either in the Hebrew Bible or in the Second Temple literature. I will then examine the so-called "foundational documents" of the Qumran community in order to demonstrate the marked preference for self-identification with "Israel" rather than "Judah."[1] Finally, I will discuss the significance of the self-identification with "Israel" for understanding the worldview of the Qumran community.

1. Terminology

"Israel" and "Judah" and their respective gentilic formations are not synonyms in the Hebrew Bible. This may seem obvious, but it is necessary to review the data on this issue, since even in academic biblical scholarship the terminological distinctions are frequently blurred.[2]

In the Hebrew Bible, the term "Israel" usually has one of three referents: (1) the patriarch also called "Jacob"; (2) the nation composed of his descendants, that is, all twelve tribes of "Israel," including Judah; and (3) the Northern Kingdom, composed of the ten northern tribes, *to the exclusion of Judah*.[3] This last meaning, in which "Israel"

---

1 The term "foundational documents" is taken from S. Talmon, "The Community of the Renewed Covenant: Between Judaism and Christianity," *The Community of the Renewed Covenant: The Notre Dame Symposium on the Dead Sea Scrolls*, eds. Eugene Ulrich and James C. Vanderkam; Christianity and Judaism in Antiquity Series 10 (Notre Dame, Ind.: University of Notre Dame Press, 1995), 3–24, especially 11. Talmon identifies these documents as: the Community Rule (1QS), the Rule of the Congregation (1QSa), the Damascus Document (CD), the Pesher on Habakkuk (1QpHab), the War Scroll (1QM), the Temple Scroll (11QT), and "to some extent" the Hodayot Scroll (1QH).

2 For discussion of the issues one may see G. Harvey, *The True Israel: Uses of the Names Jew, Hebrew & Israel in Ancient Jewish & Early Christian Literature*, AGAJU 35 (Leiden: E.J. Brill, 1996), which surveys a wide body of literature but frequently renders superficial judgments. Much more useful, though narrower in scope, is Shaye J. D. Cohen, *The Beginnings of Jewishness: Boundaries, Varieties, Uncertainties* (Berkeley: University of California Press, 1999).

3 There are exceptions to these three uses. Some argue that in a few instances in Chronicles,

denotes the Northern Kingdom as opposed to the Southern Kingdom "Judah," predominates in the Former and Latter Prophets. Thus, "Israel" is frequently *contrasted* with "Judah," as in Ezekiel 4:4–8, where the prophet is told to lay on his left side 390 days for the "House of Israel" (Hebrew: *bêth yisra'el*) and on his right side forty days for the "House of Judah" (Hebrew: *bêth yehûdah*). Even the term "all Israel" (*kol yisra'el*) frequently does not include Judah. For example, in 1 Kings 12:20, Jeroboam is made king "over all Israel" (*'al kol yisra'el*), but this obviously does not include the tribe of Judah (or Benjamin either, if they are distinguished from each other).

The exact equivalent of the gentilic "Israelite," (Hebrew: *yisra'eli*), is actually quite rare in the Hebrew Bible, occurring only in Leviticus 24:10–11 and possibly 2 Samuel 17:25.[4] Otherwise, a different genitilic phrase is used, most commonly *b'nê yisra'el* (sons of Israel). It may denote (1) any descendant of Israel, including those from Judah (Exod. 1:17, etc.), or (2) a descendant of the northern ten tribes, excluding those from Judah (1 Kings 12:24, etc.).

Likewise, the term "Judah" (*yehûdah*) in the Hebrew Bible usually denotes either (1) the patriarch of that name (Gen. 29:35, etc.), (2) the tribe composed of his descendants (Num. 1:7, etc.), or (3) the Southern Kingdom under the House of David (1 Kings 15:1), which also included Levites and Benjaminites (1 Kings 12:21, 23).

The gentilic of "Judah," namely *yehûdî* (sg.) or *yehûdîm* (pl.), is rare and late in the Hebrew Bible. Most of the biblical occurrences (77 of about 92) are in Esther, Ezra, or Nehemiah—three of the least-attested biblical books at Qumran. There need be little doubt that all of the biblical texts in which *yehûdî* occurs were composed in the exile or afterward, and with one exception (1 Chron. 4:18) all purport to describe events in the very late Judean monarchy, the exile, or the post-exilic period.[5] Josephus asserted the exilic origin of the term:

> From the time they went up to Babylon they were called by this name [*ioudaioi*] after the tribe of Judah. As the tribe was the first to come from those parts, both the people themselves and the country have taken their name from it. (Ant. 11:173)

"Israel" refers to the southern kingdom of Judah (2 Chron. 24:5; but compare 2 Chron. 10:19). I would argue that the Chronicler's use of "Israel" in relation to the kingdom of Judah reflects his view that Judah had within it an Israelite (that is, Northern) population (see 2 Chron. 10:17), consisting in part of devout Yahwists of all twelve tribes who relocated to the south after the division of the kingdom (2 Chron. 11:13–17). Thus, the population of Judah is representative of "all Israel." In Ezra-Nehemiah, "Israel" frequently refers to the post-exilic community in Judah: Ezra 6:16; Neh. 7:73; etc. However, Ezra is poorly attested at Qumran and Nehemiah not at all.

4   The term occurs four times in Lev. 24:10–11. Many commentators believe *yisra'eli* in 2 Sam. 17:25 is a corruption of *yishma'eli*.

5   Outside of Esther and Ezra-Nehemiah, the term occurs in 2 Kings 16:5; 25:25; Jer. 32:12; 34:9; 38:19; 40:11, 12; 41:3; 43:9; 44:1; 52:28; Zech. 8:23; Dan. 3:8, 12.

From the Greek *ioudaîos* through the Latin *Judaeus* we derive the English word "Jew." But Shemaryahu Cohen warns that "Jew" in English has become an exclusively religious term—one is a Jew rather than a Christian, Muslim, Hindu, etc.[6] It should be used with great care when translating the Hebrew *yehûdî* and Greek *ioudaîos*, because in antiquity these terms more commonly mean a "Judean" in an ethno-geographic or political sense, not a "Jew" in the religious sense.[7] After analysis of the relevant ancient texts, Cohen concludes:

> All occurrences of the term *ioudaîos* before the middle or end
> of the second century BCE should be translated not as "Jew", a
> religious term, but as "Judaean", an ethnic-geographic term.[8]

Thus, Cohen argues, the Greek term *ioudaîos* begins to be applied to non-Judeans as a description of either religion or politics only with the rise of the Maccabean state, which coincided (roughly) with the foundation of the Qumran community. This raises the question, explored below, of whether the Qumranites would have characterized themselves as *yehûdîm* or *ioudaîoi*.

In any event, despite the clear non-synonymity of "Israel" and "Judah" and their respective gentilics in the Hebrew Bible, terminological precision is not maintained in this matter even in professional biblical scholarship. The English term "Jew" is often used (inaccurately and anachronistically) to describe Judeans who are merely ethnically or politically associated with Judea, as well as Israelites of any time period.[9] This confusion begins already with Josephus, who employs *ioudaîoi* indiscriminately to describe the people of Israel back to the time of Samuel at least (e.g. Ant. 6:30 *et passim*). Despite the antiquity of this conflation of terminology, it should be avoided, inasmuch as it leads to confusion and blurs the distinction between ancient Israel and the various forms of Judaism in the minds of students and even scholars themselves.

---

6   Cohen, *Beginnings*, 69.

7   Cohen, *Beginnings*, 69–70. See also E. P. Sanders, "The Dead Sea Sect and Other Jews: Commonalities, Overlaps, and Differences," *The Dead Sea Scrolls in their Historical Context*, ed. Timothy H. Lim (Edinburgh: T&T Clark, 2000), 7–44. Sanders has a rich theological discussion that would benefit from being informed by Cohen's work on the etymology and sociology of the term *ioudaîos*.

8   Cohen, *Beginnings*, 70.

9   For an example of this (errant) usage, see Niels P. Lemche, "The Understanding of the Community in the Old Testament and in the Dead Sea Scrolls," *Qumran between the Old and New Testaments*, eds. Frederick H. Cryer and Thomas L. Thompson; Journal for the Study of the Old Testament, Supplement Series 290; Copenhagen International Seminar 6 (Sheffield: Sheffield Academic Press, 1998), 181–193, especially 188: "Biblical Israel is founded on the Torah ... presented to the Jews [sic] by God on Mount Sinai"; and 189: "According to the Deuteronomistic History ... the Israelites of pre-exilic times were not really Jews [sic], as they almost never fulfilled the requirement of the Covenant and the Law."

In sum, *ioudaioi* (Hebrew *yehûdîm*) and its equivalents should be (and will be in this article) rendered as "Judahites" to avoid unnecessary connotations and confusion.

2. "Israel" and "Judah" as Self-Identifiers in the "Foundational Documents"

The term *yehûdî* occurs only three times in the Dead Sea Scrolls, and never as a term of self-identification. The occurrences are in 4Q242 3:4 (Aramaic fragment of the Prayer of Nabonidus); 4Q333 2 i 1 (unidentified); and 4Q550c 1 i 3 (Esther-like document). Surprisingly, neither *yehûdî* nor *yehûdîm* occurs in what Shemaryahu Talmon calls the "foundational documents" of the community, which "reveal the Covenanter's self-understanding":[10] the Community Rule (1QS), the Rule of the Congregation (1QSa), the Damascus Document (CD), the Temple Scroll (11QT), the War Scroll (1QM) and the Pesher Habakkuk (1QpHab).

The members of the "community" (Hebrew *yahad*) preferred to identify themselves as Israelites, using various phrases such as "the repentant of Israel" (*shavê yisra'el*), the "men of Israel" (*anshê yisra'el*), or "the majority of Israel" (*rôv yisra'el*).

Qumran's Four "Foundational" Documents

The members' self-identification is incontestably evident in Qumran's four "foundational" documents, 1QS, 1QSa, 1QM, and 11QT. In 1QS and 1QSa, the tribe of Judah is never mentioned. The community is identified as "Israel" and its members as "Israelites" in various phrases. We may note the following examples:

> (1) The "rank and file" members of the *Yahad* (community) are denoted as "Israelites," as in this passage describing the order of procession of the community:

> 1QS 2:19 They shall do as follows annually, all the days of Belial's dominion: the priests shall pass in review 20 first, ranked according to their spiritual excellence, one after another. Then the Levites shall follow, 21 and third all the people by rank, one after another, in their thousands and hundreds 22 and fifties and tens. Thus shall *each Israelite* (*kôl 'îsh yisra'el*) know his proper standing in the *Yahad* of God.[11]

> (2) Elsewhere, the *Yahad* is equated with "Israel":

---

10   Talmon, "Community," 11.

11   Unless otherwise noted, all English translations of the scrolls throughout this paper are from Michael O. Wise, Martin G. Abegg, and Edward Cook, *The Dead Sea Scrolls: A New Translation* (San Francisco: HarperSanFrancisco, 1996), available electronically through Accordance® Bible software. Any and all emphasis is my own. I have provided the Hebrew in parentheses for the key phrases on which my arguments are based.

1QS 5:5 ... Together they shall circumcise the foreskin of this nature, this stiff neck, and so establish a foundation of truth *for Israel—that is to say, for the Yaḥad of the Eternal 6 Covenant (l'yisra'el l'yaḥad b'rîth 'ôlam).*

(3) The assembly of the community is described as "the majority of Israel," as in this text prescribing the testing of prospective members:

1QS 5:21 ... They shall investigate his understanding and works vis à vis the Law, guided both by the Sons of Aaron ... 22 ... and by *the majority of Israel (rôv yisra'el)* who have volunteered to return, as a community, to His covenant.

(4) The *Rule of the Congregation* addresses itself from the beginning to the "congregation of Israel":

1QSa 1:1 This is the rule *for all the congregation of Israel (l'kôl 'edath yisra'el)* in the last days.

(5) Members of the congregation are expected to be "native-born Israelites":

1QSa 1:6 The following is the policy for all the troops of the congregation, and it applies *to every native-born Israelite (l'kôl ha'ezrach b'yisra'el).*

(6) The governing structure is based on the ideal of tribal Israel:

1QSa 1:13 ... When he is thirty years old, he may begin to take part in legal disputes. 14 Further, he is now eligible for command, whether of the *thousands of Israel ('alphê yisra'el),* or as a captain of hundreds, fifties or 15 tens, or as a judge or official *for their tribes and clans.*

Suffice it to say that the identification of the *Yaḥad* with "Israel" in 1QS and 1QSa is very strong—but one must also recognize that the community acknowledges an "Israel" that is larger than their community, *in which* and *for which* they exist.[12] Thus, they are an "Israel" within "Israel."

---

12   For example, 1QS 5:6 describes the community as a "house of truth *in* Israel" (*b'yisra'el*); 1QS 6:13 states that "anyone *from* Israel" (*miyyisra'el*) may freely join the community; 1QS 8:5 describes the community as a "holy house *for* Israel" (*l'yisra'el*). Similar statements may be found in the Damascus Document.

In the Temple Scroll (11QT) and the War Scroll (1QM), we see portrayed a utopian vision of the restored twelve-tribe nation of Israel:

> 11QT 24:10 After this burnt offering he shall offer that of the tribe of *Judah* separately. Just as 11 he has performed the burnt offering of the *Levites*, so shall he perform that of the sons of Judah, after the Levites. 12 Then on the second day he shall offer the burnt offering of *Benjamin* first, and afterwards 13 that of the sons of *Joseph* as one, Ephraim and Manasseh. On the third day he is to offer 14 *Reuben's* burnt offering separately, and that of *Simeon* separately. On the fourth day 15 he shall offer the burnt offering of *Issachar*, then that of *Zebulon*, separately. On the fifth day 16 he shall offer *Gad's* burnt offering, then *Asher's*, separately. Finally, on the sixth day 25:1 he shall offer [*Dan's* burnt offering, then *Naphtali's*, separately.]

> 1QM 3:13 Rule of the banners of the whole congregation according to their formations. On the grand banner which is at the head of all the people they shall write, "People of God," the names "Israel" and 14 "Aaron," and the names of the *twelve tribes of Israel* according to their order of birth.

> 1QM 5:1 and on the sh[ie]ld of the Prince of the Whole Congregation they shall write his name, the names "Israel," "Levi," and "Aaron," and the names of *the twelve tribes of Israel* according to their order of birth, 2 and the names of the twelve chiefs of their tribes.

Some might object that the Temple and War Scrolls do not directly address the self-identity of the *Yaḥad*. Instead, they present us with eschatological ideals. However, these eschatological ideals are precisely what the *Yaḥad* wishes to become, and to the extent possible, they are actualizing their ideals in the present. Therefore it should be uncontroversial to say that the War and Temple Scrolls do contribute to our understanding of Qumran self-identity. The *Yaḥad* endeavors to become the functioning, restored twelve-tribe entity of Israel portrayed in these documents.

The evidence from 1QS, 1QSa, 1QM, and 11QT is, taken by itself, strong enough to establish that the community *prefers* an "Israelite" self-appellation over a "Judahite" one. However, the evidence from all the scrolls permits an even stronger claim, namely, that *there is no unambiguous self-identification of the Yaḥad with Judah in the scrolls.*

This claim runs counter to the common assertions that the *Yaḥad* sees itself as "the remnant of Judah" or "the true Judah."[13] Such assertions do not capture the ambition and sweep of the Qumran vision of a restored Israel. More importantly, they are not supported by the texts.

The two key documents from which scholars argue for an identification of the community with "Judah" are the Damascus Document and the *pesharim*.

The Damascus Document

In the Damascus Document (CD), the word "Israel" is used about forty times, of which about fourteen occurrences are either direct or indirect identifications of the community very similar to those found in 1QS and 1QSa. For example, the rank-and-file members of the community are identified as "Israel," as can be seen from the stipulation in CD 10:5 that the judges of the congregation must be composed of ten men, four "from the tribe of Levi and Aaron, and six *from Israel*."[14] Like the Community Rule, the order of procession in the CD is "priests first, Levites second, the *children of Israel* third ..." (CD 14:5–6). The community is also called "the company of Israel": no member is to "take any of their [the gentiles'] riches, lest they blaspheme, except on the advice of *the company of Israel*" (CD 12:8). Another term of self-identification is the "seed of Israel": "In accordance with this regulation shall the *seed of Israel* walk" (CD 12:21–22).

The word "Judah," by contrast, occurs only nine times in CD, of which four are simply quotations of Scripture. Of the remaining five independent uses of "Judah," three are sometimes taken as indicating the identity of the community.

In CD 3:21–4:4 one finds the well-known allegorical interpretation of Ezekiel 44:15:

> CD 3:21 God promised them by Ezekiel the prophet, saying, The priests and the Levites and the sons of 4:1 Zadok who have kept the courses of My sanctuary when the children of Israel strayed 2 from Me, they shall bring Me fat and blood (Ezekiel 44:15). "The priests": they are the *returnees* (or *repentant*) *of Israel*, 3 who go out of the land of Judah and the Levites are those accompanying them; "and the sons of Zadok": they are the *chosen*

---

13   See Ben Z. Wacholder, "Historiography of Qumran: The Sons of Zadok and their Enemies," *Qumran between the Old and New Testaments*, eds. Frederick H. Cryer and Thomas L. Thompson; Journal for the Study of the Old Testament Supplement Series 290; Copenhagen International Seminar 6 (Sheffield: Sheffield Academic Press, 1998), 375; Stephen Goranson, "Others and Intra-Jewish Polemic as Reflected in Qumran Texts," *The Dead Sea Scrolls After Fifty Years: A Comprehensive Assessment*, 2 vols.; eds. Peter W. Flint and James C. Vanderkam (Leiden: E.J. Brill, 1999), 2.534–551, here at 537, 543.

14   The English translations of the CD in this paragraph are from Florentino García Martínez and Eibert J. C. Tigchelaar, *The Dead Sea Scrolls Study Edition*, 2 vols. (Leiden: E. J. Brill, 1997–98).

of 4 Israel, the ones called by name, who are to appear in the last days.

The phrase *shavê yisra'el*, rendered variously as the "repentant," "converts," "return-ees" or "captives" of Israel,[15] is an important self-identification for the community of the Damascus Document. [16] It is repeated elsewhere: for example, in CD 6:2, while commenting on Numbers 21:18, the writer asserts:

> CD 6:2 ... But God remembered the covenant of the forefathers; and He raised up from Aaron insightful men and *from Israel* 3 wise men and He taught them and they dug the well: the well the princes dug, the nobility of the people 4 dug it with a rod (Numbers 21:18). The Well is the Law, and its "diggers" are 5 the *returnees of Israel who went out of the land of Judah* and dwelt in the land of Damascus. . . .

In these passages the Israelite self-appellation is quite apparent: the members of the community are "wise men from Israel," the "returnees of Israel," and the "chosen of Israel."

However, when the Damascus Document describes the community members as those "who went out of the land of Judah" (CD 4:3; 6:5), does this indicate that the authors considered their origins to be from Judah and therefore wished to be considered "Judahites" (*yehûdîm*)?

The response is likely negative. If the authors of the CD wished to be considered *yehûdîm*, they would have called themselves the "returnees of Judah." Indeed, the phrase "who went out of the land of Judah" may well express a desire to *dissociate* with Judah. For example, in Exodus alone there are around thirty variants of the expression "to go/bring out from the land of Egypt," using the same verb-preposition-noun combination found here (see, for example, Exodus 12:41). The Exodus was surely a desire to dissociate with Egypt.

Moreover, the "returnees of Israel" are mentioned in the Damascus Document only four times. Twice the "returnees of Israel" are said to "have gone out from the land of Judah" (4:3; 6:5) and twice they have "turned aside from the path of the people":

> CD 8:16 Such is the verdict on the *returnees of Israel, those who turn away from the way of the people* [repeated at CD 19:28–29].

---

15   Compare the Hebrew of Isa. 20:4; 59:20; Ezra 6:21, Neh. 8:17.

16   See Wacholder, "Historiography," 357. Wacholder opts for "captives." See also Samuel Iwry, "The Exegetical Method of the Damascus Document Reconsidered," *Methods of Investigation of the Dead Sea Scrolls and the Khirbet Qumran Site: Present Realities and Future Prospects*, eds. Michael O. Wise et al.; Annals of the New York Academy of Sciences 722 (New York: New York Academy of Sciences, 1994), 329–338, especially 333–334, where he argues for "returnees."

The two phrases (the *"returnees of Israel"* and *"who went out of the land of Judah"*) may describe the same action—the leaving of the land of Judah indicates dissatisfaction with the "path" the people in Judah were following.

Only a few lines after the first mention of the "returnees of Israel who go out from the land of Judah" in the Damascus Document (i.e. CD 4:2–3), we encounter the text that scholars commonly cite as "proof" that the community self-identifies with "Judah":

> CD 4:10 ... When the total years of this present age are complete, 11 *there will be no more joining with the House of Judah*, but instead each will stand on 12 his own tower (or "siegeworks").

The most common interpretation of these lines identifies the House of Judah as the community. Thus the passage supposedly asserts that in the last days—after the present period of tribulation—it will no longer be necessary to join the *Yaḥad*. The text, however, does not explicitly identify the House of Judah with the community. The identification arises in interpretation. Furthermore, the *Yaḥad's* view of itself, so clearly presented in other documents, is as the vanguard of the eschatological restoration of Israel. In fact, in the eschaton the *Yaḥad* and Israel will be one. How then could CD 4:10–12 be asserting that in the last days, there will no longer be any joining with the *Yaḥad*-Israel?

The passage is admittedly obscure, but there are several alternative interpretations. For example, we have already observed that the designation "returnees of Israel" emphasizes that the community saw themselves as having "left the land of Judah," which probably indicates dissociation from Judah, in parallelism with "turning away from the path of the people." Perhaps in CD 4:10–12, the "House of Judah" stands for the corrupt society that the "returnees" have left.[17] The passage thus asserts that when the present age is over, not only the "returnees" (i.e. the community) but everyone else will no longer join in the sins of the House of Judah. There are other possible interpretations, but, in any event, there is no clear equation of the community with the House of Judah in CD 4:10–12.

There remains one more passage in the CD which gives rise to the scholarly opinion that the community identifies itself with the returned Judean exiles of Babylon. Martin Abegg and others read the following passage as an allegory of the Babylonian exile:[18]

---

17 Talmon seems to take "House of Judah" as a reference to the majority of the people who followed the Pharisees and their form of Judaism. See Talmon, "Community," 22.

18 See Martin Abegg, "Exile and the Dead Sea Scrolls," *Exile: Old Testament, Jewish, and Christian Conceptions*, ed. J. M. Scott; Supplement to the Journal for the Study of Judaism in the Persian, Hellenistic, and Roman Periods 56 (Leiden: E. J. Brill, 1997), 111–125, especially 113–115, 118, 125.

> CD 7:11 … "Days are coming upon you and upon your people and upon your father's house that 12 have never come before, since the departure of Ephraim from Judah" (Isaiah 7:17), that is, when the two houses of Israel separated, 13 Ephraim departing from Judah. All who backslid were handed over to the sword, but all who held fast 14 escaped to the land of the north, as it says, I will exile the tents of your king 15 and the foundation of your images beyond the tents of Damascus (Amos 5:27). The books of Law are the tents of 16 the king, as it says, I will re-erect the fallen tent of David (Amos 9:11). The king is 17 the congregation and the "foundation of your images" is the books of the prophets 18 whose words Israel despised. The star is the interpreter of the Law 19 who comes to Damascus, as it is written, a star has left Jacob, a staff has risen 20 from Israel (Numbers 24:17). The sceptre is the prince of the whole nation; when he appears, he will shatter 21 all the sons of Seth (Numbers 24:17). They escaped in the first period of God's judgment, 8:1 but those who held back were handed over to the sword.

Abegg and others take "Damascus" to mean Babylon, and understand this whole narration as a cryptic description of the Judean exile to Babylon. Thus, the *Yaḥad* is said to view itself as the true remnant of Judah.

However, for CD 7:10–8:1 to refer to the Babylonian exile, "Damascus" has to mean Babylon, "North" has to mean East, and "escaped" has to mean "taken captive." It is difficult to accept all this. As Samuel Iwry,[19] Norman Golb,[20] Ben Zion Wacholder,[21] and others[22] have argued, there are cogent reasons for interpreting "Damascus" as meaning the actual city of *Damascus*.[23]

---

19   See Iwry, "Exegetical Method," 330–332.

20   Golb, quoted in Iwry, "Exegetical Method," 338

21   Wacholder, "Historiography," 357.

22   For example, Phillip R. Callaway, "Methodology, the Scrolls, and Origins," *Methods of Investigation of the Dead Sea Scrolls and the Khirbet Qumran Site: Present Realities and Future Prospects*, eds. Michael O. Wise et al.; Annals of the New York Academy of Sciences 722 (New York: New York Academy of Sciences, 1994), 409–427, at 422; also J. T. Milik, quoted in Iwry, "Exegetical Method," 332; Hartmut Stegemann, quoted in Iwry, "Exegetical Method," 338.

23   I argue here against the "Babylonian exile" interpretation of this passage, but the other common alternative, the "Qumran migration" interpretation (see, for example, Michael A. Knibb, "The Place of the Damascus Document," *Methods of Investigation of the Dead Sea Scrolls and the Khirbet Qumran Site: Present Realities and Future Prospects*, eds. Michael O. Wise et al.; Annals of the New York Academy of Sciences 722 [New York: New York Academy of Sciences, 1994], 149–162, especially 159; compare with 161–162), which sees "Damascus" as a cipher for Qumran as a place of study of the Law (based on Zech. 9:1), is even less likely. Then the claim of the CD that the community "went out from the land of Judah and escaped to the north, to Damascus" *really* means that the community "moved to a different part of Judah, migrating

First, the "sectarian" scrolls speak freely and literally about Babylon and the exile in at least a dozen other passages, including the first column of the Damascus Document itself.[24] There is no reason why the authors of the CD should feel compelled to use a cipher here, especially one as arbitrary as "Damascus." Second, there is no biblical passage that would serve to link Damascus with Babylon.[25] Third, the one element of Amos 5:27 which is *not* allegorized in the CD's interpretation is "Damascus." Therefore, the literal meaning of Damascus is the reason the verse was deployed. The author was seeking some Scriptural justification for a rather bizarre emigration—one to Damascus. Amos 5:27 was the best he could do—but in order to press it into service as a prophecy of a positive sojourn to Damascus, he had to allegorize all the elements of the text *except* the name of the city itself, *whose literal sense he wishes to retain.*

To sum up our review of the Damascus Document: it can be confidently asserted that it contains no unambiguous identification of the community with the "remnant of Judah" or some similar concept.

The Pesharim

There is a consensus that in the *pesharim*, the three groups designated "Judah," "Ephraim," and "Manasseh" correspond to the Essenes, Pharisees, and Sadducees respectively.[26] Stephen Goranson calls this identification one of the most "assured results" of scrolls scholarship.[27] On the basis of the *pesharim*, he asserts "the Essenes saw themselves as the true Judah." It follows that since the Qumranites were Essenes they too saw themselves as the "true Judah."

---

to the southeast of Jerusalem, to Qumran." See the critique of this view by Iwry, "Exegetical Method," 330–332.

24 CD 1:6; 1Q20 21:23; 4Q163 4–6 ii 2; 4Q163 8–10 i 1; 4Q163 25 i 1; 4Q242 1–3 i 1; 4Q244 12 i 3; 4Q266 2 i 11 (=CD 1:6); 4Q385b 16 i 4–6; 4Q386 1 iii 1–3; 4Q552 1 ii 5; 4Q553 6 ii 4; 4Q554 2 iii 19.

25 Callaway, "Methodology," 422.

26 See Ida Frölich, "Qumran Names," *The Provo International Conference on the Dead Sea Scrolls: Technological Innovations, New Texts, and Reformulated Issues,* eds. D.W. Parry and E. Ulrich; Studies on the Texts of the Desert of Judah 30 (Leiden: E.J. Brill, 1999), 294–305, especially 300–303; also George J. Brooke, "The Pesharim and the Origins of the Dead Sea Scrolls," *Methods of Investigation of the Dead Sea Scrolls and the Khirbet Qumran Site: Present Realities and Future Prospects,* eds. Michael O. Wise et al.; Annals of the New York Academy of Sciences 722 (New York: New York Academy of Sciences, 1994), 339–353, especially 346–347; Graham Harvey, *The True Israel,* 41–42; H.J. Zobel, "yᵉhûdâ," *Theological Dictionary of the Old Testament* 5.485–486.

27 Goranson, "Others," 543–544. For some healthy skepticism to balance the "assurance," see Callaway, "Methodology," and Lester Grabbe, "The Current State of the Dead Sea Scrolls: Are There More Answers than Questions?" *The Scrolls and the Scriptures: Qumran Fifty Years After,* eds. Samuel E. Porter and Craig A. Evans; Journal for the Study of the Pseudepigrapha, Supplement Series 26 (Sheffield: Sheffield Academic Press, 1997), 54–67, especially 58–60.

However, when one examines the key *loci* in the *pesharim* that pertain to the relationship of the *Yahad* with this group known as "Judah," the situation becomes more complex than a simple equation between the two. For example, a key passage from 1QpHab 7:17–8:1 reads:

> 1QpHab 7:17 [... "As for the righteous man, by loyalty to him one may find life" (Habakkuk 2:4b).] 8:1 This refers to *all those who do the law in the house of Judah* whom 2 God will rescue from among those doomed to judgment, because of their suffering and their loyalty 3 to the Teacher of Righteousness.

The "doers of the law" are generally understood as the Essenes, based on the derivation of the term "Essene" from Hebrew *'asah*, "to do."[28] What is the relationship of the "doers of the law" to the "House of Judah"? At least some of them are *in it*. They are not simply the "House of Judah," they are "*in* the House of Judah." The text does not specify whether *all* "doers of the law" are "in the House of Judah," nor whether all "in the House of Judah" are also "doers of the law." All that can be known is that the "House of Judah" includes some who "do the law" and are sympathetic to the Teacher of Righteousness. If these are Essenes, then the "House of Judah" includes at least some Essenes.

Another important text from the *pesharim* is found in 1QpHab 11:17–12:1:

> 11:17 ["For the crimes perpetrated against Lebanon he will bury you, for the robbery of beasts,] 12:1 he will smite you; because of murder and injustice in the land, he will destroy the city and all who live in it" (Habakkuk 2:17). The passage refers to the Wicked Priest, that he will be paid back 3 for what he did to the poor, for "Lebanon" refers to 4 *the council of the Yahad*, and "beasts" refers to *the simple of Judah who do* 5 *the Law*.

Here the "council of the *Yahad*"—which is probably a circumlocution for the *Yahad* viewed as a "committee of the whole"—is distinguished from "the simple of Judah." The relationship between the two is not made clear: apparently they are two different groups. There is no equation of the *Yahad* with Judah. The simple of Judah "do the law," so they are presumably Essenes. Whatever "Judah" is, here again we find that it includes "doers of the law."

Also germane to this discussion is another text from the *pesharim*, 4QpPsª:

> 4QpPsª (4Q171) 1 ii 13 "The wicked plots against the righteous and gnashes [his teeth against him. But the Lo]rd laughs at him,

---

28   See, for example, J. C. Vanderkam, "Identity and History of the Community," *The Dead Sea Scrolls After Fifty Years: A Comprehensive Assessment*, eds. P. W. Flint and J. C. Vanderkam (Leiden: E. J. Brill, 1999), 2.487–533, especially 2.490–499; Goranson, "Others," 537–540.

for he knows 14 his day is coming" (Psalm 37:12–13). This refers to *the ruthless of the covenant in the House of Judah* who 15 plot to destroy those who do the Law in the council of the *yaḥad*.

This passage indicates that in addition to "simple folk" and "doers of the law," the "House of Judah" includes "ruthless ones" who wish to destroy the *Yaḥad* (or at least, the "doers of the law" within it).

Based on the above three passages from the *pesharim*, one can safely assert that from the perspective of the *Yaḥad*, the category "Judah" is a mixed bag.[29] "Judah" includes some who are sympathetic to the Teacher of Righteousness, and some who want to destroy the *Yaḥad*. Nowhere is there a one-for-one identification of the *Yaḥad* with "Judah" or even an identification of the "doers of the law" with "Judah." All that can be known with certainty is that there are "doers of the law" in "Judah" and there are "doers of the law" in the *Yaḥad*. There are also enemies of both the *Yaḥad* and the "doers of the law" in "Judah." In sum, the assertion that in the *pesharim* "the Essenes saw themselves as 'the true Judah'" is tenuous at best. Even more tenuous is the assertion that the Qumran *Yaḥad* saw itself as such.[30]

3. Significance

My thesis has been that in the foundational documents of the community, the Qumranites show a marked preference for identifying themselves as "Israel" or "Israelites," even though they implicitly acknowledge that, in the present, "Israel" is a bigger category from which they have come, in which they exist, and for which they exist. In no place is there any clear identification of the community with Judah alone or as composed mainly or solely of "Judahites." That does not mean the community is anti-Judahite. On the contrary, the tribe of Judah has an honored place with the *Yaḥad*. The *Yaḥad*, however, aspires to be all of "Israel," not just "Judah."

How can we explain this evidence? Why does the community avoid simple identification as "Judahites" or "Judeans" when they are in fact living in the land of Judah?

First, the leadership of the community is composed, not of *yehûdîm* (Judahites) but of *levi'îm* (Levites). This is a society governed by priests who are proud of their

---

29 Harvey's assessment on this point is accurate: "'Judah' is applied to both 'good' and 'bad' in Qumran Literature. ... It is applied to both the producers of Qumran Literature and their opponents in other groups" (Harvey, *True Israel*, 41). Despite this insight, Harvey curiously refers to "a distinctive use of the phrase 'House of Judah' as a name for the Community" on the same page (Harvey, *True Israel*, 41).

30 One other passage of the *pesharim* merits discussion: 4QpNah (4Q169) 3:2–5: The "glory of Judah" I take to be the royal messiah, and the "majority of Israel"—which the simple of Ephraim join—is clearly a technical term for the *yaḥad* (cf. 1QS 5:22). That "Ephraim" contains "simple folk"—a class of people elsewhere described as "doers of the law" [Essenes] and included in "Judah" (compare 1QpHab 12:4–5)—militates against a simple equation of "Ephraim" with the Pharisees. Whatever "Ephraim" is in the *pesharim*, it is a complex category, including (like Judah) both good and bad, both (evil) deceivers and (innocent) deceived.

Levitical, Aaronic, and Zadokite lineages. The tribe that consistently is given primacy in the documents is Levi, *followed by* Judah. Since the Levitical/Zadokite leadership of the *Yaḥad* probably wrote many of the documents themselves, they strongly resist suppressing their own tribal heritage under that of Judah.

Second, the *Yaḥad* exhibits what Talmon calls "self-implantation in the world of biblical Israel."[31] They are living in the biblical world, and they use their terms as the Bible uses them. Thus, they realize that "Judah" does not mean "Israel" and vice-versa, even if some of their contemporaries were beginning to mix the terms.

Third, the *Yaḥad* is actively anticipating the *eschatological, pan-Israelite restoration of the twelve tribes*. In terms of their self-identity, they are the vanguard, the spearhead of the incoming of the lost tribes in the eschatological era. After all, the restoration and reunification of the Northern and Southern Kingdoms, of all twelve tribes, was consistently proclaimed by the three great prophets (Isaiah, Jeremiah, and Ezekiel):

> In that day the LORD will extend his hand yet a second time to recover the remnant which is left of his people, from Assyria, from Egypt, from Pathros, from Ethiopia, from Elam, from Shinar, from Hamath, and from the coastlands of the sea. He will raise an ensign for the nations, and will assemble the outcasts of Israel [Northern Kingdom], and gather the dispersed of Judah [Southern Kingdom] from the four corners of the earth. (Isa. 11:11–12 RSV)

> Therefore, behold, the days are coming, says the LORD, when men shall no longer say, 'As the LORD lives who brought up the people of Israel out of the land of Egypt,' but 'As the LORD lives who brought up and led the descendants of the house of Israel [Northern Kingdom] out of the north country and out of all the countries where he had driven them.' (Jer. 23:7–8 RSV)

> Say to them, Thus says the Lord GOD: Behold, I am about to take the stick of Joseph (which is in the hand of Ephraim) and the tribes of Israel associated with him; and I will join with it the stick of Judah, and make them one stick, that they may be one in my hand. ... and I will make them one nation in the land, upon the mountains of Israel; and one king shall be king over them all; and they shall be no longer two nations, and no longer divided into two kingdoms. (Ezek. 37:19–22 RSV)

---

31   Talmon, "Community," 12.

Fourth, the *Yaḥad* did not see the Hasmonean or Herodian Judean state as the true successor of biblical Israel. Nor was the return of the *yehûdîm* from Babylon the fulfillment of the prophecies of restoration as foretold in the prophets. It could not have been: only one tribe returned—or, at best, three, if Levi, Judah, and Benjamin are counted separately. But the prophets foresaw a pan-Israelite restoration which included the ten northern tribes.

In conclusion, although in our academic schemas we place the Qumran community into the category "Second Temple Judaism,"[32] their own worldview is more accurately described as Second Temple *Israelitism*.[33] This is not an issue of small importance, for as Talmon remarks:

> We should avoid applying a vocabulary to the description of the Community of the Renewed Covenant which tends to obfuscate its specific identity and which is prone to predetermine the conclusions of the proposed analysis.[34]

The *Yaḥad* anticipated the eschatological regathering of all twelve tribes. This finding sheds light on pan-Israelite restoration motifs in the New Testament, including at least the following: (1) Jesus' choice of twelve apostles to represent a reconstituted Israel; (2) Paul's use of the term "all Israel" in Romans 11:26 and his concept of "Israel of God" in Galatians 6:16; (3) the significance of the *ioudaîoi* in the Gospel of John as "Judahites" or "Judeans" (an ethno-geographic designation) rather than "Jews" (a religious designation);[35] (4) James' deployment of the phrase "the twelve tribes in dispersion" in James 1:1. In their self-identity, the Qumran community anticipated the theology of the early Church, which would also understand herself to be the restored Israel.

---

32   See, for example, P. R. Davies, "The Judaism(s) of the Damascus Document," *The Damascus Document: A Centenniel of Discovery*, eds. J. M. Baumgarten et al.; Studies on the Texts of the Desert of Judah 34 (Leiden: E.J. Brill, 2000). Davies, in an otherwise thoughtful article on Qumran self-identity, never asks whether it is appropriate to describe the Qumran religion as a form of "Judaism" at all.

33   Or, as John Collins has pointed out, *Third Temple Israelitism*, inasmuch as the community was dissatisfied with the Second Temple and eagerly anticipating a third, eschatological one (personal communication with author). Also, if one may digress, another community which sits with great discomfort in the category "Second Temple Judaism," or Judaism generally, is the Samaritans, who consider themselves neither Jews nor Judeans, and do not trace their history from the Southern Kingdom and the return from Babylon. Along with the Qumran community, they would much more accurately be described as practicing a form of "Israelitism." On Qumran's dissent from Pharisaic/Rabbinic/Normative Judaism, see Talmon, "Community," 22–24.

34   Talmon, "Community," 10. In my opinion this has to some extent already taken place: the (understandable) categorization of the community as a form of "Judaism" has encouraged, consciously or subconsciously, the identification of the *yaḥad* with "Judah" in various texts.

35   "Judean" (*ioudaîos*) in John should be contrasted with "Israelite" (John 1:27), "Samaritan" (John 4:9), or "Galilean" (John 4:45), but not with "Christian," which would be anachronistic.

Letter & Spirit 8 (2013): 161-188

Divine Pedagogy and Covenant Memorial
The Catechetical *Narratio* and the New Evangelization[1]

~: Sean Innerst :~

St. John Vianney Theological Seminary

Introduction

In the 1997 *General Directory for Catechesis* (GDC) from the Sacred Congregation for the Clergy[2], the ancient catechetical *narratio* [narration] finds a surprisingly prominent place. The narration was a standard part of the evangelization and cat-echesis of the Church of the fourth and fifth centuries, but had all but ceased to be a standard part of the Church's pedagogy. The catechetical narration of salvation history is mentioned first, explicitly, in number 39 of the GDC and there in the form of an imperative:

> Catechesis, for its part, transmits the words and deeds of Revelation; it is *obliged* to proclaim and *narrate* them and, at the same time, to make clear the profound mysteries that they contain (my emphases).

While the GDC will go on to make the character of that narration clearer in suc-ceeding paragraphs (even numbering the three parts of the historical narration among the "seven foundation stones" of catechesis at number 130), already here in its introduction it has made of it an obligation for Catholic teachers of the faith. Despite the weight of that clear imperative, no one would claim that in the sixteen years since the GDC's promulgation by Blessed John Paul II this ancient disclosure of what the GDC calls the "mysteries" of salvation history has been treated as an obligatory part of the curriculum for any part of the catechetical regime in our parishes. Perhaps this lack of response is because very few of the underpaid staff and volunteers who serve the catechetical ministries in our parishes read Vatican documents. Even if they did, very few would have recognized what the GDC was referring to. The ancient *narratio* is unknown, so unpracticed, and that is the

---

1   Some small portions of the following were previously published as "Time for Liturgy: 'Appointed Times' in Judaism and Christianity," in *Catholic for a Reason III: Scripture and the Mystery of the Mass*, Scott Hahn and Regis Flaherty, eds. (Steubenville, OH: Emmaus Road Publishing, 2004).

2   *General Directory for Catechesis*, Citta del Vaticano: Libreria Editrice Vaticana, 1997, (Washington: United States Catholic Conference, 1998). All references will be taken from this English edition, and the citations for this and all ecclesial documents will be made with the internal numbering system, rather than by page number.

problem I hope to address, in some small measure, in the pages that follow. What is the *narratio* and why does the GDC oblige us to use it?

This article will explore the history and character of the *narratio* and suggest ways in which it might be applied today so as to make possible a positive response to the call of the *General Directory for Catechesis*. Specifically, I hope to show that the enduring value of the narration of salvation history in evangelization and catechesis generally, and in the New Evangelization in particular, rests upon its capacity to replicate in the ecclesial setting the pedagogy that God himself uses to incite a personal response of faith in us. This inducement to faith–according to St. Augustine of Hippo–consists in the demonstration the narration provides to its hearer that the love of God is the source of the unity and order of that history and in that same divine love shown by the catechist who recites it.

I intend to do this in three steps. First, we need to ascertain the reason for the GDC's imperative regarding the narration of salvation history. What we will find is that the *General Directory* seems to link the qualities of the *narratio* to the divine pedagogy, the original pedagogy of faith, which it asserts as the model for all catechetical forms.

Second, I will examine the *narratio* as it comes to us in its fullest expression from the patristic era in St. Augustine's seminal catechetical work *De catechizandis rudibus* (DCR). In that work Augustine describes and then demonstrates the shape of a first evangelistic catechesis given to those who are approaching the Church for the first time, preparatory to entry into the catechumenate. Augustine's work is the likely source for the GDC's own insistence upon the employment of such a catechetical narration and so this will provide important background, specifically on the rhetorical structure and methodology of the ancient *narratio*.

Then, in the third part of this article, I intend to take an unusual step by looking back at the Old Testament pattern of covenant formation and renewal as an early instance of that divine pedagogy which is declared to be normative by the GDC and which we also find reflected in Augustine's catechetical work and that of the other fathers.[3] By reflecting on the narrational pattern of the divine pedagogy in the formation of Jewish identity in the Old Testament, I hope to show that the power of the catechetical *narratio*, as a preparation for full entry into a Christian identity, gives warrant to the obligation that the GDC makes of this practice. That is, our confidence in its place in the New Evangelization ought not to be secured simply because of its presence in an important Father of the Church or the mandate in the GDC, but because it represents an ecclesial participation in the divine pedagogy itself—that means by which God has always encouraged His

---

3   See GDC 129, "The fathers model the catechumenate on the divine pedagogy; in the catechumenal process the catechumen, like the people of Israel, goes through a journey to arrive at the promised land: Baptismal identification with Christ."

people to memorialize His love for them and so celebrate and maintain covenant communion with Him.

I. *"Pedagogy of God, Source and Model of the Pedagogy of the Faith."*[4]

As the quote just cited in the subtitle of this section suggests, a signal theme in the GDC—and one as surprising, in some ways, as its imperative on the *narratio*[5]—is that the method best suited to evoking a personal response of faith, and the primary pedagogical point of reference for all catechesis is the divine pedagogy.

> God, in his greatness, uses a pedagogy to reveal himself to the human person: he uses human events and words to communicate his plan; he does so progressively and in stages, so as to draw even closer to man. God, in fact, operates in such a manner that man comes to knowledge of his salvific plan by means of the events of salvation history and the inspired words which accompany and explain them.[6]

The reference to "events and words" is drawn from *Dei Verbum* 2 which speaks of revelation as "realized by deeds and words, which are intrinsically bound up with each other."[7] In describing the interplay between the deeds and words of the economy, *DV* goes on to say, "as a result, the works performed by God in the history of salvation show forth and bear out the doctrine and realities signified by the words; the words, for their part, proclaim the works, and bring to light the mystery they contain." Importantly, *DV* asserts that revelation is not a merely verbal phenomenon, but salvation historical, as well.[8] The events and words are

---

4   GDC, title of Chapter I of Part III. The citations made in the footnote to this chapter title (n.1) in the GDC represent the genealogy of the theme of the divine pedagogy in previous documents from the magisterium.

5   The GDC is markedly different from its immediate predecessor, the 1971 *General Catechetical Directory*, Congregation for the Clergy (Washington: United States Catholic Conference, 1971), which highlights that the historical revelation, in prophecy and figure and which finds its fulfillment in Christ, should yield to an ecclesial pedagogy which begins with simple, "summary formulas." (See numbers 33 and 38.)

6   GDC 38.

7   *Dei Verbum* [The Word of God], The Second Vatican Council Dogmatic Constitution on Divine Revelation, (November 18, 1965), in *Vatican Council II: The Conciliar and Post Conciliar Documents*, Austin Flannery, ed., (Boston: St. Paul Editions, 1975).

8   The significance of this assertion is, of course, not confined to catechetics. It is a bedrock principle for a specifically Catholic fundamental theology and responds to the sundering of word and event that we see both in Francisco Suarez in the 16th and in Rudolph Bultmann in the 20th centuries. See Joseph Ratzinger, *Principles of Catholic Theology: Building Stones for a Fundamental Theology* (San Francisco: Ignatius, 1987), 185 et seq. See also Tracey Rowland's incisive recounting of the origins of *DV* 2 as a response to the word/event dualism of Suarez and as an attempt to recover the participatory faith of the classical Thomist position which it distorted, in *Ratzinger's Faith* (Oxford/New York: Oxford University Press, 2008), 48–52. See also *Catechism of the Catholic Church*, 2d. ed. (Vatican City: Libreria Editrice Vaticana, 1997),

mutually interpretive. The history is even said to "bear out the doctrine." Even that which most often is conceived of as primarily verbal or propositional, that is, doctrine, is shown to percolate up out of the history of salvation. Even the words of revelation—again, most often considered to be the bearers of doctrinal content—are described as proclaiming and bringing to light the mystery behind the events.

In accord with *DV*, the GDC asserts the necessarily "historical character of the mystery of salvation."[9] "The salvation of the person, which is the ultimate purpose of Revelation, is shown as a fruit of an original and efficacious 'pedagogy of God' throughout history."[10] Here the GDC makes clear that the reason for that temporal, historical quality of the divine pedagogy is that it is personal. God makes use of the history in which we humans are ensconced to make a personal overture to us. Although entirely transcending history, God deigns to use history for our good, as the very language of his demonstration of love.

In number 139 the GDC returns over and over to the term "person" to show that the divine pedagogy is an accommodation to the needs of human persons in order to invite them to a personal relationship with God, such that God "assumes the character of the person," "liberates the person," "causes the person to grow." "To this end," the GDC states, "as a creative and insightful teacher, God transforms events in the life of his people into lessons of wisdom, adapting himself to the diverse ages and life situations."[11] The GDC concludes, "Truly, to help a person to encounter God, which is the task of the catechist, means to emphasize above all the relationship that the person has with God so that he can make it his own and allow himself to be guided by God."[12]

So, the divine pedagogy (in word and deed) is gradual and historical, as an accommodation to persons who live and act in history. In the GDC the central paradigm for discerning this gradual and personal divine pedagogy is Christ himself "who determines catechesis as 'a pedagogy of the incarnation.'"[13] Christ is "the center of salvation history. . . . the final event toward which all salvation

---

no. 53, which quotes *DV* 2, calling the interplay of "deeds and words" in the "plan of Revelation" "a specific divine pedagogy." On the importance of a propositional revelation to the Church's apostolicity and indefectibility and so also the necessary primacy of the catechetical over the theological order in the ministry of the Word, see Eugene Kevane, "Apostolicity, Indefectibility, and Catechesis," *Divinitas, Pontificae Academiae Theologicae Romanae Commentarii*, Rome (September 1985): 207–233.

9   GDC 107, title. "The *economy of Salvation* has thus an historical character as it is realized in time: ... *in time past it began, made progress, and in Christ reached its highest point; in the present time it displays its force and awaits its consummation in the future*" (citing, GDC 44, emphasis in original).

10   Ibid., 139.

11   Ibid.

12   Ibid.

13   Ibid., 143.

history converges."[14] It is in Christ's incarnation that the pedagogy of God as a carefully ordered series of words and deeds in the economy of salvation comes to be known in its fullness. His advent gives intelligibility to the events of the Old Testament economy and so "the catechetical message helps the Christian to locate himself in history and to insert himself into it, by showing that Christ is the ultimate meaning of this history."[15] The centrality of Christ as the fulfillment and continuation of the pedagogy of God is shown in the first chapter of Part Three, "The pedagogy of the faith." There, after asserting Jesus as the "one Master," in accord with Matthew 23:10, the GDC notes that by uniting his action with "Jesus the Teacher," the catechist is joined to the "mysterious action of the grace of God," and so also to the "original pedagogy of the faith."[16]

In so saying, the GDC makes clear that the divine or original pedagogy and the work of the catechist can be expressed in a concursus—that they can function together in an intimate way. The GDC sees so great a concurrence of the two pedagogies that it can say that "the Church actualizes the 'divine pedagogy'" in local catechisms[17] or that a "divine education" is "received by way of catechesis," so long as the action of the Holy Spirit is received by "teachers of the faith ... who are convinced and faithful disciples of Christ and his Church."[18] At GDC number 143 catechesis is said to be "radically inspired by the pedagogy of God." Thereafter the divine pedagogy is described in its holistic dimensions as being personal and interpersonal, progressive, Christocentric, communal and relational, didactic and experiential, truthful and loving. At 144 the GDC references "the wonderful dialogue that God undertakes with every person," stating that for our catechesis this "becomes its inspiration and norm," and goes on to assert that, of this dialogue with God, "catechesis becomes an untiring echo."[19] At number 141 the GDC goes so far as to say that the Church's mission itself is "a visible and actual continuation of the pedagogy of the Father and the Son."

It is this original, divine pedagogy, which is to be the standard for all other catechetical activity, that grounds the GDC's insistence on the *narratio*. At number 129 the GDC notes that "the fathers model the catechumenate on the divine pedagogy; in the catechumenal process the catechumen, like the people of Israel, goes on a journey to arrive at the promised land: Baptismal identification with Christ." This immediately precedes the GDC's mention of the importance of the

---

14 Ibid.

15 Ibid.

16 Ibid., 138, citing John Paul II, *Catechesi Tradendae* [On Catechesis in Our Time] (Washington: United States Catholic Conference, 1979), 58.

17 GDC 131.

18 Ibid., 142.

19 The GDC is here quoting from number 11 of the *Message to the People of God*, the document from the 1977 Synod of Bishops, and also cites *Catechesi Tradendae* 58, which it inspired.

"organization of the content of catechesis in accordance with the stages of that [catechumenal] process" and another mention of the "primary role" assigned to the *narratio* in patristic catechesis. Catechesis, then, "radically inspired" by the divine pedagogy, should itself take the "form of a process or journey"[20] and the terrain of that journey, so to speak, is disclosed to the catechumen by the *narratio*.

The journey of Israel in history, the very locus for the exercise of the original divine pedagogy, must be narrated in order for the catechumen to fall under the power of that same pedagogy. It is also critical to note that the trajectory of the journey of the catechumenate is, as noted in 129, toward Baptism. As we know from the modern practice of the *Rite of Christian Initiation of Adults*, the journey is ritual all along the way; in fact, it is a kind of continual liturgical procession.

Having ascertained the important place of *narratio* to the GDC's program for a modern ecclesial catechesis—modeled, as it is, on the divine pedagogy as historical and so gradual, staged, personal, and ritual—we can now turn to Augustine's practice of the *narratio* to see how he witnesses to this concurrence of the divine and catechetical pedagogies.

II. Augustine's Evangelistic Catechesis: De Catechizandis Rudibus

The term, *narration/narratio*—as we've seen, so prominent in the GDC—is applied to the recitation of the history of salvation made to those who approach the Church to enter the catechumenate by Augustine of Hippo in his *De catechizandis rudibus [Instructing Beginners in the Faith]*.[21] While it is here that the term *narratio* seems to have first been applied in this catechetical sense (at least so far as the documentary evidence shows), it was a standard part of the classical oration, as we see in Quintilian's *Institutio Oratoria [Institutes of Oratory]*, the handbook for Roman rhetoric and other educational practices from the first century AD.[22]

---

20   GDC 143.

21   *De catechizandis rudibus* could be translated "On the catechizing of the uninstructed" or, as Raymond Canning renders it in his 2006 annotated translation, *Instructing Beginners in the Faith*. See Augustine of Hippo, *Instructing Beginners in Faith*, Translation, Introduction, and Notes by Raymond Canning (Hyde Park, NY: New City Press, 2006). The translation of *De catechizandis rudibus* used throughout this work is Canning's, unless otherwise noted, but the reference numbers cited will be those which are internal to DCR itself, rather than Canning's page numbers. Where Canning's commentary on the work is cited, the page numbers will be used.

22   Quintilian, *Institutio oratoria* [Institutes of Oratory], H. E. Butler, trans., vols. 1–4 (London: Loeb Classical Library, 1953), IV, 1–2; see also Cicero, *De inventione* [On Invention] I, 19–21. *De inventione; De optimo genere oratorum; Topica* [On Invention; On the Best Kind of Orators; Topics], H. M. Hubbell, trans. (Cambridge, MA and London: Loeb Classical Library, 1949). See also the description in William Harmless, *Augustine and the Catechumenate* (Collegeville, MN: Liturgical Press, 1995), 123–124. See Raymond Canning on the three forms of *narratio, fabula, historia,* or *argumentum,* the second of which—"a credible account of actual occurrences"—Canning concludes, is what Augustine had in mind in using the term. *Instructing,* 17.

In using the term *narratio*, Augustine may have been simply drawing from his background as a *rhetor* [rhetorician] in the classical pagan tradition or he may have been using a term which had already found a place in the Christian catechetical vocabulary.[23] This latter possibility may well be indicated in that *De catechizandis rudibus* was penned at the request of a deacon of Carthage named Deogratias who appears, from Augustine's response, to have specifically asked about the place to start and finish the narration and whether it should be followed by an exhortation or a mere list of precepts.[24] Given that *exhortatio* [exhortation] was also a standard element in classical orations,[25] Deogratias' question about the inclusion of *exhortatio* may indicate that he assumed that something called *narratio*, even if catechetical rather than rhetorical, *ought* to be followed by *exhortatio*, as was common in formal discourses, thus suggesting that the term *narratio* had already become standard in catechesis, at least in the Churches of Latin North Africa.

The essential point for the present study, however, is that Augustine's *narratio* is more than just one element of the elaborated formal rhetorical presentation (*dispositio* in Latin or, in the Greek, *taxis*, both referring to the ordering of a speech).[26] In the Aristotelian rhetorical system it belongs to one of the three "*entechnoi*, the artistic or internal modes of proof"[27] (*pistis*). The three forms are usually designated by the three terms *ethos* [ethical appeal], *logos* [rational appeal], and *pathos* [emotional appeal]. The *narratio* belongs to the second category, *logos*, the appeal to reason by way of a disclosure of the facts of the case; in that capacity it represents the substance of an argument. The full Augustinian catechetical address is really a very lean piece of rhetoric, with only vestigial elements of *ethos*, in the introductory *exordium* [appeal for a hearing], in the *pathos*, in the closing *exhortatio* [exhortation to action], and even less of the other explicit elements of the more elaborated classical Ciceronian *dispositio*.[28]

---

23 See Joseph Patrick Christopher's 1926 commentary *S. Aureli Augustini Hipponiensis Episcopi de Catechizandis Rudibus Liber Unus* [St. Aurelius Augustine, Bishop of Hippo's, *On Catechizing the Uninstructed*] Joseph Patrick Christopher, trans.; The Catholic University of America Patristic Studies vol. VIII (Washington: Catholic University of America Press, 1926), 128.

24 DCR 1,1.

25 Harmless notes that while an *exhortatio* was not a formal part of the Ciceronian model, as he outlines it on page 124 of *Catechumenate*, "exhortatory digressions were both common and expected," citing Cicero's *De inventione* 1, 97.

26 For what follows, see Edward Corbett and Robert Connors, *Classical Rhetoric for the Modern Student* (New York, Oxford: Oxford University Press, 1999), 11–24 and George Kennedy, *Classical Rhetoric and Its Christian and Secular Tradition from Ancient to Modern Times* (Chapel Hill: University of North Carolina Press, 1980), 63–74.

27 Kennedy, *Classical Rhetoric Christian and Secular*, 68.

28 See William Harmless' attempt to show the elaborated parts of the classical *dispositio* in DCR in his chart on page 155 of *Augustine and the Catechumenate* (Collegeville, MN: Liturgical Press, 1995). It is striking that the only ones clearly identifiable are the *exordium*, the attempt to render the audience well-disposed [corresponding to *ethos*], the *narratio*, the facts of the case [*logos*], and the *exhortatio*, the arousal to action [*pathos*], corresponding to the fundamental Aristotelian

Augustine's *narratio* is historical and inductive, neither fabulous nor abstractly argumentative—as would be characteristic of the more juridical forms. With reference, again, to the Aristotelian rhetorical pattern—this time with reference to the type of audience addressed—it belongs to that category of orations called deliberative, that sort of appeal made to a hearer who is being invited to judge a proposed future course of action, in this case, entry into the Church's catechumenate.[29]

With reference to a renewed application of *narratio* in the modern setting as called for by the GDC, it is important to stress that the *narratio* makes for compelling catechesis not on the basis of rhetorical panache, nor even just because it makes an appeal to *logos*, but because it discloses the work of *the Logos*, demonstrating that Christ is what the *Catechism of the Catholic Church* calls "the key, the center, and the purpose of the whole of man's history."[30] Augustine is very much concerned with winning the soul in front of him, and that by the use of his considerable rhetorical skills if they will serve that purpose. But he is utterly convinced of the truth of his case and so seems to think that it requires not much rhetorical adornment, if the bare-bones product we have in DCR is the real measure of the question.[31]

In the Prologue to DCR, Augustine tells us that the *narratio* is intended to display "the central points of the faith" and that it "gives us our identity as

---

schema. On the character of Augustine's rhetorical concerns in this regard, see also Canning, *Instructing*, 16–17, n. 14; Harmless, *Catechumenate*, 155 and Kevane, Augustine *the Educator: A Study in the Fundamentals of Christian Formation* (Westminster, MD: Newman Press, 1964), 235–243; as well as R. A. Markus, *Saeculum: History and Society in the Theology of St. Augustine* (Cambridge: Cambridge University Press, 1970), 11 et seq.

29   Kennedy, *Classical Rhetoric Christian and Secular*, 68: "logos [is] that mode of proof found in the argument and most characteristic of rhetoric." And on page 70, "poof by example is more suitable to deliberative than to judicial oratory, since we must predict the future on the basis of our knowledge of the past." And on page 74, "Much of Christian oratory is deliberative." Quoting from Augustine's *De doctrina Christiana*, Kennedy sees the classical Aristotelian scheme still operative in this most deliberatively rhetorical of his works in noting that "the Christian teacher should 'conciliate those who are opposed [ethos], arouse those who are remiss [pathos], and teach those ignorant of his subject [logos],"156.

30   *Catechism*, no. 450.

31   In *Rhetoric in the Middle Ages: A History of Rhetorical Theory from St. Augustine to the Renaissance* (Berkley, CA: University of California Press, 1974), 48 and following, James Murphy explains the way in which Augustine, whose distaste for the crass rhetoric of what is called the Second Sophistic would have been a commonplace among the Christian commentators of the fourth century, nevertheless in *De doctrina Christiana* [On Christian Teaching] he encourages the Christian orator not to "stand unarmed in the fight against falsehood" (4,1,2) and so to take up the art of eloquence in the service of wisdom. In this, Augustine charts the course of a western appropriation of the classical patrimony but, like his contemporaries, he always asserts the superiority of wisdom over mere eloquence ("Eloquent speakers give pleasure, wise ones salvation." 4,6,9). See further Murphy, *Rhetoric in the Middle Ages*, 42 and DCR 9,13 where Augustine speaks disparagingly of those who, like himself, "have been to the run of the mill schools of grammar and rhetoric" and who must be especially enjoined to "clothe themselves with Christian humility."

Christians."[32] He goes on to say that it represents an "initial grounding in the faith" and then, that through it, "the content of the faith is communicated" to these newcomers.[33] That a half-hour to an hour-and-a-half discourse could do all that might seem a rather exalted claim, but Augustine is clear that in either a shorter or longer form, when constructed properly, the *narratio* will be "at all times perfectly complete."[34]

What becomes clear in *DCR* is that an effective narration of salvation history has no less to do with the character of content than with a particular methodological choice: the willingness on the part of the catechist to ally his will with that of God in the pursuit of His pedagogical purposes.

There are certainly constants to the content of the Augustinian address, what we could call its essentials: a Christological and ecclesial centrality in the narration, the importance of encouraging moral rectitude in accord with Church teaching, the alluring mystery and cogency added by the allegorical or typological interpretation of the letter of the Scriptural story, the importance of enabling the hearer to join his journey to that which he sees in the scriptural story, and the ultimate purpose of disclosing the love of God in Christ and so encouraging the hearer to receive the *sacramenta,* or the initial ritual signs of entry into the catechumenate and the journey toward full Church membership by way of the rites of initiation.[35]

But despite this stability of content, Augustine is equally insistent upon an absolute methodological agility on the part of the catechist in docility to the need of the hearer of the address. He repeatedly indicates that Deogratias must strive to meet the needs of the individual in front of him and not merely rely upon a stock fund of tools.

In fact, this fundamental methodological principle makes up a large part of the advice he gives in this last portion of Augustine's "directions for formulating the address."[36] Even his extended advice on overcoming discouragement and encouraging cheerfulness in the catechist is actually entirely ordered to the end that the words of the discourse may "be drunk in with pleasure" by the inquirer.[37] In fact, one of the very causes of discouragement in this sort of catechesis, according to Augustine, can be just the imperative to "improvise and adapt our words to another person's way of thinking."[38]

---

32 *DCR* 1,1. Christopher translates this, "that truth, the belief in which makes us Christians."

33 Ibid., 2,4.

34 Ibid., 2,4. In *DCR* Augustine gives a longer example of a *narratio* and a shorter one.

35 See Ibid., 26,50.

36 Ibid., 10,14.

37 Ibid., 14,22. See also 2,4: "we are given a much more appreciative hearing when we ourselves enjoy performing our task" and "our greatest concern is much more about how to make it possible for those who offer instruction in faith to do so with joy. For the more they succeed in this, the more appealing they will be."

38 Ibid., 10,14.

Augustine's advice about how to overcome discouragement in the catechist, as well as his tips on measuring the class, education, and motives of the candidate, aim entirely at preparing the soil of the soul of the student for the *narratio*.[39] His concern for the receptivity of the audience is what informs the first part of his oration, the *exordium*, the appeal for a hearing that aims to make the hearer "well disposed, attentive and receptive."[40] According to the Aristotelian rhetorical paradigm that I have set out above, this is *ethos*.

At 3,5 Augustine says that the *narratio* is "telling the story in our own words." But that doesn't mean that the catechist is free to tell the story in only one way, as from a script he has prepared. Although such a summary of the sacred history describing the journey of Israel will be one that keeps to the "most well-trodden path," and will inevitably include "oft-repeated phrases,"[41] it must still be a case of fitting "our own words to the actual circumstances" which the state of the listener presents to the catechist. Again, Augustine acknowledges that

> even when we know how to make our address attractive, we still
> prefer to hear or read something which has been better expressed
> and which can be delivered without effort or uneasiness on our
> part rather than to have to improvise and adapt our words to
> another person's way of thinking.[42]

For the catechist to surrender his preferences and make this adaptation is a work of accommodation in which he imitates the divine condescension. Augustine insists on this precisely because "what we dispense is God's, and the more we love those to whom we speak, the more we want them to find acceptable what is offered them for their salvation."[43] Augustine strings together a series of Pauline texts to illustrate the Christological kenotic principle that must be at play in such a catechesis[44] and concludes that

> the more love goes down in a spirit of service into the ranks of
> the lowliest people, the more surely it rediscovers the quiet that
> is within when its good conscience testifies that it seeks nothing
> of those whom it goes down but their eternal salvation.[45]

---

39 See Damian Halligan, "Augustine: A Teacher's Teacher," *Lumen Vitae* 22:2 (June 1967): 281–292.

40 Cicero, *De inventione* 1,20, cited in Harmless, *Catechumenate*, 141–142, who notes that Augustine cites this phrase in *De doctrina Christiana* 4,4,6.

41 DCR 11,16 and 12,17.

42 Ibid., 10, 14.

43 Ibid., 10, 14.

44 1 Pet. 2:21; Phil. 2:6–8; 1 Cor. 9:22; 2 Cor. 9:22; 2 Cor. 5:13–14 and 1 Thess. 2:7.

45 DCR 10,15. This suggests again the way in which *ethos*, while "arising from the speaker's personal

This accommodation to the person can even take rather extreme forms, for example, the case of an inquirer who comes professing the best motives while actually seeking some worldly advantage in becoming a Christian, to curry favor with the powerful or to gain some financial advantage. Augustine counsels that Deogratias "make the matter of the lie itself the starting point of your address . . . . to the point that he actually enjoys being the kind of person that he wishes to appear."[46] Such adaptation may also mean departing from the narration to supply "authoritative statements and rational arguments" when we find that the hearer holds to some error[47] or to ask probing questions of the hearer when the catechist finds him unresponsive due to boredom or a possible lack of comprehension.[48]

When the catechist commits himself to this imitation of the divine condescension for the sake of the salvation of the inquirer, whatever his state or need, "fluent and cheerful words will then stream out from an abundance of love."[49] When the good steward (*dispensatore*) of the kingdom opens up the "oracles of the scriptures"[50] to his charges, offering "the address that [he is] actually called to deliver,"[51] rather than the one he might prefer, then the catechist becomes himself an oracle, such that "he who is listening to us—or more precisely, listening to God through our agency—begins to make progress on his way of life and in his understanding and to advance eagerly along the way of Christ."[52] This accommodation to the needs of the student unites the teacher and his student in such a way that

> when our listeners are touched by us as we speak and we are touched by them as they learn, each of us comes to dwell in the other, and so they as it were speak in us what they hear, while we in some way learn in them what we teach.[53]

---

qualities" (Murphy, *Rhetoric in the Middle Ages*, 4), can help to determine the receptivity of the audience.

46　DCR 5,9. One is reminded here of Chesterton's definition of hypocrisy as the compliment that vice pays to virtue.

47　Ibid., 11,16.

48　Ibid., 13,18.

49　Ibid., 14,22.

50　Ibid., 1,2 Augustine obliquely refers to Deogratias as among "the stewards (*dispensatores*), my companions in service." In this regard, Canning refers to 1 Cor. 4:1–2, and 1 Pet. 4:10–11 at *Instructing*, 55 n.7. These texts refer to the figure of the *oikonomos* who in the latter reference from 1 Peter "utters oracles of God." One might also suggest that the *oikonomos* as the catechetical oracle is the one who can "bring out of his treasure what is new and what is old" in disclosing the shape of the divine *oikonomia* (see Matt. 13:55). See also Harmless, *Catechumenate*, 180–181, on these "monetary metaphors," that is, on the catechist dispenser as the bursar of the word of God.

51　DCR 11,16.

52　Ibid., 7,11.

53　Ibid., 12,7. See Canning's note on the proverbial quality and import of this expression, which

Augustine avers that if catechists will "cheerfully allow him to speak through us," God will work through their words.[54]

In short, Augustine's program for a personal grounding in the faith by the *narratio* calls for the catechist to put himself at the complete disposal of God, to make God's goal of love his or her own and so to draw the student to align his or her own goal with that same divine love. This all is expressive of the establishment of the authority of the speaker (the catechist), which is the aim of the classical *exordium*, and that Aristotelian mode of proof called *ethos*.

That first part of a rhetorical presentation that establishes trust on the part of the audience is, in Augustine's view, nothing less than a participation in the divine love showed by God, shared in by the catechist, and which is now offered to the hearer. For the Christian *rhetor* the authority proposed is not, in fact, that of the speaker, as would have been the case in the classical oration, but of the loving God in which both the catechist and the inquirer are to trust.[55]

Augustine's view of the *content* of salvation history is that it is a fundamentally Christocentric and unified whole, the very integrity of which discloses the love of God and moves us to love him in return for the love he has shown us in ordering it so. His *methodology* demands that the kenotic condescension of the divine love, as shown in the historical content, must be imitated by the catechist in his or her willingness to adapt the particulars of the address to the person being addressed in such a way that the divine love is communicated to the hearer in both content and method.

Augustine sums up the "manner in which the historical exposition is to be presented" in the following two ways:

> The historical exposition should then begin from what is written about God's having created all things very good and continue, as we have said, down to the present period of the Church's history. Our account should focus on explaining the deeper meaning of each of the matters and events that we describe: a meaning that is brought out when we relate them to the goal constituted by

---

Augustine may have borrowed from Ambrose in *Instructing*, 97, n. 123.

54   DCR 11,16.

55   See Kennedy, *Classical Rhetoric Christian and Secular*, 120–121. There he notes that "in its purest form Judeo-Christian rhetoric shows similarity to philosophical rhetoric: it is the simple enunciation of God's truth, uncontaminated by adornment, flattery, or sophistic argumentation; it differs from philosophical rhetoric in that this truth is known from revelation or established by signs sent from God, not discovered by dialectic through man's efforts," 121. See DCR 10,14: "what we dispense is God's." For a fuller argument on the differences between Augustinian and Ciceronian rhetoric based upon his intention to teach *doctrina*, rather than merely to persuade, see Ernest Fortin, "Augustine and the Problem of Christian Rhetoric," *Augustinian Studies*, 5 (1974): 85–100.

love; and whatever we are doing or saying, our eyes should never be turned away from this goal.[56]

Earlier, at 4,8, he gives another summary in which the theological virtues serve as a form and the measure for the proper delivery of the address, with love again as the ultimate goal:

> Keeping this love before you then as a goal to which you direct all that you say, recount every event in your historical exposition in such a way that your listener by hearing it may believe, by believing may hope, and by hoping may love.[57]

This, then, describes in sum the manner and the desired outcome of the whole historical exposition. I would contend that this seminal dictum at 4,8 also expresses a theological description of the three modes of proof, *logos* [in *narratio*], *pathos* [in *exhortatio*], and *ethos* [in *exordium*], as ordered, respectively, to faith, hope, and love.[58]

Although in examining Augustine's *narratio* I've been most concerned with his methodological dispositions, because we have been looking for likeness with the divine pedagogy, we mustn't forget that the love toward which the whole catechesis is aimed as its methodological principle is not just a feeling, but an holistic experience. Augustine's *narratio* is ordered toward conversion and to the *sacramenta* that signal reception into the catechumenate.[59] These could be described as an "enactment" or "performance" of the story that the *narratio* tells.[60] Augustine's historical exposition clearly has a sacramental trajectory. Those who enter into the catechumenate through the *sacramenta* will undergo a long apprenticeship in the word before they will be allowed to receive Baptism, Confirmation and, finally, *the* Word in the Holy Eucharist. His whole concern with the proper content and delivery of the narration is ordered toward not just enabling his hearers to see the love of God, but seeing those he addresses surrounded by the love of God in the sacramental embrace of the Church.

---

56 DCR 6,10.

57 *Hac ergo dilectione tibi tamquam fine proposita, quo referas omnia quae dicis, quidquid narras ita narra, ut ille cui loqueris audiendo credit, credendo speret, sperando amet.*

58 The attentive reader of *DCR* will note that this pattern at 4,8 of faith, hope, and love in relation to *narratio* (3,5–6,10), *exhortatio* (7,11–8,12) and *exordium* (8,12–9,13), viz. the hearer, and then 10,14–14,22, viz. the speaker) fits the overall pattern of the work itself.

59 DCR 26,50.

60 For example, "Christ's passion symbolically foreshadowed in that people when they were ordered to kill and eat a sheep, and to mark their doorposts with its blood, and to celebrate this event every year, and to call it the Passover of the Lord. ... With the sign of his passion and cross you are today to be marked on the forehead—your doorpost, so to speak—and all Christians are marked in the same way." DCR 20,34.

III. The Divine Pedagogy in the Old Testament

In what follows I will explore the way in which the historical prologue of the ancient covenant formularies functioned in the Old Testament as a ritual act of memorialization to form the covenant people of Israel and how that was then reflected in the liturgical life of ancient Israel. This is admittedly a catechetical reflection on Scripture by a catechist, aided by a few scholars who are much more than catechists. My intention is to suggest in broad strokes the tenor of the world-view that informed the ancient Jewish communities and those who sought to enter them. Obviously, I can't claim by this to settle any exegetical questions beyond my competence and the scope of this article, but only to apply what scholars have taught me to the realm of catechetical content and practice, with particular reference to how what they teach applies to our understanding of the pedagogy of God and the *narratio*.

1. History as Prologue

In his now classic 1962 study on *Memory and Tradition in Israel*, Brevard Childs, commenting upon Deuteronomy 8, which commands at verse 2, "And you shall remember all the ways which the Lord your God has led you these forty years in the wilderness," says, "In this passage historical memory establishes the continuity of the new generation with the decisive events of the past. God's plan for Israel unfolds in her history."[61] He goes on to note, "Memory plays a central role in making Israel constantly aware of the nature of God's benevolent acts as well as of her own covenantal pledge."[62] Childs, who stands at the beginning of what came to be called canonical criticism, uses form critical skills to establish the centrality of *zeker* (remember) and *zikaron* (remembrance) to the covenantal relationship between YHWH and Israel.[63]

---

61 Brevard Childs, *Memory and Tradition in Israel* (Naperville, IL: Alec C. Allenson, Inc., 1962), 51. This now classic study of the terms surrounding the concept of memory in the Old Testament is an indispensable starting point for a theology of memory and history. Building upon the work of James Barr, Childs concludes that "*zkr*" and related terms possess a wider semantic range than is common in the English term "memory," but that the breadth of the term is not suggestive of a so-called "primitive" Hebrew psychology, as J. Pedersen (*Israel*, 1926) had concluded. Childs adds to this semantic evaluation a close "form-critical analysis of the passages which employ the important words describing the role of memory" (30).

62 Childs, *Memory and Tradition*, 51.

63 See H. Eising, "*zākhar; zēkher; zikkārôn; 'azkārāh*," *Theological Dictionary of the Old Testament* Vol. IV, G. J. Botterweck and H. Ringren, eds., David Green, trans. (Grand Rapids, MI: Wm. B. Eerdmans, 1980), 64–82. This scholarly treatment of *zkr*, its etymology and various forms, explains the mode and purpose of Israel's remembering and then also of God's remembering with a close evaluation of the context in each case, along with the recounting of special instances of the acts of remembering and forgetting. See also Lawrence Hoffman's "Does God Remember? A Liturgical Theology of Memory," in Michael A. Signer, ed., *Memory and History in Christianity and Judaism* (Notre Dame, IN: University of Notre Dame Press, 2001), 41–72. He argues that *zekher/zikaron* are both best rendered as "memorial."

In *Sinai and Zion*, Jon Levenson focuses our attention on the "Sinaitic event" as that moment when Israel passes from a "prehistorical" or "protohistorical" stage to one which records an "awesome" and "transcendent" event which "occurred on the plain of human history."[64] That event was the formation of a covenant between Israel and YHWH which we find in compressed form in Exodus 19:3–8.

> 3 And Moses went up to God, and the Lord called to him out of the mountain, saying, "Thus you shall say to the house of Jacob, and tell the people of Israel: 4 You have seen what I did to the Egyptians, and how I bore you on eagles' wings and brought you to myself. 5 Now therefore, if you will obey my voice and keep my covenant, you shall be my own possession among all peoples; for all the earth is mine, 6 and you shall be to me a kingdom of priests and a holy nation. These are the words which you shall speak to the children of Israel." 7 So Moses came and called the elders of the people, and set before them all these words which the Lord had commanded him. 8 And all the people answered together and said, "All that the Lord has spoken we will do." And Moses reported the words of the people to the Lord.

Levenson calls these verses an "introduction to the entire revelation on Sinai."[65] Following the earlier work of G. E. Mendenhall and K. Baltzer, and later scholars of covenant like D. J. McCarthy, Levenson sees in this prophetic announcement from Exodus an abbreviated form of the typical covenant formulary of the Late Bronze Age Hittite suzerainty treaty.[66] Although "covenant" or "*berit* indicates different kinds of agreements or relationships, political, social, tribal, familial, etc.,"[67] Levenson focuses on the suzerainty form. The elaborated formulary would

---

64   Jon Levenson, *Sinai and Zion* (San Francisco: Harper Collins, 1985), 24.

65   Levenson, *Sinai and Zion*, 24.

66   Levenson, *Sinai and Zion*, 26–32. Although Levenson stresses the suzerainty covenant form, what follows ought to be understood, too, with reference to the larger kinship model that other scholars explore. See Frank Moore Cross, "Kinship and Covenant in Ancient Israel," in F. M. Cross, ed., *From Epic to Canon: History and Literature in Ancient Israel* (Baltimore: Johns Hopkins University Press, 1998), 3: "The social organization of West Semitic tribal groups was grounded in kinship. Kinship relations defined the rights and obligations, the duties, status, and privileges of tribal members, and kinship terminology provided the only language for expressing legal, political, and religious institutions. Kinship was conceived in terms of one blood flowing through the veins of the kinship group." See also Scott Hahn's extensive treatment of this in *Kinship by Covenant: A Canonical Approach to the Fulfillment of God's Saving Promises* (New Haven: Yale University Press, 2009). Hahn distinguishes between kinship-type, treaty-type, and grant-type covenants. Kinship-type covenants involve two persons of equal status who both come under the covenant obligations (parity). Treaty and grant-type covenants are formed between a superior and inferior parties and the obligations are unequally distributed (vassalage), 29.

67   Paul Kalluveettil, *Declaration and Covenant: A Comprehensive Review of Covenant Formulae from*

typically have included six parts: 1. a preamble or titulary in which the suzerain identifies himself; 2. the historical prologue or antecedent history, which states the past relationship between the two parties to the covenant and is aimed at instilling a sense of gratitude and obligation on the part of the vassal to the suzerain; 3. stipulations or terms of the treaty to ensure the *personal* fidelity of the vassal to his one lord[68]; 4. the deposition of the text of the treaty, often in the temple of the god who would serve as the witness of the treaty, with some treaties requiring a periodic, "liturgical"[69] rereading by the vassal; 5. the list of witnesses, these being the gods who witness and guarantee covenant fidelity, sometimes also "mountains, rivers, heaven and earth, stand in witness,"[70] too; 6. lastly, the blessings and curses which provide a "moral mechanism," "reward for the faithful, punishment for the faithless."[71]

While in Exodus 19:3–8 Levenson only finds "reflexes of the formulary,"[72] particularly the historical prologue in verse 4, the stipulation in verse 5, and the oath in verse 8, he goes on to analyze Joshua 24:1–28 (with some supporting instances from Deuteronomy and Leviticus) in which all the six elements of the formulary can be found in some measure. He also notes that the Joshua text is a covenant renewal rather than a covenant formation ceremony. Based on his analysis of these relatively early fragments he concludes that the "covenantalization of Israelite religion was so thoroughgoing that we are almost reduced to hypothesis in our effort to reconstruct the prior stages."[73] Levenson cites Baltzer's work on the covenant formulary in the Old Testament to support his assertion that, apart from the two samples that he evaluates, "there are dozens and dozens of other texts whose structure and setting become lucid in the light of the discoveries about covenant."[74]

For our purposes, Levenson's concern with "the theology of the historical prologue" is primary. He says of the function of the historical prologue as the ground of the covenant obligations of Israel that "the unstated assumption is that meaning can be disclosed in history."[75] "The present is the consummation of the

---

the *Old Testament and the Ancient Near East*, Analectica Biblica 88 (Rome: Biblical Institute Press, 1982), 15. Recent scholarship has found that "a 'covenant' is, in its essence, a legal means to establish kinship between two previously unrelated parties." *Catholic Bible Dictionary*, Scott Hahn, ed. (New York: Doubleday, 2009), 168.

68   Levenson notes that the "ubiquitous metaphor" in these treaties describing the suzerain/vassal relationship was that of shepherd and flock. *Sinai and Zion*, 28.

69   Ibid., 29.

70   Ibid.

71   Ibid., 30.

72   Ibid., 31.

73   Ibid., 36.

74   Ibid., 37.

75   Ibid.

past, the assurance that it can continue."[76] The recital of the history has as its major function "to narrow the gap between generations," says Levenson.[77] In this way it serves as the engine for the formation and maintenance of the collective identity of Israel:

> History is telescoped into collective biography. What your ancestors saw is what *you* saw. God's rescue of them implicates *you*, obliges *you*, for *you*, by hearing this story and responding affirmatively, become Israel, and it was Israel whom he rescued. Telling the story brings it alive. The historical prologue brings the past to bear pointedly on the present. In the words of the rabbinic Passover liturgy (*Haggadah*), "Each man is obliged to see himself as if he came out of Egypt."[78]

This is not an expression of a deductive or existential philosophical system. The Jews do "not determine who they are by looking within, by plumbing the depths of the individual soul," one does not find a "philosophical system" or "theorem" in the Hebrew Bible; rather, Israel infers and affirms her identity "by telling a story."[79] The public, the historical, determines the private and the personal, "[o]ne's people's history becomes one's personal history."[80] This is nearly the polar opposite of the modern view that "history is man's self-understanding."[81] This is not the autonomous person as the arbiter of the meaning of history but history as the determinative prologue of human destiny. "Israel affirms the given."[82] And, as Alasdair MacIntyre has shown in his description of classical heroic cultures and their heirs in the tragedians and philosophers of ancient Greece, this is the formative quality of tribe and tradition among premodern peoples.[83] History is determinative of one's personal relations and moral obligations; history yields covenant and not the reverse. And it is history that establishes the trustworthiness of God, who he is, not a philosophical or religious system.[84]

---

76   Ibid.

77   Ibid., 38.

78   Ibid. It is interesting to note here the confluence of collective identity and individual obligation. The association of the covenant historical prologue and the Passover *Haggadah*, albeit allusively, in Levenson is important for understanding this as precursor for Augustine's *narratio*. Covenant formation and renewal, even in the new covenant, calls for a return to the historical recital of the grounding covenantal events.

79   Ibid., 38–39.

80   Ibid., 39.

81   Gabriel Moran, *Catechesis of Revelation* (New York: Herder and Herder, 1966), 45.

82   Levenson, *Sinai and Zion*, 39.

83   Alasdair MacIntyre, *After Virtue: A Study in Moral Theory*, 3d. ed. (Notre Dame: University of Notre Dame Press, 2007).

84   If there is a philosophical dimension to be found here, it is best expressed by Brevard Childs,

Levenson shows that although a covenantal theology of history takes shape around the Exodus event, the entire *Torah* can be read as a covenant text. Even though the historical prologue that we see in the covenant formulary arises later, the creation account and the migrations of Abraham are folded into its horizon.[85] "Most of the recapitulations of the sacred history begin, like Joshua 24, sometime in the Patriarchal period."[86]

Levenson is also eager to allay the sense that the telling of salvation history is anything like an end in itself. He rejects the classical Lutheran reading in which law and grace are opposed. In the view of ancient Judaism, the historical prologue is to incite the sense of obligation, to encourage observation of the covenant stipulations, the commandments, in *mitzvot* [righteous deeds]. He disputes the Lutheran reading of Romans 10:4 of Christ as "the end of the law,"[87] asserting as the Old Testament position that *mitzvot* are the proper goals of covenant formation and a loving response to the gratuitous acts of God toward Israel. What Levenson misses, however, is that the Greek of Romans 10:4 has Christ not *ending* the law, but serving as its *telos* [end as goal].[88] In the older Christian understanding, which is beginning under scholarly scrutiny to be the more widely accepted view of the arguments that Paul is making in Galatians 3 and Romans 4, the "obedience of faith," with which Paul begins and ends his presentation in Romans,[89] represents a very similar vision to the Old Testament vision advanced by Levenson.[90]

"It [memory] serves in making Israel noetically aware of a history which is ontologically a unity. There is only one redemptive history." *Memory and Tradition*, 52. Lawrence Hoffman suggests this dimension from the perspective of Jewish moral reflection: "Halakhah is a synchronic medium, a mode of discourse in which eternal truths are spelled out much as in the philosophy of essences. Verbs in halakhic debate are present participles, implying what one does or does not do, not just now but forever. What eternal truths are for the philosophers, halakhic propositions are for the Rabbis." From "Does God Remember? A Liturgical Theology of Memory" in Michael A. Signer, ed. *Memory and History in Christianity and Judaism* (Notre Dame, IN: University of Notre Dame Press, 2001), 56.

85   Scott Hahn, in *A Father Who Keeps His Promises* (Ann Arbor, MI: Servant Books, 1998), elaborates the covenantal elements latent in the symbols of the creation account in his second chapter "Creation Covenant and Cosmic Temple." He supplies a smattering of scholarly support for these (from R. Murray, R. de Vaux, and J. Ratzinger) in endnotes 7 and 8 on pages 270–271.

86   Levenson, *Sinai*, 40.

87   Where "end of the Law" would mean that the Law, now that Christ has come, is no longer needed and is therefore terminated.

88   On this and what follows, see Michael Wyschogrod's arresting analysis of St. Paul's treatment of the Law in Galatians and Romans in light of the decision of the so-called Council of Jerusalem in Acts 15 which binds the gentile Christians to the requirements of the Noachide law (vv. 19–20) but says nothing about the abrogation of the requirements of the Law for Jewish Christians. *Abraham's Promise: Judaism and Jewish-Christian Relations*, R. Kendall Soulen, ed. (Grand Rapids, MI and Cambridge, UK: William B. Eerdmans, 2004), 188 et seq.

89   Rom. 1:5 and 16:26; see also 15:18 and Paul's charge to "win obedience from the Gentiles."

90   See also N.T. Wright, *Paul: In Fresh Perspective* (Minneapolis, MN: Fortress Press, 2005); and, again, Hahn, *Kinship By Covenant* on what Paul means by "works of the law."

Levenson's theology of the historical prologue suggests that the proper order in Old Testament covenant formation is *Haggadah* (telling the story), *Torah* (teaching on the obligations covenant requires), and *Halakah* (walking in covenant fidelity).[91] In this connection, Donald Gowen in his work *Theology in Exodus* makes clear that despite their universalization in later Jewish reflection, the commandments of Exodus are only for Israel.[92] That might seem a surprising claim until one realizes that the experience of the exodus, whether had directly or by way of liturgical covenant renewal, as in the Passover *Haggadah*, is the necessary pedagogical precursor to the acceptance and living of the stipulations of covenant life.

The commandments are *covenant* stipulations. God first saves Israel (as he reminds them in the titulary and historical prologue) and then invites them to obedient covenant relation, not the other way around.[93] And that is not only a necessity of plot, but of anthropology and psychology. Any law which is imposed apart from the narrative circumstances of human experience will be treated as an imposition. This is also just the order that we saw in Augustine's *narratio: exordium, narratio,* then *exhortatio.* First, the catechist invites a hearing in the *exordium,* then tells the story of God's saving work in the *narratio,* and only then advances to an appeal for a loving response in the *exhortatio.* Parenesis follows *narratio,* just as *Torah* and *Halakah* follow *Haggadah.*

As Levenson helps us to see, the intimate covenantal knowing (*yada*) of God that comes by way of walking (*halakah*) in the commandments is not merely a cognitive thing but historical from start to finish, past history bestowing intelligibility upon present and future obligations.[94]

---

91 Levenson, *Sinai and Zion,* 50–56. Jacob Neusner provides simple definitions of these three on pages 216 and 218 of *The Emergence of Judaism* (Louisville and London: John Knox Press, 2004). For his seven meanings of *Torah* see chapter four, notably called, "Torah: The Worldview of Judaism," 57 et seq. The arrangement that I'm proposing here: *Haggadah, Torah, Halakah,* depends upon Levenson's identification of the importance of the historical prologue in covenant formation and renewal. I'm not suggesting that the *Haggadah,* understood as the "narrative read at the Passover banquet (Seder)" [Neusner, 16], occurs first in the scriptural history. I'm proposing that the historical experience of Israel is itself preparatory to the reception of the *Torah* and covenant stipulations at Sinai and that the later Seder *Haggadah* stands in for that experience in the ongoing life of Judaism and its catechetical formation of the young.

92 Donald E. Gowan, *Theology in Exodus: Biblical Theology in the Form of a Commentary* (Louisville, KY: Westminster John Knox Press, 1994), 180–182. The *Catechism* notes the same point at paragraphs 2057 and 2060. The commandments, to be understood and accepted, need the context of the exodus and covenant.

93 R. Kendall Soulen, in his commentary on the theology of Michael Wyschogrod says of it, "Even the *Torah,* for many interpreters Judaism's center of gravity, arises from the prior reality of God's election of the Jewish people. Israel is not the accidental bearer of the *Torah.* Rather, the *Torah* grows out of Israel's election and God's saving acts performed for his people." *Abraham's Promise,* 9.

94 The obverse of this can be seen in an essay called "Jewish Thought as Reflected in the *Halakah*" by Louis Ginzberg. Commenting on the phrase from the Talmud, "He who studies the *Halakah* daily may rest assured that he shall be a son of the world to come," Ginzberg says, "he who

That is nowhere more apparent than in Deuteronomy 6 where we read:

> When your son asks you in time to come, "What is the meaning
> of the testimonies and the statutes and the ordinances which
> the LORD our God has commanded you?" **21** then you shall say
> to your son, "We were Pharaoh's slaves in Egypt; and the LORD
> brought us out of Egypt with a mighty hand; **22** and the LORD
> showed signs and wonders, great and grievous, against Egypt
> and against Pharaoh and all his household, before our eyes; **23**
> and he brought us out from there, that he might bring us in and
> give us the land which he swore to give to our fathers. **24** And
> the LORD commanded us to do all these statutes, to fear the
> LORD our God, for our good always, that he might preserve us
> alive, as at this day. **25** And it will be righteousness for us, if we
> are careful to do all this commandment before the LORD our
> God, as he has commanded us."[95]

In this explicit Old Testament directive on catechesis of the young, the answer to
the question "Why should I live like a Jew?" is not "Because I said so." or "Because it
is the virtuous thing to do." or "Because you are the author of your own history." or
"Because you will bring about the workers' paradise." or even "Because Yahweh said
so."[96] but, rather, "We were Pharaoh's slaves in Egypt; and the LORD brought us
out." Marc Brettler, in agreement with Levenson about the preparatory character
of the recollected salvation history, notes that the phrase

> "you shall remember that you were slaves in Egypt" and its vari-
> ants ... appear five times in Deuteronomy. The phrase never ap-

---

studies the *Halakah* may be assured that he is a son of the world—the Jewish world—that has
been. Not that *Halakah* is a matter of the past; but the understanding of the Jewish past, of
Jewish life and thought, is impossible without a knowledge of the *Halakah*." From *The Jewish
Expression*, Judah Goldin, ed. (New Haven and London: Yale University Press, 1976), 164.

95   Deut. 6: 20–25.

96   I don't mean by this that obedience to God, as such, is unimportant to the Jew. See, for
example, Abraham Joshua Heschel's essay, "The Meaning of Observance" in *Understanding
Jewish Theology: Classical Issues and Modern Perspectives*, Jacob Neusner, ed., (New York: KTAV
Publishing House, 1973). He notes that "To say that the *mitzvoth* have meaning is less accurate
than saying that they lead us to wells of emergent meaning" (99). He means that "Divine meaning
... is experienced *in acts*, rather than in speculation" (98, emphasis in original). Note, that, just
as *Torah* surfaces out of the lived experience of Israel as expressed in the *Haggadah*, the meaning
of both surface out of the lived experience of *Halakah*. History yields covenant, covenant means
obedience, but that obedience is only fully meaningful when lived. Again, history and the
tradition it bears is not opposed to the vital experience of God in the present, as some suggest,
but is the very source of the meaning of the present when lived anew. So the *narratio* and the
doctrine which percolates up out of it can only be understood fully by an experience of lived
faith. And that experience testifies to the meaning, the veracity of the *narratio* and its doctrinal
grammar.

pears in isolation; this too suggests that the act of memory itself
is not central. Rather, it appears as a motivation of five different
laws . .... Here, too, "remembering leads to doing."[97]

But in the life of Israel the thing remembered didn't disappear after it was ef-
fected. "Thus, life in the covenant is not something merely granted, but something
won anew, rekindled and reconsecrated in the heart of each Israelite in every
generation."[98] Levenson cites the form of Psalm 81, which Jews today chant on
Thursday mornings, as a holdover of a regular liturgical re-presentation of the
Sinaitic covenant event.[99] He notes the urgency with which the current generation
of wanderers is addressed in Deuteronomy 5:1–4 as indicative of the importance of
retaining the immediacy of the covenant with the passage of time: "It was not with
our fathers that YHWH made this covenant, but with us—us!—those who are
here today, all of us living. Face to face YHWH spoke with you on the mountain,
from the midst of the fire" (vs. 3–4). Levenson suggests that this is to allay any
sense that they are only "obliged in a distant way by the covenant of Sinai/Horeb,
but not as direct partners in it."[100]

2. The Sevening of Time: Ritual Remembrance

Because that act of memorialization which is essential to covenant formation and
preservation must be renewed and can't be left to chance, the divine pedagogue
included among the stipulations of the covenant itself not just the Passover celebration but the seven feasts of the liturgical year of ancient Judaism.[101]

---

97 Marc Brettler, "Memory in Ancient Israel," in Michael A. Signer, ed., *Memory and History in Christianity and Judaism* (Notre Dame, IN: University of Notre Dame Press, 2001), 5–6. It is important to note that for scholars like Marc Brettler the Old Testament is not history in the modern sense but a "premodern history," which as memory presents not necessarily "*the* past," but rather, "*a* past." (Brettler, *Memory and History*, 10–11).

98 Levenson, *Sinai*, 81.

99 Levenson, *Sinai*, 80. For the historical-paradigmatic quality of Psalm 89, which "comprehends at once the history and destiny of the Jewish faith," see Jacob Neusner's early essay, "The Eighty–ninth Psalm: Paradigm of Israel's Faith," in his *History and Faith: Essays on Jewish Learning* (New York: Schocken Books, 1965) and his later, mature reflections on the emergence of the "paradigmatic thinking" which makes for the "presence of the past" and the "pastness of the present," in chapter seven of Jacob Neusner, "The Story Judaism Tells," in *Judaism When Christianity Began: A Survey of Belief and Practice* (Louisville, KY and London: Westminster John Knox Press, 2002).

100 Levenson, *Sinai*, 81. Levenson goes on to argue that the *mitzvah* [command] to twice daily recite the *Shma* prayer "is the rabbinic way of actualizing the moment at Sinai when Israel answered the divine offer of covenant . .... In short, the recitation of the *Shma* is the rabbinic covenant renewal ceremony," 85–86.

101 The cursory treatment here of the ancient feasts as *zikaron* or memorial of the exodus has as its background Lawrence Hoffman's concise treatment of *zekher/zikaron* in liturgical use in "Does God Remember?" 41–72.

These are delineated in the twenty-third chapter of Leviticus. There the Lord tells Moses, "Say to the people of Israel, The appointed feasts of the LORD which you shall proclaim as holy convocations, my appointed feasts, are these."[102] The first bedrock observance is, of course, the Sabbath of solemn rest that sanctifies each week. The Sabbath observance had been enjoined in the Ten Commandments.[103] It is also assumed in the event of the provision of manna in Exodus 16. That miraculous bread, which normally went foul if kept until the next day, was both unavailable for gathering on the Sabbath and was preserved for the Sabbath from the previous day. Further, and importantly, the Pentateuch sees the roots of the Sabbath observance in the account of creation itself, as seen in Genesis 2:3: "So God blessed the seventh day and hallowed it, because on it God rested from all his work which he had done in creation."[104]

This blessing of the seventh is played out again and again in the process of sanctifying time in the Old Testament. In Leviticus 25, God commands that every seventh year be a "Sabbath" year of solemn rest for the land—a solemn rest from plowing and pruning, for man and beast. God even calls for a jubilee year after "seven weeks of years" ($7 \times 7 = 49$), that is, in the fiftieth year, beginning on the first day of the feast of Atonement, during which the Jews are to rest from labor for a whole year and to offer return of land and freedom to those who had lost either because of debt or sale since the last major jubilee.[105] In Deuteronomy 31 Moses commanded, in keeping with the fourth part of the typical covenant formulary that we saw above (deposition of the text), that on the Feast of Booths in the jubilee year "you shall read this law before all Israel in their hearing."[106]

This "sevening" of time can be seen, too, in the yearly feasts of Israel, of which there were seven commanded in Leviticus 23.[107] Three of these, Passover (*Pesach*)[108],

---

102 Lev. 23:2.

103 Exod. 20:11. "The same *Kiddush* prayer that gives us the Sabbath as a 'memorial of the work of creation' says also that it is a *zekher li'tsiyat mitsrayim*, 'a memorial of the Exodus.'" Hoffman, "Does God Remember?" 55.

104 Exod. 31:12–17. For a brief but comprehensive account of the scriptural roots and rabbinical reading of the Sabbath see Baruch Levine and Jacob Neusner (respectively) in chapters seven and eight of Jacob Neusner, Bruce Chilton, and Baruch Levine, *Torah Revealed, Torah Fulfilled: Scriptural Laws in Formative Judaism and Earliest Christianity* (New York and London: T&T Clark, 2008).

105 For the Sabbath and Jubilee as a return to the perfection of Eden and as a desist from creation, see Neusner, *Judaism When Christianity Began*, 67–78.

106 Deut. 31:10–11. See Levenson, *Sinai*, 29 and 34.

107 Hoffman ("Does God Remember?" 55), citing the *Kiddush al hakos*, relates that "'It [the Sabbath] is the day [that marks] the first of the sacred convocations [*mikra'ei kodesh*], a memorial of the Exodus . . . .' Technically, then, all sacred convocations, not only the Sabbath, are memorials of the Exodus." The OT citations identifying the following feasts as sacred convocations and so also as memorial (*zikaron*), as indicated in the paradigmatic text for Passover which Hoffman cites from Exodus 12:14–16, will be cited below.

108 Lev. 23:7–8; Num. 28:18, 25.

Unleavened Bread (*Matzot*), and First Fruits (*Bikkurim*), were celebrated in the first month of the Jewish calendar, Nisan, which falls in the spring. They combined the commemoration of the first Passover with a memorial of the first harvest in the Promised Land. One other feast, that of Weeks (*Shavuot*),[109] fell one day beyond seven weeks after First Fruits (again, 7 x 7 days + 1, or 50 days) and so was, and still is, called Pentecost, from the Greek for fifty days. It celebrates both the full harvest and the giving of the law at Mount Sinai.

The three other feasts, Trumpets (*Rosh Hashanah*),[110] Atonement (*Yom Kippur*),[111] and Tabernacles or Booths (*Sukkot*),[112] were celebrated during Tishri, the seventh month of the year. These seven feasts divide the year into two great blocks of feasts in the first and seventh months, in the spring and fall, with Pentecost standing on its own in late May or June.[113] Three of the seven feasts, Passover, Pentecost, and Tabernacles, were called pilgrim feasts because able-bodied men were expected to come to Jerusalem for their observance.[114] In this way, the year was punctuated by religious celebrations that served as a kind of life breath of Judaism as she inhaled her pilgrims into the Jerusalem Temple and exhaled them out again into the towns and villages of Israel, and even into the diaspora beyond.[115]

These feasts were commanded by God. By them, he was claiming a place in the lives of his people and was hallowing time. These feasts served to keep the founding events of Mosaic Judaism—the events of the exodus—deeply etched in the memory of the Jewish people. As I've already mentioned, the Jewish feasts recalled the mysteries of God's saving action among His chosen people. God's command to celebrate memorial feasts of this kind acknowledge an important psychological principle. Stated simply, (and forgive the apparent tautology) when we don't remember God and what he has done for us, we tend to forget him. As Childs notes, to remember or keep the festival (which is to recall the event it recalls)

---

109 Lev. 23:21; Num. 28:26.

110 Lev. 23:24; Num. 29:1. The monthly New Moon celebration, of which Rosh Hashanah is the first of the (civil) year, is cited at Isa. 1:13.

111 Lev. 23:27; Num. 29:7.

112 Lev. 23:35, 37; Num. 29:12.

113 Phillip Sigal gives a very helpful description of the feasts in *Judaism: The Evolution of a Faith*, revised and edited by Lillian Sigal (Grand Rapids: William B. Eerdmans Publishing, 1988), 19–25.

114 Exod. 23:14–17.

115 "Pesach, Shabuot (or Shabbuoth), and Sukkot (or Sukkoth) are known as the "pilgrimage festivals" because of the biblical requirement that pilgrimages to the sanctuary be made at those crucial times in the agricultural calendar. They were times of harvest, and gifts of first fruits were to be presented to the priests." Sigal, *Judaism*, 21. See also Neusner, *Judaism When Christianity Began*, 135–146.

means "to act in obedience toward" God. Likewise, to forget is commensurate with covenant failure, to "go after other gods and serve them and worship them."[116]

Whenever Israel became lax in observing God's ritual commands, it tended to forget altogether the covenant with him. For example, at the time of the sweeping religious reforms of King Josiah in the seventh century B.C., as the author of 2 Kings notes, "[N]o such passover had been kept since the days of the judges who judged Israel, or during all the days of the kings of Israel or of the kings of Judah."[117] So, in direct opposition to God's command in Exodus 12 and Leviticus 23 that the Passover be kept as the principal yearly memorial feast of God's saving work, there had been no such official celebration of it for four centuries!

During that same period, the kings of Israel and Judah consented to or directly engaged in horrendous acts of idolatry, including ritualized sexual misconduct, and even child sacrifice.[118] It was this continual and wanton disregard of the covenant, in part caused by the disregard of the covenant liturgy, that had occasioned the reforms of King Josiah, who "put away the mediums and the wizards and the teraphim and the idols and all the abominations that were seen in the land of Judah and in Jerusalem, that he might establish the words of the law that Hilkiah the priest found in the house of the Lord."[119] And despite Josiah's best efforts to draw the southern kingdom of Judah back to covenantal fidelity, disobedience and idolatry would eventually lead Israel into exile, this time to Babylon rather than Egypt, beginning in 586 B. C.

In accord with the educational dictum that repetition is the mother of learning, it seems that God was saying to Israel, "If you won't ritually recall the last time I saved you from (Egyptian) bondage, I'll just have to exile and save you again to refresh your memory." In this respect the regime of Christianity is no different than that of Judaism: to fail to memorialize God's works will tend to lead to negligence. Therefore, it is no surprise that when Jesus fulfills and perfects the Passover, he will command, "Do this in memory of me," to ensure that by liturgical recollection of his salvation, Christians, too, would be moved to covenantal fidelity.

In this regard, the Bible seems to suggest a psychological imperative of human nature that the God of the Bible feeds by commanding Israel to memorialize his saving work in acts of worship throughout the year.[120] The biblical view

---

116 Childs, *Memory and Tradition*, 54. See Deut. 18:18–19.

117 2 Kings 23:22.

118 The prophet's chilling indictment of Judah over the "Topheth" in Jer. 19 includes the charge that "they have filled this place with the blood of innocents, and have built the high places of Baal to burn their sons in the fire as burnt offerings to Baal" (vv. 4–5).

119 2 Kings 23:24. This suggests that the part of the covenant formulary called the deposition of the text, which required both the placement of the covenant text in the temple and then its periodic reading, had only been observed in regard to the first requirement.

120 The Hebrew root term *mo'ed* refers to appointed times of worship and immediately suggests to Jewish ears a time of a specifically religious assembly for liturgical purposes. It is this word

of time is that its seasons and cycles are, from their creation, precisely *for* the ritual remembering that was intended to help Israel remain covenantally faithful. Creation itself, and the movements of the stars and planets, are ordered to these "appointed times."[121]

IV. Conclusion

As we have seen, Levenson associates the covenant historical prologue with the Passover Seder *Haggadah*. Both are expressive of the conviction that "telling the story brings it alive, actualizes it, turns it from past into present and bridges the gap between individual and collective experience."[122] In God's command to Israel to keep the Passover as a perpetual ordinance he says, "This day shall be for you a memorial day, and you shall keep it as a feast to the Lord; throughout your generations you shall observe it as an ordinance forever."[123] In regard to this paradigmatic memorial of the Jewish ritual cycle the *Catechism of the Catholic Church* says:

> In the sense of Sacred Scripture the *memorial* is not merely the recollection of past events but the proclamation of the mighty works wrought by God for men.[184] In the liturgical celebration of these events, they become in a certain way present and real. This is how Israel understands its liberation from Egypt: every time Passover is celebrated, the Exodus events are made present to the memory of believers so that they may conform their lives to them.[124]

Christians, of course, hold that it was in conformity with this command for a perpetual memorial that Christ Jesus, on the night he was betrayed, said, "Do this in remembrance of me."[125] And in so doing Jesus was acting exactly in accord with the thought-world of ancient Judaism. Sacred memorials of the saving events of God's acts in history are an essential part of covenant formation and maintenance and so the "new covenant in my blood" that Jesus references would presumably require the same. Lawrence Hoffman confirms this by saying that encouragement for a proper ritual memorial of the Passover that we find in rabbis like Hillel is the same thing we find in Rabbi Jesus' "Do this in memory of me." "They are of a piece,

---

that is used in Genesis 1:14 ("for signs and for seasons"[RSV]) and Leviticus 23:2 when God commands that the seven feasts be kept at the "time appointed." See K. Kock, "*mô'ēd*," *Theological Dictionary of the Old Testament* Vol. VIII, G. J. Botterweck and H. Ringren, eds., David Green, trans. (Grand Rapids, MI: Wm. B. Eerdmans, 1980), 167–173.

121 See Ps. 104:19, "Thou hast made the moon to mark the seasons (*moadim*); the sun knows its time for setting."

122 Levenson, *Sinai*, 42.

123 Exod. 12:14.

124 *Catechism*, no. 1363, emphasis in original.

125 Luke 22:19.

each being a set of words that accompany a ritual act . ... In both cases, we have liturgy as the Rabbis understood it, liturgy as *zikaron*, liturgy as memory, or better, as pointer, drawing God's attention to what matters."[126] What this suggests to us is that the divine pedagogy is thoroughly covenantal, memorial, and so also historical, as well as thoroughly ritual.

What we've seen so far comports roughly with the list of the features of the divine pedagogy that I presented from GDC 143. The ritual, memorial, covenantal system that constitutes the Judaism of the Bible is dialogical, but by God's initiative. The treaty form of the covenant is bilateral, although between unequals: God playing the role of the liege sovereign and Israel the role of lesser vassal king. God's Old Testament pedagogy is progressive and adaptable. He alters his approach based upon the fidelity or infidelity of his people. It is a pedagogy of signs, or what Hoffman calls "pointers," which is the more literal translation of the *zekher/zikaron*. The liturgical life of Israel is woven out of these memorial signs. It is both communal and interpersonal, the collective history supplying the collective identity into which each Jew is incorporated with each celebration of the yearly Passover.[127]

Levenson's work suggests that the covenantal nature of the relationship, which requires an historical prologue to establish relationship and obligation, may in some measure be the very reason for the whole of the Old Testament corpus. The narrative portions and certain Psalms supply the historical prologue or the *Haggadah*; the legislative portions or *Torah* represent the covenant stipulations; the prophets regulate covenant fidelity and measure *Halakhic* conformity. The very preservation of the texts through the ages suggests the importance of deposition and ritual recital of the covenant documents. As Levenson makes clear, all of this depends upon the recitation of the tribal or national history of Israel as the engine of covenant formation and maintenance.

This all suggests, as Jacob Neusner puts it, that "Israel's history is taken over into the structure of Israel's life of sanctification, and all that happens to Israel forms part of the structure of holiness built around cult, *Torah*, synagogue, sages, Zion, and the like."[128] To put it in the succinct formulation borrowed from narrative theology, the story is performative in character. According to the telling of that story in the Old Testament, as well as its haggadic retelling in Judaism, this is all at God's direction. In this sense we could conclude that the divine pedagogy of the Old Testament is very much what I have called narrational.

---

126 Hoffman, "Does God Remember?" 66. Hoffman, after surveying the post-biblical rabbinical literature, concludes that the terms *zekher* and *zikaron* really mean "pointer" and these things can be both signifiers and the thing signified, these things can be events, places, objects, which point to the mercy of God, who is both remembered and the one who remembers Israel.

127 The Christocentric character of the pedagogy, as cited at point 3 in the list from GDC 143 will obviously have to wait for the "fullness of time."

128 Neusner, *Judaism When Christianity Began*, 88.

Further investigation would show that the New Testament practice is expressive of the characteristics of the divine pedagogy that the GDC elaborates as well. Of course, in the New Testament pedagogy we see the Christocentric dimension (or what GDC 143 calls a "pedagogy of the incarnation") that a Christian faith would add to the Jewish reading of the Old Testament. This Christocentric addition highlights the progressive and gradual nature of the divine pedagogy as a whole. The enduring importance given to the types of the Old Testament in the New suggests, too, that this is not a pedagogy that rushes to the punch line, so to speak, without allowing the story to unfold.

The story matters all along the way, just as the stages of the journey toward faith must each be given their season. Again, doctrine and morals, *Torah* and *Halakah*, don't come before the story, the *Haggadah*. They don't supersede it, but percolate up out of it in the lived "community experience of faith."[129] Even in the canonical arrangement of the New Testament this can be seen. The epistolary doctrine and its parenesis follow the narrative Gospels and Acts, while the apocalyptic and mystagogical Revelation draw up the rear.[130] Even the *Catechism of the Catholic Church* follows this narrational pattern of the divine pedagogy: first it presents the Creed and sacraments preceding the commandments and prayer (*Haggadah, Torah, Halakah*), making sure in its echo of the divine pedagogy that the telling of God's saving history in the Creed and our graced entry into those saving works in the sacramental liturgies precede the application of the covenant stipulations and our observance of them in the moral life and prayer.

This is why the GDC enjoins so strongly the telling of the *narratio*. It is the elaborated story of the Creed, which represents the doctrine which percolates up out of that story and which serves as the grammar to our proper reading of it. Without the story, we lose the "why" of doctrine and morals. I would suggest that much of the work of the New Evangelization will involve providing the answer to the question "*why* should I be a Christian?" A very similar question is posed in Deuteronomy 6: "What is the meaning of the testimonies and the statutes and the ordinances which the LORD our God has commanded you?" The Old Testament answers, not with a rational apologetic, but with a story, a *narratio*: "We were Pharaoh's slaves in Egypt; and the LORD brought us out of Egypt with a mighty hand; and the LORD showed signs and wonders, great and grievous, against Egypt and against Pharaoh and all his household, before our eyes. …"[131]

This deeper exploration of the divine pedagogy in the Old Testament would suggest that the GDC's imperative regarding the *narratio* is telling us that if we hope to help the West regain its Christian identity in this New Evangelization, we

---

129 GDC 143.

130 See Scott Hahn's *The Lamb's Supper: The Mass as Heaven on Earth* (New York: Doubleday, 1999) for the Book of Revelation as a kind of mystagogy of the Eucharist.

131 Deut. 6: 20–22.

must first help it regain its memory. It is the central place of memory and ritual remembrance to the construction of both Jewish and Christian identity that establishes the importance of a narrated rehearsal of the past works of God.

I would suggest that the New Evangelization of those peoples from cultures formerly committed to Christianity but which have now given up the faith requires that that they be helped to overcome the amnesia of the divine favor so clearly shown in salvation history. Without that recovery of memory there will be no hope of a return to Christian practice, nor even to the exercise of the moral patrimony of the West. What we need in the New Evangelization is to regain the capacity to tell the story that God tells in history, so that his love might be manifest again to people who have forgotten it, and so refuse to return it.

Letter & Spirit 8 (2013): 189-221

HISTORICAL CRITICISM AS SECULAR ALLEGORISM
The Case of Spinoza

~: Jeffrey L. Morrow :~

Immaculate Conception Seminary School of Theology

Introduction

Biblical scholarship at the beginning of the twenty-first century includes an incredibly diverse array of methodologies under its ever-broadening canopy. A whole host of postmodern, feminist, liberationist, postcolonial, and many other adjectival neologisms modify the hermeneutics of biblical scholarship in the academy.[1] Notwithstanding such a disparate panoply of interpretive frameworks, historical biblical criticism continues its hegemony in modern biblical studies.[2] As with the modern academic discipline of history, modern biblical scholarship in general tends to operate under the false assumption that the methods used are comparable to the Baconian laboratory methodology of the hard sciences like chemistry and physics. *L'esprit géométrique* [the spirit of geometry] has won the day. Geometric reason and the discipline of mathematics, with its language of "proof," remains the paradigmatic example of rationality to many Bible scholars, Catholic or otherwise.

With the advent of the university in the medieval period, Scripture was studied and taught as Sacred Doctrine—theological by its very nature. Explicitly theological interpretation continues to exist in the academy, but it does so as a minority

---

1 A brief sample of the titles of program units represented at the 2012 annual meeting of the Society of Biblical Literature (SBL) illustrates this hermeneutical breadth: "African Biblical Hermeneutics"; "African-American Biblical Hermeneutics"; "Asian and Asian-American Hermeneutics"; "Ecological Hermeneutics"; "Feminist Hermeneutics of the Bible"; "Gender, Sexuality, and the Bible"; "Islands, Islanders, and Scriptures"; "Latino/a and Latin American Biblical Interpretation"; "LGBT [Lesbian, Gay, Bisexual, Transexual]/Queer Hermeneutics"; and "Postcolonial Studies and Biblical Studies." A sample of the titles of papers presented at this meeting likewise displays a diversity unthinkable a century ago: "Adam as Alpha Male: Genesis 1–3, Christian Domestic Discipline, and the Erotics of Wife Spanking"; "'Dude Looks Like a Lady': Queering Wisdom in Proverbs 1–9"; "Isaiah the Tree-Hugger: Prophetic Protests of Deforestation and Visions of Ecological Restoration (Then and Now)"; "Translation Matters: A 'Womanist-Postcolonial' Reading of John 4:29–42"; "'When She Goes to Serve Her House': Pre-Coital Vaginal Examination in Palestinian and Babylonian Rabbinic Law"; "The 'Witch' of Endor and Postcolonial Magic Theory"; and "Why is Xena Naked or Veiled? The Gender Logic of Female Drag in the Ancient Near East." I use the example of the SBL because it represents the world's largest scholarly association for the study of the Bible.

2 See, for example, the 1987 Presidential Address at the SBL, Elisabeth Schüssler Fiorenza, "The Ethics of Biblical Interpretation: Decentering Biblical Scholarship," *Journal of Biblical Literature* 107 (1988): 3–17.

among a cacophony of voices.[3] By and large Catholic biblical scholarship follows this same trend. Although examples of feminist and liberationist hermeneutics can be found, Catholic biblical scholarship remains heavily historical-critical.[4] By the phrases historical-critical, historical biblical criticism, historical critical method, and the like, I do not mean simply any historical method, but rather the various methods termed source criticism, form criticism, and redaction criticism. These are more properly labeled *literary* methods than *historical* methods, as they rely more upon hypothetical literary theories of compositional origin and editorial activity than they do upon archaeology, philology, and comparative ancient historiography.

In an article on allegorical interpretation, Robert Louis Wilken recaps the odium modern Bible scholars have had for figurative and spiritual exegesis, including a personal anecdote from his student days. He aptly sums up the situation when he writes: "For generations now, biblical interpreters have scorned allegory, anagogy, tropology, and all their works. Only the literal or historical sense, presented to us by the tools of historical criticism, can claim the allegiance of modern exegetes."[5]

Attention to the literal-historical sense is the only sense that matters for historical-critical exegesis.[6] This overemphasis on the literal sense by the canons of modern biblical criticism stands in stark contrast to the official guidelines of Catholic biblical interpretation as set forth in the *Catechism of the Catholic Church*. In the *Catechism*, traditional senses of Scripture—literal and spiritual, with the subdivisions of the spiritual into allegorical/typological, moral/tropological, and anagogical—ensure the wealth of spiritual riches to be gained from exegesis.[7]

---

3   Thus, the SBL includes units like "Christian Theology and the Bible" and "Theological Interpretation of Scripture." Of course many of the other units, including those cited above, are also theological, but they are almost always representative of a secularized theology inextricably bound to non-theological methodological frameworks like Marxist philosophy, etc.

4   One need only read through any number of examples of such postmodern approaches to exegesis to see the underlying assumptions that take for granted modern historical critical (for example, source critical) assumptions about the real history behind the texts. See, for example, the groundbreaking work of feminist biblical criticism by Phyllis Trible, "Depatriarchalizing in Biblical Interpretation," *Journal of the American Academy of Religion* 41 (1973): 30–48, where she adopts classical source critical distinctions between Genesis 1 as a Priestly text and Genesis 2–3 as a Yahwistic text.

5   Robert Louis Wilken, "In Defense of Allegory," *Modern Theology* 14 (1998): 197–212, at 197.

6   In this discussion, I am indebted to Michael C. Legaspi, "The Literal Sense According to Historical Criticism" (Paper Presented at the Annual Meeting of the Society of Biblical Literature, Chicago, November 17, 2012), where he notes the difficulty of finding explicit mention of the literal sense among early modern and Enlightenment exegetes because a literal sense only makes sense in comparison to other senses, which such exegetes reject.

7   See the *Catechism of the Catholic Church*, 2nd ed. (Vatican: Libreria Editrice Vaticana, 1997 [1994]), no. 115–117. See also the comments in William S. Kurz, S. J., "Patristic Interpretation of Scripture within God's Story of Creation and Redemption," *Letter & Spirit* 7 (2011): 35–50, at 36–38; William M. Wright IV, "Patristic Biblical Hermeneutics in Joseph Ratzinger's *Jesus of Nazareth*," *Letter & Spirit* 7 (2011): 191–207, at 204–205; and Michael Maria Waldstein, "*Analogia Verbi*: The Truth of Scripture in Rudolf Bultmann and Raymond Brown," *Letter & Spirit* 6 (2010): 93–140, at 126–135.

With regard to the spiritual sense of applying the text's meaning to our lives, Pope Benedict XVI explains, "The seriousness of the historical quest is in no way diminished by this: on the contrary, it is enhanced."[8]

Despite pretenses to exclusive reliance upon the literal-historical sense—and thus to the quest for objective truth, as modern interpreters maintain—historical criticism at times results in exegesis that appears more like allegory on steroids than the plain sense of the text. Indeed, precisely by denying the plain meaning of the text in search of a more authentic history behind the text as we have it, historical criticism often results in fanciful reconstructions, more allegorical than literal, that would make Origen blush.[9] Historical criticism, especially in its source critical and form critical attire, often begins with a hermeneutic of suspicion, is guided by a hermeneutic of discontinuity, and results in a reconstruction of the imaginary history behind the text. This historical reconfiguration envisions distinct compositional histories of the biblical texts, histories that conflict with received tradition and are only discernable to scholarly eyes devoid of theological commitment. Such methods were forged especially in the wake of seventeenth century theo-political conflicts which engulfed Europe, were honed in the Enlightenment, and perfected in the nineteenth century.

It should not come as a surprise that these hypothetical literary theories were grounded in the politics of the time. The result is that the very theological diversity that confronts critics across confessional boundaries in the modern world is imposed on the text. This takes place by the allegation that such theological (and political) diversity represents the true history-behind-the-texts; that is, we are led to believe that the presence of both positive and negative elements of particular biblical figures (for example, David), or stylistic diversity of any kind, are positive evidence of different theo-political communities within ancient Israel. These communities wrote different conflicting versions of their history, portions of which were later spliced together by teams of editors, for the purpose of supporting the

---

8   Joseph Ratzinger/Pope Benedict XVI, *Jesus of Nazareth: The Infancy Narratives*, trans. Philip J. Whitmore (New York: Image, 2012), xi. The context is Pope Benedict's opinion on what he believes to be the two key stages of biblical exegesis: "I am convinced that good exegesis involves two stages. Firstly one has to ask what the respective authors intended to convey through their text in their own day—the historical component of exegesis. But it is not sufficient to leave the text in the past and thus relegate it to history. The second question posed by good exegesis must be: is what I read here true? Does it concern me? If so, how? With a text like the Bible, whose ultimate and fundamental author, according to our faith, is God himself, the question regarding the here and now of things past is undeniably included in the task of exegesis. The seriousness of the historical quest is in no way diminished by this: on the contrary, it is enhanced."

9   Origen of Alexandria is typically associated with allegorical exegesis, and for good reason. He also engaged in literal exegesis, which is often forgotten. See, for example, Peter W. Martens, *Origen and Scripture: The Contours of the Exegetical Life* (Oxford: Oxford University, 2012), especially 63–67; Peter W. Martens, "Origen Against History? Reconsidering the Critique of Allegory," *Modern Theology* 28 (2012): 635–656; and Hermann J. Vogt, "Origen of Alexandria (185–253), in *Handbook of Patristic Exegesis: The Bible in Ancient Christianity*, ed. Charles Kannengiesser (Leiden: Brill, 2006), 536–574, at 546–547.

theological politics of the editors. This sort of theory assumes that these ancient texts were composed and redacted by rival communities and thus that such competing politics was at the root of Scripture. Communities were responsible for composing and redacting what were essentially theo-political texts, which became our Scripture.

As an example of this kind of compositional theory, which becomes what I will refer to as a "secular allegory," I have selected the work of Baruch Spinoza, who stands out as a key figure involved in these early debates about the quest for an objective method of biblical interpretation. Spinoza is one of the earliest figures to attempt to articulate a "scientific" method of biblical exegesis.[10] Jonathan Israel explains Spinoza's significance within the broader Enlightenment project as a whole:

---

10   Richard E. Averbeck, "Pentateuchal Criticism and the Priestly Torah," in *Do Historical Matters Matter to Faith? A Critical Appraisal of Modern and Postmodern Approaches to Scripture*, eds. James K. Hoffmeier and Dennis R. Magary (Wheaton: Crossway, 2012), 151–180, at 152–153; Dominique Barthélemy, "The History of Old Testament Textual Criticism from Its Origins to J. D. Michaelis," in *Studies in the Text of the Old Testament: An Introduction to the Hebrew Old Testament Text Project: English Translation of the Introductions to Volumes 1, 2, and 3 Critique textuelle de l'ancien testament*, by Dominique Barthélemy, trans. Stephen Pisano and Peter A. Pettit for vol. 1, Joan E. Cook and Sarah Lind for vol. 2, and Sarah Lind for vol. 3 (Winona Lake: Eisenbrauns, 2012), 2–81, at 30, 52–54, and 64; Pierre Gibert, *L'invention critique de la Bible: XVᵉ–XVIIIᵉ siècle* [*The Invention of Criticism of the Bible: 15ᵗʰ–18ᵗʰ Century*] (Paris: Éditions Gallimard, 2010), 10, 148–175, 178–179, 184, 186, 197–198, 265–268, 292, 297, 302, and 304; Nicolai Sinai, "Spinoza and Beyond: Some Reflections on Historical-Critical Method," in *Kritische Religionsphilosophie: Eine Gedenkschrift für Friedrich Niewöhner* [*Critical Philosophy of Religion: A Festschrift for Friedrich Niewöhner*], eds. Wilhelm Schmidt-Biggemann and Georges Tamer (Berlin: de Gruyter, 2010), 193–213; Jean-Louis Ska, *The Exegesis of the Pentateuch: Exegetical Studies and Basic Questions* (Tübingen: Mohr Siebeck, 2009), XV–XVI, 257–259; Magne Sæbø, "From the Renaissance to the Enlightenment—Aspects of the Cultural and Ideological Framework of Scriptural Interpretation," in *Hebrew Bible/Old Testament: The History of Its Interpretation Volume II: From the Renaissance to the Enlightenment*, ed. Magne Sæbø (Göttingen: Vandenhoeck & Ruprecht, 2008), 21–45, at 41–42; Niels Peter Lemche, *The Old Testament between Theology and History: A Critical Survey* (Louisville: Westminster John Knox Press, 2008), 259; V. Philips Long, "Historiography of the Old Testament," in *The Face of Old Testament Studies: A Survey of Contemporary Approaches*, eds. David W. Baker and Bill T. Arnold (Grand Rapids: Baker Academic, 1999), 145–175, at 148; Gerhard Maier, "Wahrheit und Wirklichkeit im Geschichtsverständnis des Alten Testaments" ["Truth and Reality in the Historical Understanding of the Old Testament"], in *Israel in Geschichte und Gegenwart* [*Israel in History and the Present*], ed. Gerhard Maier (Basel: Brunnen, 1996), 9–23, at 10–11; Paolo Sacchi, "Le pentateuque, le deutéronomiste et Spinoza" ["The Pentateuch, the Deuteronomist and Spinoza"], in *Congress Volume: Paris 1992*, ed. J. A. Emerton (Leiden: Brill, 1995), 275–288, at 278; L. Alonso Schökel, "Arte narrative en Josue-Jueces-Samuel-Reyes" ["Narrative Art in Joshua-Judges-Samuel-Kings"], *Estudios Bíblicos* 48 (1990): 145–169, at 149; Moshe Goshen-Gottstein, "Bible et judaïsm" ["Bible and Judaism"], in *Le Grand Siècle et la Bible* [*The Great Century and the Bible*], ed. Jean-Robert Armogathe (Paris: Beauchesne, 1989), 33–38; John H. Hayes, "The History of the Study of Israelite and Judaean History," in *Israelite and Judaean History*, eds. John H. Hayes and J. Maxwell Miller (London: SCM Press, 1977), 33–69, at 45; and Hans-Joachim Kraus, *Geschichte der historisch-kritischen Erforschung des Alten Testaments* [*A History of the Historical-Critical Study of the Old Testament*], 2ⁿᵈ rev. ed. (Neukirchen: Vluyn, 1969 [1956]), 64.

... it is impossible to name another philosopher whose impact on the entire range of intellectual debates of the Enlightenment was deeper or more far-reaching than Spinoza's or whose Bible criticism and theory of religion was more widely or obsessively wrestled with, philosophically, throughout Europe during the century after his death. If the great *Encyclopédie* of Diderot and d'Alembert allocates twenty-two columns of text to Spinoza, the longest entry for any modern philosopher, in its entry about him, as against the remarkably low figure of only four to Locke and three to Malebranche, in their corresponding entries, this was assuredly not because the editors of the *Encyclopédie* were so utterly unaware of what was relevant to their Enlightenment that they got their editorial priorities stupendously wrong or owing to some wholly inexplicable aberration that historians can in no way account for. The simple fact is—however much this runs counter to certain commonplace notions—that Spinoza was deemed by them to be of greater relevance to the core issues of the *Encyclopédie* not just than Locke and Malebrance but also Hobbes or Leibniz.[11]

Thus, in this article I begin by situating Spinoza within his theo-political context. I then proceed to examine Spinoza's treatment of priesthood as an example of his exegesis. Finally, I conclude with a few comments about the need for a more faithful hermeneutic. Pope Benedict XVI has shown how, "From a purely scientific point of view, the legitimacy of an interpretation depends on its power to explain things."[12] That is, the better model (on scientific grounds) will have more explanatory power. The traditional theological explanation has better explanatory power than Spinoza's.[13] In the end, we need a liturgical or sacramental hermeneutic which

---

11   Jonathan Israel, "The Early Dutch and German Reaction to the *Tractatus Theologico-Politicus*: Foreshadowing the Enlightenment's More General Spinoza Reception?" in *Spinoza's Theological-Political Treatise: A Critical Guide*, eds. Yitzhak Y. Melamed and Michael A. Rosenthal (Cambridge: Cambridge University, 2010), 72–100, at 72–73. Elsewhere Israel claims that, "... Spinoza and Spinozism were in fact the intellectual backbone of the European Radical Enlightenment everywhere, not only in the Netherlands, Germany, France, Italy, and Scandinavia but also Britain and Iceland." See Jonathan I. Israel, *Radical Enlightenment: Philosophy and the Making of Modernity 1650–1750* (Oxford: Oxford University, 2001), vi. In his sequel, he continues this sustained argument, contending that, "it was ... the freethinkers, *esprits forts*, and *matérialistes*, particularly adherents of something called 'Spinozism' (which was not quite the same thing as Spinoza's philosophy), who set the pace and framed the agenda of scholarly and intellectual discussion not only during the Early Enlightenment but throughout the Enlightenment era." See Jonathan Israel, *Enlightenment Contested: Philosophy, Modernity, and the Emancipation of Man 1670–1752* (Oxford: Oxford University, 2006), 40.

12   Joseph Cardinal Ratzinger, *Behold the Pierced One: An Approach to a Spiritual Christology*, trans. by Graham Harrison (San Francisco: Ignatius Press, 1986 [1984]), 44.

13   In context, Ratzinger explains that, "the less it [an interpretation] needs to interfere with the

leads to mystagogical exegesis. What is needed is a method which is historical, theological, canonical, following the rule of faith, making sense of the whole of dogma and of Scripture, and follows the guide of the Magisterium so that we can read the Bible from the heart of the Church in light of the sacred mystery of Scripture's dual authorship. Such a method should allow for and facilitate use of the full senses of Scripture, and should lead mystagogically from the signs to the deeper and hidden divine realities they signify. The study of Scripture, after all, is ordered to sanctity. The Bible's purpose, its *raison d'être*, is that those who read from its pages or who attend to its proclamation become saints.

In contrast to all of this, much of what passes as historical in modern biblical criticism is not so much literal exegesis as it is *secular allegory*. It does not result so much from careful attention to the final form of the text, or even to textual vari- ants in the manuscript tradition, the only forms in which we know for certain the texts ever existed; but results rather from elaborate hypothetical literary theories guided by specific theological and philosophical assumptions (which were shaped by the Enlightenment) that predetermine the conclusions. The greatest example of this concerns the prevailing Enlightenment assumptions about priesthood, cult, temple, and sacrifice. As the Enlightenment version of the pristine history of Israel gradually comes into focus, it curiously resembles the theo-political ideals of lib- eral nineteenth century German Protestants, inherited from the Reformation via Europe's secular Enlightenments. It is my contention that, in this form, historical criticism amounts to secular allegorism.

A Method Forged in the Fires of Theo-Political Conflict: Spinoza in His 17th Century Context

Baruch Spinoza (1632–1677) was born to Marrano parents in Amsterdam. As Marranos, his parents had converted to Catholicism in Portugal, and these Marranos in Amsterdam were newly returning to their Jewish roots. The violence of the Thirty Years' War (1618–1648) was still being waged during the first sixteen years of his life. This context of dismay and calamity is important to keep in mind. The acknowledged disorder and hostility of this time contrasts with the older view that the seventeenth century Enlightenment was due to the greater objectivity of more "enlightened" intellectuals, on account of their greater prosperity and security than before.[14] Indeed, the carnage and terror of the so-called "wars of

---

sources, the more it respects the corpus as given and is able to show it to be intelligible from within, by its own logic, the more apposite such an interpretation is. Conversely, the more it interferes with the sources, the more it feels obliged to excise and throw doubt on things found there, the more alien to the subject it is. To that extent, its explanatory power is also its ability to maintain the inner unity of the corpus in question. It involves the ability to unify, to achieve a synthesis, which is the reverse of superficial harmonization. Indeed, only faith's hermeneutic is sufficient to measure up to these criteria" (*Behold the Pierced One*, 45).

14   See, for example, the comments in Stephen Toulmin, *Cosmopolis: The Hidden Agenda of Modernity* (Chicago: University of Chicago, 1990), 16–18.

religion," which engulfed Europe in the sixteenth and into about the first half of the seventeenth centuries, is difficult for us to comprehend, since the warfare was not conducted with as devastating an arsenal as that of our own age.[15]

These wars were of grave concern for Spinoza as he formed his political philosophy, which included his biblical hermeneutics. Indeed, the goal (at least ostensibly) of Spinoza's theo-political work was to create a biblical method that would bring peace to Europe.[16] William Cavanaugh explicitly mentions Spinoza as a key figure in the nascent development of the mythology of the wars of religion. Cavanaugh notes that, "Benedict de Spinoza's political writings were motivated largely by the divisions and wars that had plagued Spinoza's native Netherlands and the rest of Europe throughout his lifetime. ... The preface to his *Tractatus Theologico-Politicus* sets up religious violence as the problem to be solved by the rest of the treatise."[17] In Spinoza's own words we read:

> ... fear is the root from which superstition is born, maintained and nourished. ... Since dread is the cause of superstition, it plainly follows that everyone is naturally prone to it....It also follows that superstition must be just as variable and unstable as all absurd leaps of the mind and powerful emotions are, and can only be sustained by hope and hatred, anger and deception. This is because such instability does not spring from reason but from passion alone, in fact from the most powerful of the passions. Therefore it is easy for people to be captivated by a superstition. ... because common people everywhere live in the same wretched state, they never adhere to the same superstition for very long. ... Such instability of mind has been the cause of many riots and ferocious wars. ... It may indeed be the highest secret of monarchical government and utterly essential to it, to keep men

---

15 See the graphic description in Michael Allen Gillespie, *The Theological Origins of Modernity* (Chicago: University of Chicago, 2008), 129–130. For calling the allegedly religious motivations of these wars into question, see the important studies, William T. Cavanaugh, *The Myth of Religious Violence: Secular Ideology and the Roots of Modern Conflict* (Oxford: Oxford University Press, 2009), 123–180, especially 142–178; and William T. Cavanaugh, "'A Fire Strong Enough to Consume the House': The Wars of Religion and the Rise of the State," *Modern Theology* 11 (1995): 397–420.

16 Jeffrey L. Morrow, "The Early Modern Political Context to Spinoza's Bible Criticism," *Revista de Filosofía* 66 (2010): 7–24, at 10, 20, 23; Jeffrey L. Morrow, "The Bible in Captivity: Hobbes, Spinoza, and the Politics of Defining Religion," *Pro Ecclesia* 19 (2010): 285–299, at 298; Peter J. Leithart, *Deep Exegesis: The Mystery of Reading Scripture* (Waco: Baylor University, 2009), 18–19; Matthew Levering, *Participatory Biblical Exegesis: A Theology of Biblical Interpretation* (Notre Dame: University of Notre Dame Press, 2008), 108, 113, 118, 131, and 137; Daniel J. Elazar, "Spinoza and the Bible," *Jewish Political Studies Review* 7 (1995): 5–19, at 7; and Jon D. Levenson, *The Hebrew Bible, the Old Testament, and Historical Criticism: Jews and Christians in Biblical Studies* (Louisville: Westminster/John Knox, 1993), 94–96 and 117.

17 Cavanaugh, *Myth of Religious Violence*, 124.

deceived, and to disguise the fear that sways them with the spe-
cious name of religion, so that they will fight for their servitude
as if they were fighting for their own deliverance and will not
think it humiliating but supremely glorious to spill their blood
and sacrifice their lives for the glorification of a single man.[18]

Spinoza is quick to criticize what Enlightenment thinkers will denounce as
priestcraft,[19] the subtle manipulation of the laity by Machiavellian priestly rulers
and clerical aristocracy.[20] Reminiscent of Machiavelli, Spinoza identifies one of the
chief problems when he writes:

---

18   Spinoza, *TTP*, Preface, no. 4–5 and 7; Israel, 4–6; Akkerman, 58–63; and Gebhardt, 6–7. All
     citations from Spinoza's *Tractatus Theological Politicus* will be cited as follows. The first citation
     will be abbreviated as it is in this footnote, and will be to the chapter followed by the paragraph
     numbers used in Akkerman's edition of the *TTP*. The second citation will be to the English
     edition, from which all English translation in this article will be taken, Benedict de Spinoza,
     Theological-Political Treatise, ed. Jonathan Israel, trans. by Michael Silverthorne and Jonathan
     Israel (Cambridge: Cambridge University, 2007). The third citation will be to the pages of the
     current critical Latin edition established by Fokke Akkerman and the corresponding French
     translation as found in Spinoza, *Œuvres III: Tractatus Theologico-Politicus/Traité théologico-
     politique*, 2nd ed., ed. Pierre-François Moreau, text established by Fokke Akkerman, trans.
     and notes by Jacqueline Lagrée and Pierre-François Moreau (Paris: Presses Universitaires de
     France, 2012), the first edition of which was originally published in 1999. This volume is the
     most thorough and up-to-date critical edition of the *TTP*, with opposing pages of the Latin text
     with French translation. The fourth citation will be to the pages of the older 3rd volume of Carl
     Gebhardt, ed., *Spinoza Opera* (Heidelberg: C. Winters, 1925), since, although now obsolete,
     that remains the most accessible critical edition of the Latin text, a full text of which is available
     open access online. Silverthorne's and Israel's translation was chosen over, for example, R. H.
     M. Elwes' 1883 translation or Samuel Shirley's 1989 translation because of some problems with
     their translations including omissions of text, and their reliance on the only critical edition of
     the text then available, that of Carl Gebhardt from 1925. Silverthorne's and Israel's translation
     is taken from Akkerman's critical edition of *TTP*, and follows the paragraph divisions in
     Akkerman, which are less cumbersome than Spinoza's original paragraph divisions.

19   Diego Lucci, *Scripture and Deism: The Biblical Criticism of the Eighteenth-Century British Deists*
     (Bern: Peter Lang, 2008), especially 41, 55, and 127; Diego Lucci, "Judaism and the Jews in
     the British Deists' Attacks on Revealed Religion," *Hebrew Political Studies* 3 (2008): 177–214,
     at 182, 187, and 197; S. J. Barnett, *The Enlightenment and Religion: The Myths of Modernity*
     (Manchester: Manchester University, 2003), 45–67; S. J. Barnett, *Idol Temples and Crafty
     Priests: The Origins of Enlightenment Anticlericalism* (London: Macmillan, 1999); and J. A. I.
     Champion, *The Pillars of Priestcraft Shaken: The Church of England and its Enemies 1660–1730*
     (Cambridge: Cambridge University, 1992).

20   In this context, with regard to Machiavelli, Scott Hahn and Benjamin Wiker explain that,
     "The gap between the appearance of holiness and the underlying reality of corruption in the
     Curia became, for Machiavelli, the paradigmatic form of princely deception. ... Machiavelli
     inferred that the same gap exists in the Biblical text itself. His discovery of the 'key' to the
     underlying motives of biblical figures created a new mode of exegesis, and Machiavelli therefore
     can rightly be considered as one of the earliest, and certainly the most influential, sources of the
     hermeneutics of suspicion." See Scott W. Hahn and Benjamin Wiker, *Politicizing the Bible: The
     Roots of Historical Criticism and the Secularization of Scripture 1300–1700* (New York: Crossroad,
     Herder, 2013), 144.

In searching out the reason for this deplorable situation, I never doubted that it arose because, in the religion of the common people, serving the church has been regarded as a worldly career, what should be its unpretentious offices being seen as lucrative positions and its pastors considered great dignitaries. As soon as this abuse began in the church, the worst kind of people came forward to fill the sacred offices and the impulse to spread God's religion degenerated into sordid greed and ambition.[21]

Spinoza's personal and educational background had him positioned in the right place to make a contribution to the development of modern biblical criticism within the seventeenth century.[22] Although never having been a convert to Christianity himself, Spinoza was raised among Marrano returnees to Judaism who were relearning how to live as Jews in the Dutch Republic which granted them a great deal of relative autonomy. Marrano patterns of thought and cultural habits almost certainly shaped Spinoza's thought as he grew up.[23] In 1656, four months before his 24th birthday, Spinoza was formally excommunicated from the Jewish community in Amsterdam.[24] The actual cause of his excommunication is

---

21 Spinoza, *TTP*, Preface, no. 9; Israel, 7; Akkerman, 64–65; and Gebhardt, 8.

22 Two of the most accessible, insightful, and brief biographies of Spinoza are Richard H. Popkin, *Spinoza* (Oxford: Oneworld, 2004); and Steven Nadler, *Spinoza: A Life* (Cambridge: Cambridge University, 1999). To my mind, the best treatments of Spinoza's biblical criticism are Scott W. Hahn and Benjamin Wiker, "Chapter 9: Spinoza and the Beginning of the Radical Enlightenment," in *Politicizing the Bible*, by Hahn and Wiker, 339–393; and David Laird Dungan, "Baruch Spinoza and the Political Agenda of Modern Historical-Critical Interpretation," in *A History of the Synoptic Problem: The Canon, the Text, the Composition, and the Interpretation of the Gospels*, by David Laird Dungan (New Haven: Yale University, 1999), 198–260. It should be noted, however, that Dungan's chapter is fraught with a number of historical problems, including that the over-confident case he makes for the relationship between Spinoza and Jan De Witt overreaches the actual evidence. I am guilty of this same mistake regarding De Witt in my earlier, "Early Modern," 20.

23 Wiep van Bunge, *Spinoza Past and Present: Essays on Spinoza, Spinozism, and Spinoza Scholarship* (Leiden: Brill, 2012), 1–15; Yirmiyahu Yovel, *The Other Within: The Marranos: Split Identity and Emerging Modernity* (Princeton: Princeton University, 2009), entire book, especially 334–336 which deals specifically with Spinoza; Popkin, *Spinoza*, 5–16; Yirmiyahu Yovel, *Spinoza and Other Heretics I: The Marrano of Reason* (Princeton: Princeton University, 1989), entire book; and Gabriel Albiac, *La sinagoga vacía: un estudio de las fuentes marranas del espinosismo* [*The Empty Synagoguge: A Study of the Marrano Sources of Spinozism*] (Madrid: Hiperión, 1987), whole book. It should be noted that Albiac's otherwise fine and incredibly thorough book includes a vast array of uneven sources, and suffers in some places from the same problems as Dungan's chapter, especially regarding Spinoza's relationship with De Witt. It should be noted too that van Bunge's contribution to this discussion minimizes the Marrano background to understanding Spinoza. For a further critique of locating Spinoza in a Marrano context, see Travis L. Frampton, *Spinoza and the Rise of Historical Criticism of the Bible* (New York: T & T Clark, 2006), 18–22, which provides ample sources to consult.

24 Odette Vlessing, "The Excommunication of Baruch Spinoza: The Birth of a Philosopher," in *Dutch Jewry: Its History and Secular Culture (1500–2000)*, eds. Jonathan Israel and Reinier

uncertain, but whatever the cause, Jon Levenson is correct to state that after the ban, "… Spinoza turned against the Jewish tradition and even against the Jews themselves with fury."[25]

Heir to an Intellectual Heritage

Spinoza had a number of important influences on his thought and on his main theo-political work dealing with biblical exegesis, his *Tractatus Theologico-Politicus* [*Theological-Political Tractate*] (*TTP*). One of the most significant influences on Spinoza was his English contemporary Thomas Hobbes (1588–1679), whose *De Cive* belonged to his personal library. Although not certain, it is likely that Spinoza utilized the 1668 Latin translation of Hobbes' theo-political work *Leviathan* of 1651 in the final revisions of his 1670 *TTP*.[26] Hobbes' *Leviathan*, completed during

---

Salverda (Leiden: Brill, 2002), 141–172; Steven Nadler, *Spinoza's Heresy: Immortality and the Jewish Mind* (Oxford: Oxford University, 2001), 1–15; Nadler, *Spinoza*, 116–154; Odette Vlessing, "The Excommunication of Baruch Spinoza: A Conflict Between Jewish and Dutch Law," *Studia Spinozana* 13 (1997): 15–47; Odette Vlessing, "The Jewish Community in Transition: From Acceptance to Emancipation," *Studia Rosenthaliana* 30 (1996): 195–211; Asa Kasher and Shlomo Biderman, "Why Was Baruch de Spinoza Excommunicated," in *Sceptics, Millenarians and Jews*, eds. David S. Katz and Jonathan I. Israel (Leiden: Brill, 1990), 98–141; Lewis S. Feuer, *Spinoza and the Rise of Liberalism* (Brunswick: Transaction, 1987 [1958]), 1–16; and Israel S. Révah, "Aux origines de la rupture Spinozienne: nouveaux documents sur l'incroyance dans la communauté judéo-portugaise a Amsterdam a l'époque de l'excommunication de Spinoza" ["The Origins of the Spinozist Rupture: New Documents about Unbelief in the Jewish Portuguese Community in Amsterdam in the Epoque of the Excommunication of Spinoza"], *Revue des études juives* [*Review of Jewish Studies*] 123 (1964): 359–431. The actual core of the text used in the excommunication of Spinoza came from Venice in 1618 in Spanish translation. On this core text, see H. P. Salomon, "Le vrai excommunication de Spinoza" ["The Real Excommunication of Spinoza"], in *Forum Literarum* [*Literary Forum*], eds. H. Bots and M. Kerkhof (Amsterdam: Maarsen, 1984), 181–199.

25 Levenson, *Hebrew Bible*, 91.

26 Jeffrey L. Morrow, "*Leviathan* and the Swallowing of Scripture: The Politics behind Thomas Hobbes' Early Modern Biblical Criticism," *Christianity & Literature* 61 (2011): 33–54, at 34 and 49; Edwin Curley, "Spinoza's Exchange with Albert Burgh," in *Spinoza's Theological-Political Treatise*, eds. Melamed and Rosenthal, 11–28, at 13 n. 6; Warren Zev Harvey, "Spinoza on Ibn Ezra's 'Secret of the Twelve,'" in *Spinoza's Theological-Political Treatise*. Melamed and Rosenthal, 41–55, at 54; Menachem Lorberbaum, "Spinoza's Theological-Political Problem," in *Political Hebraism: Judaic Sources in Early Modern Political Thought*, eds. Gordon Schochet, Fania Oz-Salzberger, and Meirav Jones (Jerusalem: Shalem Press, 2008), 167–188, at 170, 172–173, 178–179, 183 n. 11, and 184 n. 28; Jon Parkin, "The Reception of Hobbes's *Leviathan*," in *The Cambridge Companion to Hobbes's Leviathan*, ed. Patricia Springborg (Cambridge: Cambridge University, 2007), 441–459, at 450–451; Theo Verbeek, *Spinoza's Theologico-Political Treatise: Exploring the "Will of God"* (Hampshire: Ashgate, 2003), especially 8–10; Malcolm, "Hobbes," 390–392; Theo Verbeek, "Spinoza on Theocracy and Democracy," in *Everything Connects: In Conference with Richard H. Popkin: Essays in His Honor*, eds. James E. Force and David S. Katz (Leiden: Brill, 1999), 326–338, at 336; Edwin Curley, "'I Durst Not Write So Boldly' or How to Read Hobbes' Theologico-Political Treatise," in *Hobbes e Spinoza: Scienza e politica* [*Hobbes and Spinoza: Science and Politics*], ed. Daniela Bostrenghi (Naples: Bibliopolis, 1992), 497–593; Richard H. Popkin, *The Third Force in Seventeenth-Century Thought* (Leiden: Brill, 1991),34–35; Karl Schumann, "Methodenfragen bei Spinoza und Hobbes: Zum Problem des

his self-imposed French exile to avoid the carnage of the English Civil War, helped pave the way for modern biblical criticism through its critique of the traditionally held Mosaic authorship of the Pentateuch and naturalization of spiritual realities in Scripture.

Another likely influence was the French Calvinist-turned-Catholic—perhaps of Marrano background—Isaac La Peyrère (c. 1596–1676).[27] La Peyrère's infamous work of biblical exegesis, *Pre-Adamites* (1655) was also on Spinoza's shelf, and a number of scholars, following the work of Richard Popkin, believe the two may have met each other when La Peyrère visited the Dutch Republic in 1655.[28] La Peyrère's work, which he completed by 1648,[29] represented a wholesale critique of Scripture, more thorough than that of Hobbes, although both subjugated

Einflusses" ["Methodological Issues in Spinoza and Hobbes: On the Problem of Influence"], *Studia Spinozana* 3 (1987): 47–86; and William Sacksteder, "How Much of Hobbes Might Spinoza Have Read?" *Southwestern Journal of Philosophy* 11 (1980): 25–39.

27   Andreas Nikolaus Pietsch, *Isaac La Peyrère: Bibelkritik, Philosemitismus und Patronage in der Gelehrtenrepublik des 17. Jahrhunderts [Isaac La Peyrère: Biblical Criticism, Philosemitism and Patronage in the Republic of Letters of the 17ᵗʰ Century]* (Berlin: Walter de Gruyter, 2012), entire book for situating La Peyrère and his biblical exegesis in context; Jeffrey L. Morrow, "Pre–Adamites, Politics and Criticism: Isaac La Peyrère's Contribution to Modern Biblical Studies," *Journal of the Orthodox Center for the Advancement of Biblical Studies* 4 (2011): 1–23, at 22; Jeffrey L. Morrow, "French Apocalyptic Messianism: Isaac La Peyrère and Political Biblical Criticism in the Seventeenth Century," *Toronto Journal of Theology* 27 (2011): 203–214, especially 210; H. J. M. Nellen, "Growing Tension between Church Doctrines and Critical Exegesis of the Old Testament," in *Hebrew Bible/Old Testament II*, ed. Sæbø, 802–826, at 822–823; Noel Malcolm, "Leviathan, the Pentateuch, and the Origins of Modern Biblical Criticism," in *Leviathan After 350 Years*, eds. Tom Sorell and Luc Foisneau (Oxford: Oxford University, 2004), 241–264, at 242–243, 243 n. 4, 247–248; Malcolm, "Hobbes," 392–398; Popkin, *Third Force*, 34; Richard H. Popkin, "Spinoza and Bible Scholarship," in *The Cambridge Companion to Spinoza*, ed. Don Garrett (Cambridge: Cambridge University, 1996), 383–407, at 391; Albiac, *sinagoga vacía* [Empty Synagogue], 124–129; Richard H. Popkin, "Spinoza's Earliest Philosophical Years, 1655–61," *Studia Spinozana* 4 (1988): 37–54; Richard H. Popkin, *Isaac La Peyrère (1596–1676): His Life, Work and Influence* (Leiden: Brill, 1987), especially, 26–59 and 80–93; Richard H. Popkin, "Some New Light on the Roots of Spinoza's Science of Bible Study," in *Spinoza and the Sciences*, eds. Marjorie Grene and Debra Nails (Dordrecht: Kluwer Academic, 1986), 171–188, at 171; and Richard H. Popkin, "Spinoza and La Peyrère," *Southwestern Journal of Philosophy* 8 (1977): 177–195.

28   La Peyrère's book created quite a stir just before Spinoza's excommunication. On the reception of his work in the Dutch Republic of 1655–1659, see Eric Jorink, "Reading the Book of Nature in the Seventeenth-Century Dutch Republic," in *The Book of Nature in Early Modern and Modern History*, eds. Klaas van Berkel and Arjo Vanderjagt (Leuven: Peeters, 2006), 45–68, at 63–65.

29   The final form of the text was published in 1655. La Peyrère apparently commenced drafting the text as early as 1635, the first portion of which was being circulated in unpublished form in 1643. Gabriel Naudé mentions the work in a 1642 letter. Drafts exist already from 1644. La Peyrère's *Pre-Adamites* was published bound together with his larger work *Theological System*. They were likely completed and bound together no later than 1648. Morrow, "Pre-Adamites," 5–6 and 5 n. 13–14; and Élisabeth Quennehen, "Lapeyrère, la Chine et la chronologie biblique" ["La Peyrère, China and Biblical Chronology"], *La Lettre clandestine* 9 (2000): 243–255, at 244.

Scripture for the purpose of redeploying it in their respective theo-political con-troversies: Hobbes in defense of the English monarchy and La Peyrère in defense of the political aspirations of his employer, the Prince of Condé.[30]

Spinoza's friend and in many ways disciple, Lodewijk Meyer (1629–1681), is another important figure in this discussion, since his 1666 *Philosophy as the Interpreter of Holy Scripture* was one of the most significant unnamed works against which Spinoza was arguing in his *TTP*.[31] Meyer sought to interpret Scripture via the lens of Cartesian philosophy, but he did so on fairly standard theological foundations, including the doctrine of Scripture's divine inspiration.

Spinoza's indebtedness to Descartes is overwhelming, even though Spinoza parts ways from standard Cartesian philosophy.[32] For Spinoza, "Descartes was

---

30   See the discussions in Pietsch, *Isaac La Peyrère*, 124–139 and 196–228; Morrow, "*Leviathan*," 37–40 and 42–48; Morrow, "Pre-Adamites," 16–20; Morrow, "French Apocalyptic Messianism," 208–210; R. H. Popkin, "Millenarianism and Nationalism—A Case Study: Isaac La Peyrère," in *Millenarianism and Messianism in Early Modern European Culture Volume IV: Continental Millenarians: Protestants, Catholics, Heretics*, eds. John Christian Laursen and Richard H. Popkin (Dordrecht: Kluwer Academic, 2001), 74–84; Arrigo Pacchi, "Hobbes and Biblical Philology in the Service of the State," *Topoi* 7 (1988): 231–239; and Henning Graf Reventlow, *The Authority of the Bible and the Rise of the Modern World* (London: SCM, 1984), 194–222.

31   Hahn and Wiker, *Politicizing the Bible*, 353–356; Gibert, *L'invention* [*The Invention*], 131–149 and 166; Leithart, *Deep Exegesis*, 7–11 and 15–17; Frampton, *Spinoza*, 175–195; Israel, *Radical Enlightenment*, 197–217; J. Samuel Preus, *Spinoza and the Irrelevance of Biblical Authority* (Cambridge: Cambridge University, 2001), xi, 8, 8 n. 22, 11–12, 34–67; W.N.A. Klever, "Spinoza's Life and Works," in *Cambridge Companion to Spinoza*, ed. Garrett, 13–60, at 29–31; Manfred Walther, "Biblische Hermeneutik und historische Erklärung: Lodewijk Meyer und Benedikt de Spinoza" ["Biblical Hermeneutics and Historical Explanation: Lodewijk Meyer and Benedikt de Spinoza"], *Studia Spinozana* 11 (1995): 227–300; and J. Samuel Preus, "A Hidden Opponent in Spinoza's *Tractatus*," *Harvard Theological Review* 88, no. 3 (1995): 361–338; Pierre Macherey, "Louis Meyer, interprète de l'Écriture," (1989) in *Avec Spinoza. Études sur la doctrine et l'histoire du spinozisme* [With Spinoza: Studies about the Doctrine and the History of Spinozism], by Pierre Macherey (Paris: Presses Universitaires de France, 1992), 168–172; Jacqueline Lagrée, "Sens et vérité: philosophie et théologie chez L. Meyer et Spinoza" ["Meaning and Truth: Philosophy and Theology in L. Meyer and Spinoza"], *Studia Spinozana* 4 (1988): 75–92; Jacqueline Lagrée, "Louis Meyer et la *Philosophia S. Scripturae interpres*. Projet cartésien, horizon spinoziste ["Lodewijk Meyer and *Philosophy as the Interpreter of S. Scripture*: Cartesian Project, Spinozist Perspective"], *Revue des sciences philosophiques et théologiques* 1 (1987): 31–44; Sylvain Zac, *Spinoza et l'interprétation de l'Écriture* [*Spinoza and the Interpretation of Scripture*] (Paris: Presses universitaires de France, 1965), 27–29. James Samuel Preus has done a lot to help us see that Spinoza's criticisms of Maimonides in his *TTP* is also a veiled critique of Spinoza's friend and contemporary Meyer. However, it is also clear that Spinoza is in fact taking on Maimonides himself, and specifically his *Guide of the Perplexed*, as James Arthur Diamond has recently demonstrated by examining carefully Spinoza's discussion of the word "spirit." See James Arthur Diamond, "Maimonides, Spinoza, and Buber Read the Hebrew Bible: The Hermeneutical Keys of Divine 'Fire' and 'Spirit' (*Ruach*)," *Journal of Religion* 91 (2011): 320–343, at 321–336.

32   See Hahn and Wiker, *Politicizing the Bible*, 259, 281, 342–343, 388, 546; Susan James, *Spinoza on Philosophy, Religion, and Politics: The Theologico-Political Treatise* (Oxford: Oxford University, 2012), 9–11, 92, 144–147, 150, 155, 218; Brad S. Gregory, *The Unintended Reformation: How a Religious Revolution Secularized Society* (Cambridge: Harvard University, 2012), 48, 60, 116;

his ticket to modernity."[33] Hahn and Wiker explain that, "… Meyer's *Philosophia* and Spinoza's *Tractatus* often travelled together as one book, a marriage that made perfect sense. Meyer provided the framework as a prolegomenon, and Spinoza … spelled out the full consequences, consequences all the more radical precisely because of Spinoza's radicalizing of Descartes."[34] I think this is generally correct, even though Meyer's work is almost certainly one of the main implied targets of Spinoza's criticism in his *TTP*, and although Spinoza disagrees with Descartes. Descartes' methodic doubt was an important underlying tool for Spinoza's biblical criticism. Moreover, although Spinoza took issue with Meyer's particular application of Cartesian philosophy to biblical interpretation, it likely had more to do with the traditional theological views concerning inspiration that Meyer retained than rationalism. As Preus makes clear, Meyer was "attempting to show how scripture's divine truths might be recovered through a philosophical method."[35] To drive the point home, Hahn and Wiker correctly identify Spinoza's debt to Descartes when they state that, "… Spinoza's entire philosophical approach, which undergirds his exegetical method, is based upon a radicalization of Descartes's project, one that itself rests on a presumed identity of being (nature) and the mathematical mode of human knowing."[36] Descartes' universe was Spinoza's universe.[37]

Michael Mack, *Spinoza and the Specters of Modernity: The Hidden Enlightenment of Diversity from Spinoza to Freud* (New York: Continuum, 2010), 7 and 11 n. 1; Michelle Beyssade, "Deux latinistes: Descartes et Spinoza" ["Two Latinists: Descartes and Spinoza"], in *Spinoza to the Letter: Studies in Words, Texts and Books*, ed. Fokke Akkerman and Piet Steenbakkers (Leiden: Brill, 2005), 55–68; Wiep van Bunge, *From Stevin to Spinoza: An Essay on Philosophy in the Seventeenth-Century Dutch Republic* (Leiden: Brill, 2001), entire book, especially 34–121, for situating Spinoza within his Dutch Cartesian context; Margaret D. Wilson, "Spinoza's Theory of Knowledge," in *Cambridge Companion to Spinoza*, ed. Garrett, 89–141, at 89–90; Don Garrett, "Spinoza's Ethical Theory," in *Cambridge Companion to Spinoza*, ed. Garrett, 267–314, at 267; Michael Della Rocca, "Mental Content and Skepticism in Descartes and Spinoza," *Studia Spinozana* 10 (1994): 19–42; Edwin Curley, *Behind the Geometrical Method: A Reading of Spinoza's Ethics* (Princeton: Princeton University, 1988), entire book; Edwin M. Curley, "Spinoza's Geometric Method," *Studia Spinozana* 2 (1986): 151–169. Susan James writes that, "Just as Descartes urges us to shed our prejudices about the natural world and only to accept ideas that we cannot doubt, Spinoza extends this project to theology by setting out to shake off his preconceptions about what Scripture says, and only accept claims that he is absolutely sure it asserts" (144–145).

33 Yovel, *Spinoza and Other Heretics I*, 206.

34 Hahn and Wiker, *Politicizing the Bible*, 355. On the following page, Hahn and Wiker explain, "Clearly, Spinoza's philosophy and hence his treatment of Scripture were part of a larger, more general philosophical movement rooted in the new mechanist-materialist worldview as interpreted according to a mathematical-mechanical approach, and which had direct implications for a radically new approach to Scripture. Spinoza would go on to provide one" (356).

35 Preus, *Spinoza*, 38 n. 14.

36 Hahn and Wiker, *Politicizing the Bible*, 546.

37 Moreover, as Spinoza begins his *TTP* by lamenting wars that have come about on account of

As important as Descartes was for Spinoza's initial philosophy and for apply-ing Cartesian methodic doubt to Scripture, Francis Bacon was probably even more significant for Spinoza's purposes of developing a historical method, patterned on the then burgeoning hard sciences.[38] The hidden influence here is that of nominal-ism (and also Averroism).[39] Michael Waldstein sums up the history by explaining how William of Ockham took Scotus' voluntarism further, transforming it into nominalism. Luther was completely indebted to nominalism and passed it on to Protestants. Both Descartes and Bacon learned nominalist philosophy and be-queathed it to modernity through their reconceptualization of the world.[40] What is missing from this brief summary is the role of Francisco Suárez mediating the scholastic tradition filtered through nominalism to both Bacon and Descartes.[41]

---

religious strife, so too Descartes situates his own *Discourse on Method* within the milieu of the Thirty Years' War. See the comments on this in Gillespie, *Theological Origins of Modernity*, 185.

38   See for example, Juan Francisco Manrique Charry, "La herencia de Bacon en la doctrina spinocista del lenguaje" ["The Heritage of Bacon in the Spinozist Doctrine of Language"], *Universitas Philosophica* 54 (2010): 121–130; Preus, *Spinoza*, 7 n. 19, 24 n. 73, 26 n. 80, 38, 158 n. 9, 159 n. 12, 161–168, 163 n. 20–21, 181, and 195; Alan Gabbey, "Spinoza's Natural Science and Methodology," in *Cambridge Companion to Spinoza*, ed. Garrett, 142–191, at 170–172; Alan Donagan, "Spinoza's Theology," in *Cambridge Companion to Spinoza*, ed. Garrett, 343–382, at 343; Alan Donagan, *Spinoza* (Chicago: University of Chicago, 1989), 16–17; and Zac, *Spinoza*, 29–32.

39   See Hahn and Wiker's very good chapter, "The First Cracks of Secularism: Marsilius of Padua and William of Ockham," in *Politicizing the Bible*, 17–59, which lays the groundwork for both how Averroist (via Marsilius) and nominalist (via Ockham) philosophy will undergird later biblical criticism as it develops, especially in the Reformation and its aftermath leading up through the Enlightenment. Their later chapters do a good job of integrating this material, showing how it plays out throughout history as biblical scholarship becomes critical. See also Gillespie's chapter, "The Nominalist Revolution and the Origin of Modernity," in *Theological Origins of Modernity*, 19–43.

40   Waldstein, "*Analogia Verbi*," 99–101. See also Gregory, *Unintended Reformation*, 36–38, 49; Steven Matthews, *Theology and Science in the Thought of Francis Bacon* (Aldershot: Ashgate, 2008); and Gillespie, *Theological Origins of Modernity*, 37–41.

41   For example, Gregory, *Unintended Reformation*, 53; Roger Ariew, *Descartes Among the Scholastics* (Leiden: Brill, 2011), entire book for the late medieval scholastic context for Descartes' thought, but especially 3–4, 49–54, 71–72 for Suárez's influence; Gillespie, *Theological Origins of Modernity*, 174, 190; Emmanuel Faye, "Dieu trompeur, mauvais génie et origine de l'erreur selon Descartes et Suarez" ["Deceptive God, Evil Genius and the Origin of Error According to Descartes and Suárez"], *Revue philosophique de la France et de l'étranger* 126 (2001): 61–72; J.-L. Marion, "A propos de Suarez et Descartes" ["On Suárez and Descartes"], *Revue internationale de philosophie* 50 (1996): 109–131; and Norman J. Wells, "Objective Reality of Ideas in Descartes, Caterus, and Suárez," *Journal of the History of Philosophy* 28 (1990): 33–61. Reviewing some of the reference material in Étienne Gilson, *Index scolastico-cartésien* (New York: Burt Franklin, 1912) is instructive here. Gilson's introduction mentions how neither Bacon, Descartes, nor Spinoza thought in a complete vacuum, but were in fact all three indebted to prior philosophical work within late medieval scholasticism. At one point Ariew insightfully hints that Suárez "seems to have been as much a Scotist as a Thomist (or perhaps may be better understood as neither Thomist nor Scotist)" (*Descartes*, 87). Indeed, it seems that although St. Thomas is certainly one of Suárez's primary masters, he filters St. Thomas through his other masters, Scotus and Ockham, as well as the general Jesuit reading of the

Michael Allen Gillespie situates Bacon firmly within his nominalist context and details the "extent of the power sought by Bacon" (in Waldstein's words).[42] This picture lifts the veil which Spinoza carefully placed over his hermeneutic. As we shall see below, as Bacon called for the torture of nature for the sake of power, so Spinoza sounds the call to eviscerate Scripture, with a specific political power in mind.[43] His use of history as the sharpened instrument will be the tool he will use.

Wielding History as a Weapon

For Spinoza, history did not so much have to do with development over time, rather, "The meaning of the term 'history,' for Spinoza, corresponded to the fundamental basis of the Greek *historein*, the critical examination of facts. For him there was a close analogy between the sphere of nature and the past events as facts to be transmitted. More precisely, history has to do with obtaining the true definition of the phenomena that were common in nature."[44] More than Herodotus or Thucydides, however, Spinoza was adapting a Baconian method to redeploy in the study of the history of the text of the Bible, or, more appropriately, he was using a Baconian method applied to the history *behind* the biblical texts.

What Spinoza presents us with in his *TTP* is a sort of Magna Carta of modern biblical criticism. He presents a fundamental shift in how the study of the Bible is to proceed. James Kugel claims that, "In a few pages of his remarkable little book the *Tractatus Theologico-Politicus* (1670), Spinoza outlined a new proposal for *how* the Bible was to be read, and this program became the marching orders of biblical scholars for the next three centuries."[45] Indeed, modern biblical critics would

---

Dominican Scholastic tradition. I am indebted to Victor Velarde-Mayol for bringing this to my attention. Significantly, Jakob Freudenthal's very important but apparently all-but completely forgotten 1887 essay on Spinoza provided important background information highlighting the influence of medieval scholasticism (including Suárez) on Spinoza. See J. Feudenthal, "Spinoza und die Scholastik" ["Spinoza and Scholasticism"], in *Philosophische Aufsätze. Eduard Zeller zu seinem fünfzigjährigen Doctor-Jubiläum gewidmet* [*Philosophical Essays: Festschrift on the Occasion of Eduard Zeller's Fifty-Year Anniversary of his Doctorate*] (Leipzig: Fues's Verlag, 1887), 84–138.

42 Gillespie, *Theological Origins of Modernity*, 38–39.

43 Whether or not Bacon actually envisioned "torturing" nature through experimentation can be questioned. Peter Pesic challenges this notion, arguing instead that Bacon envisioned experimentation with nature to be a mutually difficult "trial" between the scientist and nature. See Peter Pesic, "Wrestling with Proteus: Francis Bacon and the 'Torture' of Nature," *Isis* 90 (1999): 81–94. Nevertheless, the fact remains that the description of the experimentation of nature in Bacon's method is that of being physically ripped apart, dissected. No such physical dissection and thus destruction is envisioned on behalf of the scientist.

44 Henning Graf Reventlow, *History of Biblical Interpretation Volume 4: From the Enlightenment to the Twentieth Century*, trans. by Leo G. Perdue (Atlanta: Society of Biblical Literature, 2010 [2001]), 101.

45 Kugel, *How to Read*, 31. See also Dominique Barthélemy's comments that "Spinoza ... presents a sort of 'discourse on method' for biblical criticism in chapters seven to ten of his *Tractatus*" ("History of Old Testament," 53). And later, in the same introductory essay, "... Spinoza clearly formulated for the first time the agenda of what would later be called 'higher criticism'" (54).

follow the rough outlines of Spinoza's method even when they departed from his conclusions and from his philosophical starting points. It should be made clear, however, that far from merely attempting to construct an objective method for the scientific study of the Bible, Spinoza intended his method to serve his politics, as Shlomo Pines so clearly states, "The exegesis and the critical historiography of Spinoza aided him well in his polemic and political propaganda. And in fact, this was without a doubt the principal intention for which he invented his exegetical and historical method."[46]

This is the danger in any attempt to distance oneself from the biblical narratives in order to secure a neutral or objective stance towards Scripture; to be neutral is to pick a side, it is to have a specific secular commitment. It is impossible to be completely free of theological and philosophical commitments when approaching Scripture. Spinoza's method, despite the ostensible intent to be of use to common people over and against the ruling theological political elite, requires a tremendous amount of education and effort. Israel comments that, "Perhaps the most formidable aspect of the *TTP*, viewed from a historical perspective, however, was precisely that it set out a new critical methodology and expertise in Hebrew philology resulting in a set of extremely challenging propositions designed to curtail theology's sway which are then pressed into the service of a general system and a body of moral philosophy that is in turn integrally linked to a particular kind of republican political thought."[47] The political motivations are ever present in Spinoza's *theo-political* work, as Menachem Lorberbaum clarifies, unmasking Spinoza's hidden purpose: "The agenda of the *TTP* is hence twofold: it seeks to destroy, to the extent possible, the theological foundations of institutionalized religion, and concomitantly to salvage a significant kernel that would enable the channeling of the elements of existing historical religions for the purposes of the sovereign."[48]

Spinoza did not invent wholesale the technical principles of the criticism that he wielded in his theo-political battle; they had already existed for some time. He inherited (in some cases directly in other cases indirectly) specific arguments against traditional attributions of authorship from much earlier traditions—

---

46 Shlomo Pines, "Spinoza's *Tractatus theologico-politicus*, Maimonides and Kant," *Scripta Hierosolymitana* 20 (1968): 3–54, at 17. My own English translation.

47 Israel, "Early Dutch and German Reaction," 85. See also Magne Sæbø's comment that, "The critical philosophy of Spinoza—and of the subsequent Spinozism—not only encouraged rationalization and secularization but promoted even a shift of authority, from theology to philosophy, from biblical revelation-based faith and ecclesiastical tradition to the scepticism of critical minds" ("From the Renaissance," 41).

48 Lorberbaum, "Spinoza's Theological-Political," 169.

Gnostic sources,[49] Porphyry,[50] Ibn Hazm,[51] Ibn Ezra,[52] et al. Further textual and source critical issues had already emerged in the work of Peter Abelard,[53] Lorenzo Valla,[54] Erasmus,[55] et al, as well as from Spinoza's contemporaries Louis Cappel,[56] Isaac Vossius,[57] et al. Even his lengthy comments concerning the introduction of

49 Jeffrey L. Morrow, "The Politics of Biblical Interpretation: A 'Criticism of Criticism,'" *New Blackfriars* 91 (2010): 528–545, at 530; and Jeffrey L. Morrow, "The Modernist Crisis and the Shifting of Catholic Views on Biblical Inspiration," *Letter & Spirit* 6 (2010): 265–280, at 267.

50 Morrow, "Politics of Biblical Interpretation," 530; and Morrow, "Modernist Crisis," 267.

51 Morrow, "Politics of Biblical Interpretation," 530–532; Morrow, "Modernist Crisis," 267–268; and R. David Freedman, "The Father of Modern Biblical Scholarship," *Journal of the Ancient Near Eastern Society* 19 (1989): 31–38.

52 Barthélemy, "History of Old Testament," 3–5; Gibert, *L'invention [Invention]*, 230–236; Henning Graf Reventlow, *History of Biblical Interpretation Volume 2: From Late Antiquity to the End of the Middle Ages* (Atlanta: Society of Biblical Literature, 2009 [1994]), 234–246; Uriel Simon, "Abraham ibn Ezra," in *Hebrew Bible/Old Testament Volume I: From the Beginnings to the Middle Ages (Until 1300) Part 2: The Middle Ages*, ed. Magne Sæbø (Göttingen: Vandenhoeck & Ruprecht, 2000), 377–387; Shlomo Sela, *Abraham Ibn Ezra and the Rise of Medieval Hebrew Science* (Leiden: Brill, 2003); and Angel Sáenz-Badillos, "Abraham ibn Ezra: Between Tradition and Philology," *Zutot* 2 (2003): 85–94.

53 Constant J. Mews and Micha J. Perry, "Peter Abelard, Heloise and Jewish Biblical Exegesis in the Twelfth Century," *Journal of Ecclesiastical History* 62 (2011): 3–19; Reventlow, *History of Biblical Interpretation 2*, 143–151; and Ulrich Köpf, "The Institutional Framework of Christian Exegesis in the Middle Ages," in *Hebrew Bible/Old Testament I/2*, ed. Sæbø, 148–179, at 160.

54 J. Cornelia Linde, "Lorenzo Valla and the Authenticity of Sacred Texts," *Humanistica Lovaniensia* 60 (2011): 35–63; Gibert, *L'invention [Invention]*, 39–46; Michael C. Legaspi, *The Death of Scripture and the Rise of Biblical Studies* (Oxford: Oxford University, 2010), 12 and 22; Debora Kuller Shuger, *The Renaissance Bible: Scholarship, Sacrifice, and Subjectivity* (Waco: Baylor University, 2010 [1994]), 17–20 and 47–49; Preus, *Spinoza*, 32 n. 101 and 181; Ronald K. Delph, "Valla Grammaticus, Agostino Steuco, and the Donation of Constantine," *Journal of the History of Ideas* 57 (1996): 55–77; and Jerry H. Bentley, "Biblical Philology and Christian Humanism: Lorenzo Valla and Erasmus as Scholars of the Gospels," *Sixteenth Century Journal* 8 (1977): 8–28.

55 Arnoud Visser, "Thirtieth Annual Erasmus Birthday Lecture: Erasmus, the Church Fathers and the Ideological Implications of Philology," *Erasmus of Rotterdam Society Yearbook* 31 (2011): 7–31; Gibert, *L'invention [Invention]*, 47–63; Legaspi, *Death of Scripture*, 12–17; Shuger, *Renaissance Bible*, 17 and 19–22; and Erika Rummel, "The Textual and Hermeneutic Work of Desiderius Erasmus of Rotterdam," in *Hebrew Bible/Old Testament 2*, ed. Sæbø, 215–230.

56 Barthélemy, "History of Old Testament," 16–24, 27–30, 33–35, and 51–52; Gibert, *L'invention [Invention]*, 94–101; Legaspi, *Death of Scripture*, 19–22; Reventlow, *History of Biblical Interpretation 4*, 75–77; Shuger, *Renaissance Bible*, 14–15; Stephen G. Burnett, "Later Christian Hebraists," in *Hebrew Bible/Old Testament 2*, ed. Sæbø, 785–801, at 789–792; Preus, *Spinoza*, 32 n. 100 and 97 n. 90–91; Popkin, "Spinoza and Bible Scholarship," 390; and M.H. Goshen-Gottstein, "The Textual Criticism of the Old Testament: Rise, Decline, Rebirth," *Journal of Biblical Literature* 102 (1983): 365–399, at 372–376 and 374 n. 34.

57 Eric Jorink and Dirk van Miert, "Introduction: The Challenger: Isaac Vossius and the European World of Learning," in *Isaac Vossius (1618–1689): Between Science and Scholarship*, eds. Eric Jorink and Dirk van Miert (Leiden: Brill, 2012), 1–14; Colette Nativel, "Isaac Vossius, entre Philologie et Philosophie" ["Isaac Vossius, between Philology and Philosophy"], in *Isaac Vossius*, eds. Jorink and van Miert, 243–254; Eric Jorink, "'Horrible and Blasphemous': Isaac La Peyrère, Isaac Vossius and the Emergence of Radical Biblical Criticism in the Dutch Republic,"

vowel pointing in the Hebrew text of the OT shows his awareness of the more recent debates from Elias Levita to the Buxtorf brothers.[58] Unfortunately, insufficient attention has been paid to the influence of medieval Muslim philosophy and biblical criticism on Spinoza, although some wonderful studies in this regard do exist.[59] Spinoza's knowledge of both Maimonides and Ibn Ezra would be one clear means of having such thought mediated to him, but he likely was aware of segments of medieval Muslim thought more directly.[60]

---

in *Nature and Scripture in the Abrahamic Religions: Up to 1700 Volume 1*, eds. Jitse M. van der Meer and Scott Mandelbrote (Leiden: Brill, 2008), 429–450, at 433 and 441–447; and Popkin, "Spinoza and Bible Scholarship," 390.

58 Barthélemy, "History of Old Testament," 13–20, 28–29, 34, and 36; Gibert, *L'invention* [*Invention*], 27, 237–245, 281–283; Legaspi, *Death of Scripture*, 19–20; Reventlow, *History of Biblical Interpretation 4*, 73–76; Deena Aranoff, "Elijah Levita: A Jewish Hebraist," *Jewish History* 23 (2009): 17–40; Burnett, "Later Christian Hebraists," 787–789; James L. Kugel, *How to Read the Bible: A Guide to Scripture, Then and Now* (New York: Free Press, 2007), 697–698 n. 60; Zelda Kahan Newman, "Elye Levita: A Man and His Book on the Cusp of Modernity," *Shofar* 24 (2006): 90–109; Preus, *Spinoza*, 32 n. 100, 97 n. 90–91, 181; Stephen G. Burnett, *From Christian Hebraism to Jewish Studies: Johannes Buxtorf (1564–1629) and Hebrew Learning in the Seventeenth Century* (Leiden: Brill, 1996); Goshen-Gottstein, "Textual Criticism," 371–372, 375, 375 n. 38; and Richard A. Muller, "The Debate Over the Vowel Points and the Crisis in Orthodox Hermeneutics," *Journal of Medieval and Renaissance Studies* 10 (1980): 53–72.

59 Youcef Djedi, "Spinoza et l'islam: un état des lieux" ["Spinoza and Islam: The State of the Question"], *Philosophiques* 37 (2010): 275–298; Carlos Fraenkel, "Spinoza on Philosophy and Religion: The Averroistic Sources," in *The Rationalists: Between Tradition and Innovation*, eds. Carlos Fraenkel, Dario Perinetti and Justin Smith (Dordrecht: Springer, 2010), 58–81; Rafael Ramón Guerrero, "Filósofos hispano-musulmanes y Spinoza: Avempace y Abentofail" ["Hispano-Muslim Philosophers and Spinoza: Avempace and Ibn Tufail"], in *Spinoza y España: Actas del Congreso Internacional sobre «Relaciones entre Spinoza y España» (Almagro, 5–7 noviembre 1992)* [*Spinoza and Spain: Acts of the International Congress about "Relations between Spinoza and Spain" (Almagro, 5–7 November 1992)*], ed. Atilano Domínguez (Almagro: Ediciones de la Universidad de Castilla-La Mancha, 1994), 125–132; Juan Antonio Pacheco, "El 'Mahâsim al-mayâlis' de Ibn al-Arif y la Etica de Spinoza" ["The 'Mahâsim al-mayâlis' of Ibn al-Arif and the Ethics of Spinoza"], *La Ciudad de Dios* 203 (1990): 671–687; Roger Arnaldez, "Spinoza et la pensée arabe" ["Spinoza and Arabic Thought"], *Revue de Synthèse* 99 (1978): 151–174; Irving I. Horowitz, "Averroism and the Politics of Philosophy," *Journal of Politics* 22 (1960): 698–727; Stephen Chak Tornay, "Averroes' Doctrine of the Mind," *Philosophical Review* 52 (1943): 270–288; and Harry Austryn Wolfson, *The Philosophy of Spinoza: Unfolding the Latent Processes of His Reasoning: Volume I* (Cambridge: Harvard University, 1934), 8–13, 30, 125–126, 157, 189–190, 190 n. 3, 197–199, 284.

60 Carlos Fraenkel, "Reconsidering the Case of Elijah Delmedigo's Averroism and its Impact on Spinoza," in *Renaissance Averroism and its Aftermath: Arabic Philosophy in Early Modern Europe*, eds. Anna Akasoy and Guido Giuglioni (Dordrecht: Springer, 2012), 213–236; Carlos Fraenkel, "Could Spinoza Have Presented the *Ethics* as the True Content of the Bible," *Oxford Studies in Early Modern Philosophy* 4 (2008): 1–50; and Craig Martin, "Rethinking Renaissance Averroism," *Intellectual History Review* 17 (2007): 3–28. Youcef Djedi concludes, "A modern philosopher, Spinoza nevertheless is an heir of Judeo-Islamic thought" ("Spinoza," 298, my own translation).

Spinoza's Discourse on Method: Philosophy and Politics Unite

One key move Spinoza makes in his criticism is a more developed criticism of the sources. Spinoza employed his Cartesian doubt to the traditional attributions of authorship in the OT. The purpose was not to ascertain who actually was responsible for writing the books—for which he tentatively credits Ezra—although this was one central quest for which his method explicitly calls. Rather, Spinoza's source criticism served a different purpose. Dominique Barthélemy clarifies how, "Spinoza, as La Peyrère before him, thought, therefore, that if it could be shown that the books of the Old Testament had not been written by Moses and the Prophets but by much later compilers, one would be obliged to question the sacred nature of this collection of books."[61]

In his *TTP* Spinoza outlines the contours of his method of biblical interpretation, on what he argues must be followed in order to arrive at the true meaning of the text.[62] At the outset of his work, Spinoza explains how he came about writing the *TTP*. He was upset with religious strife and the dearth of recourse to "the natural light of reason" around him. Thus, he writes, "I resolved in all seriousness to make a fresh examination of Scripture with a free and unprejudiced mind, and to assert nothing about it, and to accept nothing as its teaching, which I did not quite clearly derive from it. With this proviso in mind, I devised a method for interpreting the sacred volumes."[63] One of the key moves Spinoza makes—indeed,

---

61   Barthélemy, "History of Old Testament," 63.

62   On Spinoza's method, see Spinoza, *TTP*, Preface no. 10, Ch. 7 no. 2–18; Israel, 8–9, 98–111; Akkerman, 68–71 and 278–311; Gebhardt, 9, 98–112; Steven Nadler, *A Book Forged in Hell: Spinoza's Scandalous Treatise and the Birth of the Secular Age* (Princeton: Princeton University, 2011), 134–142; Barthélemy, "History of Old Testament," 53–57; Gibert, *L'invention* [*The Invention*], 161–165; Sinai, "Spinoza and Beyond," 196–203; Robert Barron, "Biblical Interpretation and Theology: Irenaeus, Modernity, and Vatican II," *Letter & Spirit* 5 (2009): 173–191, at 181–182; Steven Nadler, "The Bible Hermeneutics of Baruch de Spinoza," in *Hebrew Bible/Old Testament II*, ed. Sæbø, 827–836, at 831–834; Paul J. Bagley, *Philosophy, Theology, and Politics: A Reading of Benedict Spinoza's Tractatus Theologico-Politicus* (Leiden: Brill, 2008), 16; Walther, "Biblische Hermeneutik" ["Biblical Hermeneutics"], 227–299; Manfred Walther, "Biblische Hermeneutik und/oder theologische Politik bei Hobbes und Spinoza: Historische Studie zur Theorie der Ausdifferenzierung von Religion und Politik in der Neuzeit" ["Biblical Hermeneutics and/or Theological Politics in Hobbes and Spinoza: A Historical Study of the Theory of Differentiation of Religion and Politics in the Modern Age"], in *Hobbes e Spinoza* [*Hobbes and Spinoza*], ed. Bostrenghi, 623–669; Yirmiyahu Yovel, *Spinoza and Other Heretics II: The Adventures of Immanence* (Princeton: Princeton University, 1989), 14–19; Pierre-François Moreau, "Le méthode d'interprétation de l'Écriture Sainte: déterminations et limites" ["The Method of Interpretation of Sacred Scripture: Demarcations and Limits], in *Spinoza: science et religion* [*Spinoza: Science and Religion*], ed. Renée Bouveresse (Paris: Vrin, 1988), 109–114; and Juan José Garrido, "El método histórico-crítico de interpretación de la Escritura según Spinoza" ["The Historical-Critical Method of Interpretation of Scripture according to Spinoza"], in *El método en teología. Actas del primer Simposio de Teología e Historia (29–31 mayo 1980)* [*Method in Theology: Acts of the First Symposium of Theology and History (29–31 May 1980)*], ed. The Faculty of Theology of Saint Vincent Ferrer (Valencia: The Faculty of Theology of Saint Vincent Ferrer, 1981), 269–281.

63   Spinoza, *TTP*, Preface, no. 10; Israel, 8–9; Akkerman, 68–69; and Gebhardt, 9.

many scholars see this as the main purpose in writing his *TTP*—is the radical and absolute separation of faith from reason and of theology from philosophy.[64] Spinoza claims that he had no intent on making faith and theology subordinate to reason and philosophy. Indeed, his 15th chapter is entitled, "Where it is shown that theology is not subordinate to reason nor reason to theology, and why it is we are persuaded of the authority of Holy Scripture."[65] Nevertheless, since, for Spinoza, theology and faith tend to deal solely with interior matters, often with matters of the imagination, and reason deals with objective reality, for those who do not share his mechanistic worldview, who resist the privatization of their faith, Spinoza's program takes theology and faith into exile.

The weapon of Spinoza's method is the acid of his historical enquiry. Scripture is to be studied historically, using "no other light than that of natural reason," as with any other ancient book.[66] Levenson remarks, "History supplied Spinoza

---

64   Spinoza, *TTP*, Ch. 14 no. 1–14, Ch. 15 no. 1–10; Israel, 178–194; Akkerman, 464–503; Gebhardt, 173–188; James, *Spinoza on Philosophy*, 57, 94, 134–135, 142, 218; Nadler, *Book Forged in Hell*, 20, 65; Bagley, *Philosophy, Theology, and Politics*, 10, 12; Brayton Polka, *Between Philosophy and Religion: Spinoza, the Bible, and Modernity Volume I: Hermeneutics and Ontology* (Lanham, MD: Lexington Books, 2007), 3 and 25; Richard H. Popkin, *The History of Scepticism: From Savonarola to Bayle*, rev. and expanded ed. (Oxford: Oxford University, 2003), 244; Preus, *Spinoza*, 15 n. 45, 74, 81, 194, and 207; George M. Gross, "Reading the Bible with Spinoza," *Jewish Political Studies Review* 7 (1995): 21–38, at 29; Harvey Shulman, "The Use and Abuse of the Bible in Spinoza's *Tractatus Theologico-Politicus*," *Jewish Political Studies Review* 7 (1995): 39–55, at 44 and 46; and Sylvain Zac, "Philosophie et théologie chez Spinoza" ["Philosophy and Theology in Spinoza"], *Revue de Synthèse* 89–91 (1978): 81–95.

65   Spinoza, *TTP*, Ch. 15 title; Israel, 186; Akkerman, 482–483; and Gebhardt, 180.

66   Spinoza, *TTP*, Ch. 7, no. 18; Israel, 111; Akkerman, 310–311; and Gebhardt, 112. Matthew Levering comments astutely, "Spinoza's key principle corresponds, in a certain way, to the parallel that the medieval (and some patristic) theologians had drawn between 'the book of Nature' and 'the book of Scripture.' He argues that one must interpret nature and Scripture by using the same methods. ... The difference with patristic-medieval interpretation thus begins with a different understanding of 'nature': for the patristic-medieval tradition, nature is a created participatory reality that signifies its Creator and possesses a teleological order; for Spinoza nature simply yields empirical data within the linear time-space continuum. It is not that the medieval rejected empirical study of nature; rather the difference is that Spinoza's 'nature' is metaphysically thin" (*Participatory Biblical Exegesis*, 115). See also Hahn and Wiker, *Politicizing the Bible*, 280–281, 361–362, 364–368, 385, 391–392, 544; James, *Spinoza on Philosophy*, 54, 142, 145, 148, 161, 178; Nadler, *Book Forged in Hell*, 32, 66, 76–103, 132–135, 137, 139; Yitzhak Y. Melamed and Michael A. Rosenthal, introduction to *Spinoza's Theological-Political Treatise*, eds. Melamed and Rosenthal, 1–10, at 1; Thomas Hippler, "Spinoza et l'histoire" ["Spinoza and History"], *Studia Spinozana* 16 (2008): 155–176; Preus, *Spinoza*, ix, 2, 16–17, 22, 54, 98, 100, 156, 158; Gilbert Boss, "L'histoire chez Spinoza et Leibniz" ["History in Spinoza and Leibniz"], *Studia Spinozana* 6 (1990): 179–200; Richard H. Popkin, "Philosophy and the History of Philosophy," *Journal of Philosophy* 82 (1985): 625–632, at 626–627; and Sylvain Zac, "Durée et histoire chez Spinoza" ["Time and History in Spinoza"], *La Nouvelle Critique* 113 (1978): 29–36.

with the coffin into which he placed the Torah."[67] Spinoza's method required an exhaustive account of the history and philological points of each text, after which discussion he proceeds to tell his readers that such an attempt is impossible.[68] The main points of his method are as follows:

A. The construction of a "natural history" of the Bible: "The [correct] method of interpreting nature consists above all in constructing a natural history, from which we derive the definitions of natural things, as from certain data. Likewise, to interpret Scripture, we need to assemble a genuine history of it and to deduce the thinking of the Bible's authors by valid inferences from this history, as from certain data and principles."[69]

B. To construct this history from Scripture alone.[70]

C. Constructing a history of Scripture will proceed via several steps:

(1) it "must include the nature and properties of the language in which the biblical books were composed and in which their authors were accustomed to speak."[71]

This step will further involve:

(1.a) to "investigate *all* the possible meanings that *every* single phrase in common usage can admit."[72]

(2) it "must gather together the opinions expressed in each individual book and organize them by subject so that we

---

67 Levenson, *Hebrew Bible*, 95.

68 Hahn and Wiker, *Politicizing the Bible*, 375–377; Barthélemy, "History of Old Testament," 56–58; Morrow, "Early Modern," 17–20; Reventlow, *History of Biblical Interpretation 4*, 102–103; Morrow, "Bible in Captivity," 296 and 299; Bagley, *Philosophy, Theology, and Politics*, 16; and Dungan, *History of the Synoptic Problem*, 172.

69 Spinoza, *TTP*, Ch. 7, no. 2; Israel, 98; Akkerman, 278–281; Gebhardt, 98.

70 Spinoza, *TTP*, Ch. 7, nos. 2–5; Israel, 98–100; Akkerman, 280–283; Gebhardt, 98–99.

71 Spinoza, *TTP*, Ch. 7, no. 5; Israel, 100; Akkerman, 282–283; Gebhardt, 99–100.

72 Spinoza, *TTP*, Ch. 7, no. 5; Israel, 100; Akkerman, 282–283; Gebhardt, 100. Emphasis added. Here Spinoza sees Hebrew as being the most important language, including for the New Testament.

may have available by this means *all* the statements that are found on each topic."[73]

(2.a) then the exegete must "make note of any that are ambiguous or obscure or seem to contradict others."[74]

(3) the exegete "must explain the circumstance of *all* the books of the prophets."[75]

This final step will involve:

(3.a) investigating all aspects of "the life ... of the author of each individual book."[76]

(3.b) investigating all aspects of the "character ... of the author of each individual book."[77]

(3.c) investigating all aspects of the "particular interests of the author of each individual book."[78]

These include:

(3.c.i) "who exactly" was "the author of each individual book."[79]

(3.c.ii) "on what occasion ... the author of each individual book" wrote their book.[80]

(3.c.iii) "for whom ... the author of each individual book" wrote their book.[81]

---

73 Spinoza, *TTP*, Ch. 7, no. 5; Israel, 100; Akkerman, 282–285; Gebhardt, 100. Emphasis added.
74 Spinoza, *TTP*, Ch. 7, no. 5; Israel, 100; Akkerman, 284–285; Gebhardt, 100.
75 Spinoza, *TTP*, Ch. 7, no. 5; Israel, 101; Akkerman, 286–287; Gebhardt, 101. Emphasis added.
76 Spinoza, *TTP*, Ch. 7, no. 5; Israel, 101; Akkerman, 286–287; Gebhardt, 101.
77 Spinoza, *TTP*, Ch. 7, no. 5; Israel, 101; Akkerman, 286–287; Gebhardt, 101.
78 Spinoza, *TTP*, Ch. 7, no. 5; Israel, 101; Akkerman, 286–287; Gebhardt, 101.
79 Spinoza, *TTP*, Ch. 7, no. 5; Israel, 101; Akkerman, 286–287; Gebhardt, 101.
80 Spinoza, *TTP*, Ch. 7, no. 5; Israel, 101; Akkerman, 286–287; Gebhardt, 101.
81 Spinoza, *TTP*, Ch. 7, no. 5; Israel, 101; Akkerman, 286–287; Gebhardt, 101.

(3.c.iv) "in what language ... the author of each individual book" wrote their book.[82]

(3.d) the exegete must investigate "the fate of each book."[83]

This includes:

(3.d.i) "how it was first received."[84]

(3.d.ii) "whose hands it came into."[85]

(3.d.iii) "how many variant readings there have been of its text."[86]

(3.d.iv) "by whose decision it was received among the sacred books."[87]

(3.d.v) "how all the books which are now accepted as sacred came to form a single corpus."[88]

D. "*All* this, I contend, has to be dealt with in a history of the Bible."[89]

Spinoza then emphasizes that, "Only when we have this history of Scripture before us and have made up our minds not to accept anything as a teaching of the prophets which does not follow from this history or may be very clearly derived from it, will it be time to begin investigating the minds of the prophets and the Holy Spirit."[90] Immediately after this, Spinoza emphasizes that this too "requires a method."[91] He then proceeds to enumerate the steps involved in this method, after which he examines how to study philosophical questions in Scripture (again with a proper method in hand).

---

82 Spinoza, *TTP*, Ch. 7, no. 5; Israel, 101; Akkerman, 286–287; Gebhardt, 101.

83 Spinoza, *TTP*, Ch. 7, no. 5; Israel, 101; Akkerman, 286–287; Gebhardt, 101.

84 Spinoza, *TTP*, Ch. 7, no. 5; Israel, 101; Akkerman, 286–287; Gebhardt, 101.

85 Spinoza, *TTP*, Ch. 7, no. 5; Israel, 101; Akkerman, 286–287; Gebhardt, 101.

86 Spinoza, *TTP*, Ch. 7, no. 5; Israel, 101; Akkerman, 286–287; Gebhardt, 101.

87 Spinoza, *TTP*, Ch. 7, no. 5; Israel, 101; Akkerman, 286–287; Gebhardt, 101.

88 Spinoza, *TTP*, Ch. 7, no. 5; Israel, 101; Akkerman, 286–287; Gebhardt, 101.

89 Spinoza, *TTP*, Ch. 7, no. 5; Israel, 101; Akkerman, 286–287; Gebhardt, 101. Emphasis added.

90 Spinoza, *TTP*, Ch. 7, no. 6; Israel, 102; Akkerman, 288–289; Gebhardt, 102.

91 Spinoza, *TTP*, Ch. 7, no. 6; Israel, 102; Akkerman, 288–289; Gebhardt, 102.

He then concedes some serious obstacles involved that make his method prohibitively difficult: (1) "it requires a *perfect* knowledge of the Hebrew language";[92] (2) there is also "our inability fully to reconstruct the history of Hebrew";[93] (3) moreover, "the very nature and structure of the [Hebrew] language create so many uncertainties that it is impossible to devise a method which will show us how to uncover the true sense of all the statements of Scripture with assurance";[94] (4) "numerous ambiguities [in Hebrew] are inevitable, and ... no method will resolve them all";[95] and finally, (5) the method "requires a history of the vicissitudes of all the biblical books, and most of this is unknown to us."[96] One of the purposes of all of this tedium is to narrow down the point of Scripture to a few general moral principles (love of neighbor and obedience to the state) which in turn served both his religious and political ideals.[97]

Sola Scriptura = Nulla Scriptura

Within his method, Spinoza appears to adopt the Protestant notion of *sola Scriptura*; he claims to interpret Scripture by recourse to Scripture alone. His advocacy of a sola scriptura-like position is aimed against ecclesiastical authorities.[98] To adapt Jaroslav Pelikan's witticism, Spinoza's adherence to *sola Scriptura* notwithstanding, he "showed that the 'Scriptura' has never been 'sola.'"[99]

---

92   Spinoza, *TTP*, Ch. 7, no. 11; Israel, 106; Akkerman, 296–299; Gebhardt, 106. Emphasis added.

93   Spinoza, *TTP*, Ch. 7, no. 12; Israel, 106; Akkerman, 298–299; Gebhardt, 106.

94   Spinoza, *TTP*, Ch. 7, no. 12; Israel, 106; Akkerman, 298–299; Gebhardt, 106–107.

95   Spinoza, *TTP*, Ch. 7, no. 14; Israel, 108; Akkerman, 302–303; Gebhardt, 109.

96   Spinoza, *TTP*, Ch. 7, no. 15; Israel, 109; Akkerman, 304–305; Gebhardt, 109.

97   Hahn and Wiker, *Politicizing the Bible*, 368–370, 373–374, 377–379; James, *Spinoza on Philosophy*, 188, 189 n. 9, 194, 196, 203, 205; Nadler, *Book Forged in Hell*, 141–142, 154–156; Moira Gatens, "Spinoza's Disturbing Thesis: Power, Norms and Fiction in the *Tractatus Theologico-Politicus*," *History of Political Thought* 30 (2009): 455–468; Dungan, *History of the Synoptic Problem*, 174, 216, 238, and 253; Andrew Fix, "Bekker and Spinoza," in *Disguised and Overt Spinozism Around 1700: Papers Presented at the International Colloquium, Held at Rotterdam, 5–8 October 1994*, eds. Wiep van Bunge and Wim Klever (Leiden: Brill, 1996), 23–40, at 30; and Norman O. Brown, "Philosophy and Prophecy: Spinoza's Hermeneutics," *Political Theory* 14 (1986): 195–213, at 199.

98   Preus, *Spinoza*, 12, 12–13 n. 38, 134, 134 n. 91; and Martin Greschat, "Bibelkritik und Politik: Anmerkungen zu Spinozas Theologisch-politischem Traktat" ["Biblical Criticism and Politics: Notes on Spinoza's Theological-political Treatise], in *Text—Wort—Glaube: Kurt Aland Gewidmet* [*Text—Word—Faith: Festschrift for Kurt Aland*], ed. Martin Brecht (Berlin: Walter de Gruyter, 1980), 324–343, especially 331–332, show the differences between the Reformers' understanding of *sola Scriptura* and Spinoza's.

99   Jaroslav Pelikan, *The Christian Tradition: A History of the Development of Doctrine 4: Reformation of Church and Dogma (1300–1700)* (Chicago: University of Chicago, 1984), vii, where he writes, "Despite their protestations of 'sola Scriptura,' the Reformers showed that the 'Scriptura' has never been 'sola.'"

This brings us to another key interpretive move by Spinoza, and that is his exaltation of literal exegesis.[100] Indeed, Yirmiyahu Yovel labels Spinoza "the enemy of allegorization,"[101] and his biblical hermeneutic as "an anti-allegorical method of interpretation."[102] And yet, Spinoza's literal exegesis smacks of the secular allegorism I described in the introduction.[103] Spinoza rapidly turns shades of Machiavelli when we examine his "literal" exegesis in *TTP*. His literal exegesis, or rather his secular allegorization—ostensibly an attempt to unmask the powerful politics at play barely discernable between the lines of the Hebrew text—is a façade for his political machinations.

In order to understand Spinoza's theo-political project, we must understand that he is writing in the midst of his contemporary Dutch political situation.[104]

---

100 For example, Spinoza, *TTP*, Ch. 7, no. 5; Israel, 100–101; Akkerman, 284–285; Gebhardt, 100–101; Comments in Legaspi, "Literal Sense"; Nadler, *Book Forged in Hell*, 131; Daniel J. Lasker, "Reflections of the Medieval Jewish–Christian Debate in the *Theological-Political Treatise* and the *Epistles*," in *Spinoza's Theological-Political Treatise*, eds. Melamed and Rosenthal, 56–71, at 69; Howard Kreisel, "Philosophical Interpretations of the Bible," in *The Cambridge History of Jewish Philosophy: From Antiquity Through the Seventeenth Century*, eds. Steven Nadler and T.M. Rudavsky (Cambridge: Cambridge University, 2009), 88–120, at 114; Barron, "Biblical Interpretation and Theology," 181–182; Nadler, "Bible Hermeneutics," 834; Kugel, *How to Read*, 32; Preus, *Spinoza*, 95, 189; Popkin, "Spinoza and Bible Scholarship," 306; Yovel, *Spinoza and Other Heretics I*, 29, 144, 151, and 231 n. 5; Yovel, *Spinoza and Other Heretics II*, 17; Sylvain Zac, "Spinoza et le langage" ["Spinoza and Language"], *Giornale critic della filosofia italiana* 8 (1977): 612–633; and Hans W. Frei, *The Eclipse of Biblical Narrative: A Study in Eighteenth and Nineteenth Century Hermeneutics* (New Haven: Yale University, 1974), 42–46.

101 Yovel, *Spinoza and Other Heretics I*, 144. In context, Yovel is showing how Spinoza uses allegory despite the fact that he opposes allegorical interpretation in general.

102 Yovel, *Spinoza and Other Heretics I*, 231 n. 5.

103 Jon Levenson demonstrates this basic point when he unmasks Spinoza's hermeneutic of suspicion and discontinuity: "The Bible in Spinoza's naturalistic theology becomes another political text, and its real meaning lies not in its textuality, but in its historical message, of which its own authors may have been unaware. The *meaning* of the Bible belongs to the contemporary moralizing historian. And when the message is derived from the underlying history and not from the manifest text that it often contradicts, then we are very much in the world of modern historical criticism and far indeed from the world of traditional religion ..." (*Hebrew Bible*, 96).

104 James, *Spinoza on Philosophy*, entire book, especially 2, 4, 13, 30, 40, 52, 141; Nadler, *Book Forged in Hell*, 21–25, 33, 110–111, 130; Justin Steinberg, "Spinoza's Curious Defense of Toleration," in *Spinoza's Theological–Political Treatise*, eds. Melamed and Rosenthal, 210–230, at 222; Preus, *Spinoza*, 2, 5, 24, 108; Henri Krop, "Spinoza and the Calvinistic Cartesianism of Lambertus Van Velthuysen," *Studia Spinozana* 15 (1999): 107–136; Steven B. Smith, *Spinoza, Liberalism, and the Question of Jewish Identity* (New Haven: Yale University, 1997), entire book; Ernestine Van der Wall, "The *Tractatus Theologico-politicus* and Dutch Calvinism, 1670–1700," *Studia Spinozana* 11 (1995): 201–226; Feuer, *Spinoza*, 70, 119–135; Sylvain Zac, "Le chapitre XVI du *Traité théologico-politique*" ["Chapter 16 of the *Theological-political Treatise*"], *Tijdschrift voor de studie van de Verlichting*, Bruxelles 6 (1978): 137–150; Sylvain Zac, "Spinoza et l'état des Hébreux" ["Spinoza and the Hebrew State"], *Revue Philosophique* 80 (1977): 201–232; and Zac, *Spinoza*, 166.

As Susan James explains, "in seventeenth-century Holland the interpretation of Scripture was ... a subject of tense theologico-political conflict."[105] Steven Nadler likewise explains Spinoza's goal for inserting his newly refined method into this ongoing theo-political debate: by deconstructing Scripture's supernatural and divine status Spinoza renders the Bible a dead letter, a natural literary work from which some moral profit may be derived, but one which will be unusable for state politics.[106]

Through his *TTP*, which he shrewdly published anonymously, Spinoza was able to attack several battlefronts at the same time. Through his evisceration of the Torah and his exaltation of the NT and of Jesus in place of Moses, as well as through his stringent critique of Maimonides and the Pharisees (a slightly less-than-veiled reference to Spinoza's Jewish contemporaries), Spinoza was able to exact revenge on the Jewish community that had excommunicated him. His evisceration of the Torah, and his more heavily veiled critique of Christian dogma and NT history, as well as his overt dismissals of Roman Catholic papal authority, struck out against both the Catholic Church and Catholic lands who had threatened to control the Netherlands in the not-so-distant past, as well as against the Calvinist orthodoxy which threatened to take tyrannical control of the Dutch Republic and perhaps convert it into a new Geneva. Finally, his more subtle critique of Maimonides and his comments on philosophy could be taken as pedagogical or collegial jabs at his intellectual sparring partners and comrades in philosophical arms—the Collegiants, Quakers, and other heterodox Protestants with whom he exchanged ideas, especially Meyer.

From Theocracy to Democracy: Spinoza on OT Priesthood

Spinoza's discussion of the change in the OT priesthood from firstborn sons within the tribes of Israel to the sons of Aaron within the priestly tribe of Levi provides a useful examination of Spinoza's method. Here we see clearly the influence of Machiavelli, among others. Machiavelli exerted a great influence on

---

105 James, *Spinoza on Philosophy*, 141.

106 See Nadler, *Book Forged in Hell*, 111, where he pens the following: "By showing that the Bible is not, in fact, the work of a supernatural God—'a message for mankind sent down by God from heaven,' as Spinoza mockingly puts it—but a perfectly natural human document; that the author of the Pentateuch is not Moses; that Hebrew Scripture as a whole is but a compilation of writings composed by fallible and not particularly learned individuals under various historical and political circumstances; that most of these writings were transmitted over generations, to be finally redacted by a latter-day political and religious leader—in short, by naturalizing the Torah and the other books of the Bible and reducing them to ordinary (though morally valuable) works of literature, Spinoza hopes to undercut ecclesiastic influence in politics and other domains and weaken the sectarian dangers facing his beloved Republic."

Spinoza, whom he read assiduously.[107] Graham Hammill has recently argued that, "Machiavelli enables—and Spinoza develops—a critical assessment of absolutism based on its attempt to manipulate and control the theological imaginary upon which political community depends."[108] Moreoover, Machiavelli championed the very secular allegorization this present article seeks to examine in Spinoza.[109]

Spinoza demystifies the Bible, naturalizing the supernatural.[110] He argues forcefully for the impossibility of miracles and demonstrates with sustained argument (spanning an entire chapter) that the prophets, rather than receiving divine oracles from God as a matter of public revelation, were simply possessed

---

107 Hahn and Wiker, *Politicizing the Bible*, 342–343, 388; Graham Hammill, *The Mosaic Constitution: Political Theology and Imagination from Machiavelli to Milton* (Chicago: University of Chicago Press, 2012), 1, 21–22, 32, 66–68, 72, 78, 85–87, and 99; Jacqueline Lagrée and Pierre-François Moreau, introduction to Spinoza, *Œuvres III: Tractatus Theologico-Politicus*, ed. Moreau, 3–17, at 14; Maurizio Viroli, *Machiavelli's God* (Princeton: Princeton University, 2010), 17–18; Filippo Del Lucchese, *Conflict, Power, and Multitude in Machiavelli and Spinoza* (London: Continuum, 2009), whole book; Lorberbaum, "Spinoza's Theological-Political," 170–171, 173, 177, and 183 n. 19; Vittorio Morfino, *Il tempo e l'occasione. L'incontro Spinoza Machiavelli* [*The Time and the Occasion: The Encounter between Spinoza and Machiavelli*] (Milan: LED, 2002), entire book; Nadler, *Spinoza*, 111 and 270; Douglas J. Den Uyl, "Power, Politics, and Religion in Spinoza's Political Thought," *Jewish Political Studies Review* 7 (1995): 77–106, at 83; Étienne Balibar, "Spinoza: From Individuality to Transindividuality," *Mededelingen vanwege Het Spinozahuis* 71 (1997): 3–36; Smith, *Spinoza*, 34–38; Edwin Curley, "Kissinger, Spinoza, and Genghis Khan," in *Cambridge Companion to Spinoza*, ed. Garrett, 315–342, at 315–317, 327–329, 332–333, and 341 n. 35; Bernard Septimus, "Biblical Religion and Political Rationality in Simone Luzzato, Maimonides and Spinoza," in *Jewish Thought in the Seventeenth Century*, eds. Isadore Twersky and Bernard Septimus (Cambridge: Harvard University, 1987), 399–433; Eco Mulier, *The Myth of Venice and Dutch Republican Thought in the Seventeenth Century* (Assen: Van Gorcum, 1980), 170–181; and Carla Gallicet Calvetti, *Spinoza lettore del Machiavelli* [*Spinoza a Reader of Machiavelli*] (Milan: Università Cattolica del Sacro Cuore, 1972), entire book.

108 Hammill, *Mosaic Constitution*, 99. Hammill's third chapter, "Spinoza and the Theological Imaginary" (67–99) shows how Spinoza, "one of Machiavelli's most perceptive readers" (22), developed, honed, and took further Machiavelli's work, following the theo-political trajectory Machiavelli initiated.

109 Indeed, Hahn and Wiker insightfully underscore how, "In future exegesis, Machiavelli's mode of procedure is repeated, but in the service of other philosophies. ... The pattern set is one in which the philosophy, no matter how far removed it is from the assumptions of the biblical text, becomes the secret knowledge that allows the exegete to wield the exegetical threshing tool. Passages that fit become the key to illumination; passages that do not must either be reinterpreted against the apparent meaning, or inferred to have some less than noble source. ... The task of the enlightened exegete, then, is to ferret out all the 'real' passages—the ones that fit the philosophy—and reinterpret the rest, giving some *other* explanation for their appearance in the text" (*Politicizing the Bible*, 145).

110 Hahn and Wiker, *Politicizing the Bible*, 364–368; James, *Spinoza on Philosophy*, 139–184; Gregory, *Unintended Reformation*, 60; Nadler, *Book Forged in Hell*, 76–103; Michael A. Rosenthal, "Miracles, Wonder, and the State," in *Spinoza's Theological-Political Treatise*, eds. Melamed and Rosenthal, 231–249, at 231; J. Garrido Zaragoza, "La desmitificación de la Escritura en Spinoza" ["The Demystification of Scripture in Spinoza"], *Taula* 9 (1988), 3–45; Richard H. Popkin, "Hume and Spinoza," *Hume Studies* 5 (1979): 65–93, at 87–89; and Zac, "Spinoza et le langage" ["Spinoza and Language"], 612–633.

of vivid imaginations.[111] As Scott Hahn and Benjamin Wiker put the matter, "Here, Spinoza revealed the key to his method of interpreting Scripture, even while concealing the ultimate reasons. ... *Since* miracles are impossible, *therefore* the scientific exegete must look for another explanation of their common occurrence in Scripture."[112] Unsurprisingly, that explanation was political. In the style of Machiavelli, Spinoza argued that so-called miracles, which in reality must simply have been nothing more than natural phenomena, were described as miracles, not only on account of the piety of the people, but at root on account of the sheer political power of their rulers. Michael Rosenthal explains that, in Spinoza's mind, "Miracles are especially useful not only in producing veneration but also in consolidating and maintaining political power."[113]

Spinoza shared with many of his contemporaries a disdain for the priesthood and any priestly class.[114] This should not simply be read as a criticism of the synagogue officials (although this is certainly true in part), but rather, shares much in common with later 18th and 19th century criticisms of OT priesthood as a guise for attacks on the Catholic priesthood—only for Spinoza, all Christian clergy are in sight. Yovel writes that, "When Spinoza describes the political rule of God through his priestly representatives, he thinks more of the rabbis in the Diaspora than of Moses and the Levites. But his chief targets lie in the Christian world. He aims at the political claims of the pope and the Catholic establishment; at the demands of the Dutch Calvinist *predikanten*" (ministers), among others.[115]

Likewise, Spinoza's views on prophecy are "clearly derived from Spinoza's own scientific account of the nature of prophecy; and although he attempts to find support for it in the Bible itself, in fact this is a general rationalistic presupposition derived from his philosophy and then superimposed on the text."[116] Again, this serves his political program even as it violates his own methodological principles. Just as it is impossible to have the Scripture alone without a tradition to iden-

---

111 Hahn and Wiker, *Politicizing the Bible*, 364–368, 371–373; Hammill, *Mosaic Constitution*, 13–14, 72–81; James, *Spinoza on Philosophy*, 51, 94, 130–133; Nadler, *Book Forged in Hell*, 76–103; Rosenthal, "Miracles," 231; Gross, "Reading the Bible," 22–36; Popkin, "Hume and Spinoza," 87–89, where he shows that Spinoza's demonstration of the impossibility of miracles is even more forceful than Hume's; André Malet, *Le traité théologico-politique de Spinoza et la pensée biblique* [*The Theological-Political Treatise of Spinoza and Biblical Thought*] (Paris: Sociéte les belles letters, 1966), 118; and Zac, *Spinoza*, 69–82.

112 Hahn and Wiker, *Politicizing the Bible*, 365.

113 Rosenthal, "Miracles," 241.

114 James, *Spinoza on Philosophy*, 202. Israel explains, "Freethinkers, in short, followed Spinoza in depicting priesthood as professional agents of prejudice, uncritical thinking, and ignorance" (*Enlightenment Contested*, 102).

115 Yovel, *Spinoza and Other Heretics I*, 196. See also Preus, *Spinoza*, 4–5; and Feuer, *Spinoza*, 69.

116 Yovel, *Spinoza and Other Heretics II*, 195 n. 21.

tify what constitutes Scripture and how Scripture should be interpreted, so it is impossible to have a biblical interpretation without philosophical and theological assumptions. As with many later practitioners of historical criticism, Spinoza does not articulate his philosophical assumptions.

Spinoza's political views, like Hobbes's, fit broadly in the Erastian camp—what would be Gallicanism and other forms of Conciliarism in the Catholic world—a theo-political view that ultimately placed power in the hands of the state sovereign. Spinoza emphasized this using his discussion of the Hebrew state to bolster this claim, which included official biblical interpretation (as well as all public expression of religion) to rest in the hands of the head of state.[117] Yovel explains that, "By making the political authorities the sole interpreters of what is considered the word of God, Spinoza grants the secular government a monopoly over the normative domain as a whole—that is, over right and wrong, justice and injustice in all their valid applications."[118]

Starting with the biblical Hebrew state, the "Hebrew Republic," was familiar territory in early modern European political discourse.[119] In *TTP*, Spinoza understands the Israelite theocracy instituted by Moses in the wilderness after the exodus from Egypt as an attempt by Moses to bring civil order to their newly formed nation. The golden calf episode reduced Israel to a wretched servitude. The angry God of the wilderness unleashed his wrath against Israel. The Levites thus replaced the firstborn priests. Priestly rule proved a disaster in the history of Israel, instigating rebellion and virtual anarchy. After the monarchy takes over, to bring peace to Israelite society, a new strife ensues, that of throne vs. altar, state ruler vs. priest.[120] Michael Legaspi explains the upshot, that, "Spinoza's Moses harnessed powerful religious impulses and kept dangerous social forces in check by creating

---

117 Hahn and Wiker, *Politicizing the Bible*, 382, 386; Nadler, *Book Forged in Hell*, 202–203, 262 n. 9; Steinberg, "Spinoza's Curious Defense," 219; Eric Nelson, *The Hebrew Republic: Jewish Sources and the Transformation of European Political Thought* (Cambridge: Harvard University, 2010), 130–134; Legaspi, *Death of Scripture*, 132; Levering, *Participatory Biblical Exegesis*, 112 and 137; Joseph B. Sermoneta, "Biblical Anthropology in 'The Guide of the Perplexed' by Moses Maimonides, and its Reversal in the 'Tractatus Theologico-Politicus' by Baruch Spinoza," *Topoi* 7 (1988): 241–247, at 245–246; and Zac, "chapitre XVI" ["Chapter 16"], 137–150.

118 Yovel, *Spinoza and Other Heretics I*, 134.

119 James, *Spinoza on Philosophy*, 120, 265–269, 271–273; Nelson, *Hebrew Republic*, entire volume; and all of the essays in Schochet, Oz-Salzberger, and Jones, ed., *Political Hebraism*.

120 Spinoza, *TTP*, Ch. 17, no. 7–15 and 26–29; Israel, 213–220 and 225–229; Akkerman, 544–563 and 574–583; Gebhardt, 205–212 and 217–220; Hahn and Wiker, *Politicizing the Bible*, 383–386; Nadler, *Book Forged in Hell*, 144–146; Legaspi, *Death of Scripture*, 133–134; Bagley, *Philosophy, Theology, and Politics*, 37; Étienne Balibar, "*Jus-Pactum-Lex*: On the Constitution of the Subject in the *Theologico-Political Treatise*," in *The New Spinoza*, eds. Warren Montag and Ted Stolze (Minneapolis: University of Minnesota Press, 1997), 171–206; Martin D. Yaffe, "'The Histories and Successes of the Hebrews': The Demise of the Biblical Polity in Spinoza's

a free and equal society held together by piety and common morality. He demonstrated how religion could serve noble political ends."[121]

A Secular Allegory for Political Ends

Spinoza's discussion of the wilderness period, discussed above, provides a useful example of secular allegory. The text seems to say one thing, but for Spinoza it "really" means something else. His literal exegesis amounts to little more than a secular theo-political allegory; what the text "really" means is *Realpolitik*. Levenson notes that, "Now any student of the Hebrew Bible knows that priests, prophets, and kings all take it on the chin quite a bit in that book, and the very worth of all three institutions was questioned at times. But what Spinoza does not respect is the claim of the text itself that each of them was divinely ordained and the fact that, on balance, the Bible is positive about them all."[122]

Spinoza's method is far too restrictive; so much so that it fails miserably on the grounds of explanatory power. This is unsurprising, of course, since Spinoza constructed his method to restrict the range of possible conclusions to support his theo-political project. Part and parcel of this project was to keep Scripture in the past; indeed to distance the exegete from the world of the text as much as possible. As Robert Barron, following Levenson, rightly notes, "this hyperconcentration on the intention of the historical author within his historical period, and in abstraction from the wider literary, theological, and metaphysical context, has led effectively to the relegation of the Bible to the past."[123] For Spinoza, biblical exegesis is "an offensive weapon."[124] In his mind, "biblical hermeneutics is an aggressive activity, offering the philosopher a mode of involvement in the social and cultural processes of his time."[125]

His method has been fairly left intact throughout the centuries since his death. Scholars in the Enlightenment and, later in the midst or wake of the *Kulturkampf*, built upon Spinoza's hermeneutic, honing various aspects while standing on his Machiavellian shoulders to construct theo-political tools of their own to denigrate the Judaism of the other in their midst, and utterly stomp out the Catholic bogeyman they feared might cause harm to the State. Since the end of the nineteenth century, scholars without any hidden agendas—from all backgrounds including Jewish, Protestant, and Catholic—have embraced Spinoza's heritage: historical biblical criticism. They typically do so without much knowledge of its

---

Theologico-Political Treatise," Jewish Political Studies Review 7 (1995): 57–75, at 62–63 and 65–68; and Zac, "Spinoza et l'état" ["Spinoza and the State"], 213.

121 Legaspi, *Death of Scripture*, 134.

122 Levenson, *Hebrew Bible*, 96.

123 Barron, "Biblical Interpretation and Theology," 182.

124 Yovel, *Spinoza and Other Heretics II*, 11.

125 Ibid.

history, and under the assumption that the method itself is neutral. What matters, they think, is how the method is used. To a considerable extent, this is true. The main difficulty is that the method carries within itself problems that have not yet been fully assessed. Pope Benedict XVI called for a purification of historical criticism, whereby it would shine its critical light upon its own historical origins and philosophical assumptions, so as to root out detrimental aspects.[126]

Conclusion

Spinoza contributed to turning the Bible into a material book, like any other.[127] If it is true that the canon originated in the liturgy—as scholarship is increasingly demonstrating—then a proper biblical hermeneutic will naturally be liturgical and sacramental.[128] Although open to history, indeed requiring vigorous historical investigation, such a hermeneutic will starkly contrast with contemporary historical critical ones, which remain grounded in a suspicion of the sources. Spinoza launched criticism in the direction which it has followed. Regarding the titles of *TTP* chapters 7–10, Pierre Gibert notes that they "mark a significant change of paradigm in the critical approach of the biblical corpus."[129]

---

126 Joseph Cardinal Ratzinger, "Biblical Interpretation in Conflict," in *God's Word: Scripture—Tradition—Office*, by Joseph Cardinal Ratzinger, eds. Peter Hünermann and Thomas Söding, trans. by Henry Taylor (San Francisco: Ignatius Press, 2008 [2005]), 91–126. See also Michael Maria Waldstein, "The Self-Critique of the Historical-Critical Method: Cardinal Ratzinger's Erasmus Lecture," *Modern Theology* 28 (2012): 732–747; and Scott W. Hahn, *Covenant and Communion: The Biblical Theology of Pope Benedict XVI* (Grand Rapids; Brazos, 2009), 25–40.

127 Hammill, *Mosaic Constitution*, 81; James, *Spinoza on Philosophy*, 128; and Morrow, "Bible in Captivity," 288.

128 That the canon was formed in and for liturgy, see Robert Louis Wilken, *The First Thousand Years: A Global History of Christianity* (New Haven: Yale University, 2012), 43. On the same page Wilken also shows how the Latin word, *testamentum* (testament), came to be used to translate the Greek word, *diathēkē* (covenant), but even still the idea of the New Covenant/New Testament (*Kainē Diathēkē/Novum Testamentum*) was applied to the Eucharist and only hesitatingly began to be applied to the documents gradually. He cites Origen, and observes that Origen's phraseology suggests "that the terminology was still novel in his day."

129 Gibert, *L'invention* [*The Invention*], 170. My own translation. Jean-Louis Ska similarly notes that: "Spinoza is undoubtedly the father of the historical-critical method and of modern exegesis although he is more a philosopher than a real exegete. To be sure, there is a great distance between the *Treatise* and, say, the *Prolegomena zur Geschichte Israels* [*Prolegomena to the History of Israel*] or *Die Composition des Hexateuchs und der historischen Bücher des Alten Testaments* [*The Composition of the Hexateuch and the Historical Books of the Old Testament*] by Julius Wellhausen. But, to appreciate the novelty of Spinoza's 'natural' interpretation of Scripture (*interpretation naturae*), we should not look first of all for precise exegetical methods and even less for hypotheses about the formation of single biblical books. Spinoza's main contribution to modern exegesis is to be found in his systematic *secular* approach to the *Holy* Scripture. He brought the Bible down to earth and made it possible to hear the different, sometimes discordant, voices which resonate within this literary work" (*Exegesis of the Pentateuch*, 259).

Levenson too emphasizes Spinoza's significance when he clarifies that what Spinoza pioneered "was the systematic transference of the normativity of the Bible from its *manifest text* to its *underlying history* (at least as he reconstructed it)."[130] Were such a method sought for the sake of better understanding the text, were it bereft of anemic Cartesian doubt and nominalistic historical enquiries masking deeper political and often anti-theological agendas, the cause for concern would be far less. With regard to Spinoza and his method, however, Yovel reminds us that this was precisely Spinoza's point, to be a work which had a concrete effect in the politics of his day and for future generations. Spinoza was attempting to make an effective intervention in the course of the social and political events in the Dutch Republic.[131]

The purpose? The evisceration of Scripture. Spinoza wanted the text dissected endlessly to support a particular form of politics in his age and for future generations. Hahn and Wiker make clear: "the historical-critical method as originally designed by Spinoza is neither neutral nor scientific, but is rather the form of biblical studies that purposely transforms the Bible to act as a political support to keep order in a secular state. ..."[132] In other words, "To keep the elite from turning against the philosophers, Spinoza fashions an exegetical method that produces the conclusions that reduce Scripture to a merely moral prop for civil order, one that allows the greatest freedom for philosophy."[133] In the end, this would serve other exegetes, often in the very midst of church and state conflicts, in support of ever more secular nation-states over and against the Catholic Church, and later any religious communities who refused the privatization of their faith.

Hahn and Wiker spell out the consequences of Spinoza's method, which we have seen played out in the university, the academy at large, as well as in the public eye in the realm of politics and media, on popular television and in literary works of popular fiction:

> Spinoza implied that illustrating the enormity of the task might "provoke him [the reader] into a hopeless undertaking," the reduction to hopelessness, it seems, being part of Spinoza's overall design. That is, Spinoza defined this exegetical exercise by the nearly hopeless task of recovering the historical origin of the Bible's original, preedited sources. A unified interpretation ever recedes because the flow of exegesis is toward maximum *disunity*

---

130 Levenson, *Hebrew Bible*, 96.
131 Yovel, *Spinoza and Other Heretics I*, 136.
132 Hahn and Wiker, *Politicizing the Bible*, 364.
133 Ibid., 388.

of the text, and it therefore produces an endless multiplication of ever larger technical commentaries focused on ever-shrinking textual shards.[134]

A Catholic response to this situation is not to give up on the importance of history and retreat solely to the realm of allegory. Rather, we need to unmask how claims that do away with traditional, patristic, medieval, spiritual exegesis and instead focus exclusively on the literal-historical level often mask a secular allegory at the service of another kingdom, not the Kingdom of God. We should take history seriously, and need not fear the disciplines of philology, textual criticism, archaeology, and even the hypothetical source theories of historical biblical criticism like source, form, and redaction criticism—which often prove to be incredibly useful heuristic devices. But we must be fully aware, when we engage in biblical exegesis, that we tread on sacred ground.

Those Catholics engaged in pre-theological biblical scholarly tasks like textual criticism need not abandon their posts; a re-orientation may be all that is necessary. It may require a purification of intention and purpose, always being aware that we work in the presence of God, and that our labor, especially regarding the understanding and interpretation of Scripture, should be handled with care. The ultimate goal, even in text criticism, sorting through variants in the manuscript tradition, is to become saints and help others do the same. Our goal is the Beatific Vision, and thus our very work must be mystagogical. We need to bring people to the divine waters of Scripture and the Sacraments so that they might quench their divine thirst while accompanying us as wayfarers through our heavenly pilgrimage on this earth.[135]

---

134 Hahn and Wiker, *Politicizing the Bible*, 377.

135 I am indebted to Victor Velarde-Mayol for fruitful conversations on Spinoza as well as nominalism and late medieval scholasticism, and for bringing to my attention some important sources. I owe thanks to Nicolai Sinai for providing me a copy of his work, to Michael Legaspi for providing me with a copy of his SBL presentation, and to Scott Hahn and Benjamin Wiker for their generosity in providing me with copies of their work prior to publication as well as for many fruitful conversations on the themes brought up in this article. Finally, I owe Maria Morrow special thanks for critiquing a draft of this manuscript.

Letter & Spirit 8 (2013): 223-245

Purchasing the Rewards of Eternal Life:
The Logic of Resurrection and Ransom in Matthew's Gospel[1]

Nathan Eubank
Notre Dame Seminary, New Orleans

> O God, whose only-begotten Son, by his life, death, and resurrection, has purchased for us the rewards of eternal life …
> Traditional concluding prayer of the Rosary

> Blessed are you when they insult you and persecute you and falsely say all kinds of evil against you because of me. Rejoice and be glad because your wage is great in the heavens.
> Matthew 5:11–12[2]

Introduction

The traditional English translation of the Lord's Prayer used in the liturgy diverges from the Greek of Matthew 6:9–13 in a number of respects, the most striking of which is the omission of the Greek prayer's petition for the cancellation of debts: "Forgive us our debts (*ta opheilēmata*) as we also forgive our debtors (*tois opheiletais*)."[3] The restatement of the petition in verses 14–15 ("For if you forgive people their trespasses, your heavenly Father will also forgive you") shows that "debt" is used here to refer to sin. This may be Matthew's most well-known example of sin as debt, but it is hardly an isolated occurrence. For instance, Matthew repeatedly describes divine recompense as a settling of accounts and describes the fate of unforgiven sinners as debt-bondage.[4] In the parable of the unforgiving servant (18:23–35), God is compared to a king who will forgive even the most astronomical debts of his servants. Yet the parable also warns that those who refuse to forgive the debts of their fellow servants will be thrown in prison until they "repay all that is

---

1 This essay is adapted from portions of my book, *Wages of Cross-Bearing and Debt of Sin: The Economy of Heaven in Matthew's Gospel*, Beihefte zur Zeitschrift für die neutestamentliche Wissenschaft und die Kunde der älteren Kirche 196 (Berlin/Boston: Walter de Gruyter, 2013).

2 All translations are my own unless otherwise noted.

3 Debt cancellation is preserved in the Vulgate: *dimitte nobis debita nostra, sicut et nos dimittimus debitoribus nostris.*

4 For settling of accounts see 16:27 (compare to Mark 8:38 and Luke 9:26); 18:23–35; 19:16–20:16; 25:14–30. The phrase "to settle accounts" (*synairein logon*) appears in Matt. 18:23–24 and 25:19, but nowhere else in the LXX or NT. It is common in Greek documentary papyri. See, for example, *P.Bad.* II 42.6–7; *BGU* III 775.18.

owed" (18:34). Similarly, Matthew 5:21–26 warns that those who are found with unresolved sin against a "brother" will be thrown into prison until they repay the last penny (5:25–26). In Matthew 7:2 Jesus echoes the language of loan contracts when he warns that the measure (*metron*) that a person uses for recording the sins of others will be used to measure that person's sins.[5]

Why would Matthew have such an affinity for debt-language? The recent work of Gary Anderson has shown that financial language provided the conceptual framework for speaking of good and bad deeds in the later strata of the Hebrew Bible as well as in early Judaism and Christianity.[6] In Aramaic, Anderson notes, "the word for a debt that one owes a lender, *ḥôbâ*, is the standard term for denoting sin. This term comes into Second Temple Hebrew and has the same double meaning."[7]

Closely related to the idea of sin as debt was the belief that good deeds, especially almsgiving, earned wages or merits with God. Though the idea of wages from God is well-attested in early Judaism and Christianity, it is particularly prominent in the First Gospel.[8] New Testament scholars have not been unaware that Matthew has much to say about treasure in heaven and the like, but they have tended to treat this material as a theological embarrassment to be minimized or ignored.[9] One of the most prominent themes of the First Gospel has, therefore, been left largely unexplored.

One of the most interesting features of Matthew's economic language is the way that Jesus is repeatedly portrayed as doing the very things he taught would earn treasure in heaven. Those who endure insults and persecution have "great wages in the heavens" (5:11–12); Jesus endures insults and persecution (20:19; 26:67–68; 27:27–44). Those who pray privately will receive a wage from their Father in the heavens (6:1, 5–6); Jesus withdraws to pray alone (14:23; 26:36). Those who do not store up their treasure on earth are able to store up treasure in heaven (6:19–21; 19:21) and those who leave their property behind will receive "a hundred times as much" (19:29); Jesus has no place to lay his head (8:20). Those who bear crosses, who lose their lives, will find their lives in the coming eschatological repayment of deeds (16:24–27); Jesus bears his cross and is raised from the dead. In return for

---

5   For example, see *P.Amh.* II 46. See also Eubank, *Wages of Cross-Bearing*, 53–67 for more on sin as debt in Matthew.

6   See Gary Anderson, *Sin: A History* (New Haven: Yale University Press, 2009).

7   Anderson, *Sin*, 27.

8   To be more precise, it is a particularly prominent theme in the Synoptic Gospels, and especially in Matthew. Much of Matthew's economic language is found in parables which only appear in Matthew and in Matthean "pluses" in pericopae with parallels in Mark and/or Luke.

9   See, for example, Günther Bornkamm, "Der Lohngedanke im Neuen Testament" [Wage-thought in the New Testament], in *Studien zu Antike und Urchristentum: Gesammelte Aufsätze*, 2 vols. (Munich: Kaiser Verlag, 1963), 2.69–92. Kant's contention that reward is antithetical to virtue has played an important role in making Jesus' teaching on reward a neuralgic issue for New Testament scholars. See Eubank, *Wages of Cross-Bearing*, 4–11.

forsaking everything and following Jesus the apostles will receive twelve thrones alongside the throne of the Son of Man (19:27–28); Jesus himself is enthroned as Son of Man from the time when he gives his life (26:64; 28:18).

The purpose of this article is to delve deeper into Matthew's portrayal of Jesus as an earner of treasure in heaven by analyzing three key passages which occur after the pivotal moment when Jesus begins predicting his death and resurrection (16:13–28; 19:16–29; 20:17–28). Particular attention will be given to the ransom saying in 20:28. I shall argue that careful attention to Matthew's economic language and use of the Old Testament illuminates the logic of Jesus' resurrection and enthronement and explains how Jesus saves his people from their sins (Matt. 1:21).

Cross-bearers Will Be Repaid with Eternal Life (16:13–28)

Matthew has a particular concern to describe the parousia as the time when debts are collected and deeds are repaid. There are hints of a coming settling of accounts in earlier passages such as the Sermon on the Mount, but it is not until Jesus begins predicting his passion that this concern takes center stage.[10] After Peter confesses Jesus as "the Christ, the Son of the living God" (16:16), Jesus begins to explain to the disciples what this means: "From then Jesus began showing his disciples that it was necessary for him to go to Jerusalem and to suffer many things from the elders and chief priests and scribes and be killed and on the third day be raised" (16:21).[11] This prediction is repugnant to Peter: "And taking him aside Peter began to rebuke him saying 'Far be it from you Lord! This will certainly not happen to you!' But turning, Jesus said to Peter, 'Get behind me, Satan! You are a trap to me because you are not thinking the things of God (*ta tou theou*) but the things of people (*ta tōn anthrōpōn*)'" (16:21–23).[12] Peter's seemingly reasonable objection is condemned by Jesus as human rather than divine thinking.

In the teaching that follows in 16:24–28, Jesus commences a bit of remediation for the disciples in "the things of God." He begins by explaining that the path of death and resurrection is not his alone but theirs as well: "Then Jesus said to his disciples, 'If anyone wants to come behind me, let him deny himself and take

---

10 See Nathan Eubank, "Storing up Treasure with God in the Heavens: Celestial Investments in Matthew 6:1–21," forthcoming in *Catholic Biblical Quarterly*.

11 At first glance Matt. 16:21–28 would seem to have a tenuous relationship to the preceding material. The words "from then on he began ..." make the break between Peter's confession (16:13–20) and the first passion and resurrection prediction (16:21–28) stronger than in the Markan parallel (8:27–31). Moreover, verse 21 marks the beginning of Jesus' decisive turn to Jerusalem and the cross. Nevertheless, verses 21–28 continue both the topic (Jesus' identity) and the central players (Jesus and Peter) of the preceding section. Ulrich Luz notes that 16:21–28 is a chiastic reversal of 16:13–20; see Ulrich Luz, *Das Evangelium nach Matthäus* [The Gospel according to Matthew], 4 vols.; Evangelisch-katholischer Kommentar zum Neuen Testament 1/1–4 (Düsseldorf: Benziger, 1990–2002), 2.486.

12 Note "the things of God" (*ta tou theou*) that one must "repay" (*apodote*) in 22:21.

up his cross and follow me'" (16:24). He then goes on to unfold the logic of these strange words:

> For whoever wants to save his life (*psychē*) will lose it, and whoever loses his life (*psychē*) for my sake will find it. For what will it profit a person if he gains the whole world but forfeits his life (*psychē*)? Or what will a person give in exchange for his life (*psychēs*)? For the Son of Man is about to come in the glory of his Father with his angels, and then he will repay to each according to his deeds. (16:25–27)

Verses 24–26 are nearly identical to the Markan parallel (8:34–37). Matthew, however, goes on to provide a detail in v. 27 that is not found in Mark or Luke: "For the Son of Man is about to come in the glory of his Father with his angels, and then *he will repay to each according to his deeds.*" Only in Matthew's Gospel is cross-bearing necessary because of the coming "repayment."[13]

To understand Jesus' explanation of the necessity of cross-bearing it is also important to note the wordplay on the two different meanings of *psyche*: (1) present earthly life, and (2) eternal life.[14] Jesus' disciples must follow him in losing their earthly lives to be repaid with eternal life. Verse 26 explains why one should take the bold step of following Jesus in his cross-bearing: "For what will it profit a person if he gains the whole world but loses his [eternal] life?" It is folly to cling to "the world," including one's present life, because the more precious possession is one's *psychē* in the world to come. The next line develops this further: "Or what will a person give in exchange for his [eternal] life?" (16:26). The implied answer to this rhetorical question is, of course, "nothing." No matter how much earthly wealth one amasses it can never purchase eternal life. As Psalm 49:7–9 puts it, "Truly, no ransom avails for one's life, there is no price one can give to God for it. For the ransom of life is costly, and can never suffice that one should live on forever and never see the grave" (NRSV).[15] In the day of judgment no one can present

---

13 Though the parallel passages in Mark and Luke do not describe the recompense of cross-bearing as "payment," the idea that eternal life would be "repaid" to the righteous is fairly well-attested in early Jewish and Christian texts. For instance, 2 Macc. 12:45 refers to resurrection as the "splendid favor that is stored up for those who sleep in godliness." Wisd. 2:22 describes the afterlife of the godly as the "wages of holiness." *Pss. Sol.* 9:5 says that "the one who does righteousness treasures up life for himself with the Lord." 1 Tim. 6:19 says that those who give alms store up a foundation that allows them to take hold of true life.

14 This is an example of the rhetorical device known as *antanaclasis*. For another example of *antanaclasis* in the synoptic tradition see T. J. Lang, "'You will desire to see and you will not see [it]': Reading Luke 17.22 as Antanaclasis," *Journal for the Study of the New Testament* 33 (2011): 281–302.

15 Davies and Allison link Matt. 16:26 to Ps. 49. See W. D. Davies and Dale C. Allison, *A Critical and Exegetical Commentary on the Gospel according to Saint Matthew*, 3 vols., International Critical Commentary (Edinburgh: T&T Clark, 1988–1997), 2.674.

God with earthly treasures and purchase eternal life.[16] Thus, while cross-bearing may seem ridiculous to those "thinking the things of people," it is in fact the more prudent course of action. No one can store up enough earthly treasure to purchase eternal life. It makes more sense to follow Jesus in giving one's present life in order to be repaid with eternal life in the resurrection.

One other detail in this passage needs to be noted. When Jesus says that anyone who would follow him must give his life and so receive it in the coming repayment, he is explaining not only the logic of Christian faithfulness and resurrection but also his own mission. There is a tight, organic unity between Jesus' first passion and resurrection prediction in 16:21–23, and the explanation that follows in verses 24–28.[17] The latter section is an explanation of the path that Jesus and all who follow him must take, over against Peter's "human" thinking: total self-abandonment is necessary because stockpiles of earthly possessions will be useless in the eschatological repayment of deeds. An important implication of the unity of verses 21–28 is that it is not only the eschatological repayment of Jesus' followers under discussion but the repayment of Jesus himself as well—indeed, it is Jesus' claim that he will die and be raised that initiates the discussion.

It is the message of Jesus' coming death and resurrection to which Peter objects and which Jesus defends. Thus, it is not only followers of Jesus who will be repaid for their cross-bearing with eternal life but also Jesus, as the passive infinitive *egerthēnai* ("to be raised") indicates.[18] As noted above, Matthew repeatedly portrays Jesus doing the very things that Jesus says earn heavenly treasure. In other words, the life to which the Matthean Jesus calls his disciples is the life that he himself lives. An important and neglected implication of verses 21–28 taken as a whole is that Jesus' resurrection is the repayment he will receive from his Father for obediently submitting to rejection and death (26:39, 42).

The Thrones of the Son of Man and the Apostles (19:16–29)

The close link between Jesus' fate and the fate of the disciples continues to unfold in the account of the rich young man. After telling the disciples about his coming death and resurrection for the first time in 16:21, he repeats the prediction in Galilee in 17:22. Then they go to Judea where they encounter the rich young man (19:16–22). Jesus then predicts his death and resurrection for the third time (20:17–19), and they ascend to Jerusalem.

The passage begins with the man's quest for "eternal life": "Teacher, what good must I do to have eternal life?" (19:16). Jesus responds by first telling him to obey the commandments and then by calling him to "go sell your possessions

---

16 See Luke 12:13–21; 17:33.

17 Luz, *Matthäus*, 2.486–87.

18 This point is obscured by the scholarly habit of referring to Jesus' passion and resurrection predictions as "passion predictions."

and give to the poor, and you will have treasure in the heavens, then come, follow me." This call to renunciation recalls Jesus' earlier words to the disciples: "If anyone wants to come behind me, let him deny himself and take up his cross and follow me" (16:24). Self-denial, for the rich man, means giving away all his possessions. Like 16:21–27, this passage describes the self-denial that is necessary to follow Jesus and earn the heavenly treasure required to enter the kingdom. Moreover, like the Markan parallel, the passage appears after the first two passion and resurrection predictions and immediately before the third. The placement of the story suggests it is a specific example of how a would-be follower of Jesus may take up his cross.[19]

The discussion that ensues after the young man goes away offers further illumination of the links between cross-bearing, heavenly treasure, and eternal life. When Jesus declares the impossibility of a rich person entering the kingdom, Peter asks, "Behold, *we* have left everything (*hēmeis aphēkamen*) and followed you. What then will there be for us?" (19:27). Jesus replies,

> Truly I say to you that you who have followed me, in the new age, when the Son of Man sits on his throne of glory, you yourselves also will sit on twelve thrones judging the twelve tribes of Israel. And whoever left houses or brothers or sisters or father or mother or children or fields on account of my name will receive a hundred times as much and will possess eternal life. (Matt. 19:28–29)

Jesus' response underscores again what he had said in 16:13–28: those who follow Jesus will be recompensed like Jesus. A new element emerges in this passage, however; Jesus says that in the new age the apostles will share not only in his resurrection but also in his rule as Son of Man. For the moment Jesus does not address the disciples' ongoing failure to grasp that following him means bearing crosses. Instead, he responds quite straightforwardly to Peter, promising the apostles thrones alongside the Son of Man.

What does this mention of the enthronement of the Son of Man evoke at this point in the narrative? Most agree that Daniel 7 has had some influence on this passage, though opinions differ as to whether this is a clear allusion or a faint echo.[20] Daniel 7 depicts four beasts that represent Gentile kings making war against "the holy ones" (Dan. 7:25; OG [Old Greek] 7:8). Then Daniel goes on

---

19   Commenting on the Markan parallel, Gary Anderson (*Sin*, 167–168) notes that the juxtaposition of this encounter with the passion predictions is not without significance: "The giving up of all one's wealth was construed to be one way of losing one's life on behalf of the gospel. Just as the inner core of the disciples found the crucifixion to be shocking, so the young man finds the giving up of all his wealth to be a sacrifice beyond calculation."

20   For example, Hagner (*Matthew 14–28*, Word Biblical Commentary 33b [Dallas: Word Books, 1995] 565) says that this saying "alludes to Dan. 7:9." Robert Gundry (*Matthew: A Commentary on his Handbook for a Mixed Church under Persecution*, 2d ed. [Grand Rapids, MI: Eerdmans,

to describe "thrones" and one like a son of man coming (*ērcheto*) on the clouds of heaven to the Ancient of Days and receiving authority (*edothē autō exousia*) over all people (Dan. 7:9–17).

Many have argued that in Daniel the one like a son of man is a symbol for all Israel rather than a messianic figure, noting that the kingdom given to him is subsequently given to "the holy ones of the Most High."[21] At least as early as the first century, however, Jews and Christians read this passage as an enthronement of the Messiah.[22] Daniel 7 is an important messianic text in Matthew, conspicuously recurring at a number of key points in the narrative, including three unmistakable occurrences after 19:28, namely, 24:30, 25:31, and 26:63–64. The recurrence of allusions and quotations from Daniel 7 in passages referring to Jesus' coming triumph increases the likelihood that other, less obvious allusions are significant, such as the risen Jesus' claim in 28:18 that "All authority in heaven and on earth has been given to me (*edothē moi pasa exousia en ouranō kai epi tēs gēs*)," or the reference in 16:27 to the Son of Man "coming" (*erchesthai*) in glory to render judgment on all people.[23] James D. G. Dunn notes:

> Within the Gospel tradition, the influence of Dan 7:9–14 is most noticeable in regard to Matthew. ... [T]hree of Matthew's allusions to Daniel 7 are distinctive to Matthew [10:23; 25:31; 28:18], Matthew strengthens the Daniel 7 allusion in another four verses [16:27–28; 19:28; 24:30], and two verses show awareness of the way the Similitudes of Enoch developed Daniel's son of man vision [19:28; 25:31].[24]

1994], 393) is less confident: "Jesus seems to have drawn his promise from Dan 7:9–27." Other commentators simply make no mention of Daniel 7 here.

21 See Joel Marcus's appendix on "the Son of Man" in Joel Marcus, *Mark 1–8: A New Translation with Introduction and Commentary*, Anchor Bible 27a (New Haven: Yale University Press, 2000), 528–532, especially 528. Others have suggested that the holy ones are angels. See John J. Collins, *Daniel: A Commentary on the Book of Daniel*, Hermeneia (Minneapolis: Fortress Press, 1993), 304–318.

22 See Donald Juel, *Messianic Exegesis: Christological Interpretation of the Old Testament in Early Christianity* (Philadelphia: Fortress, 1988), 162–164; Marcus, *Mark 1–8*, 528–532.

23 The argument from recurring or clustering was articulated first by Richard B. Hays, *Echoes of Scripture in the Letters of Paul* (New Haven: Yale University Press, 1989), 30. The concise formulation in *The Conversion of the Imagination: Paul as Interpreter of Israel's Scripture* (Grand Rapids, MI: Eerdmans, 2005), is helpful: "When we find repeated Pauline quotations of a particular OT passage, additional possible allusions to the same passage become more compelling" (37).

24 James D. G. Dunn, "The Danielic Son of Man in the New Testament," in *The Book of Daniel: Composition and Reception*, 2 vols.; eds. John J. Collins and Peter W. Flint (Leiden/Boston: Brill, 2001), 2.538. Juel (*Messianic Exegesis*, 158–161) considers Matthew 16:27–28; 19:28; 24:27–44; 25:31; and 26:64 all "indisputable" allusions to Daniel 7. He considers 10:23, 24:44, and 28:18 "likely" allusions.

Dunn's redactional argument complements the argument from recurrence; Matthew depicts Jesus' triumph in language drawn from Daniel 7's narrative of a triumphant "Son of Man" to whom authority and kingship are given.

The probable Danielic background of Jesus' words in 19:28–29 illuminates Jesus' claim that the twelve will receive thrones when the Son of Man sits on his throne of glory. The plural "thrones" in Daniel 7:9 has engendered a great deal of speculation about who exactly would sit on them.[25] For Matthew, the thrones are for Jesus, who will sit at the right hand of his Father (26:64; compare Ps. 110:1), and for the twelve apostles who will receive them as recompense for following Jesus. In addition to this, anyone who leaves possessions behind will receive a hundred times as much and eternal life. Matthew underscores once again the unity between the path that Jesus takes and what he requires from his followers. In 16:21–28, Jesus explains that, just as he must die and be raised to life, all who would follow him must lose their lives and so regain them when the Son of Man returns to repay everyone for their deeds. The discussion following the departure of the rich young man brings further clarity to this picture; those who leave everything behind and follow Jesus will be repaid with a share in his rule as Son of Man.

The tone of 19:27–29 is almost triumphalistic. Despite the unwarranted conjecture of numerous scholars, there is no hint that Peter's question is in any way unseemly.[26] Jesus' response is disarmingly straightforward; Peter and the other apostles will take thrones alongside of the Son of Man, and everyone who leaves their possessions behind will receive a hundred times as much.

The contrast with 16:21–28 is striking; that passage also spoke of the recompense that followers of Jesus would receive, but the accent was on the necessity to follow Jesus in giving one's life in order to receive it back, a message that disturbs the apostles (see also 17:22–23) and incites conflict between Jesus and Peter. In 19:16–29, however, there is no explicit mention of the cross—though Jesus defined "following" as cross-bearing in 10:38 and 16:24—and Peter seems blithely unaware that following the Son of Man and sharing his enthronement means giving one's life.

This passage leaves one loose thread that will become important in Matthew 20:17–28. While the emphasis of 19:16–29 is on the danger of wealth and the generous repayment awaiting those who renounce their possessions, verse 26 dangles a hint that some provision will be made for those who, like the rich young man, do not store up treasure in heaven because "all things are possible with God." This point is further developed in the following parable, which indicates that God will

---

25   On the interpretation of the "thrones" in the NT and rabbinic literature see Craig A. Evans, "Daniel in the New Testament: Visions of God's Kingdom," in *The Book of Daniel: Composition and Reception*, 2 vols.; eds. John J. Collins and Peter W. Flint (Leiden/Boston: Brill, 2001), 2.516–519.

26   For example, see France, *The Gospel of Matthew*, New International Commentary on the New Testament (Grand Rapids: Eerdmans, 2007), 741.

indeed pay his workers as he promised, but that he is also inclined to pay those who have done less work far more than they deserve.[27] At this point in the narrative this generosity is hinted at, but not explained in detail, though Matthew has already indicated that Jesus has come to save his people from the debt of their sin.[28] The logic of this salvation finally emerges with full clarity in 20:17–28.

Thrones Are the Recompense of Cross-bearers (20:17–28)

The discourse following the rich young man's departure concludes with the parable of the workers in the vineyard. It is followed by the third, final, and most detailed passion and resurrection prediction (20:17–19), which marks Jesus' decisive and final move toward Jerusalem.[29] Immediately afterward Jesus is accosted by the mother of the sons of Zebedee, who has apparently heard about the thrones the Twelve are to receive in the coming kingdom and wants the best ones to be given to her sons. While Mark 10:17–45 features a similar discussion of cross-bearing and repayment, Matthew's inclusion of Jesus' promise in 19:27—that the Twelve will sit on thrones—foreshadows the coming dispute about who will have the best places alongside Jesus in 20:20–28, thereby tightening the narrative unity and increasing the Danielic overtones.

Since 16:21 Jesus has explained to the disciples that he and everyone who would follow him must give their lives in order to be repaid with eternal life. Yet, it appears that James and John are fixated on one aspect of this teaching, namely, that they are to have the thrones mentioned in Daniel 7. Jesus' response cuts straight to the heart of the matter: "You [plural] do not know what you are asking."[30] If James and John had understood what Jesus taught them, they would have realized that enthronement with the Son of Man is the repayment for following him in his cross-bearing.[31] Jesus then clarifies the nature of James' and John's misapprehension: "Are

---

27 See Nathan Eubank, "What Does Matthew Say about Divine Recompense? On the Misuse of the Parable of the Workers in the Vineyard (20:1–16)" forthcoming in *Journal for the Study of the New Testament*.

28 See the discussion of Matt. 1:1–3:12 in Eubank, *Wages of Cross-Bearing*, 109–132.

29 Apart from 20:17–19, all of 19:16–20:28 is united by the theme of God's repayment for following Jesus. For this reason, W. F. Albright and C. S. Mann consider this final passion and resurrection prediction a foreign insertion that breaks the flow of thought (see W. F. Albright and C. S. Mann, *Matthew: A New Translation with Introduction and Commentary*, Anchor Bible 26 [Garden City, NY: Doubleday, 1971], 239). Yet, from the first prediction in 16:21 onward, Matthew shows that it is those who follow Jesus in cross-bearing who have treasure in heaven and eternal life. Thus, Albright and Mann ironically repeat the failure of the disciples to see that heavenly thrones are attained by way of the cross.

30 Unlike the Markan parallel (10:35), Matthew portrays the mother of the sons of Zebedee asking for the best thrones on behalf of her sons (20:20). Jesus' responds in the plural, thereby including the sons in his rebuke.

31 This point is further underscored by the language of sitting at Jesus' right and left, which is the same as the description of the revolutionaries crucified at Jesus' right and left in 27:38. Craig Keener, *A Commentary on the Gospel of Matthew* (Grand Rapids, MI.: Eerdmans, 1999), 486;

you able to drink the cup which I myself am about to drink?" In the prophets and post-biblical Jewish and Christian literature, "cup" could refer to God's judgment or more generally to a person's fate or death.[32] Raymond Brown pointed out that James and John are probably not being invited to drink the cup of God's wrath for sin but are rather challenged to drink the cup of suffering that Jesus will drink.[33] Jesus thus intimates that they are, in effect, asking to be crucified with him.[34] The thrones are to be repayment for cross-bearing.

The request incites discord among the disciples, who become angry with James and John (20:24). Jesus continues his catechesis, this time contrasting the Son of Man with the Gentile kings:

> You know that the rulers of the Gentiles rule them, and great ones (*hoi megaloi*) exercise dominion over them. It will not be so among you; but whoever wishes to be great among you must be your servant, and whoever wishes to be first among you must be your slave; just as the Son of Man came not to be served but to serve, and to give his life a ransom-price (*lytron*) for many. (20:25–28)

In correcting the disciples, Jesus draws on Daniel 7 in order to make a crucial distinction: one cannot join the Son of Man in his glory by emulating the Gentile kings he opposes.[35] If the Twelve would occupy twelve thrones along with the Son of Man then they must give their lives as he does rather than ruling as do the Gentiles.[36] Here the link between wage-earning behavior and Jesus' own actions is

---

Davies and Allison, *Matthew*, 3.88. Also, unlike Mark, Matthew says that the mother of the sons of Zebedee witnessed the crucifixion (27:56).

32   For example, see *Testament of Abraham* 1:3; 16:11–12; *Targum Neofiti* on Gen. 40:23 and Deut. 32:1; *Martyrdom of Polycarp* 14:2. Luz, *Matthäus*, 3.161–162.

33   Raymond Brown, *Death of the Messiah*, 2 vols.; Anchor Bible Reference Library (New York: Doubleday, 1994), 1.169–170.

34   See 26:39.

35   Brant Pitre's (*Jesus, the Tribulation, and the End of the Exile*, [Grand Rapids: Baker, 2005], 390) comments on the Danielic imagery in the Markan parallel apply: "The images of the disciples 'sitting' (presumably on 'thrones', see Dan. 7:10, 26; Mark 10:37) with a 'son of man' (Dan. 7:14; Mark 10:45) who has been given 'glory' (Dan. 7:14; Mark 10:37)—all of these presume the Danielic vision of the 'people of the saints of the Most High' being given the eternal 'kingdom' (Dan. 7:27, cf. 18, 22) … [E]ven Jesus' image of 'the great' (*hoi megaloi*) Gentile kings 'lording it over' [*katakyrieuō*] their subjects (Mark 10:42) may also be drawing on the Danielic images of the 'great beasts'—who are, of course, Gentile kings (Dan. 7:3)—and those Gentiles rulers who will 'lord it over many' during the end times (Dan. 11:39 LXX Theod.)."

36   Since Kenneth W. Clark's study ("The Meaning of [*kata*]*kyrieuein*" in *Studies in New Testament Language and Text: Essays in Hour of George D. Kilpatrick on the Occasion of his sixty-fifth Birthday*, Novum Testamentum Supplements 44, ed. J. K. Elliot [Leiden: Brill, 1976], 100–105) most have agreed that *katakyrieuō* lacked the negative force of the English idiom "to lord it over." The contrast in this passage, then, is not between abuse of power and right lordship, but on ruling

finally made explicit; the path to ruling with the Son of Man is one of following his example. Even the wage that Jesus earns is not for himself, at least not primarily, but is the ransom-price for others.

A brief summary is in order: in Matthew 16:13–28 Jesus announces that he is going to be killed and raised from the dead and that his followers must do likewise because cross-bearers will be "repaid" with eternal life, a treasure that no earthly possession could purchase.[37] In 19:16–29 further nuance is provided: those who renounce their possessions to follow Jesus will be repaid not only with eternal life but also with a share in the coming reign of the Son of Man, including thrones for the apostles. Then, in 20:17–28 the sons of Zebedee attempt to seize the best thrones for themselves. Jesus counters this request by intimating that they are asking to be crucified with him and telling all the apostles yet again that that they must give their lives if they are to rule with the Son of Man. In a nutshell: *these three passages indicate that Jesus and his followers must give their lives in order to be repaid with the eternal reign spoken of in Daniel 7.* Or, as Jesus puts it at the conclusion of the Beatitudes, "Blessed are those who are persecuted on account of righteousness, for theirs is the kingdom of the heavens. Blessed are you when people revile you and persecute you and say all kinds of evil against you falsely on my account. Rejoice and be glad, for your wage is great in the heavens" (Matt. 5:10–12).[38]

A new element emerges in 20:28. The repayment that Jesus earns by giving his life is described as a ransom-price for many. In other words, the "repayment" or "treasure" that Jesus' cross-bearing earns is not only for himself but for others as well. Before unpacking the significance of this for understanding how Jesus saves his people from their sins, it is necessary to take a closer look at the meaning of the ransom saying itself.

The Price of Release for Many

There is a vast amount of scholarly literature on Mathew 20:28 (the parallel is in Mark 10:45), much of which is not directly relevant here because it focuses on the pre-Markan origins of the saying and the question of whether or not the saying was originally drawn from Isaiah 53.[39] Davies and Allison list a number of intriguing parallels between the saying and the Hebrew text of Isaiah,[40] but, as has often

---

as do the Gentiles and Jesus, who gives his life. In other words, the critique of Gentile rulers is more profound than a condemnation of corruption; any that do not follow Jesus in giving in their lives cannot lead.

37 See also 5:2–12; 6:1–24; 13:44–46.

38 See the similar argument of Thomas Aquinas, *Summa Theologiae*, pt. 3, q. 48, art. 1, response.

39 See, for example, Scot McKnight, "The Authenticity of the Ransom Sayings," in *Jesus and His Death: Historiography, the Historical Jesus, and Atonement Theory* (Waco, TX: Baylor University Press, 2005). For more extensive bibliographic information see Eubank, *Wages of Cross-Bearing*, 148, n. 35.

40 Davies and Allison, *Matthew*, 3.95–97.

been noted since C. K. Barrett and Morna Hooker made their classic cases against dependence on Isaiah 53, there are few verbal links between the saying and Isaiah 53 LXX.[41] It seems likely that Isaiah's description of vicarious suffering had some influence on the saying, though neither Matthew nor Mark appears to have been interested in drawing attention to this link.

More importantly, however, the debate over Isaianic influence has distracted scholars from a number of important clues to the meaning of the saying in its Matthean context. Regardless of whether the saying alludes more or less faintly to Isaiah, Jesus' gift of his life as a ransom-price is in deep continuity with Matthew's description of the plight of those Jesus came to save and with the recompense of righteous cross-bearing.

Discussion of the ransom saying has been distracted not only by a preoccupation with Isaiah (and a corresponding neglect of its relationship to the Matthean narrative as a whole) but also by a tendency to equate *lytron* (usually translated "ransom") with several of its cognates, especially *lytroō*. Since David Hill's 1967 study, *Greek Words and Hebrew Meanings*, many scholars have claimed that the word *lytron* does not necessarily involve an actual exchange or payment.[42] Rather, it is claimed that in the Septuagint *lytron* and its cognates were used to refer to "deliverance" or "salvation" without any hint of a ransom-price being paid. For instance, while commenting on Matthew 20:28, Eugene Boring writes:

> Matthew adopts Mark's picture of Jesus' life as a "ransom," but does not elaborate it into a doctrine of the atonement (as Mark does not). The fact that Jesus' death effects forgiveness of sins and entering into a new covenant life with God (26:28) is important to Matthew, but he is not concerned to speculate on *how* this is "explained." "*Ransom*" (*lytron*) *in the LXX had already lost its specific idea of release by paying off the captor and had come to mean simply "rescue," "deliver" as an act of God's power* (e.g., Exod. 6:6; Deut. 7:8).[43]

---

41 See C. K. Barrett, "The Background of Mark 10:45," in *New Testament Essays*, ed. A. J. B. Higgins (Manchester: Manchester University Press, 1959), 1–18; Morna Hooker, *Jesus and the Servant: The Influence of the Servant Concept of Deutero-Isaiah in the New Testament* (London: S.P.C.K., 1959).

42 See David Hill, *Greek Words and Hebrew Meanings: Studies in the Semantics of Soteriological Terms* (Cambridge: Cambridge University Press, 1967). Hill concludes: "the *lytron*-words" should be interpreted "in terms of 'deliverance' or 'emancipation,' except when the context expresses or implies a payment made to gain freedom" (81). See also Stanislas Lyonnet and Léopold Sabourin, *Sin, Redemption, and Sacrifice: A Biblical and Patristic Study* (Rome: Biblical Institute Press, 1970), 79–103.

43 Eugene Boring, "The Gospel of Matthew," *The New Interpreter's Bible* 8 (Nashville: Abingdon, 1995), 399 (my emphasis).

More recently, Charles Talbert has argued that "There is nothing in the term
[*lytron*] that demands an elaborate soteriological theory. It simply means that Jesus
is acting on others' behalf in his ministry."[44] Like Boring, Talbert appeals to the
LXX to substantiate his claim:

> In Jer. 15:20–21 LXX, Yahweh says to Jeremiah, "I am with you
> to save you and to deliver you ... and I will ransom [*lytrōsomai*]
> you." In the parallelism, save, deliver, and ransom are synonyms.
> In Jer. 27:34 LXX (50:34 Eng.), when Yahweh says he is the one
> who ransoms [*ho lytroumenos*] Israel, it is in the context of his
> defeat of Israel's enemies (deliverance). In Jer. 38:11 LXX (31:11
> Eng.), when the Lord has ransomed [*elytrōsato*] Jacob, it means
> that Yahweh has delivered him out of the hands of stronger foes
> (return from exile). Ransom is, then, synonymous with salvation
> and deliverance.[45]

There is an initial plausibility to Boring's and Talbert's argument. In addition to
denoting the payment of the price of release (for example, Lev. 25:48), the verb
lytroō is indeed also used in the LXX with no apparent reference to the payment
of any price.

Surprisingly, however, neither Boring nor Talbert cites a single verse that
actually includes the noun *lytron*, the word Matthew uses.[46] There is good reason
for this odd omission: the noun *lytron* is never used in the LXX, Josephus, Philo
—or, according to BDAG[47] and Liddell and Scott, anywhere else—to mean simply
"rescue" or "deliver" as Boring and Talbert claim. It always refers to some price
or exchange.

In the LXX the noun *lytron* denotes the price paid to redeem the life of the
negligent owner of a deadly ox (Exod. 21:30), the price paid to avert a plague (Exod.
30:12), the price to redeem a slave (Lev. 19:20; 25:51–52; Isa. 45:13), the price
paid to regain land (Lev. 25:24–26), the price to recover the tithe from the land
(Lev. 27:31), the payment, paid either with money or with the lives of the Levites,
to redeem the lives of the first-born of Israel (Num. 3:12, 46, 48–49, 51; 18:15),
the price paid to redeem the life of a murderer (Num. 35:31–32), the price paid to

---

44   Charles Talbert, *Matthew*, Paideia Commentaries on the New Testament (Grand Rapids, MI:
     Baker Academic, 2010), 241. See also France, *Matthew*, 761.

45   Talbert, *Matthew*, 761.

46   For example, the verb *lytroō* is used in Exod. 6:6 (LXX), cited by Boring, where God says "I will
     deliver you from slavery and will redeem (*lytrōsomai*) you with a raised arm and great judgment."
     Similarly, Deut. 7:8 says "the Lord brought you out with a strong hand and raised arm and
     redeemed (*elytrōsato*) you from a house of slavery."

47   William F. Arndt, Frederick W. Danker, and Walter Bauer, *A Greek-English Lexicon of the New
     Testament and Other Early Christian Literature* (3rd ed.; Chicago: University of Chicago Press,
     2000).

appease a cuckolded husband (Prov. 6:35), and the money that a rich person may be forced to pay if threatened (Prov. 13:8). Other relevant literature reveals more of the same.[48] In short, *lytron* always refers to some sort of payment or exchange.[49] The claim made by Talbert, Boring, Hill and others—that no payment is in view in Matthew 20:28—is utterly without warrant.[50]

It is not difficult to ascertain why *lytroō* came to be used in contexts where there is no payment in view, while *lytron* always retained the clear sense of some payment. If *lytroō* originally meant to pay a price for deliverance it would not be hard for its range to expand to include deliverance in the generic sense. The cognates *lytrōsis* and *apolytrōsis* are abstract and could expand on the same lines. *Lytron*, however, denoted the price itself and was therefore less susceptible to being used to refer to redemption without an actual payment or exchange. For this reason, and in light of the ambiguity of the English word "ransom," which, like *lytroō*, can denote redemption with or without payment, it would seem best to translate *lytron* as "price of release" (as LSJ suggests) or as "ransom-price."

Having addressed the question of Isaianic influence and the misconceptions about the semantic range of *lytron*, we are now in a position to discuss the significance of Jesus' ransom saying in Matthew 20:28 against the backdrop of the larger narrative. The ransom saying evokes two major motifs in the Gospel: (1) the deliverance from captivity, and (2) the earning of heavenly treasure.

Deliverance from Captivity

As already noted, the word *lytron* was commonly used to refer to the price paid to free a captive, whether prisoners of war, slaves, or debtors.[51] For instance, Josephus says that Ptolemy gained the release of the Jewish slaves in Egypt by paying *lytra* to the soldiers who had captured them.[52] As noted above, the LXX also frequently uses *lytron* to refer to the money paid to redeem slaves (Lev. 19:20; 25:51–52; Isa.

---

48   For example, Josephus uses *lytron* to refer to the price paid to free captives (*The Jewish Antiquities*, 12:28, 33, 46; 14:371; 15:156; *Jewish War* 1.274, 1.384, 419), the price paid to recover a brother's dead body (*Jewish Antiquities*, 1.325), and a costly item given to save other costly items: *lytron anti pantōn* (*Ant.* 14:107).

49   Max Wilcox ("On the Ransom-Saying in Mark 10:45c, Matt. 20:28c," in *Geschichte-Tradition-Reflexion: Festschrift für Martin Hengel zum 70. Geburtstag*, eds. Hubert Cancik et al.; 3 vols. [Tübingen: Mohr Siebeck, 1996], 173–86) rightly takes the concreteness of *lytron* seriously, but then reads the saying to mean that Jesus gives himself as the ransom-price that helps his followers avoid being captured, a proposal with no merit as far as the First Gospel is concerned.

50   Hill's lengthy study adduces only one example, Prov. 13:8, of the noun *lytron* being used without any hint of payment or exchange (Hill, *Greek Words*, 61). Yet, even this verse refers to the money a rich person may be forced to pay if threatened.

51   See Lidell-Scott-Jones, *Greek-English Lexicon*, s.v. *lytron*; K. Kertelge, "Lytron," *Exegetical Dictionary of the New Testament*, 2:364-66.

52   *Jewish Antiquities*, 12:28, 33, 46. See also *Jewish Antiquities*, 14:371; 15:156; *Jewish War*, 1.274, 1.384, 419.

45:13), as well as the payment to redeem the lives of the first-born of Israel (Num. 3:12, 46, 48–49, 51; 18:15).

The link between the payment of a *lytron* and the end of captivity is strength-ened by the many biblical texts that describe God ransoming Israel from captivity using the verb *lytroō*.[53] For instance, in Exodus 6:6 God tells Moses to tell the Israelites, "I will ransom (*lytrōsomai*) you with uplifted arm." In Micah 6:4 God recalls the Exodus: "For I brought you from the land of Egypt and ransomed (*elytrōsamēn*) you from the house of slavery."[54]

Unsurprisingly, prophecies of the end of later exiles use this same language. In the promise of restoration in Isaiah 43:1 God says, "Fear not, for I have ran-somed (*elytrōsamēn*) you." Jeremiah 31:11 (38:11 LXX) says that "the Lord has ransomed (*elytrōsato*) Jacob and has delivered him from stronger hands." Similarly, Micah 4:10 promises that "the Lord your God will ransom (*lytrōsetai*) you from the hand of your enemies." Other examples could be cited.[55] Combined with Matthew's description of Jesus as the one spoken of by the prophets who would save his people from exile, it is likely that Jesus' claim to give the ransom-price for the many evokes the Septuagintal "ransoming" of the people, a biblical echo that is reinforced by the language of "the many," a term commonly used to refer to exiles.[56]

One might object that to shed light on Matthew 20:28 by appealing to the common Septuagintal use of *lytroō* is to commit the same blunder as Boring and others, namely, confusing the verb *lytroō* with the noun *lytron*. On the contrary, the suggestion here is that Jesus' gift of his life as the price of release (*lytron*) for the many echoes the numerous biblical references to God "ransoming" (*lytroō*) his people. The switch from noun to verb could weaken the strength of the echo, but not eliminate it. Boring and others note that *lytroō* is sometimes used without any sense of payment or exchange and then assume that *lytron* was used in the same way. As we have seen, this assumption is mistaken.

The ransom-price for many would seem to presuppose that "the many" are enduring some sort of captivity from which they need to be ransomed. Yet, schol-ars have generally agreed that this apparent presupposition is never fleshed out in the course of Matthew's narrative. That is, the suggestion that Jesus gives his life as the price of release suggests that "the many" endure some sort of captivity, but Matthew never develops or explains this suggestion. Davies and Allison state the problem clearly: "almost every question we might ask remains unanswered. What is the condition of 'the many'? Why do they need to be ransomed?"[57] In

---

53 Pitre, *Jesus, the Tribulation, and the End of the Exile*, 404–417.

54 See also Ps. 78:42–55; Isa. 51:10–11.

55 Zech. 3:1; 10:8; Isa. 44:21–23; 51:11; 62:12; Jer. 50:33–34; Lam. 5:8; Hos. 13:14; Zeph. 3:15.

56 See Isa. 52:14–15; 53:11–12; Dan. 12:1–3; 1Q28 VIII, 12–14; IX, 18-20. See also Pitre, *Jesus, the Tribulation, and the End of the Exile*, 413–414.

57 Davies and Allison, *Matthew*, 3.100

the absence of any explanation the ransom saying would seem to be "only an unexplained affirmation."[58]

Matthew, however, repeatedly describes the plight of those Jesus came to save in terms of captivity. Sin is debt, and the punishment for unresolved sin is debt-bondage. The prologue of the Gospel (1:1–3:12) describes Jesus' people as in exile, and promises that Jesus will save them from their sins (1:21).[59] In 5:21–26 Jesus uses the image of debt-bondage, teaching that even the smallest sins against a brother will be repaid in Gehenna down to the last penny. In the Lord's Prayer Jesus teaches his followers to pray "forgive us our debts, as we also forgive our debtors" (6:12). This claim is given vivid expression in the parable of the unforgiving servant, which says that debtors (that is, those with unforgiven sin) who do not cancel the debts of others will be thrown into prison and will not get out until they repay all that they owe (18:34). *In sum: captivity for the debt of sin is the plight of both Jesus' "people" who are in exile and of individual sinners.*

To return to Davies and Allison's question, then: what is the condition of "the many"? It is debt-bondage and exile because of their sins. To whom is the price of release paid? For Matthew, it is paid to God, the "creditor" whom Jesus' disciples ask to forgive their debts, and who will settle accounts with his servants (6:12; 16:27; 18:23–24; 25:19). This does not exclude the fact that, for Matthew, Jesus rescues his people from the power of the devil (for example, 4:1–11; 8:28–34; 12:22–28) and from wicked human authorities (for example, 2:1–23; 20:25–28; 21:12–21:46). To the perennial question of whether Jesus gives a ransom-price to God or the devil, however, Matthew gives an unequivocal answer: the *lytron* is paid to God. In sum: attention to the role of Matthew 20:28 in the narrative as a whole reveals that Jesus gives his life as the price of release for the many in debt-bondage.[60]

The Price of Release as Heavenly Treasure

Another major question raised by the ransom-saying is how Jesus generates the price of release for the many. Since *lytron* denotes some sort of payment to release captives, what does this payment consist of and how does Jesus earn it?

Jesus earns the price of release by doing the very things he told his followers they must do to earn heavenly treasure: by taking up his cross and giving his life. After the first passion and resurrection prediction in 16:21, Jesus tells the disciples

---

58   Davies and Allison, *Matthew*, 3.100. See also Luz, *Matthäus*, 3.166; John T. Carroll and Joel B. Green, "His Blood on Us and On Our Children: The Death of Jesus in the Gospel according to Matthew" in *The Death of Jesus in Early Christianity*, eds. John T. Carroll and Joel B. Green (Peabody, Mass.: Hendrickson, 1995), 44; John Nolland, *The Gospel of Matthew: A Commentary on the Greek Text*, New International Greek Testament Commentary (Grand Rapids, MI: Eerdmans, 2005), 826.

59   The prologue contains numerous hints that "exile" comes to an end when the debt of sin is repaid. See Eubank, *Wages of Cross-Bearing*, 108–132.

60   See the similar argument in Aquinas, *Summa*, pt. 3, q. 48, art. 4.

that they must take up their cross to find their lives (16:24–25). As noted above, Matthew provides a rationale for this claim: the Son of Man is about to repay everyone according to their deeds. In other words, the exhortation following the first passion and resurrection prediction is based on the promise that those who follow Jesus in his cross-bearing will be repaid at the Parousia.

As Jesus makes his way to Jerusalem this claim surfaces again: those who deny themselves and follow Jesus will receive a hundred times as much in return, and the apostles will receive thrones alongside the Son of Man (19:27–28). Immediately after this there erupts the dispute over who will receive the thrones closest to Jesus. In correcting the disciples Jesus points them again to his own mission: the Son of Man who triumphs over the Gentile kings did not come to be served but to serve and to give his life as the price of release for the many. These words recall the message that Jesus has been repeating again and again: those who give up their lives will be repaid in the eschaton. Though the pre-history of the ransom saying remains mysterious, the logic of these words in Matthew's narrative is clear. *Jesus will earn the ransom-price for those trapped by the debt of sin by giving his life, just as he calls all who would follow him to earn heavenly treasure by giving their lives.*[61]

To first-century Jews familiar with Daniel's description of the Son of Man being "given dominion and glory and kingship, that all peoples, nations, and languages should serve him" (7:14), Jesus' claim that the Son of Man came not to be served but to serve by giving his life would have been jarring, almost as if Jesus was deliberately contrasting his own identity with the figure in Daniel 7. Yet, as already noted, Matthew repeatedly describes Jesus' coming triumph as the triumph of the figure in Daniel 7, so it would seem that in applying this text to Jesus, Matthew does not deny that "all authority in heaven and on earth" is given to him (28:18). How does the Son of Man as servant relate to the Son of Man as the wielder of all authority? This is an implicit (not to mention *intriguing*) question running throughout 16:21–28, 19:16–29, and 20:17–28. How is it possible that Jesus, the Christ, who is also the Son of Man of Daniel 7, will reign if he is going to be crucified when he goes to Jerusalem?

Jesus answers this question several times while always keeping the similar destiny of his followers in view. In 16:21–28 he says that those who give their lives will be repaid with eternal life. Earthly possessions do not add up to eschatological victory. The treasure that matters is the treasure gained by cross-bearing. Then, in 19:16–20 Jesus says that those who renounce their possessions to follow him will

---

61   Thus, even if *lytron* could be used to mean "deliverance" or "redemption" with no exchange in view as Boring and others wrongly assert, the Matthean context would bring the importance of paying an actual price into to the foreground. Gustav A. Deissman noted that the ubiquity of the term *lytron* in reference to the manumission of slaves would have made it a particularly vivid image in early Christian circles. See Gustav A. Deissman, *Light from the Ancient East: The New Testament Illustrated by Recently Discovered Texts of the Graeco-Roman World*, trans. Lionel R. M. Strachan (New York: George H. Doran, 1927), 327–330.

receive a hundred times as much and eternal life, and the twelve apostles will receive twelve thrones alongside the Son of Man. Furthermore, it is implicit that the Son of Man receives his throne from God in return for his renunciation. Finally, in 20:17–28 Jesus explains again that the Son of Man, unlike the Gentile kings he opposes, conquers by giving his life. Or, if one combines this saying with the pericopae leading up to it, Jesus gives his life and is repaid with a glorious throne, eternal life, and with heavenly treasure that redounds not only to his own benefit but to those in arrears because of sin. Thus, the economy of divine recompense running throughout Matthew illuminates how the serving Son of Man becomes the triumphant Son of Man.[62]

Matthew's repeated emphasis on debt-bondage and the divine repayment of cross-bearing also sheds light on the meaning of the preposition *anti* in the phrase *lytron anti pollōn* (ransom-price for many). There are a number of possible ways to understand the price of release being given *anti* here, the most popular probably being that of "substitution," that is, Jesus dies "in place of" the many.[63] Matthew uses *anti* this way in 2:22 ("Archelaus reigned over Judea in place of [*anti*] his father Herod") and in 5:38 ("You have heard that it was said, 'An eye for [*anti*] an eye, and a tooth for [*anti*] a tooth'"). Yet *anti* could also be used with a slightly different nuance that may be more appropriate for the context in Matthew 20: that of "payment for." For example, in 17:27 Jesus tells Peter to take the shekel he finds in the mouth of a fish and "give it to them for me and for you" (*dos autois anti emou kai sou*). The shekel is given to pay the debt that Jesus and Peter are thought to owe.

As we have seen, within Matthew "the many" are in debt-bondage, and the ransom-price is paid to set them free. Thus, *anti* in Matthew 20:28 chiefly indicates "payment for."[64] At the same time, however, it would be overzealous to exclude the sense of substitution entirely. The idea of payment or exchange is but a hair's breadth away from substitution, and the various possible meanings of words are not hermetically sealed off from each other in everyday speech. Nevertheless, Matthew's emphasis is decidedly on payment; "the many" are in bondage because of the debt of sin, and cross-bearing earns the *lytron*, the price of their release. For Matthew it is not the mere fact of Jesus' death that earns the ransom-price. There is little if any hint in Matthew that the crucifixion atones by absorbing God's wrath, or that the effects of sin required that God crush someone and so Jesus received this punishment instead of the many. Rather, it is Jesus' active, obedient giving of his life that earns a surplus of heavenly treasure.[65]

---

62   See also the argument of Aquinas, *Summa*, pt. 3, q. 48, art. 1 as well as q. 49, art. 6.

63   See, for example, Hagner, *Matthew 14–28*, 583; Keener, *Matthew*, 488. See BDAG s.v. *anti* II.

64   BDAG s.v. *anti* III; LSJ s.v. *anti* III.3.

65   The words of David Bentley Hart ("A Gift Exceeding Every Debt: An Eastern Orthodox Appreciation of Anselm's *Cur Deus Homo*," *Pro Ecclesia* 7 [1998]: 333–349), written in defense of Anselm, apply with almost equal suitability to Matthew: "It must not be overlooked that for Anselm it is not Christ's suffering as such that is redemptive (the suffering merely repeats sin's

Two Objections?

I have suggested that the description of Jesus' gift of his life as the "ransom-price" be taken to mean that Jesus' obedient cross-bearing earns wages with God that repay the debt of sin of the many, thereby saving them. There are two potential objections to this conclusion that need to be addressed.

The first is that this reading is simply too clever. It is unlikely, one might protest, that Matthew would have set forth any "elaborate soteriological theory," to use Talbert's phrase.[66] There are three things to say in response to this.

First, the argument is not that Matthew provides an elaborate theory. The narrative does not evince systematic reflection on the plight of humanity before God. Matthew's "soteriology"—if such a word is appropriate—leaves a number of significant questions unanswered. But Matthew's description of Jesus' saving activity is coherent.[67] That is, it is based on a few core assumptions that manifest themselves quite predictably throughout the narrative. People find themselves in bondage due to the debt of sin. Jesus was born to save them. He teaches them to earn treasure in heaven and avoid debt-bondage, and in 20:28 he says that the gift of his life—an action that Matthew repeatedly describes as wage-earning—is the price to set the many free. This is *how* Jesus saves his people from their sins. Again, questions remain: how do debtors receive this ransom-price? How does this vicarious payment relate to Matthew's many claims that earning heavenly treasure is necessary to enter the kingdom? Matthew provides no clear answers to these and other questions. Again, this is no elaborate soteriological theory. It is only this: the people are God's debtors and they find themselves in debt-bondage. Jesus takes up his cross to earn their ransom-price while also teaching them to do likewise.

The second response to the charge that this reading is too clever is this: though I have followed primarily a narrative approach rather than a redaction-centered one, the occasional redaction-critical glance can be quite instructive. Most of the key passages informing the argument are found only in Matthew. The focus on end of exile, the repayment of wages, and the promise that Jesus will "save his people from their sins" (1:21) in the birth narrative is uniquely Matthean, and Jesus' claim that he and John the Baptist will "fill up all righteousness" is redactional.[68] Much of the material on earning treasure in heaven in the Sermon on the Mount is only found in Matthew. Matthew alone describes the fate of unresolved sinners as

---

endlessly repeated and essential gesture), but rather his innocence; he recapitulates humanity by passing through all the violences of sin and death, rendering to God the obedience that is his due, and so transforms the event of his death into an occasion of infinite blessings for those to whom death is condign" (348).

66 Talbert, *Matthew*, 241.

67 I use the word "coherent" in contradistinction to "systematic," following E. P. Sanders ("Did Paul's Theology Develop?" in *The Word Leaps the Gap: Essays in Scripture and Theology in Honor of Richard B. Hays*, eds. J. Ross Wagner et al. [Grand Rapids: Eerdmans, 2008], 325–350).

68 See Eubank (*Wages of Cross-Bearing*, 121–131) for an explanation of this translation.

debt-bondage two times (5:26; 18:23–35).[69] Only the Matthean Jesus teaches his followers to pray for debt cancellation (6:12). Matthew's discussion of the wages of missionaries and those who receive them (10:40–42) is much more extensive than in Mark and Luke. Only Matthew includes the parable of the hidden treasure (13:44), the parable of the pearl (13:45–46), the parable of the unforgiving servant (18:23–35), the parable of the workers in the vineyard (20:1–16), and the sheep and the goats pericope (25:31–46), all of which describe salvation in economic terms.

The discussions revolving around the passion and resurrection predictions and the journey to Jerusalem are quite similar to the Markan parallel, but it is Matthew alone who explains that cross-bearing is necessary because the Son of Man is about to repay cruciform lives with resurrection (16:27). Matthew alone expands the teaching on treasure in heaven in 19:27–28 to make it clear that the apostles, like Jesus, will be repaid with Danielic thrones.[70] This Matthean addition ties that passage together with the dispute over the best thrones in 20:17–28. It is impossible to deny, therefore, that Matthew has a special interest in sin as debt, cruciform deeds as earning wages, and in the redemption from sin that Jesus accomplished. The ransom-saying is of course not unique, being found in Mark and possessing a number of parallels in other early Christian literature.[71] But only the most flat-footed redaction critic could claim that Matthew drowsily copied the Markan text in 20:28 when the saying fits so perfectly with scores of uniquely Matthean details leading up to it. Is it not more plausible that this uniquely Matthean material comprises the Evangelist's interpretation of the traditional Christian belief that Christ gave himself up as a ransom-price?

A third and final response to the charge that this reading is too clever is this: New Testament scholars resist attributing elaborate soteriological theories to early Christian texts because they are rightly wary of reading later theological concerns back into early Christianity. Yet, the soteriological schema described here is not drawn from the categories of later Christian theology but from Matthew's late first-century Jewish-Christian milieu. Like many other Jewish texts, Matthew assumes that sin incurs a debt and that righteous deeds earn treasure in heaven. Moreover, like many other Jewish texts, Matthew assumes that one's heavenly account is not simply a matter between the individual and God but that it is possible to benefit from the heavenly treasure earned by others. Matthew shares these common Jewish beliefs about sin, debt, and redemption but refracts them through the

---

69 Compare to Luke 12:59.

70 See the very different treatment of a similar saying in Luke 22:28–30.

71 For example, 1 Cor. 6:19b–20; 7:21–23; 1 Tim. 2:6; Titus 2:14; 1 Pet. 1:17–19; Rev. 5:9.

decisive event of Jesus' death and resurrection.[72] Far from importing later Christian theology, then, this proposal situates the Gospel squarely in its historical context.

Now for the second potential objection: one might argue—and some have—that 20:28 cannot possess any great soteriological significance because it occurs in the context of exhortation.[73] It is a word of exhortation, some would claim, rather than speculation on how Jesus saves his people. There are two things to be said in response.

First, Matthew's moral vision is relentlessly christological. This can be seen in the myriad of connections between what Jesus himself does and what he tells his followers to do. In the series of exhortations leading up to Jesus' entry into Jerusalem Jesus repeatedly demands that his disciples follow him in losing their lives and then being repaid. Like the Christ hymn in Philippians 2:6–11, Matthew admonishes followers of Jesus to do what he did. Neither Matthew nor the letter to the Philippians reflects on Christ's kenosis and following glorification as would a systematic theologian—beginning from first principles and treating the Christ event and the Christian life in separate chapters—but this should not be confused with a lack of interest in Christ's work itself.[74] Far from undercutting its soteriological significance, the hortative context of 20:28 presents Jesus' saving work as both vicarious and as the template for the self-giving required of Jesus' followers. In Matthew, Jesus "saves" by showing his followers how to earn wages with God, but also by doing it for them.

Second, this objection assumes that the work of vicarious atonement is not something that Jesus' followers are able to participate in. As Talbert puts it, the ransom-saying "simply means that Jesus is acting on others' behalf in his ministry... If 20:28 gives Jesus's example for disciples to follow, it cannot include more than disciples can follow."[75] Talbert's idea may be correct in some theological systems, especially those that emphasize the complete inability of humankind to participate in their own salvation, but one should not assume this is the case in early Christian texts.

To take one particularly vivid example, in Colossians 1:24 Paul says "now I rejoice in my sufferings for your sake, and in my flesh I fill up what is lacking in

---

72 See the observation of Pope Benedict XVI in the encyclical *Deus Caritas Est*: "The real novelty of the New Testament lies not so much in new ideas as in the figure of Christ himself" (12).

73 See, for example, Talbert, *Matthew*, 241.

74 Keener (*Matthew*, 488), states: "As in Philippians 2:1–11, however, the evangelists treat their audiences to this summary of Jesus' mission not to rehearse soteriology but to provide an active model for Christian living." The assumption that exhortation betrays a lack of interest in Jesus' work is unwarranted. See also J. Christopher Edwards, "Pre-Nicene Receptions of Mark 10:45// Matt. 20:28 with Phil. 2:6–8," *Journal of Theological Studies* 61 (2010): 194–199.

75 Talbert, *Matthew*, 241.

Christ's afflictions for the sake of his body, that is, the church."[76] Here Paul suffers vicariously on behalf of the church, seeing his trials as somehow contributing to the benefits wrought by Christ's trials. Similarly, given that Matthean ethics are cruciform in nature, that is, the disciples are told to do what Jesus does, it is at least implicit that the apostles are to follow Jesus in storing up treasure in heaven not just for themselves but for others. Instead of rejecting the soteriological significance of 20:28 because it occurs in the context of exhortation, it makes more sense to see Jesus' words as a call to the apostles to join him in earning heavenly treasure not only for themselves but for others. They are to follow him in giving their lives and then receiving "a hundred times as much" in return, heavenly treasures that overflow to the benefit of the many, just as Paul filled up what was lacking for the sake of the church, and just as the merits of the patriarchs accrued to the benefit of Israel.[77]

Conclusion

Jesus' final admonition to the disciples before entering Jerusalem unites Matthew's depiction of Jesus as savior with the depiction of Jesus as exemplar and teacher. Before 20:28 Matthew stresses, on the one hand, what we might call salvation by imitation of Jesus, by taking up one's cross like him in order to be repaid with eternal life and a share in the rule of the Son of Man. On the other hand, there are numerous indications that, through Jesus, God would do for the people what they could not do for themselves: most notably, the prophecy that Jesus would save his people from their sins (1:21), his claim to fill up all righteousness (3:15), the hints that God is able to save those who have done little worthy of heavenly treasure (19:26; 19:30–20:16), and Jesus' claim that his blood is the blood of the covenant for the forgiveness of sins.[78]

---

76 In his commentary on Colossians (n. 61), Thomas Aquinas notes that this verse could be misunderstood to mean that the passion of Christ was not sufficient for redemption. He cites 1 John 2:2 to refute this view before offering his solution: the merits of Christ are infinite, but God has ordained that every member of Christ's body should display some merits, not because of any lack on Christ's part, but so that all the saints would be conformed to Christ who suffered for the sake of the Church.

77 On the merits of the patriarchs in rabbinic theology see Solomon Schechter, *Aspects of Rabbinic Theology* (New York: Macmillan, 1909; repr., New York, Schocken Books, 1961), 171–189. On the transferability of merits in the OT as well as rabbinic literature see Gary A. Anderson, *Charity: The Place of the Poor in the Biblical Tradition* (New Haven/London: Yale University Press: forthcoming). For another NT example see Menahem Kister, "Romans 5:12–21 against the Background of Torah-Theology and Hebrew Usage," *Harvard Theological Review* 100:4 (2007): 391–424.

78 For a discussion of how these themes play out in the passion narrative see Eubank, *Wages of Cross-Bearing*, 169–198.

In 20:28 these two motifs, which wind their separate ways through the Gospel, finally converge and illuminate each other. Jesus' righteous deed is here described not just as an example—though it is that too—but as a vicarious payment of the price of release to liberate the many trapped by the debt of sin. Sinners are in debt to God and find themselves in debt-bondage. Jesus earns the ransom-price for them by doing the very thing he taught his followers to do to earn heavenly treasure: he gives his life.

One might ask, then, why anyone would need to store up treasure in heaven to acquire eternal life when Jesus has done it for them. If Jesus has earned the ransom-price there would seem to be no "last penny" for us to repay, no need to cancel the debts of others so that God would cancel our own debts, all debts having been made equally irrelevant. Does Jesus' payment on behalf of others render moot all of Jesus' own teaching about heavenly wages and debts?

This question is too complex to answer in full here, but I conclude by offering one observation.[79] As in other early Jewish texts, the divine economy in Matthew does not work by the logic of strict necessity. For instance, those who receive itinerant missionaries into their homes will be repaid at the Parousia as if they themselves had left everything behind (10:40–42), and those who do leave everything behind are repaid "a hundred times as much" (19:29). The divine economy is less like a zero-sum game and more like a family in which the parents enjoy enabling their children to be full participants in the family's day-to-day tasks.

This can be seen even more clearly in Matthew's description of Jesus' self-giving, which—far from precluding the wage earning of the disciples—is the ground and example of their own cross-bearing. Thus, it is not a matter of God's needing to generate the heavenly currency to release the many from debt-bondage; instead, it is a matter of pulling the disciples into the ambit of Jesus' own self-giving, multiplying heavenly treasure for themselves and for others. In light of this, it would be very strange indeed if the Matthean Jesus had not told his followers how to have their debts canceled and how to store up treasure in heaven; they are to become *teleios* (perfect) as their Father is *teleios*, and the heavenly treasure that Jesus earns for them is not so much the end of this process as it is the beginning.[80]

---

79 For a more in-depth response to this question see Eubank, *Wages of Cross-Bearing*, 202–206.

80 Matt. 5:48; 19:21.

CONSUMING THE WORD

THE NEW TESTAMENT AND THE EUCHARIST
IN THE EARLY CHURCH

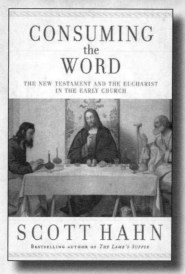

BY SCOTT W. HAHN

*"After reading Consuming the Word, I will never hear the phrase
'New Testament' in the same way again."*
— John C. Cavadini —
Notre Dame University

Long before the New Testament was a document, it was a sacrament. Jesus called the Eucharist by the name that Christians subsequently gave to the latter books of the Holy Bible. This simple and demonstrable historical fact has enormous implications for the way Christians read the Bible. In this book, Dr. Scott Hahn re-examines some of Christianity's most basic terms to discover what they meant to the sacred authors, the Apostolic Fathers, and the first hearers of the Gospel.

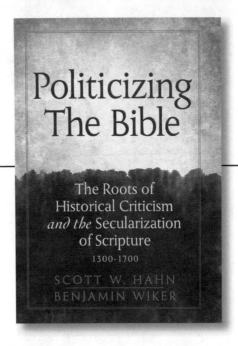

Politicizing
The Bible

The Roots of
Historical Criticism
and the Secularization
of Scripture
1300-1700

SCOTT W. HAHN
BENJAMIN WIKER

ARCHBISHOP AUGUSTINE DINOIA

Secretary of the Vatican Congregation for Divine Worship
"Historical criticism has its own history, and its development should be
subject to the scrutiny of historical method, as it is in these pages."

HADLEY ARKES

Edward N. Ney Professor of Jurisprudence and American institutions,
Amherst College
"Hahn and Wiker have not only given us a notable work in theology, but
one of the most compelling histories of political philosophy. I cannot recall any book that achieves that combination as arrestingly as this one. It
is, altogether, the most remarkable of works."

FRANCIS J. BECKWITH

Professor of philosophy and Church-State Studies, Baylor University
"This is an important work that will force its readers to readjust, and in
some cases totally reject, what they had been taught about the objectivity
and neutrality of contemporary approaches to God's Word."

JACOB NEUSNER

Professor of religion and senior fellow of the
Institute of Advanced Theology at Bard College
"Hahn and Wiker show how the study of Scripture was transformed by
centuries of conflict over the fundamentals of Western civilization. They
demonstrate their thesis in minute detail. The Bible clearly emerges as the
foundational document of western civilization and its academy."

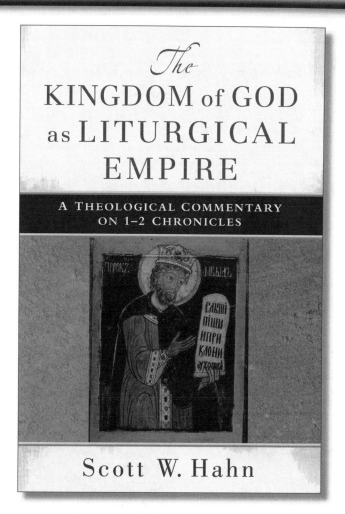

The
KINGDOM of GOD
as LITURGICAL
EMPIRE

A THEOLOGICAL COMMENTARY
ON 1–2 CHRONICLES

Scott W. Hahn

In this rich theological commentary, Scott Hahn gives a powerful account of Chronicles' inner unity. The church, the sacraments, Marian devotion—these are all shown to have their roots in Chronicles in this profoundly Catholic reading."

— *Stephen B. Chapman, Duke Divinity School*

Hahn's brilliantly illuminating commentary on Chronicles is written with extraordinary passion and intelligence. I recommend it warmly to both scholars and preachers.

— *Robert Barron, Mundelein Seminary, University of St. Mary of the Lake*

This commentary shows how the author of Chronicles reads the Old Testament as the first canonical critic; as such, the Chronicler is also the first biblical theologian. Scott Hahn identifies in the Chronicler's work a decisive biblical worldview and highlights the Abrahamic key to the Chronicler's narrative. He also explores how Chronicles provides readers with important insights into key New Testament concepts such as Jerusalem, Zion, the Temple, the church, the Kingdom, and the messianic identification of Christ as King and Priest.

KINSHIP BY COVENANT

A CANONICAL APPROACH TO THE
FULFILLMENT OF GOD'S SAVING PROMISES

SCOTT W. HAHN

"Both well-written and exhaustive, this impressive work will fascinate readers with New Testament truths about God's unyielding covenant with his chosen, fallible people." — David Noel Freedman

While the canonical scriptures were produced over many centuries and represent a diverse library of texts, they are unified by stories of divine covenants and their implications for God's people. In this deeply researched and thoughtful book, Scott Hahn shows how covenant, as an overarching theme, makes possible a coherent reading of the diverse traditions found within the canonical scriptures.

Biblical covenants, though varied in form and content, all serve the purpose of extending sacred bonds of kinship, Hahn explains. Specifically, divine covenants form and shape a father-son bond between God and the chosen people. Biblical narratives turn on that fact, and biblical theology depends upon it. With meticulous attention to detail, the author demonstrates how divine sonship represents a covenant relationship with God that has been consistent throughout salvation history. A canonical reading of this divine plan reveals an illuminating pattern of promise and fulfillment in both the Old and New Testaments. God's saving mercies are based upon his sworn commitments, which he keeps even when his people break the covenant.

ANCHOR YALE BIBLE REFERENCE LIBRARY

H608 PAGES • PUBLISHER: YALE UNIVERSITY PRESS (JUNE 16, 2009) •$50

THE ST. PAUL CENTER
FOR BIBLICAL THEOLOGY
Reading the Bible from the Heart of the Church

Promoting Biblical Literacy for Ordinary Catholics . . .

- Free Online Bible Studies
- Online Library of Scripture, Prayer, and Apologetics Resources
- Conferences and Workshops
- Popular Books and Textbooks
- Pilgrimages: to Rome, the Holy Land, and other sacred sites
- Journey Through Scripture: a dynamic parish-based Bible study program

. . . and Biblical 'Fluency' for Clergy, Seminarians, and Teachers

- Homily Helps: lectionary resources for pastors and RCIA leaders
- Reference Works: including a Catholic Bible Dictionary
- Letter & Spirit: a Journal of Catholic Biblical Theology
- Scholarly Books and Dissertations
- Seminars and Conferences
- Studies in Biblical Theology and Spirituality: reissues of classic works

ST. PAUL CENTER
FOR BIBLICAL THEOLOGY

1468 Parkview Circle
Steubenville, Ohio 43952
(740)264-9535
www.SalvationHistory.com